1ST EDITION
175⁼

~

186

Nelson
vs.
The UnitedStates of America

A
SYSTEM
IN DENIAL:
by
Marcus Giavanni

© 1998 by Marcus Giavanni

Edited by: G & B publishing L.L.C.

First Edition
1 2 3 4 5 6 7 8 9 10

Library of Congress Catalog Card Number: Pending

ISBN 0-9660928-0-5

Published by: G & B Publishing, LLC
              3208 E. WESCOTT DR.
              PHOENIX, ARIZONA
              850250

Manufactured in the United States of America

Dedication...

To My Daughters:

Catarina Ianna Marie Giavanni
AND
Devon Elizabeth Bysshe Giavanni

The tears that have fallen from my eye's and the broken heart that I carry with me every day... Will never bring me into your life... One day my dream is to see my twin angels from heaven... One day when you two are old enough to understand, I hope and pray, the third part of this book sheds light on why we were deprived of our love, and being a family...

Love,
Your Father...

Acknowledgments...

To my God, nobody will ever believe that I have counted on you so much... You are always there when I need you. I didn't need a big fancy church needing money for survival in exchange for your love and understanding... My mind and body, is my temple, protecting the soul you have given to me, for ever lasting life...

There are no words sufficient enough to express the gratitude I have for an individual that believed in me and my determination to exploit the truth, and gave me an opportunity to finally move on with my life. This individual gave me the encouragement, help, and financial guidance for this first project. Even though the serpent of negativity was always on his back, he never let it destroy the dream! "Thanks so much... Thomas Leo Bechard, Vice-President of *G & B Publishing LLC.*"

"Celina Trohoske the love of my life... We have created life... A boy or a girl... It doesn't matter to me... Cause, I'm as happy as can be...!"

To all the other believers that helped with the fruition of this book, Dave and Gail Oullete, Michael James Robinson, Ray Marshall, Donald and Dorthy Browing and Dale Schmitt. I hope all your financial dreams come true.

Not being computer literate I did not know anything about computers nor the programs I would need to complete this project. And that's when I found the Apple, my *Macintosh Performa 6400/180 PowerPC*. It changed my whole attitude about computers because it was the easiest for me to learn. The programs used for the development of this book. *Adobe PageMaker 6.0*, The *American Heritage Dictionary*. Also my *Power Look UMAX Scanner*. With out these helpful tools. This book would not have been... My teacher for the above, Robert Zusman, the best Apple man around, for always making himself available. You deserve that "Bobcat..."

Many thanks to John Prichard of *Cornucopia Publishing*, for showing me the ropes and correcting mistakes, for you are wise and caring... Dan Elders and all the staff at *Tri Star Visual*. Because you made all my visions become reality. Thanks for the Book Cover and Web Page they look great! Mike & Jason and all the staff at *Apps Software*, for teaching me all about the internet in so little time. You're worth the money I paid; you're expensive, but I now see why... "You are the best!" Pat Selcer of *Lamar Advertising Company*, thanks for giving me a break," the billboard looks great!" Richard "Ricky" Phillips the Publisher for *City AZ*, in your words, "Here's to our Empires!" Frank Ehrman for listening to me talk about my book for the last two years. "You are the only person that does not have to read this book..."

To my close friends Carr and Catharine Thompson, Tim Bryan, Tim Ritsma, Walter "Bubba" Loving Danny Wasserman and his father Mal Wasserman, John "Duke" Brickhouse, Jeff Bonadonna and Ray Schank, Tony Leparulo and Henry Ehrman, Harold Morales and his family, John and Corda Colvin, for all the help, and their paint referrals. Jay Balcon, Orlando Naverette and his family. Lynn Lanier, Gina Gina of "MTMO" and her family, Danya and her family and to all the people I forgot, I did not, I just ran out of room... Thank You, to the unnamed individuals that had helped me throughout my life... "I will see you again!"

To all that been victims of false accusations, false arrest, false prosecution and false imprisonment. I know this *Pain*...! To all Law, Fire, EMT and Medical personal, "you are the real *heroes* of the world... Just get rid of the few bad apples!"

To the staff of the Broadcast Interview Source and Mitchell P. Davis, Editor & Publisher, for allowing me to participant in the Yearbook of Experts, Authorities & spokespersons. You are America's favorite newsroom resource! To the staff of the National Register's WHO'S WHO in Executives and Professionals also thanks!

Last but not least, the man that lead me the additional 25 yards for a touch down. The final link to the books completion, Steven R. Lowy, of the law firm Lowy & Zucker. "Your definitely not a *yes* man...!"

ɪɴᴛʀᴏᴅᴜᴄᴛɪᴏɴ...

There are three parts to this book.

              Part One, unfolds a hauntingly intimate story of the vulnerability and innocence of childhood betrayed by adoptive parents.

              Part Two, is a transformation into adulthood and career decisions one makes to live in society. Which becomes a parable for the wrongful prosecution of a innocent young man as told in...   **Part Three**, The simplicity of the prose serves to expose the raw emotion occasioned by injustice and makes the author's ultimate spiritual triumph over adversity all the more dramatic and believable... A bit unorthodox in writing style, some of the actual reports and newspaper articles are tied in with the narrative flow of the story. Some times these reports and/or newspaper articles can't be read due to the quality of the original. You may choose to accept the narrative and/or read the actual report, and newspaper articles, that you may better identify with each individual character in the book. An appendix was added for the many page reports. What ever the style of reader you are, you control the pace. Enjoy the read...

TABLE OF CONTENTS

CONTENTS CONTINUED

PART ONE
THE EARLY YEARS

June 12, 1960

THE BEGINNING OF AN AMERICAN CITIZEN

A baby boy born on June 12, 1960, was immediately put up for adoption through *Catholic Social Services* in Phoenix, Arizona. Today, the temporary name given the frail infant by staff people at the adoption center is unremembered.
Identity, however, would become his.

One Saturday morning, a man and wife with the surname Nelson came to see the adoptable babies at the facility. The Nelsons were "pre-qualified" to adopt a child from the agency. They saw a particular tiny boy, a chronically ill baby. Unlike a majority of adoptive parents, however, the Nelsons were prepared emotionally, physically, and financially to adopt and care for such a child. In fact, this tiny baby was very much the sort of infant they wanted to adopt and bring into their home and lives.

Most likely though, their anticipation was to bring into their lives a child not quite so ill, and not quite so undernourished--one perhaps who would be less difficult to nurture and provide for. They had, however, agreed upon adopting a child that most other adopting parents might pass by. This baby boy surely matched their parental objective.

The Nelsons already had two children, a Caucasian boy adopted by Mrs. Nelson during her previous marriage, and an Apache Indian boy the Nelsons had adopted since their marriage.

On this particular Saturday, it was only 4 years since the Nelsons had met, fallen in love, and after a fairy tale courtship were married. They wed with a belief that they would be together forever. Mr. Nelson knew that his bride had been abused in her previous marriage. He knew also that his bride was not able to bear children because of a childhood illness that had been neglected when family circumstances made it necessary for her to care full-time for her invalid aunt instead of taking time away to get the medical attention she needed.

Undaunted, the Nelsons decided they would adopt children who would become their family. Not just any children, but children often passed over by other couples seeking to adopt. Back in the late 1950s and early 1960s, adoption wasn't new -- but realistically speaking, a Caucasian man and wife adopting sick children of a different race, while being a marvelous thing to do, was generally frowned upon.

Prior to their visit to the adoption facility on this day, the Nelsons had already made their decision that the child they would adopt would be a boy and he would be named Mark Andrew Nelson. These names were chosen out of the bible after the Apostles Mark and Andrew.

Mrs. Nelson said to her husband when she first saw the tiny child, "He looks like a true care baby. His body is frail, his arms and legs are skin and bones, and his little belly is bloated. This baby's tiny body makes his head look big and look at those huge brown eyes."

She couldn't, however, avoid wondering if she would be fully able to care for such a sickly infant. She spoke again to her husband saying, "There are other babies here, perhaps we should see them, too, before ...."

Mr. Nelson understood her concern, and with no further words, the two of them turned to leave the infant's crib.

As the Nelsons were about to exit the room to see other babies, Mrs. Nelson looked back at the woebegone, tiny June baby boy. She saw his big eyes fill with tears. His scrawny little arms were reaching toward her. Mrs. Nelson could walk no further. To her husband she said, "He's making me cry, too." She then stepped back to his crib and picked up the scrawny, malnourished baby boy.

That baby boy was me.

1961-1964
WHEN DOES "WHAT WE ARE" START

Later in life, as I approached adulthood, I often wondered how much influence those first few days of life, those days before adoption and becoming a member of the Nelson family, had in molding the nature of my character through infancy, childhood, early youth, and today's adult. The questions of life can be pondered by all of us. For orphan babies, and sickly ones in particular, the questions of "Who loved me?" "Who took care of me?," "Where did I sleep?," and "Was I ever breast fed?" Will always *haunt* us. What emotions? What bonding? What early-on feelings and sensations does an infant experience that are never to be forgotten, never totally outgrown? What happens to an infant, when there is no early presence of an every day mother or father to offer these nurturing moments? What life long developments occur within the child, emotionally and physically, in the absence of mommy and daddy and their undying love.

Maybe those first orphaned weeks were reasons or a powerful part of why, today, I hold love so precious among the emotions of my life. I will never know how I might have turned out if I had not been adopted.

I, like other "no-parents-at-hand" infants, must have in their first days of life acquired certain "deeper than normal" emotional sensitivities that simply won't go away. The sensitivities I have found to be particularly strong for me today are emotions such as difficulty in coping with rejection and infrequent spells of loneliness for no apparent reason.

I do not recall very much about my "baby years." I had a disease called Celiac that caused me to be a chronically sick baby, to cry almost continually day and night and not be able to digest food.

A pediatric specialist discovered what was wrong with me. Through time and a special diet, I was able to gain the energy, strength, size, and stamina of a

normal preteen youngster. Although it took nearly ten years to accomplish, I , out-grew the disease only to have to survive the child abuse doled out by my mother. At the time, I thought of her abuse as only extreme mental and physical cruelty by a vixen woman unable to cope with her existence and the make believe family she wanted so badly. Reflecting back, I believe her abuse to have been principally the result of her stress and frustrations brought on by the tasks of caring for two seri-ously sick children--my asthmatic sister (fourth adopted child) and me, while also giving maternal care for her two other children at the same time. Her demeanor was not bettered either by the absence of her husband, except late nights, early mornings and on Sundays because to Mr. Nelson put in long hours at work and attending school. I see now why my dad is the way he is, The lady lied to us all. To me, from childhood until the day I left home for good, I thought of her as a shrew--with an occasional gesture of kindness
 quasi affection thrown into quell guilt or to impress an observer.

As the reader continues on in this book he she might recognize that the grow-ing up of Mark Andrew Nelson could be likened to the story of the ugly duckling who became a handsome swan or the runt of a litter who grew to be a grand cham-pion.

From 1963 to 1965 we lived in a nice four bedroom house with swimming pool, an arrangement that was becoming popular for more and more Phoenix homes. Mrs. Nelson was a full time housewife who stayed home most of the time. The only time Mr. Nelson was home during hours when the kids were awake was Sundays. To support his wife, three adopted boys, and two adopted girls, he held down two jobs while taking after-work courses at Arizona State University.

My two adopted brothers, both older than me, were already in school. So on school days I was the only one left at home with Mrs. Nelson. During those hours and at other waking times as I was recovering from my infancy illness, I did the usual kid things, like play outside and ride my tricycle. My intrinsic curiosity caused me to delve deeper into why things happened like they did. If I knocked something off of a coffee table and it broke, I wanted to know, *physically*, why it broke. My memory then, as today, worked like a computer. That, of course, could be good or bad, depending upon what was to be remembered. Because of my penchant for do-ing mischievous things and wanting to know the why of particular results--I was given the family nickname *"Character,"* a appellation that stuck with me even into my teen years.

When I was two, the Nelsons adopted a baby girl. She, like me, was a very sick baby. She had asthma so severely that she was sometimes rushed to the hospital's emergency room. She almost died several times before reaching age 12.

The Nelsons in 1964 adopted another baby girl, a pretty Yaqui Indian. We became a family with five adopted children. This little daughter was another sickly child. She had a recurring heart condition. She had huge, appealing eyes and a healthy looking dark brown complexion similar to the skin tone of our older adopted brother, who is Apache Indian. He, however, has a red-brown complexion.

At age four, I was always told by my mom that I must protect my little sisters, making sure nothing bad happened to them. This proved to be my introduction to responsibility. Since my dad was not home until late in the evenings, it was as if he was never there. It was thus that I became "Mother's little helper," as she called me when she was in a good mood.

I might have become her little helper but that didn't curb my mischievous ways. I wanted to know all about everything--what it is, what it does, and how it works. And yet, I was still expected to take care of my younger sisters and look out for family interests. At age four, I was on a mission of sorts.

As a child, I recall that I had whatever most kids my age in the neighborhood had. I remember wanting a watch and wanting to learn how to tell time. My parents told me I was too young. Little did they know I came up with my own methods of telling time. I could tell what time it was by the position of the sun or by the times of certain TV shows. Daily events, too, made me aware of the time. For example, always in the afternoon, shortly after lunch, my mom would send me outside into the front yard. I was locked out at my early age with two little sisters to watch until my mom would call us back in one to two hours later. There were many times a man visited during these hours, a deputy sheriff for Maricopa County, Arizona. He was my dad's best friend and his family was friendly with all of our family members. They lived just five houses down the street. He would come over after lunch to visit with my mom, always asking before entering our home if my father was home. I never got to answer him before he would just walk in. I never did like the guy even at age 4, I didn't like the way he looked at my mom.

At that age, I was very aware of the adults' actions around me, and I did not try to hide the fact that I was confused by what I saw. I just did not know how to communicate my thoughts regarding what I'd see or hear.

June 1964

EARLY EXPOSURE TO AN UNSAVORY ASPECT OF LIFE

One day when I was four years old, some of my friends and me were outside playing and a boy asked me, "Why does the sheriff come to your house all the time?"

"To see my daddy," I replied.

Another boy said, "That's funny. Your father's never at home when the sheriff visits."

Hey, that's right, I thought. Daddy's never home when the sheriff comes by on weekdays. My gosh, this has been going on for almost a year and only now my five and six year old friends are bringing it to my attention.

Just then another six-year-old said, "I heard my mom and dad talking and they said your Mommy is sleeping with the sheriff."

"What do you mean?"

"They're playing around together like daddies and mammas do. You know what I mean, sex."

I got so mad. I stood up, all 2 feet 8 inches and 24 pounds of me, and said, "You take that back!"

"No!" he snapped back.

I punched him in his belly hard.

He fell to the ground and began crying. I didn't care. He had no right to talk about my mommy that way or did he?

I kicked him in the butt and said, "Don't ever say that about my mommy again. And get off my property!"

Well, it was minutes after I ran my playmate off of our property that the deputy sheriff came out of our house, and it was time for me to go into take my nap. I was still seething mad. I didn't want to believe that my mommy was in bed with another man. And worse, the sheriff !

In 1964, we were still taught that cops were good. We had to wave at them when we saw them and say, "Hello." They would always wave back to kids who called out a hello to them. They were, I was taught, there to protect our family from "stranger danger." You know, the tall man and the little fat man, who would take you away! My older brother said the cops and sheriff deputies even came to his school to give the kids pamphlets and short talks about how to look out for dangers. How could I accept the idea that the sheriff, a friend of my daddy's, was doing funny things with Mommy?

As I walked to my room that day for my nap, the phone rang in Mommy's room. The call was from my ex-playmate's mother telling Mommy that I had hit her son and kicked him. Even at age four, by listening to Mommy's words to the lady on the phone and hearing the flare up of her anger as she spoke, I knew what the call was about. Quickly jumping onto my bed, I pretended I was asleep.

Within seconds, Mommy stormed into my room screaming, "How dare you tell people I'm sleeping with the sheriff? Why you little . . ." Those were her words as she was slapping me and shaking me around like I was a rag doll. She added, "Why did I ever adopt you? God only knows!"

Through tears and sobs, although I was scared like hell, I tried to call out loud enough that she might hear me between her mad woman verbal blasts, "Mommy, Mommy, I never said that about you. I never would."

She didn't believe me or her anger was so severe that it didn't matter whether she believed me or not. She wanted immediate vengeance.

For the first time in my life, I experienced hate! Full blown, one hundred percent hatred vocally and physically displayed loudly and painfully!!! She became another person, a woman transposed to a witch-like demon. All I could do was beg for her to stop her madness!

After that occasion, there came many such Mommy vs. Mark (Little Character) episodes at our home. Among the five adopted children, it was only me, Little Mark, often on the receiving end of Mommy's most vicious outbursts of anger during daytime hours when the older boys were away at school and Daddy was off at work or school.

Was it me she was angry with? Was it me who committed the deception, the infidelity, the lies? Or was her anger solely at herself and me was her punching bag for guilt? From that first screaming punishment day onward, I was afraid of the woman who was Mommy, my only mother. Granted, I was the one who held her transgressions up to her face. It was certainly no fault of mine, however.

Any reader of this work needs to be told that I was brought up in a very Roman Catholic way. Unfortunately, the lessons that I was supposed to learn about my religious and family values were nearly all taught by *our church* and the Nelson family.

Some of the morality issues I learned as a small child, a school age youngster, and on into teen age years were different than those our family actually lived and sometimes different than what I heard in church, where teachings of the Lord were preached. At times, I felt what the church and what the Nelsons tried to teach me were the opposite of what should be. Yet, when I would question Mommy, I would be quickly shoved off as "looking too deep!" And on those occasions, I would be punished. This rang particularly true regarding my suspicions and (unexpressed) questioning concerning Mommy's bedroom friendship with the deputy sheriff. Often, still at age four, I would ask Mommy about something and she would tell me, "You're not old enough to know."

That "you're not old enough" response should have more truthfully come from her as, "What or why is none of your damned business, Character." And at the same time, as I look back today, I sensed what I felt to be so. In actuality, as far as Mommy and the deputy sheriff carrying on, I saw what was going on but I just didn't know who I could tell about it. To tell Daddy was such a frightful thing I never even gave it much thought.

Mommy's infidelity should have been exposed. I knew even then, not knowing adult words for a small child's thoughts, that since my suspicion existed, while still not proven, things between me and Mommy, and between me and this family, would never be the same again.

April 15, 1965
EMERGENCY ROOM AND POSSIBLE LOSS OF FINGER

I was five-years-old and I got hurt, it all started when I heard Daddy tell Mommy, "Don't use the dryer until I finish fixing it." But like always, she just did what she wanted to and was drying clothes. I wanted to see what was the big deal. Why didn't he want her to use the dryer? I opened the garage door and there it was, this big white box bigger than me. Daddy had taken the back off of the dryer and with Mommy using it, the drum container inside the big, white barrel was turning. The belt driven turning action from the motor to the inner drum was hypnotic. Overhead was a white fluorescent light that made the belt and the wheels look as if they were turning slowly. A warm breeze came from the dryer, acting somewhat like a vacuum drawing me closer and closer to the moving belt and the turning wheels. I remember staring fixated. Those turning wheels and the moving belt drive had a grasp on my desire to make the wheels turn faster...

I put my tiny hand onto the moving drive belt then it happened so fast. My finger became a lever to shift the belt flying off of its drive wheel causing a loud crash-bang sound. In seconds, the belt locked into position and commenced to burn from friction as the motor drive wheel continued to turn momentarily. I remember seeing a very bright light flame, like a camera flash. The motor stopped. I removed my hand from the dryer but my hand had no feeling at first, and I started to feel dizzy. I put my injured hand to my little forehead. That's when I began screaming and crying because I was beginning to really feel pain and there was blood everywhere. My third finger was hanging by only a small piece of skin. Still alone, I was vigorously shaking my injured hand around not knowing that I shouldn't be doing it. The pain was increasing and blood was squirting in all directions.

Hearing my screams, Mommy came rushing into the garage. After she saw I wasn't dead, she was pissed off at me. She pulled my ears and said, "I can't believe you would be so stupid! Where the fuck are your brains?"

I was in pain but forgot the pain because she frightened me so much. She was evil looking and her cigarette breath-- oh, shit, she smoked non-filtered *Lucky Strikes*!

After wrapping my bloody hand and hanging finger in a towel, she took me to the hospital. At some point, she must have called Daddy. When he arrived, she was suddenly quite pleasant. The emergency room surgeon said he couldn't sew my finger on; it was too difficult for him and he couldn't guarantee success.

"We have the insurance. You find me a surgeon right now, God damn it!" Mommy yelled furiously.

From what I was told and the portion of the event I remember, there was a well known hand surgeon participating in a seminar at *Maryvale Medical Center*. Mommy rushed over to where the seminar was being conducted and asked the hand surgeon if he would sew my finger back on. The seminar schedule canceled out so he could and with the aid of others at the hospital, he successfully reattached my finger to my hand. I don't know the surgeon's name or the names of any of the staff people who assisted him, but now, years later, I want to thank the surgical doctor and those people who assisted him for the four-hour operation to reattach the finger that is now in perfect working order. I'm so glad my finger was saved because it would have been a lot of explaining where my finger went as I grew into adulthood.

And for getting the surgery accomplished, Mom, thank you. I guess for that time at least you really did care.

February 1965

DO YOU THINK KIDS DON'T KNOW WHAT'S GOING ON

My fourth adopted sister had asthma and a red birthmark in the middle of her forehead directly between her eyes. It was reddish-pink and stood out slightly from her pretty, white skin. I remember people often asking what the mark was and all the kids making fun of it. She became withdrawn.

We would be out playing in the front yard and the boys would try to touch my sister's birthmark and call her names, too! I got so pissed off. My little sister would cry. I would yell, "Mommy said, no one is allowed to make my sister cry!" But they kept on and on.

Once, as one really upset five-year-old, I went into the house to find Mommy. I couldn't locate her throughout the house until I arrived at her bedroom door. It was locked. I sensed there was someone in there with her.

I knocked on her door. I heard talking, too soft to know what was being said. But no one came to the door so I knocked harder. Nothing. Then I called out, "Mommy, is the sheriff man in there with you?"

Boy, that door flew open! Mommy came out and came at me like a wild woman. I was scared. She started hitting me on my shoulders, chest, and head. Through the barrage of fists and verbal abuse, I managed to see into Mommy's bedroom. The reality struck me so deeply, I wanted to faint. It was the sheriff's face looking at me while he was laying on my daddy's bed naked. He had to have seen the anger and hate for him in my eyes. He knew I'd be back one day to kick his big fat sheriff's ass!! Believe me, this was exactly what I thought at five years old!

I was so intent upon seeing behind her door that her blows and her cursing seemed like nothing. Exhausted, Mommy took me to my room and said, "I was sleeping and you had no business waking me up."

I tried to tell her that the boys were picking on Little Sister but she wouldn't let me finish a sentence. She was right. I was wrong. Period.

She left me in my room. I was sobbing and trying to calm down. I then heard someone else crying outside my bedroom window. It was Little Sister. I ran back outside, and there she was, sitting in the dirt covered with mud from head to foot and weeping as if her little heart were breaking. The boys had fled for fear of getting caught or maybe even fear of me.

Mommy was back in her bedroom with the door closed and, I presumed, locked, even with my precious sister sobbing uncontrollably. It would be a cold day in hell before I'd ever knock on that bedroom door again. Beaten and cursed for no real reason - bad Mommy. Beaten and cursed again for knocking on her door, stupid me. At age five, I was naive and curious but not stupid.

I took Little Sister into the house and cleaned her up. I stuck her muddy clothes under her bed because I knew if I put them into the dirty clothes basket Mommy would find them right away. This way, even though Mommy would find them sooner or later, I was buying time from being severely punished.

How would I be able to explain to Mommy that the big boys had been doing and saying bad things to Little Sister and that when I knocked on her door she was too busy with the sheriff in Daddy's bed? That I'd only knocked to get help. And for that, she had given me a barrage of flying fists and verbal abuse because I "woke her up."

I can't even imagine what she would have done to me If I'd accused her of sleeping with the sheriff, as the older boys had said she was doing. From her side, the truth hurts. From my side, I was punished severely for seeking her protection.

So often during my early years, my little head was spinning. I wanted everyone to go away. Except Daddy? I never saw him it seemed except sometimes on Sundays. When he was home during our waking hours, Mommy did a good job keeping him busy, pulling his attention toward her and away from me and his four other adopted children. In those formative years, I didn't know Daddy hardly at all.

With Mommy's attitude toward me, because I was with her alone more than my older brothers and because she called me (among other things) "Her little helper," it was easy for my older brothers and their friends to make me the "scapegoat" for their misbehavior.

One day, I was playing out back and my two older brothers and some of their friends were out behind the garage playing with matches. When I approached them and saw what they were doing, I said, "You're not allowed to do that." Laughing at me, they commenced lighting matches and flicking them at me. Some of the flicked matches landed on my skin and hurt. Finally, my brothers stopped and told their friends to stop too. Then one of my brothers, the first adopted one, said to me, "Tell Mom you burned yourself playing with matches." Then they ran into the house and told Mommy I was out back playing with matches. Mommy came running out of the house like a mad woman to render to me another barrage of her flying fists and verbal abuse.

I couldn't believe it, my own brothers! Then I was sent to my room. It was 4:00 P.M. I knew the time because it was my cartoon watching time. I remember my brothers and their friends watching cartoons that afternoon while I sat in my room with burns that still hurt.

The very next day I awoke early; it must have been about 5:00 A.M. All was quiet; everyone in the house was sleeping but me. I wasn't allowed out of my room until someone else got up, this was a rule of the house. But I had to go to the bathroom bad, so I walked quietly, like a mouse, to the bathroom.

Chills went down my back when I looked down at the bathroom floor and saw a book of matches. I thought about how neat it looked when my brothers and their friends were lighting matches and flicking them at me. As I was relieving myself, I couldn't help but feel an urge to pick up the book of matches and light and flick some of them. I picked up the matches. The first match I flicked into the toilet looked neat, and I flicked some more. I wasn't scared, even when I burned my finger tips. I was having fun, just like the big boys.

Then one of those flaming sulphur sticks flew into the plastic garbage pail that contained a lot of used facial tissues and some left over hair die material. It started to smoke and then, poof, a flame went as high as my head.

My mind spun. Smoke was quickly everywhere. I thought I was going to die like in a movie I'd seen. As the bathroom filled with smoke, I could hardly breathe. I fell to the floor and crawled toward the door, l just as I saw on TV. I remember thinking, please don't wake up Mommy; I'm sorry! Then something stopped my crawling. Looking back, I saw the fabric of my bathrobe was caught on one of the bolts that anchored the toilet to the floor. Pulling on the bathrobe wouldn't free it. I freaked out but I couldn't scream. Five years old, and I'm going to die. I've never been able to forget those thoughts. I was more scared of Mommy than the flames.

The bathroom started to fill with black smoke; I could barely breathe. Flames from the trash can started to burn the towel set hanging from the rack! I could feel the extreme heat the flames were making! I was so scared that I prayed to my God for help. I was crying silently. I kept kicking and kicking at my belt. It would not come free! The smoke was getting thick, I could taste the burning plastic of the trash can in the back of my throat! I tried one more time; somehow I managed to kick the robe belt lose and started to crawl out on the bathroom floor.

I stood up, with the door still partly open, crying silently. I didn't want to wake anyone up, especially Mommy because she'd really be pissed off. Flames were reaching the bathroom curtains and black and brown smoke was beginning to come through the partly open door into the hallway. I was about to pass out; the smoke was making me gag! I can still smell it now as I write!

I closed the door. In a second, smoke commenced to come into the hall through the narrow space under the closed door. I opened the door again slightly to see if the flame had gone out.

A suction-like force felt as though it pulled open the door! As I fought the pressure, flames bellowed out from all sides of the door! I could barley breath; I started to cough. My head was spinning! I wanted to scream; tears were flowing down my face, and I could feel the heat drying my tears!

"Please, God," I said. "Please make it stop!"

I closed the door again, but I managed to grab a towel from a towel bar beside the door. Smoke was still coming through the crack under the closed door so I crammed the towel there to stop the smoke from coming into the hall. It worked, but only a little bit; more smoke was seeping out of the bathroom!

I then took a small rug from the hall and crammed it under the door. I was so scared! No one had awakened yet. Again, my head was spinning. I thought surely I was going to die. I couldn't breath. I simply had to lie down. I went into my bedroom, closed the door behind me, and climbed into bed, leaving the hazard behind me, and no one yet astir. I actually passed out!

Next thing I knew a fireman was waking me up. He took me outside where I saw the rest of the family. All still in sleeping clothes, my family was awaiting information on who started the fire.

Boy, two fire trucks at this five-year-old's house. I could hardly believe it. I wanted to get close up to see the big, red trucks. I wanted to talk to the firemen and ask them all kinds of questions. Then my wish seemed to be answered when one of the firemen came over beside me.

My finger was hurting where I'd burnt it with the matches that started the fire that could have killed all of my family and me. Suddenly, in that moment of childish realization, I felt sick to my stomach and dropped down to lie on the ground. The nice fireman picked me up. It was then when I told him I'd hurt my finger. He looked at my sore finger and said, "It looks like you burned it."

I remember his face. He had blonde hair, blue eyes, and a real somber expression. He looked like a Ken doll fireman who had come alive. He had real white teeth and his breath smelled like cinnamon. He looked toward the house and then back directly into my eyes. His look was kindly and his blue eyes were sparkling.

He asked me, "Do you want to tell me what you did?"

I told this nice fireman how I'd gotten up early to go to the bathroom, how I'd found the book of matches on the bathroom floor, and that I'd lit some of them and flicked them like my brother and the bigger boys had showed me how to do the day before. I told him that's what started the fire.

The fireman sat me down then walked away, saying, "Hey, kid, thanks for telling me the truth." I remember that he made me feel good for telling the truth.

Moments later, Mommy came storming up, her nostrils flaring like a horse running up hill and trying to get more air. She could make some pretty evil faces, and yet she was a physically attractive lady. The fireman liked her. She liked the Ken doll. I don't know how I knew, something inside told me. With him she became all bubbly and turned on her Miss America smile. The fireman asked me if I was okay, but before I could tell him it was hard to breathe, my Mommy cut me off. She told him, "He's okay. He just wants attention!"

To me she said softly so the fireman could not hear her words, while she looked right into my eyes, "I'll deal with you later!" I knew from the look in her eyes and the tone of her voice, soft and subtle, that the punishment I was going to receive would be the worst I'd ever gotten. The cold chill that went down my small spine actually hurt my front teeth!

The firemen began cleaning up and putting away their equipment. The neighbors, who had come out to see the early morning excitement began shuffling back to their homes. Daddy had left for work. Luckily, when I had closed the bathroom door and stuffed the towel beneath it, I had cut off the oxygen that had fed the fire. In a way, I had saved my family, although none of them would have seen it that way, least of all Mommy.

My older brothers had left for school and I was back in my room, watching and waving to the departing fireman. Suddenly, I was grabbed from behind, and I heard this horrible, rough, witch voice. I have never forgotten her words. "Okay, you little son of a bitch," she screamed. "I'm going to show you just what happens to a little boy who plays with matches in my home!!!"

I started to cry. My heart was beating fast and furious. It felt like it was getting ready to stop beating entirely.

I could still taste burnt plastic in my throat! Breathing hard was actually making it worse!

She yanked me by my scrawny little arm into her bathroom. Mommy's anger couldn't have been more if the entire house had been burned to ashes, as she pulled me I was crying out, "No, Mommy! No!

Please don't hurt me! I love you. I'm sorry, I'm sorry!!! Please, Mommy, no, no-no, no!

"Shut up," she said. "Your father will never know about this punishment." Then, as she pulled me near the sink, she added, "You're going to think twice before you burn my fuckin' bathroom down, you little prick!"

I remember her bad breath, cigarette smoke breath, and sprinkles of her saliva on my face, spat there by her forceful screaming at me. I remember, too, the veins in her neck bulging out as if they were going to pop!

I was yelling as loudly as she, the bathroom walls echoing my pain!

"Who is this lady?" I thought to myself. Through my tears and difficult breathing I said, again, "Mommy, please don't hurt me."

She answered, "You don't know what hurt is." She grabbed me by my arm and placed it under her arm to hold me. Standing tall, she literally lifted me from the floor by my arm so my legs were dangling like rag doll legs.

This five-year-old was doomed! I yelled out, "Someone help me! Please!"

She continued to hold me by my arm under her upper arm. Mommy lit her cigarette lighter! I remember she said that old, worn out phrase, "This is going to hurt me more than it does you."

I was freaking out, screaming, "No! Mommy, no!" As she moved her lighter toward my thumb, I could already feel the heat.

I cried out, "No, Mommy! Don't burn me! No!" With tears rolling down my cheeks I kept pleading, "No! Please, Mommy. No!" As I looked into her eyes, they were not pretty blue any more, they were black with a small outline of blue.
I felt and saw the true touch of evil in this lady I called "Mommy!"

Then she did it. She held the flame under my thumb.
All I could do was cry the pain was so intense. I could feel the heat burn the underneath part of my thumbnail from the inside!!!

I was breathing very hard, I was going to pass out!! I remember my head was spinning. I was reliving the fire in the bathroom! I was so scared!

"No, no-nnnno, Mommy! Don't burn my thumb!"

"Shut-up, God damn you!" she replied. As she let go of my arm, I fell to the floor. I started to crawl away, like a wounded dog, severely beaten by his master I remember this, as though it was just the other day.

She grabbed me again! And scolded me "don't you dare pull away from me, you little shit!" She pulled me by my other arm, I thought for sure she was done. But she pulled me into her sweaty arm pit.

I screamed, "Noooo! Please, Mommy Noooo! Please don't burn me! Please stop. I can't breath!" But it was too late, almost immediately the whole underneath of my thumbs had blisters that seemed to me at the time to be the size of ping-pong balls.

As a result of those severe burns I stayed in the house for one week while they healed. In fact, I'm lucky to still have thumb prints. My mother knew just how long to keep my thumbs in her flame.

When I was finally able to again play outside neighborhood, kids were not allowed to play with me because I'd almost burned the house down. I remember making mud pies in the front yard by myself. My sisters were not allowed to play with me either. I was off limits, according to Mommy!

I remember crying many of those days because I had no friends, and the friends I used to have were now playing across the street, making fun of me, and calling me "fire bug." The big question here is, was this an appropriate way to punish a five-year-old!

I guess in Phoenix, Arizona, in 1965 it was!

September 1965
THINGS DO TEND TO GO FULL CIRCLE SOMETIMES

As time passed, I became increasingly depressed because I thought by now one or a couple of my old friends would be back to be my friend again. But it wasn't happening; no parents wanted their children to be my friend. Because I played with matches, and almost burnt the house down, I was doomed. I started to hate everyone!

Then one day the light did shine. It was shortly after lunch time, during Mommy's nap time, that Daddy came home early (the sheriff had just left).

Daddy said smilingly, as he passed me in the yard, "We're moving."

I was so happy. I'd prayed for our family to move to a new house and start a new life.

After Daddy told me we were moving, I recall running to my bedroom and jumping up and down on the bed. In whatever terms I would have used at age five, I was thinking, "No more assholes, a whole new life." I could hardly wait.

We moved into the largest house in the *Phoenix Maryvale District* at the time. Our front yard overlooked the *Maryvale Golf Course*. It looked huge to a five-year-old, a new residence of six bedrooms, three bathrooms, a living room, family room, formal dining room, laundry room, kitchen with breakfast nook, and even a den! It was mansion compared to where we used to live! This house had been the sales office for a famous local community builder, John F. Long. This was a good deal. Thanks John F. Long for your sales office we called home!

 I remember being awake in bed one day just a few days after we'd moved into our new home. I was thinking how good it felt not to be around anyone who knew who we were. I figured I would keep away from the people, kids and adults, we left behind.

The first quest at our new home was to find out who the neighbors were. This pre-schooler went to every house for a block in each direction. At each house, I knocked on the door, and when someone answered, I introduced myself and told them we'd just moved into the neighborhood. All of these people were very nice to me. They gave me cookies, Koolaid, donuts, candy, and one lady even gave me a dollar. She said I had beautiful eyes. Boy, I thought I was the luckiest boy in town. My new neighbors were cool people. I went home with lots of stuff, better than Halloween.

When I got home though, it was what I expected. I told Mommy what had happened. She got so mad she started yelling at me. She screamed, "People are going to think you're poor! Looking for a handout. How could you do this to *me*?"

She took all my stuff and threw it away, and she kept my dollar. For further punishment, I had to stay in my room for two hours. It was considered a space break.

At five years old, I was very observant and continuously curious. Thus, I asked lots of questions and sometimes blurted out curiosity motivated statements as an innocent youngster, both in church and at school. I was thinking how good it felt not to be around any of our old friends, the people who said bad things about my mother. I'd hear both questions and statements such as, "How many husbands did she have?" Childishly, when I would hear this, I would yell at the top of my lungs, "See, Mommy, these ladies are saying bad things about you!" Now with a new circle of life, I thought it would be better. However when we would go to church, I would overhear such comments and blurt out loud what I heard. Then, when we'd get home, I'd see "the mad woman" yelling at me for embarrassing her. She would insist, "Those ladies are nice. Why do you keep causing problems? You always seem to get involved where you just don't belong."

After each such Mommy's ire session, I remember thinking to myself, "Am I just imagining this stuff? After all, these bad comments I hear do come from these peoples' mouths." Anyway, I resolved to stay far away from these gossipy people, far, far away. They all acted as if the time they spent at church every Sunday was their Mortal Act of Contrition to others. They seem to think, "I am aware of the sins I commit; therefore I go to church and my sins for this week have just been forgiven by God." Not everyone had this belief, just the majority.

This little five-year-old would listen to the adults speak about life telling him, "Do as I say, not as I do life styles." And yet these same adults are in complete denial that they are doing anything wrong themselves because they go to church every Sunday and give money. They do it so they can sin just a little more next week.

I couldn't figure out what kind of adults these were. It was not until later that I learned they must be called by their true name, "hypocrites."

So you can see, for me going to church was quite difficult. They would preach and teach not to sin, and yet these same teachers were not teaching adults around me not to do or say what they considered bad. When I would see or hear the opposite of what was being taught, I would speak out about it until someone listened, only to be shunned or scolded. I began to feel like an outcast or even mentally disturbed because Mommy and Daddy would tell me "You're a mentally disturbed child."

Once again my mind was spinning, too much bad information. But at the tender age of five, to whom could I tell my tales of woe? The Nelson family attended church every Sunday. Our family was like *"The Brady Bunch."* We would be the family to carry the collected offerings to the alter. Going to the alter was something I never quite understood. I wished I could have found the words to tell them they were the ones disturbing me along with "those mean people at the church!"

September 6, 1966
FIRST FLIGHT OF THE BALD EAGLE OUT OF THE NEST BY LAW

Early in 1966, I prepared for my first day of school, kindergarten. I was so scared. It was the first time away from Mommy. Even with her promiscuous ways and evil temper, I feared stepping out from beneath her protection. I did not know if I would be able to handle the pressure of leaving home on a bus.

But I had to. It was the law. Every kid had to go to school or the truant officer sent him off to jail. These were the rumors that went around in 1966. I woke up that early morning shaking with fear and went to the school they called "Sunset Elementary."

I was very small for my age. Plus, I had a hair cut from hell. It was a crew cut or flat top. I was the only kid to have one of these special hairdos, among my peers! I hated the haircut myself, but just how much the other kids disliked it, I was to find out my first day riding the school bus. The kids on the bus kept calling me "Bald Eagle." At first, I just laughed, then more kids started making fun of my hair. I started to get mad, and I stood up and told them to be quiet. Then this boy stood up and pushed me down onto my seat, saying, "You shut up, Baldly!" I wanted to stand up and hit this kid, but I'd been told, "Don't hit!" So I just ignored being pushed down and what he'd said.

Later that same morning, when I was in my classroom, a monitor came and accompanied me to the principal's office. The bus driver, I learned, said I'd "caused a lot of commotion on the bus." So I got in trouble. No one else, just me. Things like this happened to me a lot, getting blamed for things I didn't do. It hurt, but I figured that's life!

After a few days in school, I noticed that not many kids wanted to play with me, and the ones who did were scared of the other kids who seemed to be "the clique." Before long, I mustered up the courage to ask some of the boys of "the clique" if I could play bat ball with them. Their reply to me was, "We don't want you to play with us because you have a chocolate brother." They were referring to my adopted big brother, three years older than I, who is a full-blooded Apache Indian.

I got so mad I told them to take back those words.

"No!" Three of them shouted back at me. Then the big kid, who had pushed me down on the seat on the bus, said, "You're a baldly and nobody wants you around."

I demanded he take back those words. He pushed me down to the ground!

This time I got up and went off, flying fists into him. I'd learned well from Mommy and my brothers how to hit, where to hit, and to hit hard. He went to the ground, tears welled up in his eyes, and he stayed on the ground wondering what kind of little wolverine had attacked him. This bully, almost a head taller than me and a lot heavier, never bothered me again!

What was pleasantly funny was that after that occasion I became kind of a little hero! None of the kids really liked that bigger bully either. They mostly went along with him because they were scared of him. If I had known that and if I'd been equally angry at the time, I would have beaten him up on the bus when he pushed me down onto my seat and threatened to beat me up if I stood up again, in front of my classmates!

My first grade teacher was Mrs. Tomb. School was fun, all I did was play. I couldn't get enough. After six years of only my Mommy and a few people's games, this to me was a vacation.

Do you blame me? Now that I am older, and I think back, I recognize that school at this stage is extremely important. It is the foundation for more comprehensive schooling and education in years to come.

It is the parents and teachers who play key roles in the success of positive development of such young children. If during these formative years, you haven't taught your children self control and self respect because you were just too busy to concern yourself with your children's well being, consider this: Your children are reflections of the circle of life in which they grow up!

September 6, 1969
PUBLIC SCHOOL vs CATHOLIC SCHOOL

In 1969, my parents decided I would go to school at *St. Vincent De Paul*. My parents thought a private catholic school would be a better foundation compared to the public school system. It did cost more but my dad said it was worth it. He thought public schools would lead to a decline of education and social standings. I was eight years old and excited knowing that there would be new people and I could start all over again. Maybe the grass is greener on the other side of the fence? Besides, I felt I would be safer at my new church anyway. At least one would think so.

I don't remember much about the school but what I do know is that my Apache Indian brother was always picked on by the other students. No one physically abused him because they were definitely scared of him. This was why rumors were started about him that he scalped people. One afternoon on the playground, I heard some boys talking. Pointing they said, "There's that Injun." I looked where they pointed and there was my brother. One boy said, "He looks weird. What color is his skin?" Another replied, "Brownish red." Another said, "No, Red." And yet another said, "No, it's chocolate."

"Hey, what color would you say his skin is?" one asked me. "He's an Apache Indian and he's my brother!" As we spoke my brother continued walking further away from us.

I was about to follow my brother when the one Big Mouth kid said, "He's not your brother, you're a liar!"

Facing the Big Mouth, I shouted with anger, "Yes he is my brother!"

I saw that my brother was already out of sight behind a building and Big Mouth was directly in front of me inches, from my face.

"You're a liar," he said, "Do you know what we do to liars?"

Unyielding, I replied, "But I'm not a liar. He truly is my brother."

"You're a fuckin' liar," he yelled.

Another boy had kneeled behind me and then the Big Mouth shoved me backwards. I hit the ground head first. Everything went super bright for an instant and then darkness. I was out cold.

A little girl was beside me when I opened my eyes, and I remember her saying, "I woke you up. I saw what those boys did to you, and I thought you were asleep, like..., and I thought they hurt your head!"

"Yeah," I replied, still groggy. "It sure feels like a broken neck must feel. But I'll be all right."

The little girl kissed me on my cheek, saying, "I hope you'll feel better." As my senses were returning and I was able to sit up I saw how pretty the little girl was, and then she was gone. I was never to see her again.

On the way to the boy's room, I told another kid what had happened.

"You're lying," he said. "No girl kissed you."

"Yes, she did!" I shouted

"Hey, I saw that big boy push you down, but I didn't see any girl kiss you. I didn't even see a girl near you."

I remember my thought at the time, "Am I making up the girl and her kiss to rationalize the reality of other kids seeing me getting bullied, pretending that someone really cared?" I remember, too, that my head hurt and I kept my thoughts to myself for I knew what happened.

These kinds of incidents happened a lot to the members of our family. One time my sister, the one with the birthmark in the center of her forehead and who was in third grade at the time, came into my classroom crying. She found me and said, "Some boys are calling me a Martian and they want to touch my middle eye." Hearing what she said to me, the others in my classroom commenced laughing. Sister cried even louder. My teacher told my sister to go to the principal's office. That was when I stood up to my highest height, looked my teacher right in her eyes, and said, "She's not going to any office; they won't do anything anyway!"

Following those words, I took my sister by her hand and left the classroom and went to the school's south lawn where she had been playing with kids her age in the playground tunnels. I asked in a loud voice so all the kids could hear, "Who was picking on my little sister?" Not a single kid replied. Then I asked Sister who it was who called her a Martian and wanted to touch her forehead? She pointed to a boy, saying, "Him."

Sure enough, he was a lot bigger than me. But that didn't matter. At that moment, I was just plain sick of having schoolmates picking on my little sister who was a petite age seven and who suffered from frequent asthma attacks, three of which had brought her close to death before this incident. This was a scary situation; her anxiety could bring on another asthma attack. Besides, she was my first sister, and Mommy always urged me to protect her because no one else in the family was near her as much of the time as I was.

I said to the bully, "Hey, you, why are you calling my little sister names?"

He answered, "She's not your sister; you don't even look alike!"

"Well, she is, my sister. I love her and nobody's going to say bad things to her. Now you tell her you're sorry!"

"No!" he replied, "And you sure can't make me."

I hit him hard and put him into a head lock like my brothers had showed me and like I'd learned from Bruce Lee movies. He apologized, just as the Nuns came running to the play area. One of them grabbed me by my ear and literally dragged me into the office. With two nuns there, one of them hit my hands with a ruler, then paddled me. It hurt but for what I'd done to that bully it was worth it. That was until it was time to go home. Mommy was called, and she had to come pick me up. When she arrived to get me in the early afternoon, she acted as though I'd interrupted something special. She was polite to the nuns and listened to their reasoning for having her come to get me. On the way home, a ten minute ride, she said absolutely nothing. A sign to me that real trouble was brewing! Her nostrils were flaring like that horse, running uphill!

Once home, her tirade commenced. She pushed and punched me and called me names forbidden even among angry sailors and truck drivers. She was at times like what many people would call "a first class bitch!" I remember my dad calling her that once in a while and my brothers, as they got older, would call her that, too. Sometimes I even heard neighbors referring to Mommy as the bitch who has all those kids. It made me so mad. *Why* would these people talk such trash about my mother. I had gotten into a lot of fights in honor of my mother. I still loved her in spite of the way she treated me sometimes. And even when many things I personally witnessed and heard about her pointed otherwise, I still didn't believe or didn't want to believe that Mommy would ever cheat on Daddy or that her ways of punishment and discipline were actually abusive or that she was "a first class bitch."

Shit, at that time in my young life, I didn't even know what the adult definitions of those words and phrases were, let alone what they meant! Now looking back, I realize that while she would say "I love you" to me or to other family members, her actions frequently proved otherwise. Even at a tender age, however, I would simply ignore her actions and verbal abuse of family members, with me being one of her prime targets for venting frustrations and ire. Was I wrong when repeatedly accepting her abuse without outcry or mention to others? If so, in the year of 1969, where were the counselors, the special personnel trained for such unfairly handed out circumstances to this little boy of nine?

Was I, between the ages of four and eighteen, living a life of self persecution, a life of mere survival? My Mommy was the ruler of my life, and I was totally frightened of her, yet dependent upon her. I named the dependency *"love"* in a child's way. I'm sure I did love her or at least I thought of my feeling as love. Inside I was confused and scared, very, very scared! I would ask myself over and over again, whom do I tell? When can I tell someone? And then the other giant question for this kid, who would believe me over the adults? The answer was simple, no one! I wanted to run away, far away where no one could find me, where I could take care of myself. Then I would get frustrated and know that was completely stupid thinking! Is this the sort of thing an eight-year-old is supposed to be thinking about? I simply accepted the reality of my existence, crawled into a corner, and cried.

Sometime after the incident at the church school play yard tunnels, my family finally had little sister's birthmark surgically removed. They finally took my sister's and my words and deeds seriously that she was truly being picked on beyond what little ones should have to handle. Before that Daddy used the old saying, sticks and stones may break my bones, but words can never harm me. I never believed what he said to me because I saw and heard what happened between Daddy and Mommy when he called her a bitch or when she called him a bastard. Boy, did things get louder and more names were used. When the words flew, Mommy would cry and I would see her doing it, and she'd see me looking at her and say to Daddy, "My baby, Markie. Please, not in front of my baby!" My Dad was slapping around my mother, it was not the first time, and it was not the last! One time, Dad told me to go to my room.

I answered, "No. Why are you hitting Mom?" Then Mommy said to Daddy, "Yes, we are fighting!" I felt real sorry for my Mommy. I didn't like to see her cry. Her crying made me cry. Through sobs I said, "Daddy, you're bad!" Then my 6 foot 3 inch 200 pound Daddy hit me, his 3 foot 5 inch, 55 pound ten-year-old boy. Daddy would literally throw me into my room. Mommy, when this happened, stood by and did nothing more than cry. And there were times when Mommy took the offensive in their battles, times when Daddy drank eight quarts of beer a day. My Mom, on the other hand, loved her bourbon and Coke!

I was very mad when the man I call Daddy was hurting my mommy. But what could I do, who could I tell? Now I hate my Dad but I still love him, too. But when he hurt Mommy, he passed the line for me, this was when I actually wanted to hurt my Dad, but could not. I thought he'd found out about his best friend, the sheriff, sleeping with his wife, my mother. But he had not.

But whom was I supposed to tell? There was no one. The Nelsons were the best for adopting and rearing so many kids. And yet behind the door in the corner sat this little boy crying out for someone to rescue him from false accusations, serious punishment, and abuse for little to nothing bad at all--and even worse--so often they struck the punching bag to relieve pent-up tensions and frustrations brought on by those very adults' own sins, denials, and idiosyncrasies.

One day at *St. Vincent DePaul School* in my fourth grade class, there was a big fuss about some kid being hit in the head with a thrown boot. The boys athletics coach, Mr. Domiani, had never liked my Indian brother. He really didn't like anyone of a color different than his own. My Mom knew this about the coach and was quite verbal about it when talking to people about the him.

Coach Domiani told the school principal (a Nun) in her office at the school that it was my brother who threw the boot. Sadly, when my brother told the coach and principal who did throw the boot, they punished him more severely. My Mom was furious. I'd never before seen her act in a public situation as she did with the school administrators following their false accusation and punishment of my brother. Mom took all of us kids out of the school after telling the principal, her assistant, and the coach that they were all hypocrites and liars. She told them, too, that one day it would all come back to them. My Mom needed to record that speech and listen to the recording herself!

I was in the office when this argument occurred, and I was hoping Mom would yell at the one egotistical Nun (the principal), the one who had hit me before. This nun was very bitter.

The false accusation Nun was so scared of my Mom, that she appeared white as a ghost. This Nun had acted as if she thought she was Mother Mary, as the rumors went. From my understanding, though, the Nun abused her power as a Nun and as administrator of a Catholic school, and she did a very good job hiding it from her superiors. I'd seen her do other mean things to some school children of different races.

But with that happening, as with scores of other things in my life, who was I to tell about the unfair and unjust treatment of my brother? The coach, the principal, and even my Mom in some of her actions and the things she said condemning them, were they all wrong in their thoughts, words or actions? Or was it me who was wrong in my feelings and in my inability to do anything positive about my feelings and observations? I remember my brothers's face. He would never be the same again.

But the adults, essentially because they were bigger, older, and wiser in their minds always seemed to win out over my thoughts, actions or words. And yet since these adults were older, they should have fathomed the truth in such situations. I know that Coach Domiani knew dammed well that my brother did not throw the boot. I knew my brother had told the truth to everyone, only to be ignored and forced to take the blame.

Looking back, I wonder now, "How did the adults win anything from a situation like the boot throwing, and the results; what did the adults win? No, it was for nothing but to hide the little white boy who actually threw the boot. Everyone knew who did it, and it was not my adopted Apache brother, who told the school administrators he saw who did it.

I just wanted the truth and to live by it, but my problem was the adults in my life responsible for my upbringing were living a different life style. Some adults whom I overheard talking among themselves about me, referred to me as being "too deep!" It appeared to me that it was just them labeling me to avoid the truth about themselves. They would always say it was me who was wrong. *Silly people!*

My family and me after almost two years of attending the private school, were removed; we still continued to attend the *St. Vincent De Paul Church* regularly. I was glad I no longer went to school there.

During my primary *Roman Catholic* school days, I did see a lot of disrespect among parishioners at our church. Maybe this is a thought that is too harsh. Yet what can I call it other than disrespect when in church our family, the Nelsons, were praised for adopting and rearing children of mixed races and mixed cultures. Then, outside of the church these same people criticized and scoffed the existence of such a unique family. *Why?*

My Dad, still very much involved with our church, joined the church mens' mushball team. I played lots of mushball too, but I particularly liked to go watch the men play. As the men's games went into long innings, sometimes extra innings, some of the players on the bench below where I sat with Mom to watch the games would get into cursing and saying words like "fuck," "asshole," "prick," "pussy," "cock sucker," and every other dirty word known or imaginable words I was absolutely forbidden to say. Church men!

I had the gumption to point out some of these men's vocabularies to Mom, wondering why I shouldn't be able to use those words too, not to mention that we were on the church lawn! I waited until it was relatively quiet around us; then I stood up and said in a bold voice, "Mom did you hear those men? They said 'fuck you' and 'asshole.' Why can they say those words, Mom?" The words were barely out of my mouth when she slapped my face and said, "Don't you ever say those words again!"

"But the men did, Mom. Why don't you slap them, too?" People sitting near us laughed and, at the same time, I started to cry. Mom's eyes glared and her face turned red. She was seething, and I guess I was lucky there were other people around so she couldn't strike me as hard as she would have liked to.

Mom ordered me, "Go sit in the car. And don't talk back to your elders."

I stormed off to the car thinking about those eleventh inning mushball players, those drunk assholes! And then people wonder where kids pick up the back alley curse words? I know where I learned lots of those words, at the Sunday after mass mushball games.

Sometimes we'd drive the 85 miles north to Prescott, Arizona, to match our parish softball team with a church team up there. We kids enjoyed going to Prescott, up in a mountain area of Arizona, and the pregame picnic lunches. However, when the games got underway, we might as well have stayed in Phoenix. It was the same players getting drunk on beer and whatever else as the innings were played and the same dirty curse words said. I wasn't a prudish kid, and I didn't dare say anything negative about these boors. I just wanted to be away from these stupid people who, after coming from church, were disrespecting my mind and soul, not to mention Jesus and God! Was I too deep? Was I living in make believe?

At the Sunday afternoon mushball games, I remember seeing all kinds of sinful things going on after church that had nothing to do with mushball. I saw married women kissing married men who weren't their husbands and thinking to themselves they were fooling everyone, but they were only fooling themselves!

The thing that bothered me the most, that spun around endlessly throughout my thoughts, was the fact that with deception, their family and friends were adversely affected, either by ignoring the reality they experienced, and then bottling up the negative entity in their subconscious minds, soon to be released on someone else or thing the hidden parts, in the laws of *Karma*.

My religion did not teach of this law. It was a law that was taught to me by someone very long ago when I was a very small child. The teacher was a close friend of our family who moved to Australia, and I have never forgotten her or this law of *Karma*!

February 1970
A KISS WITH A PRIEST

I saw a priest who kissed a woman on her lips for a long time. I saw my own Mom kiss this same dark-haired priest. He was very handsome. Lots of the ladies I overheard talking about him and saying how good looking he was. At one Sunday service, he mentioned that since he'd been an assistant pastor, masses had been filling to capacity and the offerings were much larger. He thanked everyone at the mass but I'm sure it was his "woman appeal" that caused those things to happen. This priest had a very powerful way about him. I just cannot explain it here.

I went by myself to see that same priest at the rectory one day. I was age nine. I knocked on the rectory door. It was he who came to answer my knock. I asked, "Father, may I talk to you?"

"Certainly, son. Come right on in."

"Oh, no, I can't do that, Father. Can't you come outside where we can talk. Mommy told me I was to never go into the house where you live or into where the nuns live."

"What is your name, son?"

"Mark Nelson."

"Why, you're one of the Nelson children. I'm sure your mother won't mind if you come into the rectory for a short while. In here we have some milk and cookies and most boys like those. Wouldn't you like some, too?"

Wow! Milk and cookies. I got so happy, nothing would have kept me outside any longer. The handsome priest was going to give me a special snack. So I said, "Okay, I'll come inside, but you can't tell my mommy. Promise?"

He promised our conversation and my visit to the rectory would be our secret. We walked into the big kitchen with a table and chairs for six people. He directed me to one of the chairs, and I watched while he poured two glasses of milk and took some cookies from a big cookie jar. Four chocolate cookies on a plate were placed onto the table by the priest, then he brought us two glasses of milk. Boy, what a great place this is, I thought, but it was awfully quiet!

I asked, "Where are the other priests?"

He smiled then laughingly said, "They're out calling on people of our parish." His words reminded me that the white car, the car the priests drove around, wasn't in the driveway.

Seated at the table with me to share the cookies and milk, the good looking priest asked, "What is it you want to talk about, son?"

A small boy of few words on such occasions, I replied matter of factually, "I saw you kiss my Mom."

Dumbfounded and spilling some of the milk he was just raising to sip, he stuttered, "N-N-N-Noooo, it couldn't have been me." Then he added, "I did kiss Mrs. Nelson on the cheek one day as a token of friendship for flowers she brought us to decorate the altar. Maybe that's what you saw? I think it's just that you're young and have a wild imagination."

"No, Father. You kissed her on her lips.

He said nothing for an instant and then changed the subject to, "You're a strong boy, Mark, I've watched you at play and if you'll let me I want to teach you some things about life, about things that are good for you to learn."

"I'd like that, Father."

"One of the things you must learn, Mark, is to not be quite so open and explicit, so blunt with people. Always be honest, Mark, but tone down what you say a little."

"I guess I can do that. But I only say what's real."

"I'm sure that's true, son, but you don't always need to tell everything you know because some people don't always understand and maybe hurt or upset by things you or I too, might say. Be honest, Mark, but not so honest that you hurt someone, that you cause someone to be upset or that some people might take what you say in some other way besides how you mean it."

"I think you mean I shouldn't tell people I saw you kiss my Mom on her lips."

"Not unless you're absolutely sure of what you saw. I only remember quickly kissing your mother on her cheek. That had to be what it was, and it was your strong imagination that would have me kissing her any other way."

"I don't think so, Father, but I'll not tell anyone you kissed her." Just as I was finishing the last of the cookies he had brought to the table, he bent down to tie my shoe that had come untied. I jumped out of the chair and back from him.

"I'm only going to tie your shoe," he said.

"I have to go now, Father. Thank you for the cookies and milk."

"There's no hurry, Mark. Would you like more milk and cookies?"

"I just want to go home. My Mom's expecting me." Before I could leave, he put his arms around me and kissed me on my forehead.

He said, "Mark, you can be my little friend and come here for cookies and milk any time you would like."

"I don't think so, " was my reply. I added, "But thank you, Father." I was getting scared, and I did not know why.

We said good-bye, and I left the rectory walking out the long driveway toward the parking lot that lead to the street. I remember turning around to wave good-bye and seeing him in the doorway and calling out to me, "Come back again, Mark. Okay?"

I repeated, "I don't think so." I took off for home, running. Somehow it felt like the priest was coming right behind me. He wasn't, of course, but I had a creepy feeling like he was. Even some days after my visit to the rectory, I sometimes felt like he was right at my back following me. I would see him watching me play on the playground. I would pretend I couldn't see him. Boy, I should have never said anything to that priest.

A short time after my visit to the priest, he left the parish to go raise money for another church. I guess his special gift of raising money was needed elsewhere.

Don't get me wrong I was proud of being a *Roman Catholic*, I did my studies like a good little Christian. And what I discovered was that the majority of the people live the opposite of these studies. You, as a reader, might think I was and remain too deep, but the studies of the church were intended to make me a better servant of God. How can I serve God the way it is written if the majority are just pretending to?

I wanted so badly for my life to be as it was written, and I would try to change the circumstances surrounding my plight. But what could this nine-year-old do?

September 6, 1972
CATHOLIC SCHOOL vs PUBLIC SCHOOL

I was off to a new school *John F. Long Elementary*. Once more I was excited about the opportunity for new people, new friends. Frankly, attending the catholic school had confused the hell out of me! I did like the fact we had to wear uniforms in the catholic school. It was great because all the students looked the same and you could not tell who had money for nice clothes and who didn't. But the people there made me never want to go into the public again.

Now it was time to experience a new social dilemma I really had not before experienced, the buying of school clothes. My parents, did not like to buy the latest fashions and I always wore what we could afford. Let's just say I remember in kindergarten and first grade my classmates would make fun of my clothes. Now in fifth grade, it was happening all over again!

At my new school, I was in Mrs. Johnson's class. I'll always remember her and her husband because they seemed so much in love, so devoted to each other. It seemed like every week he sent her flowers. I remember, one day, she was talking to us, and she brought up how cute the dimple was on his chin. She'd laugh real loudly and say, "You should see him when he eats spaghetti. His dimple or cleft will fill with sauce." And she would point to the center of her own chin to help us visualize his cleft filled with sauce. We kids would all start laughing with her. She taught me a lot about being a leader, but I always seemed drawn toward a crowd of the unwanted races. School procedures for me at that time were completely boring.

Three different schools, kindergarten to the fifth grade, and I heard nothing but lies. I should have just studied and kept the world closed out. No relationships, no fun, just study. If there is one thing I learned, books certainly can't hurt you and your education is something no one can take from you. But for me, what good is a education if the world around you is in denial? At age 11, was I just being too deep!

In fifth grade I did the normal kid things, good and bad. I liked to star in class plays. I was "Hippie Short Stuff" in one play written by Lori Jones who was a classmate. She was very proud of her role that she wanted me to play. Unfortunately I don't remember the plot, I can tell you it had something to do with a hippie!

I was in the chorus, where one of my best friends was a black guy named Tony Taylor, who had a voice like Al Green. I remember we had a concert at another school; the teachers even cried and gave him a standing ovation. I wish I knew what happened to him after I left sixth grade, but I never saw him again or his brothers.

I wanted to be a law enforcement officer so I became a patrol boy in my school, I figured this would be good basic training. Boy, what was I thinking? I really took my patrol job seriously. I remember my principal sitting me in the office and telling me that I had to do the right thing by making people follow orders. I said, "I could do it." But he emphasized that my friends would try to get away with things, but I would have to report them. I remember telling him, "My friends will never do me wrong." I said that knowing that the people who were my friends truly were not real friends. But I figured that negative thinking might be wrong. Boy, was that a big mistake.

The bullies at school tried to cross the street at the crosswalk before I would give them the signal that it was okay to cross. They were supposed to wait for me to signal them to cross safely, but these guys just thought they could push their way through without waiting and that I wouldn't stop them. They were wrong. I did stop them, and they accepted my order because there was almost always a yard duty teacher there watching the crosswalk area.

Then one day there was no teacher in sight in the vicinity of the crosswalk at street crossing time when three of those bullies were crossing the street outside of the painted crosswalk. I told them to get back onto the sidewalk. All three of them came running toward me, one of them shouting, "We're going to kick your ass!"

I replied, "I'll fight all three of you, but right now I'm on duty."

They were laughing at me and one said, "Duty? What duty? You're an asshole!"

"I am not. And I can't fight you right now because I'm on duty and wearing my patrol belt."

They pushed me down right near the curb and while I was down one kicked me. As I hit the ground, I heard someone yell, "It's a fight!" All the schoolmates started to scream and shout, "Kick his ass!" I couldn't figure out who they were rooting for. I can bet it wasn't against the bullies. I got up from the ground and took my belt off and tore into one kid, fully ready and willing to fight all three, and then a teacher came running to where we were and broke up what might have been a real fight. Of course, I got into trouble because I was told, "You were there to set an example, you should have gotten a teacher," by the principal. I remember looking at the principal and saying, "You're right. And it is your responsibility to make sure the safety of kids comes first, so what's your excuse?"

He answered, "How dare you talk to me that way."

"It's the truth isn't it?" I replied.

He just sat there thinking of something to say. He was in shock.

As I turned to walk away I said, "If you don't remember, I told you a few times these bullies bothered me and fellow students after school, and you did nothing. I Quit!" I walked out of his office as he yelled for me to come back.

I told him to suck an egg! Boy, did I press a button! I ran home immediately after I quit the patrol boy job. Dad was at home when I arrived, and I told him I'd quit being a patrol boy because no one liked me. He told me he was disappointed that I had quit because Nelsons don't quit.

"I knew you wouldn't understand," I replied.

"Now what the hell is that supposed to mean?" he asked.

"Dah!" was my only reply. Dad never learned what that meant. It was a word we kids used at school, and it meant pretty much, "On the outside I'm in control, but I'm cracking up with laughter inside because of your ignorance!"

I guess the patrol boy bottom line for me was that I tried to enforce school rules, but the rule breakers were usually the bullies. You know the ones I'm talking about, because they're found in every school across America. They expose themselves at a very early age, like the first grade.

Realistically, I believe it's much earlier than that, maybe three years old. They tend to defy every rule they can and will attempt to go against rules simply to find out if they can get by with disobedience. Some of these youthful pranksters become the adults who continue to defy laws and authority throughout their lifetimes when their parents, perhaps, shouldn't have merely shrugged things off, believing their little angels would simply grow out of it.

As for me and being a patrol boy, I guess I took the easy way out by quitting but I attribute my decision to improper evaluation of my action in performance of my duty--with no adult readily there to assist me--and my discovery that some adults were just as uncaring and as poor in the situation as the bullies. At the time, still less than a teenager, I didn't know why such a posture was vented toward me--but I sensed even then that someday, as I got older, I would understand.

My parents did provide very well financially for our family. We always lived in a big house with plenty of bedrooms and bathrooms. We always had a swimming pool, and we ate the best of foods. But emotionally, affectionately, and culturally we lived in poverty. Regarding those aspects of child-rearing, we were being raised in the heart of Arizona's desert, literally and figuratively.

The Nelson's intentions were good. They were just out of balance. Why is it I could see it in their relationship, but they couldn't? In many ways, they were ignorant of the emotional and affection requirements of the 'special needs' children they adopted to become members of the Nelson family. They became so obsessed with trying to make the perfect adoptive family that they just couldn't accept the reality that we were not.

This author's problems that existed in childhood, and many of which carry over to today, were caused predominantly by uncaring or ignorant adults, who as parents or child-guidance-givers in the fields of education and of the clergy, all thought that they knew everything. In reality, they knew only what suited themselves.

Don't get me wrong. I was exposed to and did meet some very good and caring adults who came across as knowing what was wrong. Often, I'm sure, such individuals did know what this kid needed, but the principle deterrent to their being able to help me was Mrs. Nelson. After a couple of conversations with her, these might-have-helped, knowledgeable adults--many who were parents with children my same age--deemed me a lost cause and stopped trying to help. They quickly learned that Mom was a "back biter" who would criticize them to others, and who didn't want suggestions or friendly guidance from them in anyway, shape or form. Sadly, when my Mom rejected help or suggestions from these good adults, I would also lose opportunities for their children to be or become my playmates and friends as well. Yes, it was truly sad.

These are the elements that caused me to be a daydreamer and to be able to escape reality for a few hours each day. My parents, however, couldn't fathom such a thing and thought of me as being a laggard and unwilling to accept responsibilities and challenges they deemed necessary for my growth.

Little did they know that, in my daydreams, I accepted opportunities, challenges, and responsibilities on a daily basis, and accomplished everyone.

The evening dinner call to the table signaled the end of each day's dream accomplishments and the thoughts of what's next for tomorrow! I did, however, make a positive decision, a decision to create a fort around myself--a fort that was really cool inside. This decision allowed me to, in an important part of my life, cut myself away from my family, at least part of the time. I learned how to hide for dream time two to four hours every day in my fort in my backyard by myself. Mom used to say to me, "What the hell is so God damned interesting in your fort?" My reply was always, "You wouldn't understand."

I would dream about my imaginary real mother while wishing I might see her. I would talk to her and tell her that Mom and Dad Nelson meant well, but were just overloaded with too many adopted children. Too many jobs for my Dad, too many unresolved issues running around rent free in my Mom's mind. Don't get me wrong, my mother was a very pretty strawberry blonde, with crystal blue eyes! She had a Miss America smile. My friends would tell me their fathers would say how pretty she was. But to me she was not my mother, not of blood!

April 1973
THE SHOWDOWN WITH THE SHERIFF SEVEN YEARS LATER

It happened one morning right after I got on my school bus; we rode back past my house on the way to school and there was a car parked in our driveway. The driver must have been parked somewhere nearby watching for us kids to leave. I could not believe how sneaky this individual was. If my Dad ever found out he would kick his friend's ass. A friend sitting next to me saw the car at my house and commented, "There's that light blue Ford LTD in your driveway!"

"I know, the bastard's back," was my response. I kept my words soft so others on the bus wouldn't hear my reply. I became sick to my stomach. I couldn't breath and my heart was beating double time. I tried to convince myself that "No. No way. He can't be back." Then I thought, the kids who said my mother is cheating on my father were right! Mom is sleeping with that fucker! The feeling inside me was hot, I wanted to cry but was to scared to. That rat bastard sheriff!

Then I thought of all the fights I'd gotten into with kids my size and bigger to proclaim the innocence of the lady, no, the bitch, I called Mom. Once again, I asked myself who can I dare tell that my mother was a whore? Saying that word made me feel so shameful towards my Mom. I had learned what the word whore meant by the age five, it just took a long time to believe it!

When we arrived at school, before I got off the bus, the feeling came to me that I just wanted to die. I hated that sheriff. I wished I could beat his ass!

I just wanted to crawl under a bush and go to sleep for the whole day. I could feel and see the tears start to form in my eyes.

I remember thinking, my poor Dad. I hated Mom, but I also loved her. Why is it this way? Why? Why couldn't this sheriff just stay with his own wife? For nearly half my life, he'd been this dark shadow. Where is this man's honor? Has he no shame? And the deception of friendship to my father, my family, and to his wife and family. What a pig!

I was sick for a long time after that. Then one day, before my Dad went to work, I told Dad I wasn't feeling well!

He told me, "Mark, you stay home from school today. I have to leave for work, but you wake your mom up and tell her you're staying home today."

I answered, "But Dad, I don't want to wake her up. She gets mad at me when I wake her up this early."

"Son, remember she told you and me that if you are going to stay home from school we are to tell her first thing in the morning so she can plan her day," my father said gently. Today, Mark, you're going to have to wake her up and tell her because I'm already late getting started to work. You be a good boy now and go wake her up. I hope you feel better in a little while. I'll see you this evening." With those words said, Dad was out the door.

Boy, I thought, she thinks she has us under her thumb. She's so sneaky. What she wants is to know if any of us are staying home that day so she can tell her male visitor not to come to the house. Nothing changed. I hated her and I loved her.

After Dad left, I returned quietly to my bedroom, and I didn't wake Mom up. By fate or coincidence, my older Indian brother happened to stay home that day, too. My hunch was right about Mom's sneakiness. Not awakened, she made no cancellation and, sure enough, within 30 minutes after returning to my room, the front doorbell rang. I went quickly to answer the door.

It was the sheriff. My heart beat fast. In front of me, ready to enter our house, stood the big, suntanned man. He frightened me, but I think he was just as surprised and frightened by my answering the door. As I looked at him, his dark outdoor complexioned face seemed to turn white. I wasn't letting him in and he knew it.

"Oh, Mark, you're home," he began tentatively.

Ignoring his comment, I replied, "No way!"

"Where's your father?" he asked, clearly annoyed.

"You know where he is. You came to see my Mom, asshole!" I slammed the door in his face!

My big brother, who had been standing behind me, said to me, "You've got a big mouth. If Mom heard what you just said, I hate to think what she'd do to you."

"She can kiss my ass!" I shouted.

The sheriff was gone, my brother went into the kitchen, and I went to my room to watch cartoons. Fifteen minutes later, I heard the phone ring. We kids were not allowed to answer the phone, even when we knew who was calling. Mom answered the phone.

Three, maybe four minutes passed quietly, then suddenly, Mom was in our room and all over me, hitting me with a leather belt while yelling at me, "You little bastard, don't you ever, say that shit to him again!" Whop, came the belt again and again. Between blows to my butt and back came more of her words, "If you mention this to your father you'll get this all over again and more of it!" Each word was punctuated with another pelting with the belt.

Her attack lasted for nearly half and hour. I remember the time because I'd been watching the cartoons and a new show was coming on when she finally left the room. I couldn't believe then, and still can't believe today, that what happened really did happen. I was sobbing. I wished someone cared.

There did come a time in my life when I had to face a denial of my own that I was living under for a very long time. It was when I was forced to accept the fact that I was adopted. I tried to hide when the subject or even the word would pop up in conversation. I would get this horrific feeling of loneliness that would shoot through my body.

It all started when one day my fifth grade teacher, Mrs. Johnson, asked every-one in class to bring a picture of their grandparents. We were then supposed to tell the class about the picture. I was very excited because my grandfather on my Mom's side was a tour bus driver at Catalina Island. I had a picture of him in front of his bus plus my mother gave me some pictures of the island to show to my classmates. Even Mom was extremely nice and loving about helping me gather family information; she sure could turn on the charm!

Well there I was, in the classroom telling my story when this kid said, "Hey, he's not your real grandfather; you're adopted." Some of the class laughed some just gasped. Me, I got that feeling of loneliness going through my body. I yelled, "I'm not adopted!" We started to argue ,and my teacher stopped us and said, "Mark, my dear, but you are adopted." She said it in a loud, but gentle voice. I can remember looking back at her to tell her I was not adopted.

She grabbed her face and said under her hand, "You didn't know?" I bailed out of the classroom. I ran home over one mile. The feeling of despair in my body felt like the flu! I was running as fast as I could. I was going to leave. I didn't know where I'd go. I remember thinking to myself, this explains a lot of the negative-energy-surrounding people in my circle of life. At thirteen-years-old, all I could think of was it's finally time to confront my mother.

She greeted me at the door, I was so scared!

"Hello!" she said, "I've been waiting for you to come home. The school called and said you left the class."

"I'm sorry," I said.

She took me into the kitchen, and asked if I would sit down so we could talk.

The first thing I asked was if I was really adopted.

She said, "Yes, but I love you just like if you were my own." She then tried to move closer to give me a kiss and a hug, but I would not let her.

I said, "You mean, you're really not my mother, and Dad is not my father?"

She admitted to me that they were not my biological parents, but that they did love all of us kids. All I can remember is that after we talked, I just went to my bedroom. The feeling of loneliness and hopelessness filled my little body, like the blood that flowed through my veins! As I lay in my bed crying, the thought of never being born was all I could wish for! Now that I'm older, I can reflect back to that time of despair when I just wanted so badly for my parents to be my real parents and my adopted brothers and sisters to be real! But for some unknown reason, I thought that because I was adopted and did not know were I came from, that I was nonexistent.

At this particular time of my life, something died inside of me. I can't say what, but to this day that same feeling of nonexistent loneliness still lurks in the back of my mind! During those preteen years, I remember thinking that I would never forget (or fully forgive) many of the adult sins I witnessed going on about me or the many unjustified punishments meted out to me by adults, at home and at school, who refused to see my side of things. I know most kids feel this way, but for me it was near perpetual. My intrinsic bubble of youthful enthusiasm was popped early on. Again, *why*?

From ages three through twelve and even on into my early teens, I lived in complete denial concerning scores of truths that surrounded me. Would this affect me throughout my lifetime?

Mom's infidelity, known only to me, my two older brothers, and a few neighbors, continued on. It was none of my business and yet it was. I knew about it, and I needed to tell an appropriate adult about it or perhaps confront Mom. But I couldn't do either of those things; I was too scared. The effect was massive to this little kid. I couldn't do my schoolwork; I just wanted to play outside! I could not stand the adults my parents grew up to be; they thought they fooled everyone. Not me! And my friends would tell me, "It's not like they are your real parents, It's nothing to worry about!" Boy did that hurt, real deep inside, was it because it was the truth?

To me at age eleven, the most important love in my life was my family! No matter how bad my parents were or all the bad things people would say about the Nelson family. No matter how bad I would fight to change the truth, this reality was always in front of my eyes and that hurt me. So I rebelled!

1974 - 1975

MIDDLE SCHOOL YEARS IN PHOENIX, ARIZONA

I entered a new school, *Desert Sands Junior High School*, for my seventh and eight grade education. It was a great school but, again, my grades were poor, reflecting my ongoing poor parental home life and continued abuse from my mom. My favorite teachers were Mrs. Boop, Mr. Shoemacker, and Mrs. Simmons. My worst teacher was Mr. Schauntz, my P.E. coach. He used to punish certain kids with a swift blow to the top of the head, what many students called a "Schauntz knocker."

One day I got into trouble with him; he told me to stand next to him. He then grabbed the back of my neck, then "Pow," his knuckles slammed into my skull. This teacher hit me so hard it made my front teeth numb. It hurt so bad I wanted to cry, but I could not let the other students see my weakness.

Later that same day after school, I was eating dinner with my family. I had this big lump on my head, and I asked my Dad to look at it. He said, "Boy, that's some knot. Where did you get that?"

I told him I got it from my P.E. coach. Boy was he pissed off. Let's just say nobody said much after that, all nine of us were speechless. It was something I never forgot.

The next day, I told my friends how pissed off my dad was. They were surprised because no one ever told their parents on this P.E. coach. Then during P.E. class, my dad came walking up. He asked my coach if he could have a moment to speak with him. Everybody was scared of this coach, but standing next to my dad the coach looked like a midget. Nevertheless, the coach consented. Us kids stood there anxiously. The only thing I remember my dad saying was, "Do I make myself clear?" in that old drill sergeant's voice of his. It scared me, even my class got scared. You have to remember this is a teacher who thought he could bully 7th and 8th graders, even some teachers wouldn't stand up to him. As my Dad started to walk away, no one said a word. We all stood there looking at the coach. He was so embarrassed he was red and he couldn't speak. What was even worse for him was that one of the students yelled, "The coach is a pussy!" Everyone died laughing, except him.

It didn't take long for rumors to circulate throughout the school that my father had put the coach into the hospital. Though it had not really happened, I think some of my classmates, especially those who had received a "Schauntz knocker," wanted it to be true.

Reality check...

There was one important thing my Mom always used to say, "Always be as clean as you can be, because you never know what might happen." You see, I was very active and always dirty, and I just didn't care. I figured why should I take a shower every day if I'm just going to get dirty tomorrow. My philosophy changed that one day in my seventh grade class. We were playing kill the man with the football, which always got real rough.

I'm talking 200 plus kids, boys and girls. Anyway, I got the ball, and I would have run forever because not too many people could catch me, except this time my foot landed in a hole and two guys tackled me. My leg broke, everyone heard it snap. As my classmates gathered around me, the nurse arrived and took off my shoes and socks. You have to understand that the day before we had a "dirt clods and mud fight." My ankles were very filthy. Some girl yelled, "Ooohh he didn't take a bath!" I was so embarrassed I couldn't even look at my classmates. I was carted off to the hospital, and from that day forward, I was Mr. Clean...!

It turns out I had a cyst in my bone in my leg and the pressure just snapped my bone and it broke. It was so painful I wanted to cry, but once again I could not. So I bit the inside of my lip, I could taste the blood. I suffered through weeks of a painful cast. The very next day after I did finally get the cast removed, we were enjoying another dirt clod fight, and I broke my wrist. My mom was so mad, I was grounded for two weeks. From that point on, I was known as being accident prone.

August 1974
WE TRIED SETTING A WORLD'S RECORD

To maintain my sanity, from the time I was eight years old, I managed to find odd jobs around the neighborhood, mostly mowing lawns or selling candy door-to-door. I walked much of a two-mile radius around our home, pushing a lawn mower and carrying a gasoline can, rake, and a broom. I always had money I'd earned for snacks and for video games for my friends and me.

And then there were my school grades. Let's just say that I had so many worries and unresolved issues in my mind, while trying to figure out who really loved me, there was no way possible for me to concentrate on my schooling. Where are my real parents? Where are my real brothers and sisters? My real cousins and aunts and uncles? Where did I belong in this world? These were big issues for a preteen, more pressing than any classroom issues they could throw at me.

I would always pray, "Please, God, help me find the way!" There were times I couldn't even think straight, I wanted so badly to die. I would think of things to do. I was tired of working, I wanted to do something big. It was the summer of 1974 and I'd just turned 14 years old. Unfortunately, I looked nine years old. I was very small and had a baby face. That didn't ever stop me from doing things I wanted to do or things people said I couldn't do. For instance, I saw this program called "Brady Bunch," where these two children, Bobby and Cindy, wanted to break the world record in teetertottering. So a few weeks later, I decided that this summer would be one I would never forget.

I would break the world's record in swinging, I thought to myself. I had my father buy me a *Guinness Book of World Records*. I looked up swinging and there it was; the world record was set by Jim Anderson and Lyle Henderson. The record was a 100 hour marathon.

I was so excited, I can remember that rush of fury and the determination I knew I would need to see this dream into reality. My goal was to prove that I could do it, I could break a world record. But the problem I was dealing with was it took two people to break the record. I had one person ! I just had to find one more person to help me. Who would help me swing to break the record? Then how will I ask my parents? Where will I get a swing set? It was weird, I first went and asked my father, and tried to explain what I was going to do.

"Will you make a mess?" He asked.

"No!"

"Will anyone get hurt?"

"No!"

"Where are you getting the swing set?"

"Well Dad, I haven't figured that one out yet. I'm just asking for permission first."

"I really don't know where you come up with some of your hair-brain schemes!"

"Dad that's easy, the 'Brady Bunch!'

"The Brady Bunch," he bellowed.

"What's wrong with that?" I asked.

"Nothing at all," my father said, "I was just curious!"

"So does this mean I can break the record, and I don't have to ask Mom?"

"I suppose you can do it, but you still have to get a swing, and someone to go along with your plans. Plus their parents have to agree and talk with me, okay?"

I got so excited, I kissed him on his cheek and was out the door!

"Mark!" he yelled.

I came back and ask what he wanted.

He said, "Son, don't be disappointed if it doesn't work out the way you want it to. Not everyone has the same wants and goals as you."

"Don't worry, Pop!" I said. "How does one worry about something he doesn't have to worry about losing, if he doesn't have it to lose in the first place!"

"Just keep it in mind" he said.

"Sure, Dad, just remember what I said, okay." I was out the door!

It took me only a few days and Boom! I did it, I found my friend, Steven, and his mom even talked to my Dad. It was set. We were on our way to break a world's record. One thing I did notice when Steve's Mom was talking with my Dad that annoyed me; they were laughing and joking hysterically, even as far as to tell each other it would only last for 2 to 3 hours. I remember what my Dad said, not everyone will have your same wants and needs. I sure did not think it would be our parents laughing at us. I thought they would be proud of their children trying to break a world record. It was then that I realized I was on my own.

Almost a week went by, and still no luck with a swing set. I looked everywhere, but to no avail. I even went door-to-door in my neighborhood asking and telling everyone. All they did was laugh at me and tell me I was crazy.

I asked my friend, Darius, who lived a few blocks away and who had a new friend with him, named Doug, who had just moved into our neighborhood. They said they had a swing set we could use but I had to ask Doug's mom to use it. I was so excited. There were about seven of us boys there. We all ran as fast as we could to Doug's house. When we got there, I told her about us wanting to break the world record and we needed a swing, and we had been looking for almost two weeks. She told me to slow down and that we could use their swing. She then took all of us into the backyard and there it was. It was huge! The kind used at the schools. She said, "If you can move it, you can use it!"

No problem, I assured her, my dad will bring his station wagon to pick it up. At home I waited until my dad came home from work. I asked if he would pick up the swing

He said, "No, this was your idea, and it's something you should have thought of!"

"Fine," I yelled, "I will do it some other way." So I called my friends and asked them to ask their big brothers to help. A few said no and that it was too damned hot. Shit, it was only 115 degrees and that was in the shade. They said in our neighborhood in direct sun it was 25 degrees hotter. But we did it! We managed to find some strangers to help us; it took almost 10 people to move the swing to my house. It took us about two days to set everything up. We painted a four-by-eight foot sign, which read: "Attempting to break World Record in Swinging." We even called a few news stations, and they assured us they would be there at the house to report the possible breaking of a world's record in swinging.

The night before, a lot of my friends called and said good luck but nobody believed that Steve and I would break the record. This non-belief energy that we were subjected to by my friends, and even my family, at this point in my life was no surprise! This energy fueled my drive I needed to create my success.

Our goal was 101 hours, the swing never stopping one rider jumping off while the other hopped on. But Steve fell asleep on the swing, and the swing stopped at 71 hours. We had failed. It was a wonderful experience for us, and a lot of fun. I just wish the adults in my life would haven taken us more seriously! We even made the news. I think it may have been Larry Martel from KPHO TV5, who did an interview with us!

In the eighth grade, I was very bored. My friends suggested I run for class president. I should have run for class clown, that was the only thing I wanted to do was make people laugh. Even when I gave my "If you vote for me" speech that every candidate gave, mine was the most comical. I had everyone laughing, even some of the teachers. I did lose the race, but we sure had fun, and I made a few new friends. We plastered posters all over the school "Nelson for President." I lost to a girl who was very popular. It was fun.

I did manage to graduate from eighth grade. I really don't know how I did it, all I did was play and build lots of forts. The one thing I was not looking forward to was high school. I had started to believe that school was not for me, too passive, too rigid. I knew the next step in life was to graduate to high school which meant tougher gangs, more drugs, and lots and lots of fights! All the rumors I had ever heard about Maryvale High School were soon to become the reality of my tomorrow...

<u>1976 - 1979</u>
EXCERPTS FROM THE BOOK: "SOCIAL STANDINGS" CLASS OF 79'

Maryvale High School in Phoenix, Arizona, was the home of the *Maryvale Panthers*, and where I was destined to spend the next four years of my life. At Maryvale, I learned all about everything, cliques, racial dilemmas, drugs, gang fights, high school riots, beer parties and music, birth, and even *death*!

I fought my way through those years. Then three months into my senior year, 1979, this big kid beat up my little brother (the baby of the seven kids), who was walking home with two girls from his 7th grade class.

My brother and the girls had been laughing at this big kid. The girls called this guy *Ronald McDonald* because of his bright red afro style hair, not to mention his very big size. To them, he looked like *Ronald McDonald*! This guy stopped on his bike and turned around. He said, "What the hell is so fuckin, funny?"

The girls started to call him more names. Ronald (We'll call him since we don't know his name) was getting extremely angry!

He said to my brother, "You tell these fuckin bitches to shut their fuckin mouths or I will kick your fuckin ass all over this street!" Before my brother could answer, Ronald grabbed him and started severely beating him to the ground! All the while, my brother begged for him to stop. Even the girls were yelling for him to stop. But Ronald had dragged my brother to the sidewalk, and placed his mouth to the curb. He said, "If I ever see your fuckin ass again, I will give you a sidewalk sandwich! Got it!"

"And that's what happened Mark, I promise!" My little brother said, as I was cleaning up his bloody lip and bruised body. My friends wanted to know who this guy was. They wanted to go kick his ass.

"Shut up!" I told my friends. "Let my little brother finish talking!"

"I'm really sc-c-cared, Mark !" my brother said, "He really will hurt me if he ever sees me again. Please go tell him you'll kick his ass if he ever touches me again!"

With that my friends yelled, "Let's go fuck up that clown! Let's go get *Ronald McDonald*. He's got no right to kick your little brother's ass!"

One of my friends asked my little brother, "How big is this guy, *Ronald McDonald*, anyway?"

"He's a little bigger than Mark, but I know Mark can kick his ass!" my brother said.

The next day, about five of my friends and I went to the bike racks at the school. We asked everyone if anyone had seen a guy who looked liked *Ronald McDonald*. Everyone started laughing!

"Yeah," someone yelled out, "He's sick, and he did not come to school today."

I was so mad; I really just wanted to tell this guy to leave my little brother alone, but my friends started telling everyone I was looking for Ronald because he had beaten up my little brother and swore he would do it again! Boy, everyone got excited, a fight. Some kids went into a frenzy and started yelling, "A fight!"

Kids came running from everywhere, I couldn't believe my eyes! But, there I was caught in the middle of a crowd that, at any moment, might explode into a riot! The teachers showed up just as fast, and so did the police! You see, my high school with nearly 4,000 students was very rough. When the crowd became too bad, even the teachers couldn't control the students. When the students got to this level, watch out, because someone always got hurt, so they always called in the law!

Like everyone else, we took off running because that's what the teachers and police told us to do! The students who were left behind most of the time were the kids who didn't leave like they were told or the ones who stayed to witness the action. Either way, I knew that the teachers would find out that it was my friends and I who had started the commotion at the bike racks. I didn't care, this imposter *Ronald McDonald* beat up my little brother. I couldn't let it happen again, could I? We'll just see what happens tomorrow at school! For the conclusion to this story read the book: "*Social Standings: Class of 79.*"

November 1978
EXPELLED FROM SCHOOL

During November, 1978, seven months before the class of '79 would gradu-ate, my fist fighting had finally caught up with me. I was expelled from school and was told by the Dean of Students, Mr. Kendal, that my parents would have to get me back into school. Little did Mr. Kendal know my parents had informed me that if I was expelled from school for any reason, since I was 18 years old, I would no longer be welcome in their home! Boy, what am I going to do now? I was so scared, and I knew that when I got home, my belongings would be out in the frontyard!

I ran home as fast as I could, racing against the reality of me being thrown out of my home. The sick feeling rushing through my body as I ran made me feel faint!

As I rounded the corner of my block, I jumped into the air and looked over the oleanders to see if my stuff was outside. It was! I started to cry, but no tears would fall, and no noise would I make. I then fell to one knee and asked God for help!

I walked up to the front door and knocked. My mother looked out the win-dow. She said, "You've got to be kidding!"

"Where do I go, Mom?" I replied.

"That's your problem, you should have thought of that before you disobeyed direct orders!" Mom yelled.

I grabbed my stuff, all placed in four garbage bags, and I walked away! I can't remember everyone who helped me, but I was homeless. My mom was always look-ing for a way to get me out, and now she had her chance. I couldn't believe my mom only gave me my clothes, the rest of my belongings were thrown into the trash. Eighteen years of my life tossed away like an old newspaper.

My girlfriend, Judi, was my angel! She believed in everything I did; she was the most powerful person in my life! She gave me the direction and money I needed to stay alive! Her love for me shined like a diamond in the rough. Thank you, so very much, Judi!

We had been together since 1977, our sophomore year in high school. She was the only one who really cared for my well being during that time of my life! She wanted me to pursue my early career as a promoter. We made a commitment that she would help me get started.

Judi did not care if we lived in a castle or a shack, and we wanted to get married as soon as we graduated. Since I was thrown out of school, I was even forbidden to see Judi. This gave her father Clyde another reason to keep me away from seeing his daughter. I never had a problem with Judi's mom, however, she was great.

Judi and me knew that this was our chance to do something so that we could be together. I called a friend named Damen and asked what he thought of me promoting a desert party, like the ones he and his 4x4 truck buddies had done. He said it was a great idea and asked if I needed help.

Damen contacted "Jeyssca Stone," his brother in-law's band and I contacted the band, "Multi-Purpose," who were grade school buddies of mine. The location I picked out was on some private land that someone told me I could use, located right behind *Thunderbird Park*, on 59th Ave. and Pinnacle Peak Road in Phoenix. The concert date was May 31st, 1980. We had one year to raise and save 5,000 dollars, the total cost of the production.

We needed to rent stages and the big light show with a massive PA system. I contracted a deal with KAET-TV to rent their generator. The generator was so powerful, the station general manager told me it could power half the city of Phoenix. I also needed searchlights and the all-important 65 kegs of beer for the biggest free beer fest ever in the Southwest, and quite possibly the whole United States during and before this time period. People would come from all different states.

Judi and me worked hard to raise the money, because everything had to be paid for before it could be delivered. Judi baby-sat and I painted houses. My father also lent me some money. Everything we had went for this show. It had to or the show would not go on.

PART TWO

ENTREPRENEUR

May 31, 1980
DESERT CONCERTS AND NIGHTCLUBS

A week before the desert fest was to start, I took a limousine to all the high schools in metropolitan Phoenix and passed out 10,000 fliers. It took two days to complete, two days of riding around in a limousine, what a bummer! I knew I had no money for expensive advertising, so I took the poor man approach and it worked.

Then came the day of the show and everything was set; the stage, lights show, sound system, and even the port-a-potties were in place.

The generator was set up and the searchlights were in place. Everything in perfect order. Even the off-duty Maricopa County Sheriff deputies were in place for security. I figured we would make at least $15,000 and I was not sure how I was going to protect the funds. There were rumors that there was going to be a heist that evening.

One of my security measures was to have two armed individuals in two separate locations with binoculars in radio contact with security. By 5:00 P.M. everything was set, the 65 kegs of beer had just arrived and everyone was so excited. Cars were already backed up for miles in both directions, but the gates were not yet open. People were so excited for me, all they could say was, "You're going to sell out, Nelson."

Then the unexpected happened, the Department of Public Safety arrived along with members of the Maricopa County Sheriff's Office. They arrived in cars and huge vans and were dressed in full riot gear. A helicopter was flying overhead, and it even landed at one point.

My people were panicking as they became very frightened. I was told that the owner wanted me off the land, and that I would be cited and arrested for trespassing if I did not leave.

An hour before the show was to start, it was canceled. The DPS officers and

Sheriff's officers said they did not want to break up the concert, but they had no choice, and besides the traffic was backed up for miles in both directions and certain home owners could not get to their homes. A crowd control engineer was called into help unsnarl traffic and that night an estimated 30,000 people arrived throughout the night, only to be told the concert was canceled.

From that night, I thought who would have imagined that by just passing out flyers to the high schools and at night clubs and concerts, I would get such a response?

If everything worked out as planned, I would have grossed over $90,000 in one night, not the $15,000 I anticipate, Instead I lost over $5,000. My dreams were shattered. So were those of my girlfriend, my dad, and friends.

THE AFTERMATH OF A DREAM GONE BAD

The next morning after the canceled show, I woke to a ringing telephone. It was a friend, informing me that he saw on the television news last night, on ABC, CBS, NBC, and KPHO, that my show was busted, and that there were arrests made, so he called to see if I was in jail. He also informed me there was an article in *The Arizona Republic.* I told him no one was arrested, and that it was broken up peacefully.

"That's not what the news said!" my friend replied.

"You can believe what you want to believe," I told him. "I was there and no one was arrested. As a matter of fact, the police really did not want to break it up! Some of their buddies were hired to do security. So the media is wrong!" I hung up on him.

Then my girlfriend, Judi, called and said, "I saw on the news, that our party got busted, and that there were arrests made."

I told her, "No one was arrested, and the news people are lying."

She asked, "Why would the news do such a thing?"

"I don't know," I told her, "but I have to go and see what's up with the lies." I called my father, and he told me that he also saw on the news that my party was busted and some arrests were made.

"No, Dad," I explained, "no one was arrested, it all broke up peacefully before I even sold one ticket."

"Well that's not what the news is saying," my dad told me. "But once again everyone is lying, and you did nothing wrong," he added sarcastically. "All the news stations and *The Arizona Republic* are all out to get you, right?"

"How can you believe them over your own son? And if I got arrested, I would probably be calling you for some bail money, right?" My Dad paused for a second and then said, "You're right but I can't believe that these reporting news agencies would even bother with you." I was so mad. He was so freakin' ignorant, and not once did he even ask me if I was okay. I told him I would speak to him later. I was really confused. I still had some equipment out in the desert, and I still had to find my 65 kegs of beer, no one knew what happened. I then went to the store to get a paper to see exactly what everyone was talking about. I was so disappointed that *The Arizona Republic* could write such untrue statements. *Why?* And who gave them this information? I never did find out where my 65 kegs of beer went. I called the Maricopa County Sheriff's office, asking where my truck of beer was? They told me that they did not confiscate the beer and that I should contact the Maricopa County Attorney's office to see if they may know something.

I called Maricopa County Attorney, Charles Hyder's office, and spoke to either him or an assistant. He told me to come in and talk with them. I told them I hadn't done anything wrong and that I just wanted my beer back. The sheriff's people said I did not do anything wrong, and not to worry about it. I still did not get any information as to the whereabouts of my beer. I never did go see the Maricopa County attorney. I figured I didn't get arrested for anything so I'm not going to talk to anyone. I was scared. I figured if the media was reporting false claims, I was probably being set up for something. The police had said, don't worry, and I didn't.

I called *The Arizona Republic* and spoke to the city editor. I explained who I was and asked, "How can you write a story without verifying the facts reported?" He was very apologetic and said they would rewrite the story, and a writer would call me later. I agreed and thanked him. I really could not understand who would say such things.

☐ **The Arizona Republic**

Rock concert-beer parties halted by police in desert

Local law-enforcement officials halted two rock concert-beer parties Saturday in the desert north of Phoenix, and at least seven persons were reported in custody.

Sheriff's Sgt. C.M. Hoaglund said officers broke up a rock concert before it started on private land north of Thunderbird Park at 59th Avenue and Pinacle Peak Road.

Hoaglund said 30,000 persons were expected to attend the outing, which had been advertised with flyers an having four rock bands. Admission to the concert was advertised at $3 apiece

Officials moved in after the owner of the land objected, Hoaglund said. He said 65 kegs of beer were confiscated at 6:30 p.m. an hour before the event was to have started.

In the Deer Valley area, Department of Public Safety officials helped break up a similar party.

DPS Lt. Oscar Baron- said seven persons were taken into custody and a truck with about 30 kegs of beer was confiscated.

June 05, 1980
COUNTY MANAGER WILL MEET WITH ATTORNEY ON INQUIRY

Certain that D.A. Charles Hyder was looking for a high-profile case to help him with his do-nothing past, I felt confident that if I met with Hyder, I would become a victim of his wrath! The rumors were that Hyder needed something to give his office a boost, and he was trying to seek prosecution, but no one would help him in his charades. *The Arizona Republic* published the article below. You maybe asking yourself, if nothing became of this, which was the case, why does it matter? Eleven years later, it will matter a great deal!

Hyder to discuss study of his office

County mansger will meet with attorney on inquiry

Maricopa County supervisors asked County Manager Robert Mauney on Tuesday to meet with County Attorney Charles Hyder to decide what kind of study is needed of Hyder's office.

The supervisors recently granted Hyder's request for three new attorneys after months of debate   with the condition that Hyder allow his operations to be evaluated by an outside expert agreed upon by Hyder and the supervisors

Supervisors said they wanted to know if Hyder was running the office efficiently.

Supervisors Chairman Fred Koory said he wanted Mauney and Hyder to "agree to the scope of the study," then allow consultants to bid for the contract to do it.

"It ought to be done after the process, for completion after the (fall) election so there can't be any question about it influencing the election," Koory said.

Hyder said later he will meet with Mauney, but he believes a federally funded study already scheduled for his office should satisfy the requirements of the board.

"Until I talk with Mr. Mauney, my original feeling still stands," Hyder said. "I will not allow anybody to come into my office except the company that has the LEAA grant."

He was referring to the Bureau of Social Science Research inc., a Washington based organization under contract to the Law Enforcement Assistance Administration. Hyder applied April 28 for the grant, and it has been approved tentatively.

Hyder said supervisors "don't want anybody doing the study that they can't control."

Another research firm, Crisip, McCormick & Padgett, is examining Hyder's operation now as part of a study of the county's entire criminal-justice system. A report is expected in mid-July.

Rodger Golston, Hyder's chief deputy attorney who represented the office in Tuesday's meeting, accused Supervisor Hawley Atkinson of trying to influence the Crisip firm to provide a negative report.

Atkinson said he had contacted the company's research leader, but only to ask if the firm needed money from the board to complete the study.

Koory and Supervisor George Campbell criticized Hyder for making plans for the Bureau of Social Science Research study without consulting the board.

Golston said Hyder asked for the study because he believed the supervisors would not grant his budget requests until a study was done, and he wanted it done immediately!

June 05, 1980
THE ARIZONA REPUBLIC RETRACTION

The Arizona Republic, after five days of investigating the claims against their story written on Nelson of June 1, 1980, found there were perplexities to the story. The article below was written in answer to the problem. The newspaper apologized to Mark A. Nelson and passed his name on to other writers in the entertainment industry, Hardy Price and Andrew Means. *The Arizona Republic* told Nelson, "We do not support yellow journalism, and we hope this, and anything else we can help you with, should prove our sincerity."

No arrests were made at concert

A story in Sunday's *Arizona Republic* incorrectly implied that persons were arrested at a rock concert Saturday evening on private land north of Thunderbird Park

The story also incorrectly quoted a sheriff's deputy as saying that 65 kegs of beer were confiscated before the concert was to have started and that flyers advertised that four rock bands would perform.

Seven persons were taken into custody Saturday evening at another rock concert in the Deer Valley area. However none were arrested at the concert north of Thunderbird Park according to deputies

The planned concert north of Thunderbird Park was halted before it started when the owner of the land objected, deputies said.

Mark Nelson, 19, of 2454 W. Campbell, the concert promoter, said the event was canceled when the land owner demanded $5,000 for use of the land. Nelson said he previously had understood he would have free use of the land.

Saturday, June 14, 1980
THE ARIZONA REPUBLIC

During the summer of 1980, my main goal in life was to promote desert parties. After my first desert party was busted, I turned my attention to promoting nightclubs and local bands. A lot of time and energy went into this effort, as the following pages illustrate. The following editorial was published in *The Arizona Republic*, by Hardy Price. By such articles was I able to continue in my endeavors. I met a lot of interesting people and investors who contacted me after my name and address appeared in the paper.

The articles mention the concerts of "Jyssyca Stone" and "Deep Purple" at the *Celebrity Theater* produced by Mark Nelson of *Hype Production*, me. It was a big deal among my business associates, friends, and strangers because my name appeared on the same page as Jack Nicholson's story for "The Shining." It was a great time in my life, people wanted to invest in almost anything I wanted to promote. Not for my concerts as much as for the company I was associated within newspaper articles.

What was more ironic, six years later Jack Nicholson was driving his dark blue 450 SL Mercedes and pulling into the Rainbow and the Roxy parking lot on the Sunset Strip in Hollywood, California. Mr. Nicholson almost hit me with his car. Mr. Nicholson rolled his window down and said, "Sorry."

Leisure and the Arts

THE ARIZONA REPUBLIC
Saturday, June 14, 1980

C11

Stanley Kubrick 'never lets us down completely, but lets us gasp at a subtitle, jump at the sight of paper being pulled from a typewriter.'

Jack Nicholson, 'The Shining' radiate brilliance

By Michael Maza
Republic Staff

Jack Nicholson in *The Shining*.

The Shining, Stanley Kubrick's freakily paced upending of the horror movie genre, could raise goose bumps on a Georgia peach.

The script lards the framework of Stephen King's novel with the ethereal ideas of Kubrick and Diane Johnson. The result is a package that's muddled around the edges, but burning with berserk energy at its core.

The Shining is a multilevel affair. It's as much a small-family drama as an extravaganza of horror. It butts personal demons against professional spooks and overlaps psychological trauma with the occult in a deliciously shimmering — and shivering — parfait.

Jack Nicholson is Jack Torrance, a frustrated writer who has been teaching rather than writing to support his family. He resents that, far more than he can say.

Offered a job as winter caretaker of The

THE SHINING

A Warner Bros. release produced and directed by Stanley Kubrick from a screenplay by Kubrick and Diane Johnson based on the novel by Stephen King. Cinematography by John Alcott. Cast: Jack Nicholson, Shelley Duvall, Danny Lloyd and Scatman Crothers. Rated R. At Valley theaters.

Overlook, a snowbound Rocky Mountain resort, Nicholson moves in with his wife and son, expecting "five months of peace" there and plenty of time for writing.

Of course that's not what he finds.

His kindergarten-size son, Danny (Danny Lloyd), feels the danger first — even before the family arrives. Tony, Danny's "imaginary friend," warns that all is not well at Overlook.

Leaning heavily on a masterful score, Danny's visions and Torrance's physical and mental deterioration, Kubrick tells the story leisurely.

He builds tension and eases it, sometimes with humor, more often with humdrum events. He never lets us down completely, but lets us gasp at a subtitle, jump at the sight of paper being pulled from a typewriter.

From the opening, startlingly smooth aerial shots, we are absolutely in the palm of his hand.

Unlike routine haunted-house directors, Kubrick doesn't abuse us. The booming that typically signifies a spiritual presence turns out to be Torrance in the throes of writer's block, bouncing a ball off a wall.

Kubrick also makes full use of sound, picking up tonal variations as Danny, on his plastic-wheeled trike, flashes in a circular, reaching ride across tile and carpets in the hotel lobby. I can't say why, but it's ominous.

John Alcott's cameras peer at the characters from odd angles, seeking, it seems, what it is that's gotten them into their fix.

Nicholson, of course, gets the closest scrutiny, and he's totally up to it. Swinging — mostly with his face — between choirboy innocence and full-tilt loony deviance, he turns in the most stylish performance of an already distinguished career. His ability makes us believe the nude beauty in the bathtub turns into a walking, talking, rotting corpse before our eyes, and that the bartender is there when he isn't.

Ms. Duvall also is convincing as the servile, gaunt, blowzy brained Wendy, Torrance's intended victim. Danny Lloyd is consistently eerie as their son. And Scatman Crothers, the almost heroic hotel chef whose ability to communicate mentally with Danny makes him the only possible savior, is solid in the supporting role.

SECOND OPINION: "Many of the film's more bewildering nightmarish touches are ill-explained holdovers from Stephen King's novel ... which has been changed and improved considerably."

— Janet Maslin
The New York Times

Arizona's history springs back to life at pioneer museum

By Peter Rose
Republic Staff

Hazy, dusty, snoozy, remote. This is 30 miles north of downtown Phoenix, off the Black Canyon Freeway. Old, faded buildings. A four-faced clock. The blacksmith whaling away on an anvil.

Orange sparks: History makes it jump!

Wagon master Gary Garrett guides two huge black workhorses ("People say they've got a lot of Morgan in them") between tall stands of eucalyptus past an 1861 saloon from Gila Bend, an 1877 opera house from Prescott, an 1879 church from Globe, log cabins and log houses and log ranches, a stage stop, a gazebo.

That white, handsome St. Paul's Methodist Episcopal Church, recon-

Pioneer was founded 11 years ago by Jo Ann Graham and her family. The private, non-profit organization has a large volunteer force aiding its staff of 10. Their 550-acre spread includes 26 museum buildings, campgrounds for organized youth groups and a nature-study center.

The history it is preserving is pure Arizona, from 1860 to 1902.

And John Cochran is cooking with iron over in the blacksmith shop.

"A lot of people have a mistaken image about blacksmiths: all brawn and not much upstairs," he says. "It's not true. A blacksmith would never last without imagination. For every hour at the anvil, he spent an hour at the drawing board.

"Can you imagine someone coming

Hardy Price

■ PEOPLE AND PLACES — The future of Celebrity Theater has cleared somewhat. Barry Denenberg says he has indeed taken a lease on the property — a five-year lease at that. He and partner Tom Sparks, a local real estate individual, have formed Celebrityflight Productions as a management company to run the theater. Denenberg said another company of his, Phoenix Flight, will book shows in the theater and it will be open to other promoters as well. He said Mark Nelson of Hype Productions will produce a Jysayca Stone concert in the theater June 27-28 and a Deep Purple show on June 29. Additions this summer will likely include the O'Jays in August, produced by Richard Lang's Phoenix Music Group, and the Whispers, also in August and produced by Denenberg. David Manusevitz, owner of the theater, has yet to be heard from.

■ PEOPLE AND PLACES II —

June 25, 1980
PHOENIX NEW TIMES CORRECTS MISTAKES

Phoenix New Times is an alternative paper located in Phoenix. The following section from *Phoenix New Times* contains a retraction regarding certain remarks misquoted from the Sheriff's deputies. Coincidentally, the appearance of my name and company name on this page did again boost my endeavors.

PAGE 24 · NEW TIMES WEEKLY · JUNE 25-JULY 1

PROGRAM NOTES

• • •

It's looking pretty certain that **LINDA RONSTADT** will perform a big benefit concert for the campaign of Arizona congressman **MO UDALL**. Udall faces a stiff challenge this fall when he goes up against wealthy land speculator **RICHARD HUFF**, and Mo is also enlisting the aid of **GREGORY PECK** and **TIP O'NEILL** of the House. Unfortunately for us, the Ronstadt extravaganza will not take place in Tucson, but in New York City about the time of the Democratic National Convention.

Last week's boondocker story contained some misleading phraseology about the 65-keg concert at 59th Avenue and Pinnacle Peak Road. There were no arrests or beer confiscations made at the **HYPE PRODUCTIONS** gig; the show was merely *cancelled* because of a last minute hassle over the use of private land. One officer reportedly told promoter **MARK NELSON** that he hated to cancel the show because it looked like such a professional job, with four top bands scheduled to play on a concert-sized sound system. **HYPE PRODUCTIONS** is heading in a non-boondocker direction over the next few months, staging June 27 and 28 shows at the **CELEBRITY THEATRE** with **JYSSYCA STONE** and **MULTI-PURPOSE**. More big plans are in the works.

• • •

BLUE SHOES is finally out with their trick single, a three-sided disc with "Better" as the A-side.

• • •

Rock promoter **DOUG CLARK**, once rumored to be leaving for a new frontier in San Diego, is now rumored to be back in Phoenix and talking about re-entry into the concert biz here.

• • •

Pete Townshend of The Who, right, talking guitar with Cheap Trick's Rick Nielsen.

Got 'dem celluloid Blues, 3rothers

Ronstadt: Not just another campaign.

Bob Seger: Closing in on two Phoenix sellouts.

The long-awaited flash-sellout show by **THE WHO** is this Monday night at ASU, with Phoenix able to see ex-Small Faces drummer **KENNY JONES** in his first western tour as **KEITH MOON's** replacement. The band is on a new label (Warner Bros.) for the first time in their 15-year history, and both **PETE TOWNSHEND** and **JOHN ENTWHIS-TLE** are working on solo careers too. Townshend's **Empty Glass** on Atco is dynamite and Entwhistle's sessions took place earlier at Crystal Recording in L.A. Look for Townshend and **THE PRETENDERS** on this week's "Midnight Special".

• • •

BOB SEGER, due in for two big shows Thursday and Friday, is making his move on more than just the rock & roll front. True, **Against The Wind** is his best seller ever with rock devotees, but Seger also has a tune called "Nine Tonight" on the countryish **Urban Cowboy** soundtrack, and he made the cover of jazz-oriented **Musician** magazine this month.

• • •

THE BLUES BROTHERS, a musical comedy, has come to four theatres here: The Glendale 7, UA 6 Cinema, El Camino, and Scottsdale 6 Drive-In. "Gimme Some Lovin' " is the fast-rising Blues Brothers single from the soundtrack, but also making appearances on film are fellow living legends **JAMES BROWN, CAB CALLOWAY, RAY CHARLES**, and **ARETHA FRANKLIN**.

• • •

Tentative concert dates are being lined up for **MICHAEL FRANKS** (July 30), **EMMYLOU HARRIS** (August 22), **SAMMY HAGAR** (July 11), **THE COMMODORES** (October 24), as well as **JEFFERSON STARSHIP, THE ROSSINGTON COLLINS BAND**, and **MARSHALL TUCKER**. Phoenix fave **BILLY JOEL** has two days off, August 9-10, between gigs in L.A. and Salt Lake City, but so far no local commitment.

October 15, 1980

THE *ROCK SHOWPLACE* NIGHTCLUB

       This ad was published in the *Phoenix New Times*. After all the money I lost from the concerts, I wanted to open a nightclub. I was introduced to Steve Barba who had financed the *Rock Showplace*. Unfortunately, the owner of the club, Houston Turner, used the money and promotions to finance his personal debt. You will be able to read about the struggles to attain fame that I endured those 17 years ago in a soon-to-be released book, *"NIGHTCLUB$"*

November 2, 1980
NELSON YOUNG PROMOTER *THE ARIZONA REPUBLIC*

The Arizona Republic kept their promise on keeping up with my career. This story was written by Andrew Means, a respected writer in the industry.

New club tests young managers

Apart from being Arizona's self-declared "largest and newest rock nightclub," the Rock Showplace is also the testing ground for a young and relatively untried management team.

Located at 3811 W. Indian School Road, the Showplace arose from the ashes of the rhythm and blues club El Morocco III.

The r & b format apparently did not draw well in northwest Phoenix, hence the attempt to rejuvenate the location with top-40 music appealing to young rock fans.

At the helm of the new club is 20-year-old Mark Nelson. With club manager Damon Roberts and Paul Bettis, organizer of the club's Tuesday night male dance revues, Nelson also operates a booking agency, Hype Productions.

Nelson helped to promote several shows at the Celebrity Theater last year, but the Showplace is his first venture into clubs.

"Some people are really turned off," Nelson said. "They think I'm 18. But I say, give us young kids a chance."

Planned to accommodate more than 1,000 customers, the club has an ample dance floor and stage, and Nelson is bringing in live groups from Phoenix and beyond.

Glider, from Seattle, is playing the club until Nov. 29. Another Seattle group, Hot Stuff, plays after that, and then local band the School Boys takes over Dec. 16-27.

With low lighting and a dark color scheme, the club's main girth is devoted to tables for sampling alcohol, while at the end opposite the stage and dance floor there is an area with video games, easy chairs and couches. The bar extends along one wall.

A powerful sound system reproduces recorded sound when no live music is being played.

The club plans to have live groups Wednesday through Sunday evenings, remaining open until 3 a.m Friday, Saturday and Sunday, serving non-alcoholic drinks between 1 and 3 a.m.

It either will be closed on Mondays or national acts will be featured, Nelson said.

Free beer will be served on Wednesdays from 6 to 9 p.m.

April 1982
THE *STAR THEATER* NIGHTCLUB

The *Star Theater* in Phoenix, my second nightclub, was proving to be an excellent concept. This was a nonalcoholic club. I raised the money necessary to promote my presentations by placing an ad in *The Arizona Republic*. A few months later, an investor entered my life, an investor seeking such a new concept.

June 18, 1982

THE CALLING OF THE GODS

I auditioned for Surgical Steel, for the lead singer position at the *Rock Showplace*. Their singer Harley Van Kirk could not be found after the "Little Tokyo Concert." Van Kirk always thought he could never be replaced. He was in fact, a very good heavy metal singer. Jimmy Keeler and Greg Chaisson was fed up with his arrogance and his noncompliance to the band's rules. They knew to replace their singer would be very tough. They had asked around, but very few would or even could answer the call.

Then one day at the *Rock Showplace*, "Surgical Steel" was rehearsing on stage. I overheard the band talking about the replacement of Harley. I, being the assertive type, asked the band if there was a problem. At first, they said nothing was wrong, but I was persistent, and they finally admitted they were secretly looking for a replacement for the singer. I told them I could sing, even though I had never been in a band, but I was in the boys chorus in school. They all started laughing and told me, "This is far from grade school singing." I was mad at their response and challenged the band for an audition. Greg Chassion, the bass player and second in command, agreed to the audition. They gave me a tape of their music and told me to learn the song "Rivithead." The band told me "You have a couple of hours to learn the song, and when you think you can sing, we will audition you this afternoon when the club is closed."

I learned the song, and when I went on stage that afternoon, I felt something I never felt before. Then Greg counted, 1, 2, 3, 4... The band started to play, and it was almost perfect. There were about 15 people in the club, and everyone was surprised. They all started clapping. Greg and Jim, along with the other members of the band, were amazed. Greg told me, "Shit, you can sing!" That afternoon they asked me if I would like to learn more songs, that I had some untapped talent, but did need some practice. I, at that time was "scared shitless." The best band in the Southwest had asked me to learn more of their songs. I did not go any further due to the fact that I had a nightclub to oversee, and I was lacking one important ingredients to becoming a greet singer, "Confidence!" Even though everyone else said I could do it, I just was not ready for the big stage. But as time went on, the notion of being a lead singer of a band was always running wildly in my mind. That's when I joined "Voyeur Dire," soon be recognized as a vocalist.

August 1983

This ad was published in *Phoenix New Times*. I decided I would give up the night club business and pursue a musical performer career. We were: "Voyeur Dire," with me as lead singer; we found some local success. The band from left to right:

Henry Ehrman, Lead Guitar
Jim McMillan, Lead Guitar, <u>Chris Biddles' replacement</u>
Marcus Nelson-Giavanni, Lead Singer
Steve Pokorny, Drums
Harold Morales, Bass Guitar

January 1984
NIGHTLINE NIGHT CLUB

This ad was published in the *Phoenix New Times*. This was my biggest challenge, my third nightclub and the New Year's party of the decade. And my band performed that night. Everyone was there, KUPD staff and *New Times staff*. There were 1500 people that night! I achieved what I desired, but the night club business was getting to me. I wanted to be the best singer in heavy metal. I had joined the best musicians in Phoenix, to sing for "Voyeur Dire."

Additionally, the pressure was getting to Morales the bass player and the band. He wanted to concentrate on music. Morales told me and the rest of the band, "let's do a few more shows then move to Los Angeles. To get a record deal. We will open a club when we can control everything." I remember so many people thought we were full of shit. This was the secreat to our drive toward sucess...

August 1985

LEAD SINGER VOYEUR DIRE

I was faced with a serious dilemma. I was involved in a serious car accident. A drunk driver was speeding over 80 m.p.h. when he ran a red light and hit my car. I was severely injured and rushed by ambulance to a hospital. I needed surgery that included the removal of a right rib. The worst of all this was that "Voyeur Dire" had moved to Los Angeles. To try to get a record deal and were waiting for me. But now I couldn't go! I would be unable to sing for a whole year. My career was over, at least for the time being. "Voyeur Dire" was no longer a band.

My personal life was in turmoil too. I had just broken up with Judi, my girl-friend of eight years. Judi's father, Clyde was and probably still is the most ignorant know-it-all I have ever met! Clyde, on many nights and for many years, finished his days drinking *Olympia* beer. His breath stunk of beer. Clyde would constantly speak about how much of a dreamer and loser I was, and that his daughter deserved bet-ter. Clyde destroyed the love of Judi and me by continuously putting me down. He did not approve of us moving in with each other. He did not want the two of us to marry and I clearly was not welcome in their home.

All this happened because Clyde did not like where I was going with my career. Judi and me were in the ninth year of our relationship and still I was not invited to attend the big Smith family holiday gatherings. Clyde's wife, Barbra, and her parents, the Rainwaters, were from Illinois. They all liked me and so did the rest of the Smith family. They used to tell me that Clyde was being an asshole! But be-cause I wouldn't kiss Clyde's ass and had promised Clyde's daughters I wouldn't kick their father's ass, there remained a serious problem since Clyde ruled his roost of submissive family members.

Finally, enough was enough. Judi had begun to cry every night, not because of me but because of her not wanting to displease her father. There was nothing else to do. We broke up. That day was one of my saddest days, and one of Clyde's happiest.

A few months later, I married Gina Fillepi, her father's claim to fame was that he had built one of Bob Hope's homes. Gina never got to know her father because he never remained or tried to remain in their lives. He never paid child support or helped her mother with anything. Gina had remained bitter concerning the lack of a father-daughter relationship with him since she was little. When she was a little girl, she was closer to her father, but then their closeness eroded. Her father had hugged her when she was tiny. He brought friends to the house sometimes, and they were kindly toward her too. One of her father's friends was Geraldo Rivera, who used to visit sometimes. He would pick up her sister, Lisa, and her and hug them. It was nice, she recalled.

There were many nights when she would cry while saying things like, "I wish Lisa and I could get to know our father again." This went on for five and a half years and was most pronounced on birthdays and holidays. Through my whole marriage with Gina, I really knew what she was going through. I gave her everything I could give her except what I couldn't give her, her father. I think if her father was in her life, we might still be together.

December 1986 - August 1988
HOLLYWOOD CALIFORNIA GUITAR "GOD" SEARCH

Morales called me one day and told me to come out to Hollywood to sing for him. He told me we're a great team, and I had only one more chance to make it as a singer. "There are many Guitar Gods out here," he said, "And we will find the right one. Give Gina a kiss and tell her you'll send for her later. If she really loves you like she says she does, she will let you pursue your natural born career." I agreed, and we set out to find the best guitar player in Los Angeles. You can read more about this fantastic story in a book to be released in the Fall of '99 called: *Guitar Gods: Who Are They Really*? This book is about a band's every day struggle for who they want as the best guitarist and their pursuit of a record deal. I left my wife in Phoenix, but she soon moved to Los Angeles. My mother-in-law hated the fact that we moved and told me, "If Gina dies in an earthquake, I will never forgive you!"

Morales and me, at this time, worked with Chris Impellittiere, who became very big in Japan. Chris was an excellent guitarist. He worked really hard with Morales and me. Then one day, Morales began getting these symptoms. It happened so fast. He was admitted into *U.C.L.A. Medical Center* where they tried to find a cure. Morales was real sick. I loved this guy, and he looked as if he was dying. He was diagnosed with Lou Gehrig's disease. After a while, Morales and me went our separate ways, me to pursue my music career and Morales to fight the disease that took his music career away. But Morales was strong and had many people in his life who loved him, the kind of love I have yet to experience.

Morales was never to play bass again. He, however, did in 1990, become a promoter and opened a few clubs of his own; like the "Roxy" and the "Party Gardens" in Phoenix. It was the best!

At this time, I met *Jeff Bonadonna*, who worked for *NIJI Management*. Bonadonna wanted to be my manager; he pursued Ingwie Malmstien, the best guitarist I was to audition for. This guitarist was having management problem. The band was unable to rehearse at *Leads Rehearsal Studio* in Los Angeles. That's where the auditions were previously held. I ended up auditioning in Ingwie's studio in his house. I remembered seeing a picture of Ingwie's dad in uniform on the sound board. I asked him about the picture. The guitarist replied, "I loved my father." From that point on, I knew this was no guitar god, but a human being. I was still the singer who could put him back on top. I'm sure Ingwie's life-style is still the same. My quest continued for the guitar god. I told everyone back home, "I'll either try to sing for Edward Van Halen or Ingwie Malmstein. One out of two is not bad!"

BACK HOME IN PHOENIX

I was involved in two serious auto accidents in Los Angeles, again neither of which was my fault. The first one was a head-on collision on the alternate 405 route right outside of a tunnel. A female driver on an antidepressant medication crossed the center line and collided with my Porche. Given the vehicular appearances of my car, no one believed that my Apache Indian brother and I could have survived the accident.

My second accident happened within 45 days of the first, in Gina's and my brand new, 30 day out-of-the-showroom "Hundui." A truck traveling 40 m.p.h. hit us from behind while we were stopped at a red light. I had a bruised esophagus and could not eat for days. My brother, the Apache, broke his hand from the impact. He was the only passenger in the car.

I was still trying to get into a band but could not find the band with the best guitar player. Gina wanted to move back to Phoenix. Her mother was giving us pressure about the earthquake that Nostradamus predicted would happen in May, of 1988. I couldn't take any more, after the two car accidents and the extreme pressure from my in-laws about the earthquakes. The love I had for my music career was over; I loved my wife more than my music. We moved back to Phoenix. (We divorced in 1989.)

I figured I would get back into painting houses, the thing I liked, next to music. I also wanted to open another nightclub. I contacted Harold Morales, and medecided that we would open a club. We needed to find investors to finance this project. It was a lot tougher than it seemed. If you don't put together a business plan, your business won't survive. We called Tony Leparulo. We wanted his dad, Vincent Leparulo, to help with the business plan. He was very successful and his son was a partner. But the Leparulos had been burned so much, Vince was reluctant. We all decided to call Donald Trump to invest in our ideas. He was top notch for a potential business advisor/financier to finance and advise a privately owned entertainment center called *Paradise Theatre Concert Convention Center*!

We wrote him a letter and sent what we thought was a good business plan.

One of Mr. Trumps's assistants sent back a letter stating Donald Trump is not interested at this time, but thanks for bringing it to his attention. We never thought the Trump organization would even contact us but it did not hurt to try!

For a long period of time nothing seem to materialize, but Tony's dad decided to change his club to a smaller version of what he currently owned at that time. So Tony, Morales, and me put together another plan to open, *The Underworld*. The cost to open was quite a bit less than our original plan, yet Mr. Leparulo told all of us if we could do it for less than what our second plan needed, we could have the money and club.

To Tony and Morales, this was really good news. But this was not good news for me because I knew that *The Underworld* we wanted to create could not be opened for less money than we needed. I did not want the headaches this project would bring being underfinanced. I knew this in my heart, yet Tony and Harold did not see it that way, especially Morales. Let's just say no good words passed between us, and we did not part as friends.

Tony and Morales did manage to open *The Underworld* with Vince's help, and ended up closing, and reopening as the Roxy. If they would have done it right in the first time, like I said, *The Underworld* would still possibly be open today!

October 1990
WHERE ITS HOT MAGAZINE

      I went to work as account executive for Jim Keeler, the publisher for *Where It's Hot*. It was fun. What had happened was I was asked by the publisher of the magazine, to find out why sales were not like they should be, and for me to put together a few maps to track sales, and one other map for stand location. The publisher agreed with my solution, gave me a few hundred dollars to put together the maps. Nevertheless, it took me quiet a few weeks to put it together, time for which they did not pay me, but which I did to prove my point. Well, I did manage to prove my point only to find that Keeler did not like what I told the publisher. The next thing I knew, I was out the door. I have had enough of ignorant people using me and my ideas, throwing me to the curb, only to use my ideas later. Now I want to be my own publisher and do what I want to do. This was the final issue I worked. Ricky Rackman is the individual on the front cover; he also was MTV's Headbangers Ball guest VJ, and the owner of *The World Famous Cat House*. Rackman would rent *After the Gold Rush* and have surprise guests appear and perform and there would be over 1,000 people. As I reflect back now... The fact I knew these people wanted me to fail, and with their twisted two faced tales towards me. I would go no further with these individuals in my life. But the question is which individuals are they? If I only had some way of finding out the truth of the friendship around me?

May 1991

A NEW MAGAZINE VENTURE: THE ARIZONA PREMIER

I was preparing to publish my magazine, *The Arizona Premier*, an entertainment, restaurant, and fashion guide. There was a lot of interest from retailers and media, but I knew I needed some experience and advice as well as money. I read an article in *The Wall Street Journal* about the most successful alternative paper in the United States. It was *The Boston Phoenix*. The article mentioned a man named Steven Mendich; he created a niche in the market and I wanted him to publish my magazine. I knew he was the missing link. I called information in Boston and got his phone number. What was more surprising was that Steven Mendich picked up the line. He told me to send him a proposal.

Steven Mendich wrote back personally. He said that it was an interesting proposal and that I had everything I needed to be successful except for one thing: money. He said he had no time for any new projects, particularly out-of-state projects. He did pass on some advice, the same advice that his father passed on to him, "to be successful, make sure you have more coming in than you have going out. Watch your receivables!"

I decided I would wait to publish the magazine after I opened a night club; the funds to open a club were more readily obtainable because of my experience. I determined I would try to buy the nightclub *After the Gold Rush* and then launch my magazine.

RUSH FOR THE GOLD

I decided, it was time to open my own nightclub. It all started when I attended a Cathouse party at *After the Gold Rush*. I went with a girl named Jamie, and there I met a girl named Connie South who was very pretty. I liked the way she came onto me. When she put her hand onto my bare chest, I had feelings that came over me like I had never felt before. When she asked me for my phone number, I gave it to her. I felt something special with Connie. I couldn't figure it out. Now I was in a dilemma once again. I really liked Jamie, but she was a little too forward with her actions toward other males. That, when if I even looked at a another girl or said hello, she would get mad. I just wanted to be her friend. I tried to tell her before how I felt, but she did not care, she thought I was insecure. I don't see how she came up with that one. I mean, I counted 15 guys just in this one night alone who she kissed while I was supposed to just sit at our table and wait until she contacted all her male friends. We broke up that night.

The next morning, Connie called and wanted to go out with me. We did and I started to fall in love with her. We did not stay together long due to some personal problems she had and the fact that I needed to spend more time studying books on how to make a business plan that would gain me the funds to open my own night-club. I worked diligently around the clock. I wanted to buy *After The Gold Rush*, in Tempe. It proved to be a lengthy process involving many people and much time. I worked seven days a week and met with over 20 business people and City of Tempe officials.

After the Gold Rush was a 20,000 square feet nightclub with live entertainment. It had a history behind its some 20 years. It was first owned by Dick Dooley and he called the place "Dooleys." Mr. Dooley worked with promoters like Danny Zelisko of *Evening Star Production*, a Phoenix based company. Rumors were that Zelisko was backed by a big production company out of Chicago called "Jam Production." Danny Zelisko is the best promoter in Phoenix. I use to pass flyers out for him.

Dick Dooley sold his club to Sean O'Hare and his associates; they turned it into *After the Gold Rush*, which operated for many years. At the present time ,I was working with Michael (Arlie) Gross and David Hitzig. They were the real estate agents for John Hall and Associates. They lead me to all the appropriate individuals and set up meetings to help me with getting my nightclub opened.

The manager of the club, Bradley Lou, was helpful too. He gave me full access to the club so I could get the remodeling costs for my business plan. The invited construction contractors all came and gave estimates. A problem arose when the City of Tempe wanted an extensive face lift on the building and parking lot. I met with the Tempe planning and zoning people, Randy White and Steve Tinker, at the club and went over all the face lift requirements. I agreed to upgrade to their specifications; I had to in order to get an after hours permit. This club sat a few miles away from *Arizona State University*. Tempe was a college town that likes to party after hours and that's where the real money is. I was told to contact the Office of Building and Safety for the City of Tempe and talk to Paul Telles. They had one major concern, the safety of the patrons inside and outside of the club. Paul Telles suggested I have off-duty Tempe police as security. It was expensive but I agreed to his recommendation. Besides I had used off-duty officers before and they worked out great. I called Tempe police and talked with Officer Delores. He gave me the price information and his blessing for success. I really liked working with Tempe city officials. They did everything they said they would to accommodate my needs.

Now I needed an accountant to set up the books. I hired Burton Rosenthal of *American Fidelity Service Corporation*. Burton worked hard on the financial part of my business plan. Burton explained that I needed to turn over every financial rock and try hard to include all costs because he advised, "Once your business plan is done, it's hard to change." He encouraged me to make it right the first time. I also hired attorney Kevin Swartz and financial consultant Amhad Khan. I now needed a bank. I thought I would use the one next to my apartment in Scottsdale, *Bank of America*. I met with Lillian M. Carnahan. She was very excited about my new business venture.

I was ready to raise money in November of 1991. I asked my ex-girlfriend, Jamie Brown, to place ads in the, *Chicago Tribune*, the *New York Times*, the *Philadelphia Enquire* even the *Los Angeles Times*. All my professionals said these were the right papers in which to place ads for investors. Jamie paid for the ads on her credit card, and I gave her the cash. I was so glad she remained my friend.

I was really surprised. I received calls from every city where she placed an ad. After sifting through about thirty prospects, I narrowed it down to a few people, because it was not the money that was important as much as being able to work together as a team.

I selected these people: David Carpino from Kingston, New York; Steve Sbarbari in New York City; and Anthony McClendonal in Chicago at *Financial Corporation*. I was to send my business plan to these individuals, in return they arranged financing to be paid after they closed the deal and I received the funds I needed for my company.

I then contacted the area radio stations and magazines because I thought, if I opened this night club I will publish the magazine at the same time. Everyone was excited. My business plan was to be completed by March 1992.

THE DAYS PRECEDING
ALLEGED PARTICIPATION IN A
HEINOUS CRIME...
AND ARREST

EXCERPT'S FROM THE AUTHOR'S HAND WRITTEN DIARY
AS RECALLED DURING INCARCERATION AND HOME ARREST:

The events of these days illustrate the life pattern of my days, the ordinary things I did because I was an ordinary citizen. I was not a man plotting to bring harm to anyone! Are these days I describe much different than yours?

Thursday, February 6, 1992
NELSON'S DIARY

I woke up at about 8:00 A.M. I took the dogs for a walk. My girlfriend Dawn went with me. Then we came home. I ate then went to work painting at the Brian Holt's. He is a very successful businessman, who owned a few drugs stores in Las Vegas, Nevada, and in Los Angeles, California. Brian is a very nice man. I had Thanksgiving dinner with his family in 1991. He has a very pretty and classy wife, Debra. I used to watch their dog, Bridgett, a cocker spaniel, when they would go on vacation. I was even asked if I would bring in their mail and newspapers. I was there for only a few hours this day. Debra was leaving for out of town. I forgot to get the paint out of the garage. Brian asked if I could paint the front part of his house. I said I would and that I would start on his house when I finished the Cameron's house, next door.

I went to work at Cameron's house for a couple of hours. I had lunch with Dawn. She brought it over to the Camerons. My friends, Steve Ginacola and Johnny, came by and sat and talked while we ate. They were working on Lot One for the builder, Nick Lees.

Brian came by at the same time we were having lunch and said, "Marcus, the house looks great." I thanked him.

Dawn and me went home. We walked my dogs, then went to Richard Sollami's apartment and stayed there for a while. Then I took Dawn to work at 4:00 P.M., I returned to pick her up at 12:00 midnight. She wanted me to go to one of her jobs. I said okay but wait a few days. She told me she loved me, and that her job, as an escort, was not like it's portrayed. I didn't want to tell her that she was starting to disgust me I'm talking putrid!

We spent the night together and I was mad because it was supposed to rain Friday, Saturday, and Sunday. I really needed to work but painting sucked when it rains. So I figured I would use this time to put together my business plan for my investors, get my Corvette, then deal with her lying ass later. It sucks, being me right now! Why did she wait till now to tell me what she does for a living. All this time she told me that she was a waitress.

I called Burt Rosenthal, the accountant. He had already worked out the five-year projection plan with his partner. I was so excited on one hand, and yet still pissed off! My girl was an escort. What would my friends think? Shit, what do I think? She compared her job to a topless dancer.

Friday, February 7
NELSON'S DIARY

I got up at 8:00 A.M. It was cloudy out. I knew I couldn't work. I walked my dogs then got back into bed with Dawn and hugged her for a while. I got up around 10:00 A.M. This girl is so nice to me. Maybe I'm being too judgmental?

I was bored, and I started to dwell on her job. Not good, so I went to Lot One to see Steve Ginacola and Johnny. I really like these guys. I would always tell them "When I get this nightclub open, you two will work for me." Steve told me, of all the people he knows who have big dreams, he'd bet I make it. He said, "I wish I had your gift to wheel and deal!"

Steve asked how the ads I placed in the classified sections in the newspapers work out. I said I had about 30 calls from Chicago, Philadelphia, and Los Angeles.

Steve said, "See, dude, what did I tell you!"

I was thinking, I'm almost 32 years old. I've done everything I've wanted in life, things that most people just dream about. Most importantly, I learned how to put a wining business plan together and now is the time to implement it!

I stayed at Lot One for about an hour, then Nick came by and asked if I was going to paint his house where he wrecked his Porche.

I told him, "I will if you gave me a paint sample."

He said he would, and then left.

I remember telling Steve, "It must be nice to crash your $80,000 Porche into the wall of your million dollar house, and not even give it a second thought."

Steve laughed and said, "Yes that's called insurance!"

I told Steve I would talk to him tomorrow.

I went back home, and crawled back into bed with Dawn. It was about 1:00 in the afternoon.

I told Dawn, "Let's go to Los Angeles." She was still sleeping but I finally got her up. I told her that I needed to go because I had to get $300 from Brian. I begged her to go but she couldn't because she didn't know her schedule for work.

"Okay, Dawn," I said, "I'll go and you stay and watch the dogs and bird."

She said, "Okay. I'll miss you."

I told her, "I'll miss you, too."

She left to go to her mother's apartment. I was packing. I got my car all ready to go, then about five minutes before I was to leave, Dawn pulled up. She wanted to go with.

 I said, "Dawn, I've already made my plans. If I leave now I'll arrive in Los Angeles about 9:00 P.M. I don't want to get there any later."

She started to yell at me.

I asked, "How long will it take you to get ready?"

She said, "Well, I have to wash some clothes, then pack. A few hours.

I said, "Dawn, I don't have time. Why are you doing this to me?"

She got pissed, and said, "Fine. Go by yourself...!"

I was so pissed, I thought, great! Then I went back in my apartment. She followed; she started gathering all her stuff. I couldn't believe it.

She said, "You're on your own." She threw my keys at me, and I locked up my apartment. Then I went to Richard and Lea's and put my keys under their flower pot by their door.

They weren't home. I knew Lea would watch the dogs and the bird. I was so pissed, I just left for Los Angeles.

I was on my way at 3:00 P.M. I made a few calls, one to Lea's and Richard's apartment. I told them I had gotten into another fight with Dawn. I asked if Lea would please watch my dogs and not to let Dawn into my apartment unless Lea talked to me first. This message I left on their answer machine. Then I called Ray Schank in Los Angeles and told him I was coming to town and would be there by 9:00 P.M.

ARRIVAL IN CALIFORNIA

I stopped and got gas in Blythe, then was back on my way. I had called Ray about 6:00 P.M. Los Angeles time.

He said, "Come on over!" I got there about 8:30 P.M. We went to Hollywood, just drove around, then went back to his house and talked. That's when I asked about Jeff Bonadonna.

Ray told me he didn't see much of Bonadonna, just once in a while. "He got beat up!"

Ray said, "So he's has not been around." I couldn't believe it, at least him fighting, I couldn't believe him getting beat up! I didn't go to sleep until about 2:00 A.M. I was tired...

Saturday, February 8
NELSON'S DIARY

I was so tired but I woke up around 7:00 A.M. I always wake up early, it doesn't matter what time I go to bed. When light hits my eyes, I'm up. I went to wash my car with Charlie, Ray's roommate. Then we ate at *Baker's Square*, I think that's the name, then Charlie took me where he worked. I asked him for Bonadonna's phone number. He didn't have it, only Ray did.

I got Bonadonna's number when Ray woke up. I called Bonadonna around late afternoon. I got his answering machine, and I left word I was in town and heard he got the shit beat out of him by four guys. I said, "Bonadonna, that's not like you, but I haven't seen or talked to you for two years. Things do change call me at Ray's house, See yeah."

That afternoon, I called Brian Holt on his boat and talked to him personally. I told him I was in town and made arrangements to meet with him the next day about 8:00 A.M.

That night Ray called Bonadonna. I was told he was coming over to see me. We were all getting ready to go ice skating. We were just leaving when Bonadonna pulled up. I shook his hand, and he reached out and gave me a hug.

"Hey, I haven't seen you in two years," he said. "It's good to see you, you look great, nice car." He was talking 100 m.p.h., like always! Bonadonna said, "I'll meet you guys at the ice rink."

We all went ice skating, it was 10:30 P.M. I didn't skate because it was too cold and it was not what I thought it was. It was boring, not like the ice rinks in Arizona. I just waited for Bonadonna. He never showed. Ray and Allan Myers said, "He's still the same, he probably won't show."

I said, "Oh, well." I left, and drove to Hollywood by myself, I was really tired, I stopped for a while at the *Rainbow Bar and Grill*, (They serve the best lobster!) then went back to Ray's house and went to sleep.

Sunday, February 9
NELSON'S DIARY

I was supposed to be in Marina del Ray at 8:00 A.M. But before I fell asleep, I set my watch to Los Angeles time, one hour behind Phoenix. I woke up at 7:00 A.M. I looked at my watch and thought I was still on Phoenix time. So I thought it was 6:00 A.M. and went back to sleep. I woke up about 8:00 A.M. and remembered I was on Los Angeles time. So I got in my car and we drove to Marina del Ray. I knew

Brian would be disappointed; he likes punctual people. I knew he would understand me being late.

I arrived at his boat about 9:30 A.M. Brian was not there so I left and went to the beach. From there, I called Bonadonna at about noon. He finally answered the phone. He was sleeping. That's all this guy does is sleep. How does he expect to be successful if he sleeps till noon every day? He gave me his address. I went over there and we went for lunch. It started raining and my car was leaking badly. So we went back to Bonadonna's place where we hung out and watched TV movies. I had to leave for Marina del Ray later so we just hung out at his house.

This was the night Bonadonna was telling me he wanted to move. I told him to move to Phoenix, Arizona. It was going good. I told him about my new job with *Nicholas Lees Custom Development*, and that I was trying to buy a nightclub called *After The Gold Rush*. I told him he could use his degree he just received and help me build an empire. The cost of living was really cheap too, and he could stay with me until we got our shit together. "You just can't sleep everyday. Its not a productive way I want to run my business," I told him."

Bonadonna said, "Hey, maybe I can go out there sometime."

I said, "Come out now."

"I have no money," Bonadonna told me.

I said, "You could work on this house I am painting, and it would pay for your trip and a ticket back to Los Angeles.

Bonadonna said, I'll go and check it out.

Monday, February 10
NELSON'S DIARY

I got up around 8:00 A.M. I went to *McDonalds* on Wilbur. After I ate I got on the road and went east to 101 on-ramp to Topanga Canyon. I was going to take the scenic route, but it was closed. There were mud slides because of the "El Nino". I had to turn around. I went 101 to 405 South to Marina del Ray. Then Brian Holt called me on my cellular phone. He said, "Marcus come on over, and I'll give you a tour on the *777*." I think you'll really like this boat. When I arrived, Brian took me on a tour of his beautiful boat and also his condo. Then we went back to his boat. He was waiting for someone to fix his motor he was upgrading.

Then he paid me for the work on his house, $300.00, that I did previous to the trip. We talked about my interest in the club, and his interest in buying property to fix up and sell. I was excited.

This man believed in me, I was on my way to success. Brian asked if I wanted to fix the front of his house and paint it after I finished Doug Cameron's house.

I told him, I would.

I left, driving down the Pacific Coast Highway (Interstate 1). I stopped at a Chevron station and got gas and oil using my credit card.

I went also to a *McDonalds* for lunch and to use the bathroom, and went on my way. I ate as I was driving, a quarter pounder with cheese. Yum-Yum. I drove through Malibu up to *Pepperdine University*, to Zuma Boulevard, then went back to Bonadonna's. It was around 5:00 P.M. For dinner we went to eat at *Bob's Big Boy* on Reseda. By then it was raining really bad and my car was leaking real badly. I was so pissed. My new car, and it was leaking The back compartments were full of water and even my gun was under water.

We went back to Bonadonna's house and just watched TV. It was about 9:00 P.M. Bonadonna said he was tired so he went to sleep. Tomorrow we were to leave for my home. I'd read in the paper this storm was heading for Phoenix. That wasn't good since I had to work and I couldn't when it rained. I went to sleep on the couch.

Tuesday, February 11
NELSON'S DIARY

I woke up 8:00 A.M. I drove to the *7-Eleven* for something to drink. It was raining real badly. My car was flooded. So I went back to Bonadonna's.

He woke up around 11:00 AM. We watched TV. The news was on talking about the floods. It didn't look like I was going to go home, but I knew I had to. I went for another drive just because Bonadonna wasn't getting out of bed!!!

Then I went back to Bonadonna's house. He had a note on his door to come in and take a shower. He said he'd be back soon, don't leave.

So I went to his room to get my stuff. He'd put my stuff in the dining room. So I took my shower.

He then came home. He asked if I would take him to his doctor's appointment at 2:00 P.M.

I said, "Okay, where is your Dr's office?"

Bonadonna said, "It's on Wilbur, across from the *McDonalds* where you ate the other morning."

While Bonadonna was at his doctor's, I waited for an hour, then I ordered a large Coke at *McDonalds*.

When Bonadonna came out of the doctor's office, he was talking to this girl. He waved me over. I drove over. He got in the car. I asked who the girl was.

He said his girlfriend. Then we drove to his house. He got ready to go. I called my friend, Richard Sollami, and Dawn. I told Bonadonna that I just found out a few days ago that my girlfriend is an escort.

He said, "What a prostitute?"

"No asshole, she is an escort!"

"Giavanni, I don't know about you sometimes. You sure are naive for being such a ladies' man!"

"You just don't understand. She lied to me. She said she was a waitress and answered the phone for a friend's business. I don't think I really want to see her any more; the problem is I love her!"

"Yea, I don't think you need that bullshit in your life. There will be others, they never seem to have trouble finding you. I'm finished packing to depart for Phoenix, and quite possibly start a new life, too!" Bonadonna sighed.

We left for Phoenix, at around 7:00 P.M. The last call made was to Bonadonna's mom's house in Palm Springs. He told her we were going to stop in say hello. We arrived at her house at 9:30 P.M. She cooked us Chinese food, we told her about my nightclub and that Bonadonna was thinking about moving to Phoenix and work for me. Then we left about 11:00 P.M. She wanted us to stay but we wanted to move on.

Wednesday, February 12
NELSON'S DIARY

We arrived in Phoenix about 3:30 A.M. I called Dawn at her cellular phone. She was just getting off work. I got sick to my stomach. I wish she had a different job.

I asked where she was. She said Pima and Shea. She was going home. I said, "I guess I'll talk to you tomorrow." She said, "okay."

Bonadonna went to sleep on my floor, I went to sleep with my dogs in my bedroom. I woke up at about 7:30 A.M. Snuggles was licking my face. She needed to go out. Patches was still sleeping. I sure missed my dogs. I took them for their walk then went to Richard and Lea's house to tell them about my trip. Then went back home and got Bonadonna up. It was about 11:30 A.M. He sure likes to sleep!

Bonadonna wouldn't get up, so I took his covers. Then he got mad and got up. Then we tried to go to work on Doug Cameron's house. It was going to rain, but we got into the van to go to work. We stopped at Lot One then went to Lot Four. It started to rain, so I couldn't paint. I was pissed. It was supposed to be done days ago, but the rain kept me from working, and Bonadonna was getting on my nerves. Now I know why I haven't talked to him for two years. I kept that thought to myself. His cigarette smoking was killing me.

Bonadonna said, "What do we do now?"

I said, "Let's go on a little tour of Phoenix."

We went back to my apartment and got my car. I took him to South Mountain. We stopped at *Kentucky Fried Chicken*, ordered food, then proceeded to South Mountain. We stopped at a picnic area, ate, then went to the top, then we left. Then I took him to *Pinnacle Peak Patio*.

I met up with Dawn. She came over to meet Bonadonna. Dawn cooked spaghetti. It was great. Then we went to sleep.

Tuesday, February 13
NELSON'S DIARY

I woke up first as usual. I walked my dogs. Dawn asked if I wanted her to come with me. I said, "No, just sleep." How can I break up with such a nice girl? She would have gotten up from a dead sleep just to walk my dogs with me. I was so confused.

Then I went to Richard's house to say good morning to Richard and Lea. Richard was still sleeping and Lacie, their daughter, let me in. Then Lea came into the room to say, "Hello," and to ask if Dawn and me had worked things out. I said, "For now."

I left and went back home. Bonadonna and Dawn were still sleeping. These two would make a great couple all they do is sleep. I left to Lot One to talk to my friend Steve Ginacola. I went to the job site. I couldn't work because it was very cloudy and was going to rain again.

I did wash my car to get off the scum of Los Angeles. It was bad. Then I went home about Noon. Dawn was still sleeping, and so was Bonadonna. I got them both up and told Bonadonna we couldn't work because it looked like rain, and I couldn't paint. He was pissed.

Bonadonna said, "How am I going to get home?"

I said, "Don't worry. I'll pay for it."

He said, "Okay. I'll pay you back later. But not until I get back from the *Mardi Gras*, in New Orleans February 21-27." Then he asked, "Where do you go when it gets hot here in Phoenix?"

"We have different lakes" I said. "The only one I go to is *Saguaro Lake*" I told him, and that I would take him there.

Dawn said, "Well, I have to go and do something, just call me on my cellular." I said, "Okay." Bonadonna and me left. We went to Lot One, looking for Steve Ginacola, no one was there. Then I went to show Bonadonna *Saguaro Lake*.

I took him the same way I always go, I showed him Fountain Hills and explained why it's called Fountain Hills. We also stopped at the scenic view point on the right hand side of Shea heading east.

Then Bonadonna told me, "Hey I'm hungry. We haven't eaten yet, and there's a *McDonalds*! He asked if we could stop in and get some food before we went to the lake.

I said, "On the way back."

Bonadonna said, "Okay."

As I was driving, I made a call to Richard Schiables, (Subway sandwich President in Phoenix.) before I arrived at the lake, but he was on another phone. They took my message to call me back. I was explaining to Bonadonna that I wanted to build Richard's, and other houses, and buy *After the Gold Rush* nightclub.

Bonadonna said, "I hope everything works out for you, that's why I came to Phoenix. I want to work for you. I just graduated, and I need to utilize my degree... And how did you met this *Subway* sandwich guy?"

I told Bonadonna, "My friend Steve Ginacola met him and his wife at Lot One, where he was working a few days before we arrived from Los Angeles. This *Subway* sandwich guy wanted to know who built the house. Steve told them it was *Nick Lees Custom Development*. Mr. Schiables gave Steve a card and asked if someone could get back with them on some building information. Steve gave me the card and then Nick told me to follow up on the lead. This was my break , and I was not going to blow it!

Bonadonna said, "I hope not, Giavanni, your thirty-one-years old. Just don't get involved with those negative, girls and don't give up this career for some girl, like you did with your singing. Don't get me wrong, I know it was your wife, and I cared for her deeply and she knows it. It's the principle. She should have stood by her man, you know the old Italian way!"

We finally arrived at *Saguaro Lake*, it was about 3:00 P.M. as we pulled in, I showed him the marina and the sheriff's office. Then we went to the parking area. I pulled next to this car about 4 spaces down. I had my music playing loudly so when I got out of my car, I could still hear my music. After singing in a heavy metal band for years, my hearing had lost it's high end! Not to mention the constant ringing in my ears. Anyway, Bonadonna got out of the Corvette first and walked up to the car where there were two males, one white and one Hispanic. The very first thing out of Bonadonna's mouth was his favorite all time saying; he would say it to everyone he would meet for the first time, and what was funny most people thought it was real funny, even to me, after all these years!

Bonadonna said, "Hello. My name is Jeff Bonadonna. I'm from Los Angeles, and if I was married to Madonna, she would be called Madonna Bonadonna!" Bonadonna went on to say, "I just got in town. What's it like in the summer time here? Is it real hot?"

I started walking toward them but first I walked down toward the water. I put my hand in it. Then I came back toward the car. Bonadonna and the Hispanic guy went down toward the water.

Then the Hispanic started throwing rocks at these ducks that were just floating on by. Of course, I got mad at these guys who were drinking beer. By the looks of them, it seemed as though they had been drinking beer all day. So I had to be careful.

I said, "Come on Bonadonna. Let's go before I start throwing rocks, and I'm not talking about at the ducks either!" As we entered the car, the time was about 3:05

P.M.; we did not stay at the lake more than 15 minutes or so.

"Shit, Giavanni!" Bonadonna said, "Are those the type of losers that hang out here at this lake?"

"What do you mean?" I asked.

"Well it's a weekday. They're drinking beer, their car is parked sideways, and they don't seem to have any brains."

I said, "They're construction workers. When it rains, they don't work, just like me, I'm a painter. It's raining, and I'm off work!"

"Giavanni, your nothing like those bozos. It might be raining, but you're still trying to better yourself. You're calling this Subway sandwich owner to possibly build his $1,000,000 home, and there maybe other homes too! What about the night-club? If that goes well, then you are on your way to fulfilling your dreams. Maybe now we can finish what we started years ago!"

As we got to the exit from the lake. I told Bonadonna, "There is this place where you can rent inner tubes, and float down the river!"

"Show me where it's at," he said.

So I turned on to Bush Highway. I told Bonadonna that Bush Highway will lead you back to the cities of Mesa, Chandler, and Tempe. I showed him a few sites About 20 minutes later Bonadonna said, "I get the point, I have to go to the bathroom, and I'm hungry. Turn around, let's go to the *McDonalds*, so I can piss and we can get some food."

I turned around and we traveled north on the Bush Highway. As we got to the area, which is about one mile from the entrance to *Saguaro Lake*. I saw those assholes Bonadonna and me saw at the lake pulling out from this area going the opposite direction, south, on Bush Highway, headed towards Chandler, Mesa, and Tempe. We don't know where they went.

"Hey! There's those dudes, from the lake," Bonadonna bellowed.

"Screw those guys," I said.

"I thought you were going to give them a job," Bonadonna said.

"No way, like you told me, Bonadonna, they have no brains, and they're lucky I didn't start throwing rocks at their freaking heads, trying to hurt those ducks!"

We proceeded on Bush Highway from where we were, about 28 miles from the Beeline Highway. We soon arrived at the junction of Bush Highway and Beeline Highway 87. These are the only roads that lead to *Saguaro Lake*. I approached 87, and turned left heading south, heading where the *McDonalds* was located on Shea, and this is the same boulevard that leads to my former home in Scottsdale.

Bonadonna said, "Giavanni show me what this car can do. There is no excuse, there are no cars and no police for miles that I can see! Wide open road for miles!

"So you want to see how fast my little red Corvette can go, huh, Bonadonna?" I said, "You've been tormenting me to see how fast I can go since we left your house in Los Angeles. To shut you up, I'll put the pedal to the metal."

I hit 130 miles an hour. A little while later in the distance ahead, I saw two vehicles and slowed down. As I approached, I saw a light-colored four door car; it was a few hundred feet behind a Mercedes Benz. I then passed the four door car, and I looked at the occupants; they where just a couple of computer nerds. They really couldn't see Bonadonna and me to well because my Corvette had dark limousine tinted windows. Even on the brightest days, you could not see the passengers.

I then approached the Benz, it was so beautiful, a 500 SL, and my favorite color, teal blue. I slowed down, and while I was looking at this car, I told Bonadonna, "Shit dude, look at that car. Now that is success! I'm going to get one of those when either or both of my projects makes it big!"

Bonadonna said, "Well I'm sure you will, but this guy in the car looks scared."

"Fuck him. He shouldn't own a car that draws so much attention if he doesn't want the attention in the first place! He should be driving a station wagon!" We started laughing!

"Let's just go, I need to piss, and eat!" Bonadonna said. So once again I put the pedal to the metal, I was doing 90 miles a hour. We were about a mile or so from Shea Boulevard It did not take long to arrive, I turned right heading west toward the *McDonalds*, in Fountain Hills.

"I can't do the speeds we were just doing in Fountain Hills or Scottsdale. They will put me in jail," I explained to Bonadonna.

Bonadonna responded by saying, "You're not that stupid, besides I wouldn't expect you too! I'm not that stupid, we are a little crazy for going 130 miles an hour!"

"Yeah, you're right, but if Coverlet didn't want you to go faster than the legal limit, then they shouldn't have built the Corvette or any street muscle car. They should have stuck to building station wagons!"

We arrived at 4:00 P.M. I pulled into the *McDonalds* parking lot, Bonadonna got out of the car, and walked to the garbage area where he proceeded to relieve himself. I got so mad. Why didn't he go into the restaurant? Sometimes this guy had no class. When Bonadonna was through doing his classless act, he jumped into my car. I said, "Why did you piss outside for, you pig? This is Fountain Hills, they will put you in jail for that crap!"

"Don't worry. Do you see any police, anyone complaining? I just didn't want to go through the hassle of getting the bathroom key, just relax, Giavanni, and go through the drive thru!"

We got our food, then pulled into a parking space at the *McDonalds*, and we ate our food. We finished, and I told Bonadonna, "I'm tired. Let's go home and take a nap before we go out tonight." We left the *McDonalds* at 4:20 P.M. I returned to Shea Boulevard, heading west towards Scottsdale, driving in my usual manner, about 10 miles an hour over the posted limit. I traveled at this speed to keep up with traffic, the slower cars, I would just pass. We arrived at my apartments. Bonadonna said, "These are sure nice apartments. This is a very rich area, how long have you lived here?"

"Oh, about two years and I just signed a new lease too, at the beginning of the month. If you have to, you can stay with me if I get the nightclub opened."

Bonadonna said, "Sure, I think I'll like this place, I'm just scared it's going to get hot, and those guys at the lake said it's dead here in the summer."

"Yeah, in some instances, but we will have the hottest nightclub in Tempe. When you're supplying the alcoholic beverages and have kick ass music and the right promotions, it won't be dead! I promise!" I said.

"Just hurry and get it open, I need a job!" Bonadonna said.

"It all takes time, my friend, I have to get my business plan finished, but you are here, and I need a little break. Besides, I can't concentrate when I've got a guest! Especially you, you talk more than I do." I then pulled into my registered parking spot.

Bonadonna said, "I'm going to take a nap, Is Dawn coming over today?"

"I don't think so Bonadonna. I can't deal with her job like I thought I could, and I can't trust her since she lied to me. I'm too old for lies!" He fell asleep on the floor while I was talking to him. I took my dogs for a walk; they were happy! I then went to my room to take my nap.

That night, Bonadonna and me were going bar hopping among, all the top-less bars. Since I'm about to open a club, I tell the girls in these bars so they would tell all their friends, and they could show up too, if they were single; I didn't care! It's's a promotion thing; you as the reader may think I was being hypocritical to-wards Dawn, because I went to see topless dancers and yet, despise my girlfriend for being an escort. You cannot compare the two. I was inviting girls as guest when the club opens and they could even bring their boyfriends. My girlfriend on the other hand, was standing nude in all uncontrolled environment in a hotel room, with a strange man and doing, God knows what... I do not see me as being hypocriti-cal, but yet *Mr. Promotional*, in my actions...

Bonadonna was having a real good time. We did not have to pay cover. That always saves money. All the girls I knew gave us free table dances at all the clubs, and some of the patrons I knew would buy our drinks. He could not believe it! I told him, "That's part of the perks to opening a nightclub, everyone wants to be your friend, but its these people you must not forget. You have to give them back what they give you."

Bonadonna said, "I can see your plan clearly."

Dawn called me on my cellular phone; she asked if she could see me. I told her that I couldn't see her any more, I don't like her job, smoke cigarettes, and lied to me!"

She said, "Marcus but I love you. I could not tell you what I did because I knew you would not see me."

I hung up on her. I loved her so much but what could I do! Then my phone rang again; it was Dawn. She said, " Fuck off asshole!" Then silence. She hung up on me.

Why did this happen? Why do I attract such girls? I went back into the club, and got Bonadonna. He was wasted and his mouth was going a hundred miles an hour.

    We made it back to my apartment; I dragged him in on the floor..., he was out. I was scared to leave him in case he got sick. I didn't want him to *die*. I placed him face down on the floor. I would check on him from time to time. Then I went to sleep, my day was full...

PART THREE
SUDDENLY
DIVERTED
ONTO ANOTHER
TRACK

Parallel Lives
THAT COME TOGETHER

On this day, like every day before it, and every day after, there will always be, bizarre circumstances involving people, places, and things. It is only when such circumstances become exploited and turned into known realties that conform to particular situations that will, in turn, either prove positive or negative, depending on exactly what happened and the conditions or facts attending to that specific event and having some bearing on it. *The Federal Bureau of Investigation* (FBI) was in the process of investigating a crime involving two counts: "The mailing of a threatening communication with the overt act of extortion, through the United States Postal Service," and "Conspiracy."

Nelson, on this same day, following his path in life had no idea of the parallel of circumstances happening to other people, places or things around him. His life was about to be set back to near total ruin because he became a main focal point of the FBI in this investigation, according to FBI Case Special Agent Keith D. Tolhurst.

What does it take to destroy, permanently or for several years, the lives of innocent men? In these pages, Nelson will attempt to prove that a conspiracy of some kind did take place, not by two innocent men who would be arrested and accused of a heinous crime, but rather by certain U.S. Government agencies and employees', who fabricated false reports of their investigating and then released these reports to the media. As a Special Agent blatantly attempted to cover-up the false reports to his boss.

The first employee in question is FBI Case Special Agent Keith D. Tolhurst. It was his job to gather the documented facts pertaining to this case from FBI reports, to consolidate the reports, and to file his findings for the arrest and possible conviction of his suspects. Tolhurst was appointed by his boss, Special Agent James Ahearn to head the investigation of this case along with the support of some 100 FBI Special

Agents. A few Special Agents, actually prepared and submitted false reports. These facts establish credibility for an FBI conspiracy focused toward two innocent men that involved their false arrest, prosecution, and defamation of character.

The second employee in question is Assistant US Attorney Chuck Hyder, who was appointed by Roslyn Moore-Silver Chief Criminal Justice Division for the State of Arizona. Ms. Moore-Silver also gave the final approval for the arrest of Miller and Nelson; which was solely based on the Criminal Complaint filed on February 19, 1992, by SA Keith Tolhurst.

In order to prove Nelson's accusations of false arrest, prosecution, and defamation of character by an employee and/or employees of the United States of America, we must start at the beginning of this case. We commence also with the FBI Special Agent Keith Tolhurst, and his reporting Special Agents and their reports. Along with personnel of the Arizona Office of the United States Attorney, and in particular Assistant US Attorney Chuck Hyder.

The teamwork style Tolhurst and Hyder used in their efforts to prosecute two innocent men and to hide the truth from their bosses is strong evidence of a conspiracy. It was Special Agent Tolhurst's Criminal Complaint on which his bosses based their firm beliefs for the arrest, and sought conviction: with up to a 50 year prison term and $500,000 fine on both counts if Miller and Nelson were to be found guilty. Let's not forget either the hardships either family and friends suffered.

Bosses, all the way up to and including Assistant U.S. Attorney Hyder, should have read their agent's reports. Right? Yes and no. The simple fact that these bosses have appointed certain individuals to work a particular case tends to imply that the bosses have trust in the truthfulness of their Special Agents reporting their observations. It is only when unique and extraordinary cases come along, such as this one, that scrutiny beyond ordinary circumstances must be employed.

Case Special Agent Keith Tolhurst fooled everyone. *Why?* No one knows. What could have been his motive for a cover up? Was he seeking a promotion? Or was he just plain lying to hide his mistake based on first opinions or gut feelings?

And as for Assistant US Attorney Chuck Hyder, is it possible he still held a subconscious grudge against Nelson for the 65 keg beer party he promoted on May 31, 1980, while Hyder was Maricopa County Attorney. This true story began February 7, 1992.

<u>Friday, February 7, 1992</u>
A LETTER RECEIVED

Marc Kaplan
6867 Bar Z Lane   or   4545 E. Shea Blvd. Suite 150
Paradise Valley. AZ 85253   Phoenix. AZ 85283

Dear Marc,

IF YOU VALUE YOUR SON'S LIFE....READ THE REST OF THIS LETTER!

To start, let me supply you with a little information about our
little group. There are three of us who were officers in the
special forces. There we learned many of the skills that we are
now applying in real life applications. What we have developed is
a foolproof method of playing Robinhood, we take from the rich,
etc. One third of all funds are donated to disabled veterans and
to charities for children diseases. And who said the army doesn't
prepare you for civilian life? With the assistance of blackmarket
high-tech government equipment we are able to perform this task
efficiently and effectively.

SELECTION

You were selected based on our five requirements. They are:

1.   You have a young son, Brian, whom you care about. This we see
      from your involvement in his activities.

2.   Your son is involved in sports and would need to be in
      excellent shape to continue.

3.   You have a very expensive houses and cars. These are outward
      signs of wealth that we look for.

4.   We look for something extravagant, beyond the houses and cars.
      Many times its a private jet or yacht, but in your case it was
      the baseball team.

5.   You are young and can make the money back without it affecting
      your retirement.

THE REQUIREMENTS

You will pay us $250,000.00 in cash in one week or we will remove
your son's arm or leg. From our past experiences he will have a
greater than 75% chance of living using most of the methods that we
employ. We use $250,000 as the base because this amount usually
equates to the value of our client's cars. The correlation here is
a simple one: do you value your son's life or limbs more than your
cars? Almost all our previous clients have thought that their son
was more important and we feel you will think the same way.

RULES

1. If you do what we request then everyone will be left alone.

2. If the authorities are contacted to apprehend us then there is no time limit placed on removing your son's arm or leg.

3. There is nothing wrong with hiring people to protect your son.

4. You may not mark the money in anyway. That means not writing down numbers or placing invisible dyes or poison on the bills.

5. Most important...we only give you this one chance. If for any reason there is a deviation from the rules then please be prepared to face the consequences.

CONSIDERATIONS

1. We have been watching you for over a month now and know your patterns and associates. If we see others that do not fit, we will find out who they are.

2. If you do decide to call the authorities and think they can protect your son, please think this over carefully. They may be very concerned the first month or two but will become very lax soon after. That is if they do not dismiss this as a hoax to begin with.

3. The government spent many dollars training us to do exactly this type of work, and they did a very good job of it. We have the expertise to remove his arm or leg many different ways. But the big advantage is that we have time on our side.

4. If you decide that you will try to protect your son it will take a minimum of 2 very good trained men to <u>possibly</u> accomplish this task. They will run you around $150,000 - $200,000, so it is almost a break even. Plus when being guarded it requires a more risky removal method, thus decreasing his odds of survival.

5. If you decide to hide him for this year, good luck. Only 1 of our clients decided on this approach. He is a Philadelphian who sent his son to Ireland to live with a cousin. We found him about 2 weeks ago and when the Executioner responsible for him frees up he will make this trip. We actual thought about recontacting our client, but decided against it. The rule is: <u>only one chance</u> and even if we wanted to, we don't go against the rules.

6. Because we use a totally random method to select our clients it would be impossible for the authorities to make any connection to us. We pick different cities, different races and religions. This randomness is why we are so successful and confident.

TIME LIMIT

There is a time limit to this contest. If you do not call the authorities or other private concerns then you can gamble and try to hide your son from us for one year. If you are successful, we will not bother you after that date. We will also not harm any other member of your family, including yourself. However, if you call the authorities we again will not hurt any other member of your family but the time limit is removed and we will still remove his arm or leg. The reason we do this is that it gives you an option to try to hide your son which gives us pleasure in tracking him down, its all part of the game. We don't really like to hurt children but our government let us do it before so we feel we can do it now. The reason we try not to kill your son is so that every time you look at him it will be a reminder of your terrible choice.

WHAT NOW?

On Thursday, February 13, you will receive a phone call at exactly 2:00 PM at your office giving you instructions. If you follow these instructions everything will be fine, but if you do not than we will enact the next phase of the operation. The money will be all $100 bills and placed in any type of bag or suitcase. Have an additional $1000 spending money on you. This should be in smaller bills.

WHY NOT KIDNAPPING?

The reason for us is simple. Kidnapping can inflict serious mental damage to a youngster. It is riskier and carries a greater penalty if apprehended. Also, .you never have positive proof that your son is alive and well and that he'll ever come back, even if you follow all the instructions. So the bottom line is it is easier for us and less traumatic for you and your son.

OUR TEAM

The group consists of three team leaders. Each team leader rotates assignments on each new mission. These assignments are:

1.   The Scout. He checks out new client for 1 month, delivers letters and instructions and then leaves.

2.   The Executioner. Scouts with person #1 for 2 weeks on client, then spends next 2 weeks tracking the son. If the money is not delivered or the authorities are contacted, he begins his hunt and carries out the sentence.

3.   The Collector. In our group this is the only person that may be identified. This is highly unlikely given our recent accomplishments, but he is the only one exposed. To prevent any connections, he also keeps all the money. We do not distribute it among ourselves, thus keeping everything separate. This is why we rotate the assignments.

If the Collector notices police involvement, he can abort the mission and not make a phone call or he may still go ahead with the mission, which he will still be successful and again, not make the phone call. No phone call means "BEGIN THE HUNT"! The reason for the rotation is so that we each are independent and also because when you become the #3 person you are on vacation for almost 2 months.

There is no way you can determine if we are serious. When we first started, we did reckless things like shoot out a tire, etc. but there was always that risk of someone getting hurt. Now we just send this letter and try to explain our business in some detail so you will know we are serious. We now have experience on our side. It took some time to perfect this operation. The first 3 didn't go as smoothly as planned but still came off without serious injury. Since then, using this new and refined method we have been successful 8 times with only 1 person trying to hide his son and contact the authorities. There is more on this one later on. I think having the extra money from the first jobs was the key because it allowed us to purchase the best equipment for this type of work. The night scopes, listening devices and high-tech electronics have definitely helped, but as they say so often...practice makes perfect.

The confidence we have allows use to give you about a week to get the money together. In reality and in the movies the money is always due in a very short period of time. This generates a lot of stress which can cause people to make ill advised decisions.

We hope you are smart enough to make the correct decision. But for us the only difference is in the monetary amount. We would still get pleasure matching wits with you. Also, as with the case in Ireland, we will have before and after pictures in a short period of time. These can be a good references to future clients.

It would be wise to keep this to yourself, or to very few close friends. If the wrong person hears about this, they may feel they are doing you a favor by calling the authorities.

LET THE GAME BEGIN!

Monday, February 10, 1992
NOTIFYING THE FBI

FBI RESPONSE
TO THE EXTORTION LETTER

Marc Kaplan contacted the *Federal Bureau of Investigation* on Monday, February 10, 1991, two days after receiving the extortion letter filled with the horrifying demands that his child was under threat of being kidnapped and his son's arms and legs were to be removed if the demands were not met!

Kaplan did not know what to do, the letter said no police. He did however have a friend who was a policeman. His friend told him, "This is a federal crime, and that you need to call the FBI. "Kaplan followed his policeman friend's advice and called.

The FBI initiated an investigation into possible extortion activities directed at Marc Kaplan. The FBI's investigation focused on a computer-generated letter sent from an unknown individual.

The FBI thought they were dealing with a very sophisticated group of highly trained mercenaries. Upon information and belief, the investigation was overseen and administrated by Keith D. Tolhurst, a Special Agent (SA), of the FBI. SA Tolhurst immediately put a 24-hour watch on the Kaplan family and house and their work place. SA Tolhurst ordered "tap and trace" devices installed on the phones of Kaplan's home and office. Tolhurst knew there was not much more they could do but wait for the call that was mentioned in the extortion letter to take place on February 13, 1992, at exactly 2:00 P.M.

Approximately
TO COME NEAR OR CLOSE, AS IN DEGREE, NATURE, QUALITY

February 13, at 2:17 P.M., Marc Kaplan received a phone call from the supposed extortionist. In short, Kaplan was told to go to a closed down *Security Pacific Bank,* and there he would find a note taped to a flag pole giving further instructions. The call, it was learned, came from a pay phone at an *ABCO Supermarket.*

The time and place of these events as investigated by Special Agents Jason N. Deaton, William E. Hanchak, and Kenneth J. Williams can be found in the FBI report on the fallowing page.

When reading any FBI reports, look at the dates of when the investigation took place, and look at the dates of dictation, and finally look at the date of transcription. On all the reports filed by the FBI, there are days, and even weeks before these reports become a document. **All of the reports and documents in this book are copies from the actual cases involved.**

When the reporting Special Agent give a certain time for which a certain event was supposed to have happened, it is always written as an approximate. In fact, when one of the best trained information gathering agencies in the world uses this word to come close to the actual time of these events to cover up any time errors, one would have to question this style of investigation.

One of the requirements to be a Special Agent for the FBI is possessing a college degree, to identify the education level of this group of individuals, and to enhance the image they desire to portray as being the best. But appearance is not always the case as evidenced in their investigation of me.

FBI Special Agents should use the exact time of when certain activities are known to have taken place. They should not use approximate times to allow flexibility in a report.

The use of approximate times in an FBI report, whether it will benefit a prosecutor or a defendant, seems more a matter of convenience for a Special Agent and allows room for gut instincts and feeling as opposed to pure facts.

More specifically, in the *Surveillance Log,* the times reported at which individual Special Agents observed certain events are not quite correct. The log was written so the FBI could fit the approximate times of when these events are supposed to have happened to match the Criminal Complaint for the arrest and prosecution of those whom they claim to observe as being a suspect in this case. However, some of the true happenings of this case were completely ignored.

There follows a **two version breakdown** on the initial investigation and the *Surveillance Log.* **The first breakdown;** includes information filed by FBI SA Keith D. Tolhurst and his reporting Special Agents. It encompasses the FBI information (their input) everyone was lead to believe and which was used for the arrest of Mark A. Nelson.

The second version; of the investigation and *Surveillance Log* is a detailed and comprehensive study of all FBI Special Agent reports, which contain previously omitted or conflicting case information.

Thursday, February 13, 1992
SAGUARO LAKE SURVEILLANCE LOG

FBI Special Agents'
INITIAL INVESTIGATION

- 1 -

FEDERAL BUREAU OF INVESTIGATION

Date of transcription   2/27/92

On February 13, 1992, at approximately 12:00 noon, Special Agents (SAs) assigned to the Phoenix Division of the Federal Bureau of Investigation (FBI), were dispatched to various assignments related to an investigation concerning an attempt to extort MARC KAPLAN.

At approximately 2:22 p.m., all agents were advised that KAPLAN received a telephone call informing him of further instructions. The call was traced to a pay telephone located next to the ABCO grocery store, 1988 North Alma School, Chandler, Arizona.

At approximately 2:50 p.m., SA KENNETH J. WILLIAMS requested the telephone number of the telephone from radio dispatch. SA WILLIAMS was informed that the call was traced to telephone number (602) 899-6475. SA WILLIAMS and SA JASON N. DEATON secured the telephone and called the FBI collect from the telephone.

At approximately 3:06 p.m., SA SHERRY L. HANCOCK and SA WILLIAM E. HANCHAK relieved SA's DEATON and WILLIAMS and continued to maintain security of the telephone for the purpose of preserving any fingerprints.

At approximately 6:10 p.m., Crime Scene Officer (CSO) DIANE SELLIER, Mesa Police Department (PD), arrived at the aforementioned telephone and processed the telephone and immediate adjoining area for fingerprints.

SA HANCOCK and SA HANCHAK followed CSO SELLIER to the Mesa PD. CSO SELLIER turned the fingerprints she had lifted, over to RODOLFO ZAMORA, Technician, Mesa PD, telephone number (602) 644-2341.

ZAMORA was requested to compare the latent fingerprints that CSO SELLIER had lifted with the known fingerprints of MICHAEL G. MILLER.\ ZAMORA conducted his comparison and turned

Investigation on ___2/13/92___ at __Chandler, Arizona__   File # __PX 9A-PX-46497__

   SA JASON N. DEATON, SA WILLIAM E. HANCHAK,
by __SA KENNETH J. WILLIAMS, and__ _____ Date dictated __2/16/92__

71

93

N000237

Surveillance Log

After Marc Kaplan received the phone call from the *ABCO Supermarket* pay phone (2:20 P.M.), Kaplan then proceeded to the *Security Pacific Bank* (2:25 P.M.). Kaplan arrived at the bank. Kaplan retrieved the note from the flagpole at 2:28 P.M., and followed the directions to *Saguaro Lake* and the Marina Covered Picnic Area #3 (location L-3).

On the following pages are copies of the exact *Surveillance Log* created by the FBI Special Agents. These two-page reports were split up into three sections. The times listed on these logs are the exact times that the Special Agents reported observing described vents. The thing wrong is they don't match the times listed on the final FBI Criminal Complaint Affidavit filed on February 19, 1992, for the arrest of their claimed culprits; this same erroneous information was used in the indictments filed on February 27, 1992, for the two felony counts.

You may read the actual notes, left at the flagpole at the bank, and the note left for Kaplan at the lake. These events have become paraphrased in the reports, according to the beliefs of Case Special Agent Keith D. Tolhurst, who wanted his bosses to believe his reports are factual.

Case Special Agent Tolhurst based his reports and findings on unusual circumstances, these circumstances are imaginatively plausible, in the series of events paralleling others unrelated circumstances of the same times. Collectively, the circumstances could lead to a possible conviction of two innocent men.

FBI Surveillance Log
PAGE 1 AND RECORDED TIMES

      This *Surveillance Log* has the list of the personnel involved. There was a total of eight Special Agents; (SA's) listed beside "Personnel Involved:" Each SA's, has a corresponding number by their names, e.g., SA Bateman (4). Their objective is to observe all activity, and report their finding on this log sheet, in the little boxes listed, the INIT box, is for the Special Agent to sign to admit what they said, they saw. The TIME box, is for the actual time, they claim events to have happened. The OBSV box, is for the Identity of which SA's, observed what activity. This log sheet was cut in half at the 2:29 P.M. entry. The second part will start on the following page. The original is listed in the back of the book, and there were only two actual reports. The only Special Agents at this time reporting were Bateman (4) and Henderson (10).

SURVEILLANCE LOG -- PHOENIX DIVISION

DATE: 2/13/92 · DAY: THUR.

WEATHER: CLEAR   CASE #: 9A-A-46497

STARTING (Street) 4545 E. SHEA BLVD,   CASE AGENT: K. TOLHURST
LOCATION:

(City) SCOTTSDALE, AZ.

PERSONNEL BATEMAN (4), COWAN (3), MACDONALD (7), BEITER (8), PETERSON (2)
INVOLVED: RIPLEY (PC), HENDERSON (0), WHITE (1)   PAGE 1 OF 2

INIT	TIME	OBSV	ACTIVITY OBSERVED	PHOTOS ATTEMPTED ROLL #	EXP
TB&H	1:45 p	4,10	SURVEILLANCE INSTITUTED AT 4545 E. SHEA BLVD, SCOTTSDALE (L-1)		
TB&H	2:25 p	4,10	MARC KAPLAN (M-1) DEPARTS L-1 DRIVING A TEAL BLUE MERCEDES BENZ, AZ/GWS 676 (V-1).		
	2:28 p	1, PC	V-1 OBSERVED AT A CLOSED SECURITY PACIFIC BANK N.W. CORNER OF TATUM AND SHEA (L-2).		
	2:28 p	PC	V-1 OBSERVED IN THE MIDDLE DRIVE-THRU OF L-2 WITH M-1 TAKING A PIECE OF PAPER OFF THE NORTHERN POLE.		
	2:29 p	PC	M-1, AS HE DEPARTS FROM L-1, IS OBSERVED TO TALK TO THE DRIVER OF A WHITE CADILLAC, AZ/ KFT4 (V-2).		

Location And Events Map
KAPLAN MOVEMENTS MONITORED BY FBI SPECIAL AGENTS

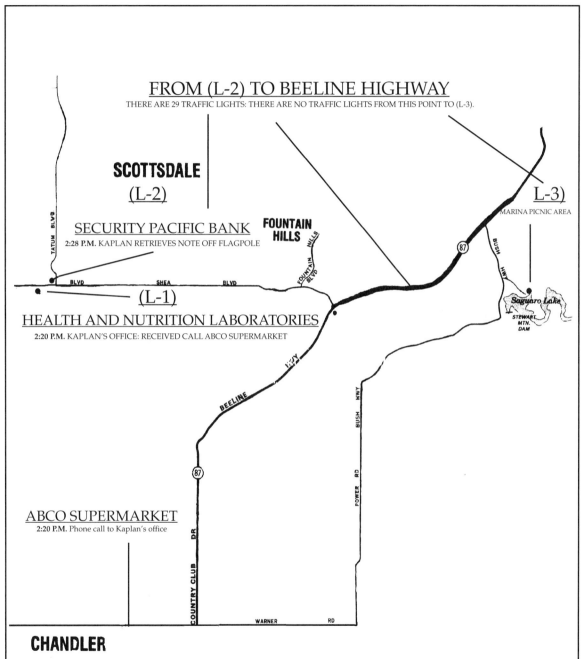

FROM (L-2) TO BEELINE HIGHWAY
THERE ARE 29 TRAFFIC LIGHTS: THERE ARE NO TRAFFIC LIGHTS FROM THIS POINT TO (L-3).

SCOTTSDALE
(L-2)

L-3)

MARINA PICNIC AREA

SECURITY PACIFIC BANK
2:28 P.M. KAPLAN RETRIEVES NOTE OFF FLAGPOLE

FOUNTAIN HILLS

TATUM BLVD

BLVD   SHEA   BLVD   FOUNTAIN BLVD

(L-1)

HEALTH AND NUTRITION LABORATORIES
2:20 P.M. KAPLAN'S OFFICE: RECEIVED CALL ABCO SUPERMARKET

Saguaro Lake

STEWART MTN. DAM

BUSH HWY

BEELINE

ABCO SUPERMARKET
2:20 P.M. Phone call to Kaplan's office

COUNTRY CLUB DR

POWER RD

BUSH HWY

WARNER   RD

CHANDLER

To travel from (L-1) to (L-2,) it is less than three blocks or 3 minutes away. From (L-2) to (L-3) it is exactly 31 miles. A driving time record was taken, it took 52 minutes to travel this distance, covering 29 traffic lights, and average speed of 60 m.p.h.., at (L-2) the estimated traffic count was 65,000 a day one way, this is a two way street.

Security Pacific Bank

2: 28 P.M. MARC KAPLAN RETRIEVED A NOTE
FROM FLAGPOLE AT THIS ABANDONED BUILDING

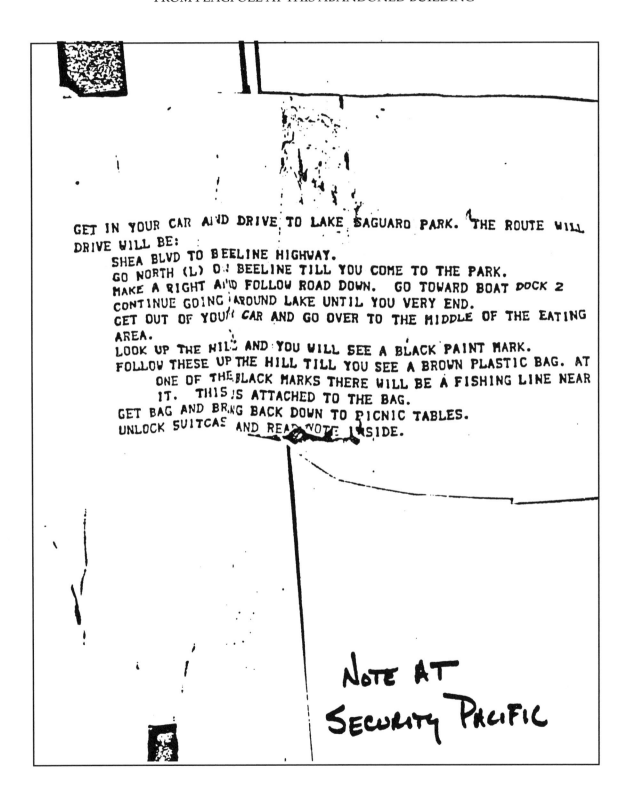

GET IN YOUR CAR AND DRIVE TO LAKE SAGUARO PARK. THE ROUTE WILL
DRIVE WILL BE:
SHEA BLVD TO BEELINE HIGHWAY.
GO NORTH (L) ON BEELINE TILL YOU COME TO THE PARK.
MAKE A RIGHT AND FOLLOW ROAD DOWN. GO TOWARD BOAT DOCK 2
CONTINUE GOING AROUND LAKE UNTIL YOU VERY END.
GET OUT OF YOUR CAR AND GO OVER TO THE MIDDLE OF THE EATING
AREA.
LOOK UP THE HILL AND YOU WILL SEE A BLACK PAINT MARK.
FOLLOW THESE UP THE HILL TILL YOU SEE A BROWN PLASTIC BAG. AT
ONE OF THE BLACK MARKS THERE WILL BE A FISHING LINE NEAR
IT. THIS IS ATTACHED TO THE BAG.
GET BAG AND BRING BACK DOWN TO PICNIC TABLES.
UNLOCK SUITCASE AND READ NOTE INSIDE.

NOTE AT SECURITY PACIFIC

Location And Events Map

KAPLAN DRIVES TOWARDS BOAT DOCK #2
AND CONTINUES AROUND LAKE TO (L-3)

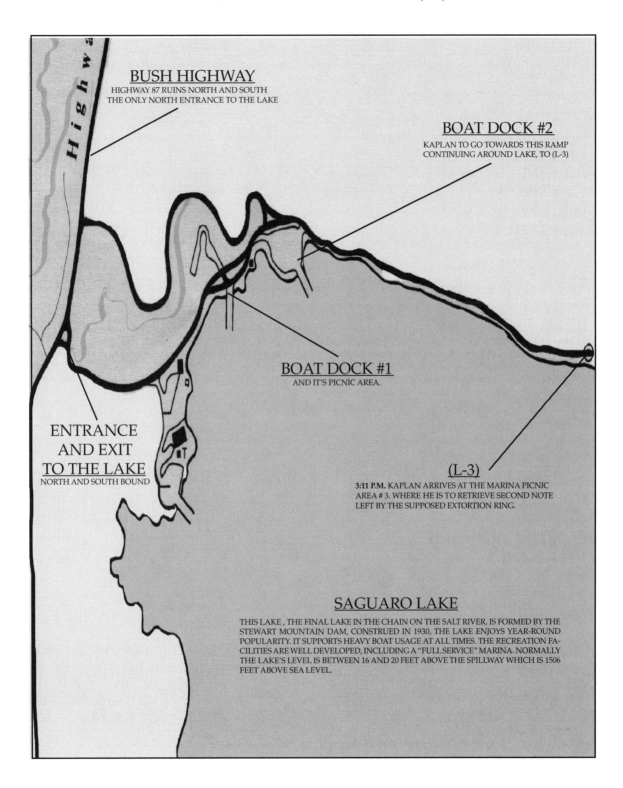

BUSH HIGHWAY
HIGHWAY 87 RUINS NORTH AND SOUTH
THE ONLY NORTH ENTRANCE TO THE LAKE

BOAT DOCK #2
KAPLAN TO GO TOWARDS THIS RAMP
CONTINUING AROUND LAKE, TO (L-3)

BOAT DOCK #1
AND IT'S PICNIC AREA.

**ENTRANCE
AND EXIT
TO THE LAKE**
NORTH AND SOUTH BOUND

(L-3)
3:11 P.M. KAPLAN ARRIVES AT THE MARINA PICNIC
AREA # 3. WHERE HE IS TO RETRIEVE SECOND NOTE
LEFT BY THE SUPPOSED EXTORTION RING.

SAGUARO LAKE

THIS LAKE , THE FINAL LAKE IN THE CHAIN ON THE SALT RIVER, IS FORMED BY THE
STEWART MOUNTAIN DAM, CONSTRUED IN 1930, THE LAKE ENJOYS YEAR-ROUND
POPULARITY. IT SUPPORTS HEAVY BOAT USAGE AT ALL TIMES. THE RECREATION FA-
CILITIES ARE WELL DEVELOPED, INCLUDING A "FULL SERVICE" MARINA. NORMALLY
THE LAKE'S LEVEL IS BETWEEN 16 AND 20 FEET ABOVE THE SPILLWAY WHICH IS 1506
FEET ABOVE SEA LEVEL.

Marc Kaplan's Next Move
ABANDONED SECURITY PACIFIC BANK BUILDING ON TATUM AND SHEA BOULEVARD

At 2:29 P.M., Kaplan reads the note at the bank. He leaves without telling any FBI Special Agents, to avoid the risk of being deemed as having involved the FBI. He was informed earlier to go where the note indicated. He'd been told by the FBI "To take it slow, but get there, we don't need any problems or someone getting hurt if you wreck your car." We (FBI) will be following behind you. It's 2:30 P.M. and Kaplan is at least 50 to 70 minutes away from *Saguaro Lake*. At this time of day, he's on a busy road in North Scottsdale, with the 29 traffic lights and 31 miles to the lake.

Kaplan knew *Saguaro Lake*, he knew the exact location of the Marina Picnic Area #3, located at the end of the road, at the far eastern end of the boating and picnic areas. When you first drive into the park, the Restaurant Marina overlooking the lake is on the right, then a few hundred feet away is the Maricopa County Sheriff's office. As you pass these buildings, you come to Boat Dock #1 and its picnic area, then Boat Dock #2 and its picnic area. Follow the road to its dead end and you had just arrived at Marina Picnic Area #3.

Kaplan departs the bank, (L-2) and proceeds to the lake (L-3) followed by FBI Special Agents.

FBI Surveillance Log
PAGE 2, SECTION 1, AND RECORDED TIMES

This *Surveillance Log*, is the second half of this *Surveillance Log*, it has the same list of the "Personnel Involved." This Log sheet entry starts at 3:01 P.M. The actual reporting Special Agents Bateman (4), White (1), MacDonald (7), and Peterson (12).

The map on the left will let you place each event at the location as how the FBI said, "they observed the following activities."

INIT	TIME	OBSV	ACTIVITY OBSERVED	PHOTOS ATTEMPTED	
				ROLL #	EXP
TB	3:01p	4	OBSERVED PARKED PAST RAMP 2 (SAGUARO LAKE		
			MARINA), FAR EASTERN END IS A DARK COLORED		
			MERCURY (V-3)		
TB	3:03p	4	A RED CORVETTE (V-4) IS NOW OBSERVED PARKED		
			NEXT TO (V-3), 4 WHITE MALES ARE OBSERVED		
			AROUND THESE VEHICLES, ONE OF THE W/M's IS CARRYING		
			A CELLULAR TELEPHONE, ANOTHER IS DESCRIBED WITH		
			LONG PERM HAIR WITH A PONY TAIL, AND ONE W/M IS		
			WEARING A BASEBALL CAP BACKWARDS.		
	3:11p	4 7/12	V-1 ARRIVES L-3,		
TB	3:14p	4	M-1 IS OUT OF V-1 AND IS OBSERVED NORTH ON THE		
			HILL FROM SAGUARO LAKE (EAST END), M-1 IS OBSERVED		
			OPENING A GREY PLASTIC TRASH BAG AND THEN		

358

Location And Events Map
KAPLAN MOVEMENTS MONITORED BY FBI SPECIAL AGENTS

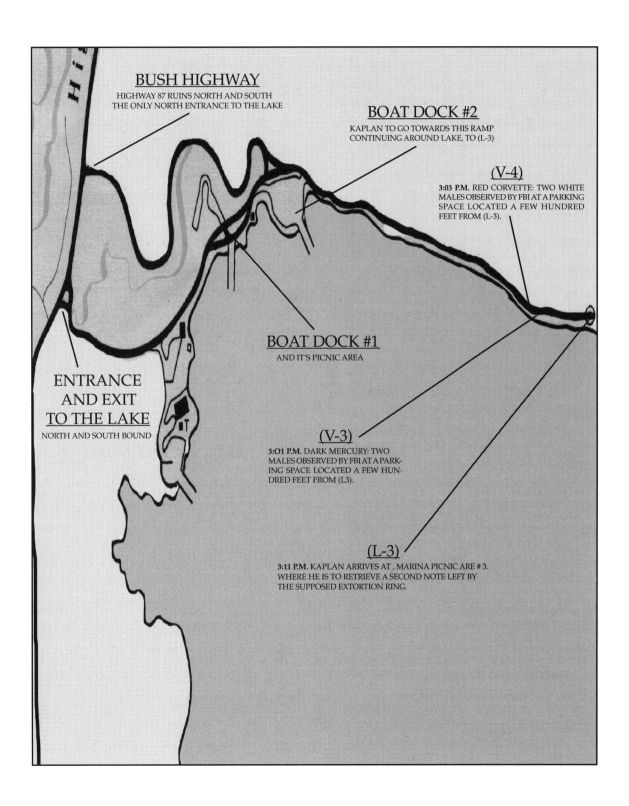

BUSH HIGHWAY
HIGHWAY 87 RUINS NORTH AND SOUTH
THE ONLY NORTH ENTRANCE TO THE LAKE

BOAT DOCK #2
KAPLAN TO GO TOWARDS THIS RAMP
CONTINUING AROUND LAKE, TO (L-3)

(V-4)
3:03 P.M. RED CORVETTE: TWO WHITE
MALES OBSERVED BY FBI AT A PARKING
SPACE LOCATED A FEW HUNDRED
FEET FROM (L-3).

BOAT DOCK #1
AND IT'S PICNIC AREA

**ENTRANCE
AND EXIT
TO THE LAKE**
NORTH AND SOUTH BOUND

(V-3)
3:01 P.M. DARK MERCURY: TWO
MALES OBSERVED BY FBI AT A PARK-
ING SPACE LOCATED A FEW HUN-
DRED FEET FROM (L3).

(L-3)
3:11 P.M. KAPLAN ARRIVES AT , MARINA PICNIC ARE # 3.
WHERE HE IS TO RETRIEVE A SECOND NOTE LEFT BY
THE SUPPOSED EXTORTION RING.

Kaplan Locates Note At Marina Picnic Area # 3

3:11 P.M. FBI SPECIAL AGENTS OBSERVED KAPLAN'S ARRIVAL
AT AND RETRIEVED THIS NOTE

NOTE AT SAGUARO LAKE

AT THIS POINT WE ARE WATCHING YOU AND CAN TELL IF YOU HAVE BEEN
FOLLOWED. PLEASE DO EXACTLY AS THESE INSTRUCTIONS TELL YOU.

TAKE OFF YOUR SHIRT AND TURN AROUND SLOWLY.

PUT YOUR SHIRT BACK ON.

REMOVE THE ROLL OF TAPE FROM THE SMALLER CASE.

PLACE ALL THE MONEY INSIDE THE MAIN COMPARTMENT OF THE SMALLER
CASE. THERE SHOULD BE ENOUGH ROOM BUT IF THERE IS NOT. USE THE
OTHER COMPARTMENTS.

CLOSE THE BAG

TAKE THE TAPE AND TAPE THE BAG ON EACH SIDE OF THE HANDLE. MAKE
ABOUT 8 TURNS AROUND EACH ONE.

TAPE WIDTH WISE AROUND BAG ABOUT 8 TIMES.

PLACE SMALLER BAG INSIDE BIGGER BAG. CLOSE AND LOCK BIGGER BAG.

TAKE THE TAPE AND TAPE THE BAG ON EACH SIDE OF THE HANDLE. MAKE
ABOUT 8 TURNS AROUND EACH ONE.

TAPE WIDTH WISE AROUND BAG ABOUT 8 TIMES.

LEAVE YOUR BAG ON THE GROUND AND TAKE THE MONEY BAG BACK TO YOUR
CAR. YOU CAN PICK YOUR BAG UP TOMORROW. IF YOU WANT.

YOU WILL DRIVE DIRECTLY TO ESTRALLA PARK. GOING BACK DOWN SHEA TO
32 ST. ONTO THE SQUAW PEAK TO I 10 , AND THEN GET OFF ON THE
ESTRALLA PARKWAY GOING SOUTH.

YOU WILL GO ABOUT 7 MILES T'LL YOU HIT THE BIG ROCK ESTRALLA SIGN.
KEEP GOING TILL YOU SEE A BLUE SIGN ON LEFT SAY "ESTRALLA MOUNTAIN
ESTATES ACRE LOTS PARCEL 1 TO 8" . MAKE A LEFT ONTO THIS ROAD -
SANTA ELIZABETH.

GO TILL YOU SEE 2 REFLECTORS NEXT TO A FIRE HYDRANT. PARK CAR AND
GET OUT. THERE WILL BE A FISHING LINE ATTACHED TO FIRE HYDRANT.
FOLLOW THIS TILL YOU HIT A BUCKET.

THERE IS A BOARD COVERED WITH DIRT. REMOVE IT. PLACE BAG AND THESE
INSTRUCTIONS IN THE BOX. COVER AND REPLACE DIRT WITH DIRT IN PAIL.
PUT ROCKS OVER THIS.

COLLECT PAIL. FISHING LINE AND REFLECTORS AND GET BACK IN CAR AND
GO DIRECTLY HOME. YOU HAVE ONLY 1 HOUR FROM THIS POINT.

IF YOU DID EVERYTHING CORRECTLY. EVERYTHING WILL BE FINE. IN TWO
WEEKS WE WILL SEND YOU A LETTER SAYING EVERYTHING WAS OK OR NOT.

Location And Events Map

KAPLAN ARRIVES AT THE MARINA COVERED PICNIC AREA #3

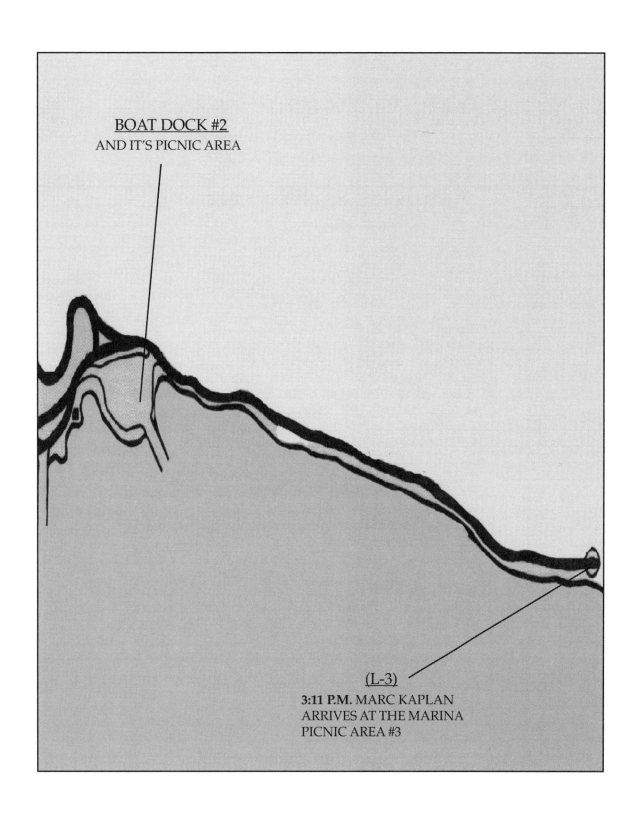

BOAT DOCK #2
AND IT'S PICNIC AREA

(L-3)
3:11 P.M. MARC KAPLAN
ARRIVES AT THE MARINA
PICNIC AREA #3

FBI Surveillance Log
PAGE 2, SECTION 1, AND RECORDED TIMES

This is the second page of the *Surveillance Log*, the only observing Special Agents were Special Agent Bateman (4), Henderson (10), and Cowan (3). The authenticity of the signatures of the FBI's Special Agents listed below needs to be approved, that on Thursday 13, 1992, these Special Agents really singed this *Surveillance Log*. The map on the left will let you place each event at the location as how the FBI said, "they observed the following activities:"

SURVEILLANCE LOG -- PHOENIX DIVISION

DATE: 2/13/92   DAY: THUR.   CASE #: 9A-PX-46497

CASE AGENT: K. TOLHURST

PAGE 2 OF 2

INIT	TIME	OBSV	ACTIVITY OBSERVED	PHOTOS ATTEMPTED ROLL #	EXP #
			REMOVING A DARK BAG FROM IT.		
TB	3⁵⁵ₚ	4	M-1 WALKS BACK DOWN THE HILL TO THE AREA WITH COVERED PICNIC TABLES WITH THIS BAG.		
TB	3⁴⁵ₚ	4	OVER THE NEXT FEW MINUTES M-1 IS OBSERVED TO GO BACK AND FORTH BETWEEN V-1 AND THE COVERED PICNIC TABLE AREA.		
TBDBCH	3²⁶ₚ	4,10	M-1 LEAVES A DARK COLORED BAG ON THE TABLE AND DEPARTS AREA IN V-1.		
TB CH	3²⁷ₚ	4,10	V-4 DEPARTS L-3 WITH 2 OF THE WHITE MALES. V-4, FURTHER DESCRIBED AS HAVING LICENSE PLATE. AZ/ EYV571, TURNS LEFT (WEST) UPON EXITING L-3 AREA.		
CH	3²⁸ₚ	3,10	V-3, FURTHER DESCRIBED AS A MERCURY ZEPHYR, AZ/ AWS 09L, DEPARTS L-3 WITH 2 WHITE MALES, HEADING IN THE SAME DIRECTION AS V-4.		
	3⁴⁰ₚ		SURVEILLANCE DISCONTINUED, LOG MAINTAINED BY CARL HENDERSON.		
			Carl T. Henderson, S.A. F.B.I. A, AZ		
			Thomas A. Bateman, SA, FBI, PX, AZ		
			Duane McDonald SA, FBI, PX, AZ		
			___ J. Peterson, SA, FBI, PX AZ		
			Daniel F. ___ SA FBI PX AZ		
			Dorn J. White SA, FBI, PX #		
			___ PX2 PX AZ		
			Ted B. Cowan, SA, FBI, PX, AZ -A-		

Location And Events Map
KAPLAN DEPARTS THE MARINA COVERED PICNIC AREA #3

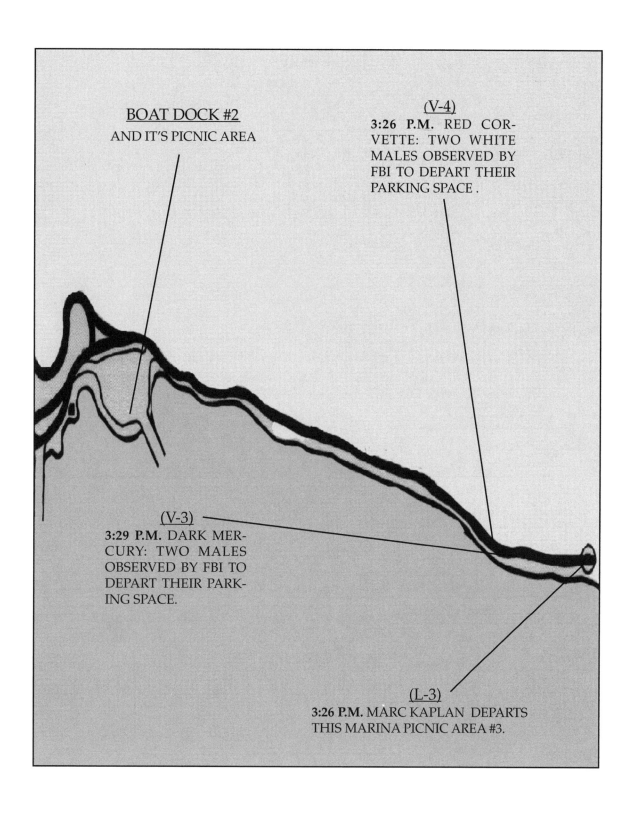

BOAT DOCK #2
AND IT'S PICNIC AREA

(V-4)
3:26 P.M. RED COR-
VETTE: TWO WHITE
MALES OBSERVED BY
FBI TO DEPART THEIR
PARKING SPACE .

(V-3)
3:29 P.M. DARK MER-
CURY: TWO MALES
OBSERVED BY FBI TO
DEPART THEIR PARK-
ING SPACE.

(L-3)
3:26 P.M. MARC KAPLAN DEPARTS
THIS MARINA PICNIC AREA #3.

Examining The Credibility Of The FBI's
SPECIAL AGENTS OBSERVATIONS

The *Surveillance Log* you have just read contains many discrepancies. It is time to examine some of them. But first, let's consider why the FBI became involved. Mailing a threatening piece of communication through the United States Postal Service is a federal offence, punishment of up to 25 years in a federal prison and an additional fine of up to $250,000. Conspiracy also federal offence punishment is the same as the Mailing offence. In all such cases, the FBI is always called into the investigation.

When the victim, Marc Kaplan, first received the extortion letter at his business location, on Friday February 7, 1992, he was understandably scared even though his children were safely with him. The Letter, of course, instructed him to not call the police. Marc Kaplan, however, had a friend who was a police officer. He called his friend who encouraged him to immediately contact the FBI. Marc Kaplan called the FBI and had them review the letter. The FBI took the threat seriously and placed the Kaplan family, his home, and his business location under 24-hour surveillance. Additional, they set up a trap and trace on all of Kaplan's phones, at home and at work. Then they waited for the phone call due on Thursday 13, 1992, as indicated in the extortion letter. The FBI kept a very low profile, they had no suspects and no further information. They merely set out to gather information and observe any developments.

At approximately 12:00 noon, Special Agents (SA's) assigned to the Phoenix Division of the *Federal Bureau of Investigation* (FBI) were dispatched to various assignments related to an investigation concerning an attempt to extort from Marc Kaplan. During this time, it was unclear where to place SA's, because the FBI did not have any information as to any location, except the fact that Kaplan was to receive a phone call at his place of business. The breakdown of this *Surveillance Log* sheet begins with page 1, part 1 below.

```
        SURVEILLANCE LOG -- PHOENIX DIVISION

DATE: 2/13/92    DAY: THUR.

WEATHER:    CLEAR              CASE #: 9A-A-46497

STARTING  (Street) 4545 E. SHEA BLVD    CASE AGENT: K. TOLHURST
LOCATION:
          (City) SCOTTSDALE, AZ.
PERSONNEL  BATEMAN (4); COWAN (3); MACDONALD (7); BEITER (8), PETERSON (12)
INVOLVED:  RIPLEY (PC); HENDERSON (10), WHITE (1)        PAGE 1 OF 2
```

INIT	TIME	OBSV	ACTIVITY OBSERVED	PHOTOS ATTEMPTED ROLL #	EXP
TAB	1:45 p	4,10	SURVEILLANCE INSTITUTED AT 4545 E. SHEA BLVD, SCOTTSDALE (L-1)		
TAB	2:25 p	4,10	MARC KAPLAN (M-1) DEPARTS L-1 DRIVING A TEAL BLUE MERCEDES BENZ, AZ/GWS676 (V-1).		

1:45 P.M.: The FBI instituted a surveillance at 4545 E. Shea Boulevard, Scottsdale, Arizona, (L-1). The observing agents were Special Agent Thomas A. Bateman (4) and Carl Henderson (10). It was also reported on this log sheet that it was a clear day when it really was overcast, and it even rained that morning, and that early evening. Both Special Agents initialed their observation time.

2:22 P.M.: At approximately this time, all Special Agents were advised that Kaplan had received a telephone call informing him of further instructions. This phone call told him to go to the closed *Security Pacific Bank* building. No other location was given, the FBI still had no location of a drop-off site, and pressure was building to keep the situation from the media. This information was omitted from this *Surveillance Log. Why?*

2:25 P.M.: Marc Kaplan (M-1) departs (L-1) driving, a teal blue Mercedes Benz (V-1). He heads toward location (L-2). Both Special Agents initialed their observation time.

Location And Events Map
FBI SPECIAL AGENTS MONITOR KAPLAN'S MOVEMENTS

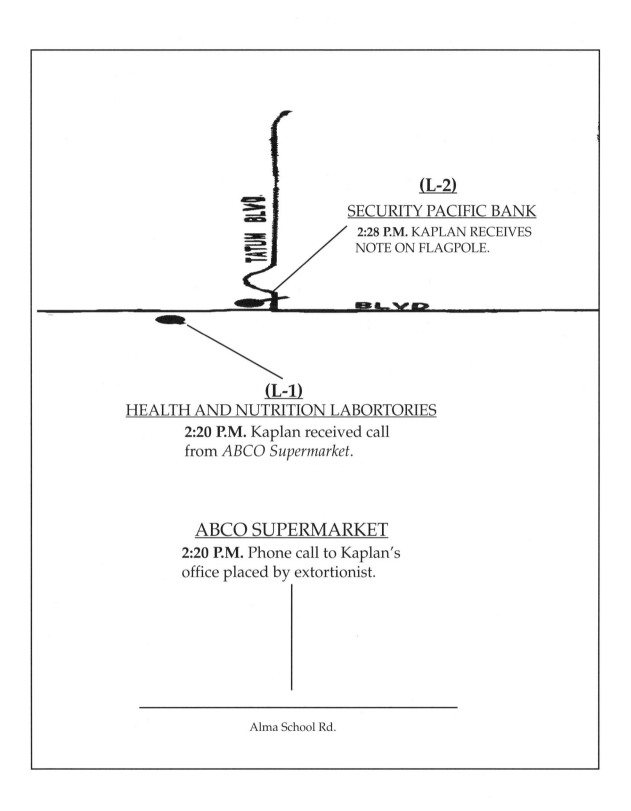

PAGE 1, SECTION 2, AND RECORDED TIMES

INIT	TIME	OBSV	ACTIVITY OBSERVED	PHOTOS ATTEMPTED ROLL # EXP	
	2:28 P	1, PC	V-1 OBSERVED AT A CLOSED SECURITY PACIFIC BANK		
			N.W. CORNER OF TATUM AND SHEA (L-2).		
	2:28 P	PC	V-1 OBSERVED IN THE MIDDLE DRIVE-THRU OF L-2		
			WITH M-1 TAKING A PIECE OF PAPER OFF THE		
			NORTHERN POLE.		
	2:29 P	PC	M-1, AS HE DEPARTS FROM L-1, IS OBSERVED TO		
			TALK TO THE DRIVER OF A WHITE CADILLAC, AZ/		
			1. KFT4 (V-2).		

2:28 P.M. Special Agent White (1) and Riply (PC) observed (V-1) at the bank.

2:28 P.M. Riply (PC) observed Kaplan (M-1) taking a piece of paper from the flagpole. The question comes up were did Special Agent White (1) go? Only one Special Agent initialed the observation time.

2:29 P.M. Ripley (PC) observed Kaplan (M-1) is observed to talk to a driver of a white Cadillac (V-2). Kaplan (M-1) departs to the undisclosed location listed on the note. At this point, Kaplan did not tell anyone about the information on the note he found. So it is believed at this point, all the Special Agents, followed the victim Kaplan, to the undisclosed area or the person in the white Cadillac was in fact an FBI Special Agent. The licence plate listed on this log is either a personal plate or FBI. It's not known for sure because this individual, you will later lean, was never interviewed. Only one Special Agent initialed his observation time. Why was this unidentified person even at this location, (L-2) a closed down *Security Pacific Bank*? Again what happened to Special Agent White (1)?

Location And Events Map
FBI SPECIAL AGENTS MONITOR KAPLAN'S MOVEMENTS

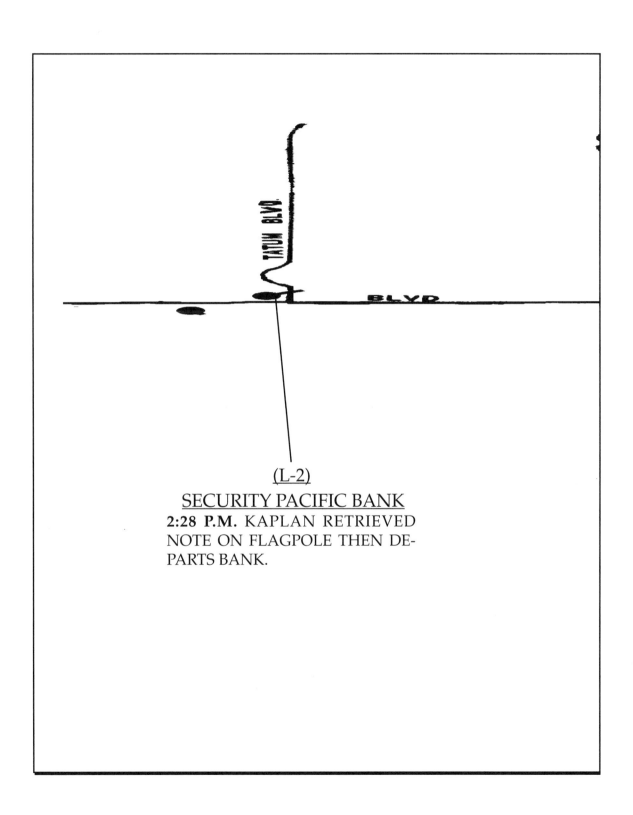

(L-2)
SECURITY PACIFIC BANK
2:28 P.M. KAPLAN RETRIEVED NOTE ON FLAGPOLE THEN DE-PARTS BANK.

PAGE 1, SECTION 3, AND RECORDED TIMES

TAS	3⁰¹	4	OBSERVED PARKED PAST RAMP 2 (SAGUARO LAKE		•
			MARINA), (L-3) FAR EASTERN END IS A DARK COLORED		
			MERCURY (V-3)		
TAS	3⁰³	4	A RED CORVETTE (V-4) IS NOW OBSERVED PARKED		
			NEXT TO (V-3), 4 WHITE MALES ARE OBSERVED		
			AROUND THESE VEHICLES, ONE OF THE W/M'S IS CARRYING		
			A CELLULAR TELEPHONE, ANOTHER IS DESCRIBED WITH		
			LONG PERM HAIR WITH A PONY TAIL, AND ONE WM IS	\.	
			WEARING A BASEBALL CAP BACKWARDS.		

3:01 P.M. SA Bateman (4) observed at *Saguaro Lake* Marina (L-3) a Mercury Sedan (V-3). This vehicle was actually *250* feet away from the location listed above. Only one Special Agent, Bateman (4), initialed his observation time.

3:03 P.M. SA Bateman (4) observed a red Corvette (V-4) parked next to the Mercury (V-3) containing four white males. Only one Special Agent, Bateman (4), initialed his observation time. Once again the question, How did the FBI Special Agent Bateman (4) know to go to *Saguaro Lake*, when he was still at location (L-1). This location (L-3) was not revealed to anyone until Kaplan (M-1) in vehicle (V-1), retrieved the note from the flagpole at the bank location (L-2). Yet, Special Agent Bateman arrived in 30 minutes at this location to report his observations. Remember, it is 31 miles from location (L-2) to (L-3) and with 29 traffic lights, and estimated 2 minute per light stop light delay, not to mention the 65,000 cars a day traffic delay time of 15 minutes. For this time of day near this location, (L-2). That's a total of 104 minutes possible drive time, at the average speed of 60 m.p.h., which SA Bateman arrived at this location, (L-3) in less than 30 minutes. "How did he, do that?" There were other individuals at this same location (L-3), at the same time as these other vehicles were too. But it's not mentioned on this *Surveillance Log*. *"Why?"* In fact, on this log sheet the FBI SA's; reported in numerical order all the vehicles they observed during this surveillance. Listing the victim Marc Kaplan's vehicle as (V-1) and then lists the white Cadillac at the bank as (V-2). The vehicles listed as (V-3), was the Mercury and the red Corvette was listed as (V-4). In fact, before the arrival of the Mercury (V-3), there was an older individual, in a blue truck at this location fishing. This individual should have been listed as (V-3) on this *Surveillance Log*. Then the Mercury should have been listed as Vehicle, (V-4). The reason it was not? FBI, SA Bateman was not at this location at the time listed, in order to report these observations? *Why?* There are still two more unidentified individuals with an vehicle and they should have been listed as Vehicle, (V-5). They were two fisherman, and as they pulled up to this location, they drove by the Mercury and said, "Hello."

Location And Events Map

FBI SPECIAL AGENTS OBSERVED MERCURY AND CORVETTE
NO MENTION OF OTHER VEHICLES IN THE LOG

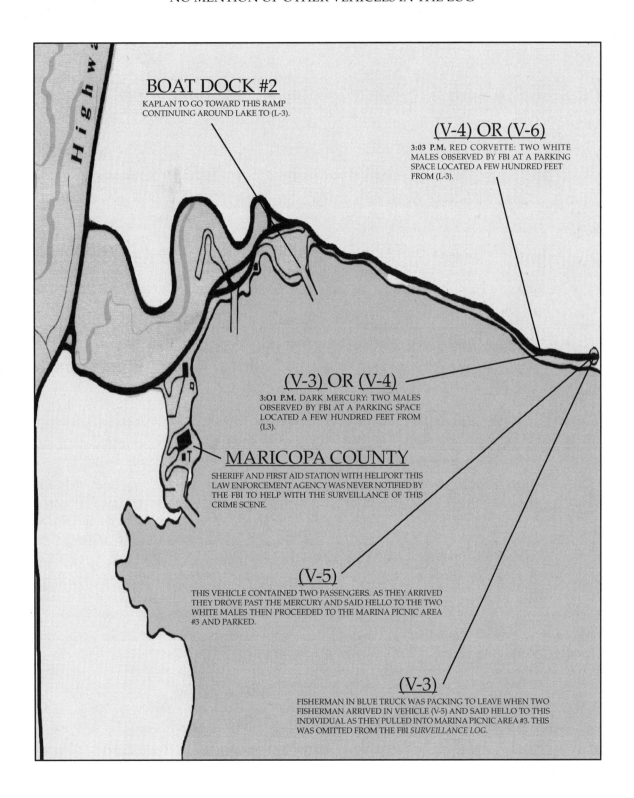

BOAT DOCK #2
KAPLAN TO GO TOWARD THIS RAMP
CONTINUING AROUND LAKE TO (L-3).

(V-4) OR (V-6)
3:03 P.M. RED CORVETTE: TWO WHITE
MALES OBSERVED BY FBI AT A PARKING
SPACE LOCATED A FEW HUNDRED FEET
FROM (L-3).

(V-3) OR (V-4)
3:01 P.M. DARK MERCURY: TWO MALES
OBSERVED BY FBI AT A PARKING SPACE
LOCATED A FEW HUNDRED FEET FROM
(L3).

MARICOPA COUNTY
SHERIFF AND FIRST AID STATION WITH HELIPORT THIS
LAW ENFORCEMENT AGENCY WAS NEVER NOTIFIED BY
THE FBI TO HELP WITH THE SURVEILLANCE OF THIS
CRIME SCENE.

(V-5)
THIS VEHICLE CONTAINED TWO PASSENGERS. AS THEY ARRIVED
THEY DROVE PAST THE MERCURY AND SAID HELLO TO THE TWO
WHITE MALES THEN PROCEEDED TO THE MARINA PICNIC AREA
#3 AND PARKED.

(V-3)
FISHERMAN IN BLUE TRUCK WAS PACKING TO LEAVE WHEN TWO
FISHERMAN ARRIVED IN VEHICLE (V-5) AND SAID HELLO TO THIS
INDIVIDUAL AS THEY PULLED INTO MARINA PICNIC AREA #3. THIS
WAS OMITTED FROM THE FBI *SURVEILLANCE LOG*.

Surveillance Log Continued
SPECIAL AGENTS HIDE THE IDENTITY OF WITNESSES

These two fisherman asked the old man who was loading his truck to leave, how the fishing was. The old man responded negatively and left. This unidentified individual and his vehicle were never mentioned on this log for one simple reason. It's believed by the evidence herewith, that the FBI Special Agents had not yet arrived at this location (L-3). This discredits FBI Special Agent Bateman's (4) reported observation at 3:01 P.M. and 3:03 P.M. Sometime thereafter, a red Corvette pulled into the area; this vehicle should have been listed as (V-6) on this log, right? Believe it or not, there was still one more vehicle (V-7) that arrived 5 minutes after the red Corvette and the Mercury left this area, and even positively before the victim Marc Kaplan arrived. This last vehicle (V-7) was actually the FBI's Special Agents arriving at the surveillance scene at the real time of 3:10 P.M. It's believed just prior to their arrival, the FBI saw the Corvette leave *Saguaro Lake,* and turn the opposite direction heading south on Bush Highway. The FBI recorded the licence plate number, and few hundred feet behind the Corvette was the Mercury, and again the FBI recorded the license plate and saw the Mercury turn left and head south on Bush Highway. Why, again were these witnesses and their actions *omitted* from this *Surveillance Log*?

So as you read, even before the victim Kaplan arrived. There were five vehicles already at this location (L-3), and you must take into consideration the fact that the Corvette and Mercury, left before Kaplan arrived. Still this was not how the FBI reported these events. *Why?*

The map on the right replicates the exact area of these activities, and approximately where all the vehicles were located.

Location And Events Map
SPECIAL AGENTS OBSERVED MERCURY AND CORVETTE
NO MENTION OF THE OTHER THREE VEHICLES

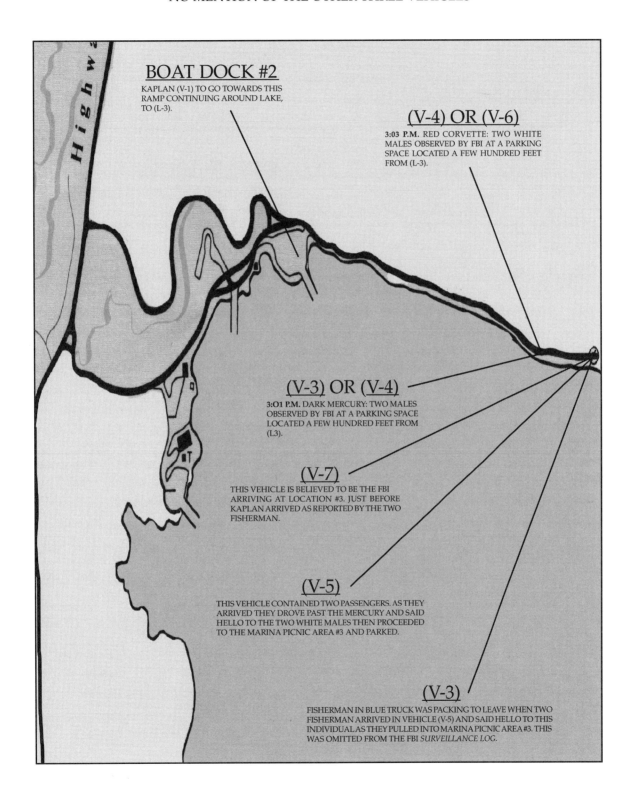

BOAT DOCK #2
KAPLAN (V-1) TO GO TOWARDS THIS
RAMP CONTINUING AROUND LAKE,
TO (L-3).

(V-4) OR (V-6)
3:03 P.M. RED CORVETTE: TWO WHITE
MALES OBSERVED BY FBI AT A PARKING
SPACE LOCATED A FEW HUNDRED FEET
FROM (L-3).

(V-3) OR (V-4)
3:01 P.M. DARK MERCURY: TWO MALES
OBSERVED BY FBI AT A PARKING SPACE
LOCATED A FEW HUNDRED FEET FROM
(L3).

(V-7)
THIS VEHICLE IS BELIEVED TO BE THE FBI
ARRIVING AT LOCATION #3. JUST BEFORE
KAPLAN ARRIVED AS REPORTED BY THE TWO
FISHERMAN.

(V-5)
THIS VEHICLE CONTAINED TWO PASSENGERS. AS THEY
ARRIVED THEY DROVE PAST THE MERCURY AND SAID
HELLO TO THE TWO WHITE MALES THEN PROCEEDED
TO THE MARINA PICNIC AREA #3 AND PARKED.

(V-3)
FISHERMAN IN BLUE TRUCK WAS PACKING TO LEAVE WHEN TWO
FISHERMAN ARRIVED IN VEHICLE (V-5) AND SAID HELLO TO THIS
INDIVIDUAL AS THEY PULLED INTO MARINA PICNIC AREA #3. THIS
WAS OMITTED FROM THE FBI *SURVEILLANCE LOG.*

PAGE 1, SECTION 4, AND RECORDED TIMES

INIT	TIME	OBSV	ACTIVITY OBSERVED	PHOTOS ATTEMPTED ROLL # EXP	
pw DN3	3 ¼ P	4,7,12	V-1 ARRIVES L-3.		
TBB	3 ¼ P	4	M-1 IS OUT OF V-1 AND IS OBSERVED NORTH ON THE		
			HILL FROM SAGUARD LAKE (EAST END). M-1 IS OBSERVED		
	"		OPENING A GREY PLASTIC TRASH BAG AND THEN		

3:11 P.M. SA White (1), SA MacDonald (7), SA Peterson (12) all observed a teal blue Mercedes (V-1) arrive at the picnic area (L-3). All three Special Agents initialed their observation time.

3:14 P.M. At first there were five possible FBI Special Agents observing this area. But on the *Surveillance Log*, the other four FBI Special Agents have been crossed out. *Why*? And only one FBI SA Bateman (4), observed Kaplan (M-1) get out of his vehicle (V-1), open a grey plastic trash bag, and removes a dark bag from it. Which Bateman (4), initialed his observation time. The question here is what happened to the other Special Agents? This part of the *Surveillance Log* lists the victim Marc Kaplan arriving at location (L-3) at 3:11 P.M. In fact, Kaplan really arrived at 3:20 P.M. This time will be listed on the Criminal Complaint Affidavit to be filed February 19, 1992, by SA Keith Tolhurst, as an approximate time, when in fact it was the actual time. In order for Kaplan to arrive at the time listed on this *Surveillance Log*, he would have to have traveled from locations (L-2) to (L-3) in less than 40 minutes, but the real facts prove he arrived at this location in 50 minutes, which is closer to a more believable travel time.

There is one very important piece of exculpatory evidence that was also omitted from this *Surveillance Log*; the victim, Kaplan, driving vehicle (V-1), would have to have passed within five feet of the red Corvette and the Mercury, in order to drive into the covered picnic area (L-3), located at the end of the road. Emphatically, it was reported that Kaplan did not see either of these described vehicles, nor did he see the four white males. *Why*? Because these individuals and their vehicles, left minutes before the FBI arrived, and minutes before Kaplan arrived. This is not however, the way it was reported by these FBI Special Agents. *Why*?

3:14 P.M. Special Agent Bateman reported that he observed Kaplan (M-1) get out of his vehicle (V-1) at location (L-3) at the picnic area located at the east end of the dead end road. How did this SA Bateman (4) observe these events when Kaplan hadn't even arrive at this location until 3:20 P.M. according to the Criminal Complaint Affidavit filed February 19, by Case Special Agent Keith D. Tolhurst?

<u>Location And Events Map</u>
SPECIAL AGENT OBSERVED KAPLAN

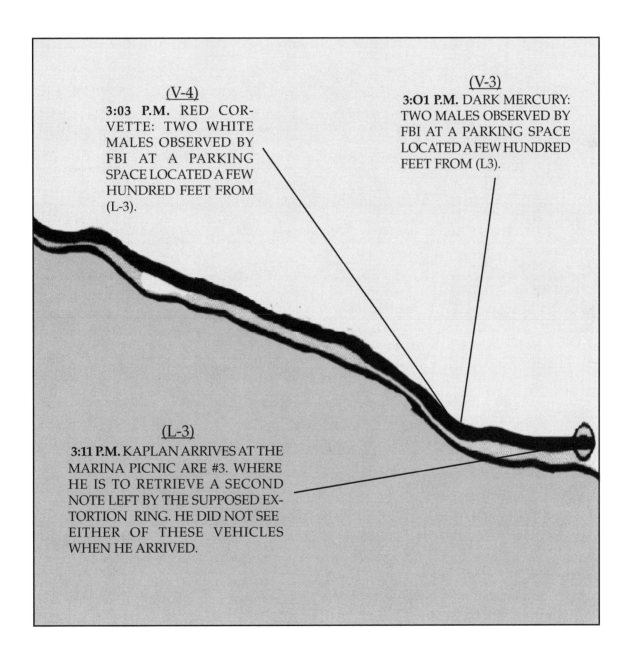

SURVEILLANCE LOG -- PHOENIX DIVISION

DATE: 2/13/9~   DAY: THUR.   CASE #: 9A-PX-46497

CASE AGENT: K. TOLHURST

PAGE 2 OF 2

INIT	TIME	OBSV	ACTIVITY OBSERVED	PHOTOS ATTEMPTED ROLL #	EXP #
			REMOVING A DARK BAG FROM IT.		
TB	3:15p	4	M-1 WALKS BACK DOWN THE HILL TO THE AREA WITH		
			COVERED PICNIC TABLES WITH THIS BAG.		
TB	3:16p	4	OVER THE NEXT FEW MINUTES M-1 IS OBSERVED		
			TO GO BACK AND FORTH BETWEEN V-1 AND THE		
			COVERED PICNIC TABLE AREA.		

3:15 P.M. SA Bateman (4) observed Kaplan (M-1) after he had opened a gray plastic trash bag and removed a dark bag from it, then walked down the hill to the covered picnic area. The question here is what happened to those other Special Agents? Special Agent Bateman (4) initialed his observation time. These observations listed above could not have happened at the times listed because the victim Marc Kaplan did not arrive at this location (L-3), until 3:20 P.M. Why were these events observed and recorded otherwise?

3:16 P.M. SA Bateman (4) observes Kaplan over the next few minutes, going back and fourth between his vehicle (V-1) and the covered picnic area (L-3). Special Agent Bateman (4) initialed his observation time. We now know the truth, based on the evidence forthwith; that Kaplan had not yet arrived at this location (L-3). Remember, the Corvette and Mercury departed this area before the FBI arrived. Kaplan too did not arrive until 3:20 P.M., The unbelievable thing here is, the chain of events that are listed in this log, are not what the true facts reflect, which becomes more shocking, as this bizarre case unfolds throughout this book! Why the cover up?

Location And Events Map
KAPLAN LOCATES NOTE AND A DARK BAG
AT THE MARINA PICNIC AREA #3

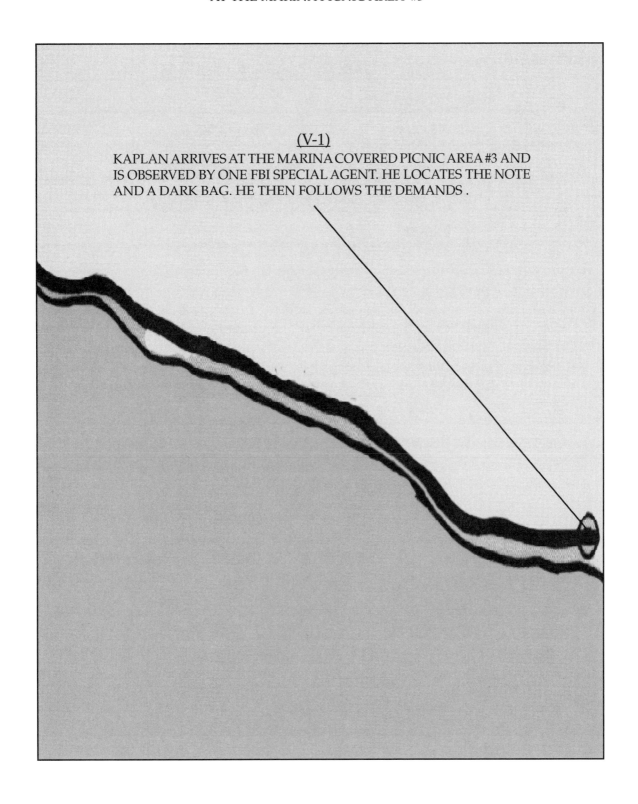

<u>(V-1)</u>
KAPLAN ARRIVES AT THE MARINA COVERED PICNIC AREA #3 AND
IS OBSERVED BY ONE FBI SPECIAL AGENT. HE LOCATES THE NOTE
AND A DARK BAG. HE THEN FOLLOWS THE DEMANDS .

PAGE 2, SECTION 2, AND RECORDED TIMES

INIT	TIME	OBSV	ACTIVITY OBSERVED	PHOTOS ATTEMPTED ROLL / EXP	
DBOt	3²⁶⁷	4,10	M-1 LEAVES A DARK COLORED BAG ON THE TABLE		
			AND DEPARTS AREA IN V-1.		
Ot	3²⁷⁷	4,10	V-4 DEPARTS L-3 WITH 2 OF THE WHITE MALES.		
			V-4, FURTHER DESCRIBED AS HAVING LICENSE PLATE,		
			AZ/ E\V571, TURNS LEFT (WEST) UPON EXITING		
			L-3 AREA.		

3:26 P.M. At this time, Special Agents Bateman (4) an Henderson (10) observed Kaplan (M-1) depart the area in vehicle (V-1). Both Special Agents initialed their observation time. Don't you as the reader find it difficult to believe their observations, not to mention the fact that Special Agent Hendersons (10) reappearance? How did this Special Agent see Kaplan put a bag on the table, and see him leaving, but fail to witness the events prior to this time period listed in the log? Or did he just arrive in a second vehicle that no one saw? Maybe this Special Agent was hiding behind a cactus somewhere?

Remember, Kaplan did not arrive until 3:20 P.M. To be on track with Kaplan's movements is not the discrepancy, it's the times, listed as they were supposed to have happen as all the questionable deceptions started. At this point of the log sheet, Kaplan is already 15 minutes into his actions. You have to add the 15 minutes, to the actual time of Kaplan's arrival of 3:20 P.M., which is 3:35 P.M. This is just another piece of evidence for the Conspiracy Theory. Here is something else that will prove positive to these contentions. Kaplan would have had to drive past the Mercury first, then three parking spaces to reach the red Corvette, then proceeded to the exit the lake. You already know by now why this could not have happened! When Kaplan arrived these individuals and their vehicles had already left. Kaplan told the FBI he did not see either vehicles or individual at this location.

3:27 P.M. At this time, Special Agent's Bateman (4) and Henderson (10) observed the red Corvette (V-4) depart with two white males, they note the car licence plates and followed this vehicle to the point of seeing the car turn left heading west. Both Special Agents initialed their observation time. One problem with this observation, These Special Agents did not have the directions correct. This would substantiate the fact these Special Agents were not at this location. The Corvette was actually heading south! How did this occur when the Corvette (V-4) left before Kaplan even arrived, plus the vehicle was not correctly numbered, it should have been (V-6), remember?

Location And Events Map

KAPLAN DEPARTS MARINA PICNIC AREA AND CORVETTE IS SUPPOSED
TO HAVE FOLLOWED, ACCORDING TO FBI SPECIAL AGENTS

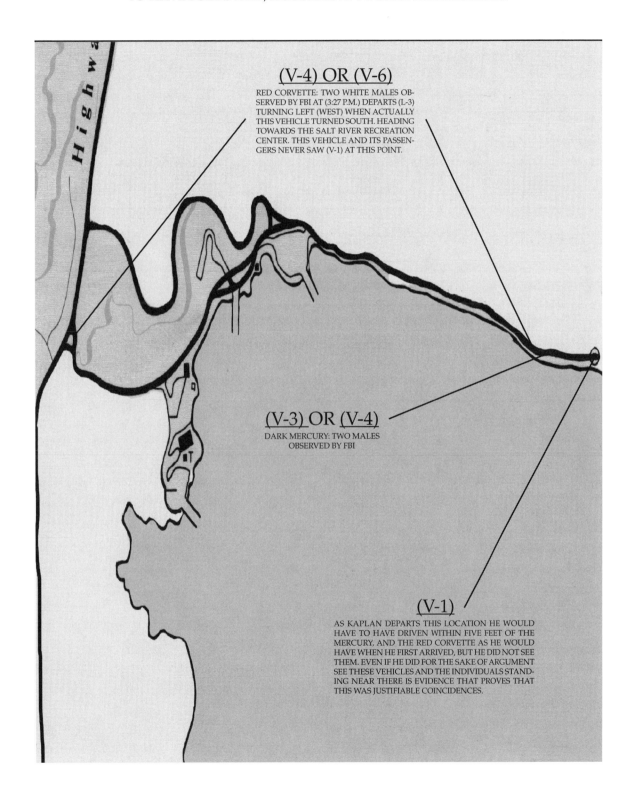

(V-4) OR (V-6)

RED CORVETTE: TWO WHITE MALES OB-
SERVED BY FBI AT (3:27 P.M.) DEPARTS (L-3)
TURNING LEFT (WEST) WHEN ACTUALLY
THIS VEHICLE TURNED SOUTH. HEADING
TOWARDS THE SALT RIVER RECREATION
CENTER. THIS VEHICLE AND ITS PASSEN-
GERS NEVER SAW (V-1) AT THIS POINT.

(V-3) OR (V-4)

DARK MERCURY: TWO MALES
OBSERVED BY FBI

(V-1)

AS KAPLAN DEPARTS THIS LOCATION HE WOULD
HAVE TO HAVE DRIVEN WITHIN FIVE FEET OF THE
MERCURY, AND THE RED CORVETTE AS HE WOULD
HAVE WHEN HE FIRST ARRIVED, BUT HE DID NOT SEE
THEM. EVEN IF HE DID FOR THE SAKE OF ARGUMENT
SEE THESE VEHICLES AND THE INDIVIDUALS STAND-
ING NEAR THERE IS EVIDENCE THAT PROVES THAT
THIS WAS JUSTIFIABLE COINCIDENCES.

Examining The Credibility
PAGE 2, SECTION 3, AND RECORDED TIMES

CH	3²⁹/P	3,10			
			V-3, FURTHER DESCRIBED AS A MERCURY ZEPHYR, AZ/		
			AWS 09L, DEPARTS L-3 WITH 2 WHITE MALES,		
			HEADING IN THE SAME DIRECTION AS V-4.		
	3⁴⁰/P		SURVEILLANCE DISCONTINUED. LOG MAINTAINED BY		
			CARL HENDERSON.		
			Carl R. Henderson, S.A. F.B.I, A, Az		
			Thomas A. Bateman, SA, FBI, PK, AZ		
			Duane Macdonald SA, FBI, PK, AZ		
			[illegible] SA, FBI, PK, AZ		
			David H. [illegible] SA FBI PK AZ		
			[illegible] white SA, FBI, PK AZ		
			[illegible] PSR AZ AZ		
			Fred B. [illegible], SA, FBI, PK, AZ. -4m		

3:29 P.M. Special Agents Cowan (3) and Henderson (10) observe the Mercury (V-3) depart location (L-3), as these Special Agents followed they recorded the license plate number. The report further describes this vehicle heading in the same directions as the Corvette. It appears that both Special Agents initialed their observation time. The confusing problem here is, how does Special Agent Henderson (10) report his observations from two different vehicles, and where did Special Agent Cowan (3) appear from? Here is another mind blowing piece of evidence that was also left off this log sheet. Remember, the two fisherman at the lake, who arrived before the FBI, Kaplan, and even before the Corvette, but not before the Mercury? Their vehicle should have been listed as (V-5). Well, one these individuals actually went through the evidence left by Kaplan; immediately after Kaplan left this area. Therefore, this area is now contaminated, this information was confessed to the FBI five days later. Why again would something this important be *omitted* from this *Surveillance Log*, unless there was a cover-up of some kind?

3:40 P.M. The *Surveillance Log* was discontinued, and maintained by Special Agent Henderson (10). Here is something real puzzling, eight Special Agents signed their full names at the bottom of the log to their activities they claimed to have observed. The question once again is, "Did all these Special Agents sign exactly on February 13, 1992 or was this *Surveillance Log* rewritten to fit the accused? Based on the witness reports and time discrepancy it had to be rewritten, and possibly the Special Agents listed above all conspired to these facts...!

Location And Events Map
KAPLAN DEPARTS MARINA PICNIC AREA LOCATION #3

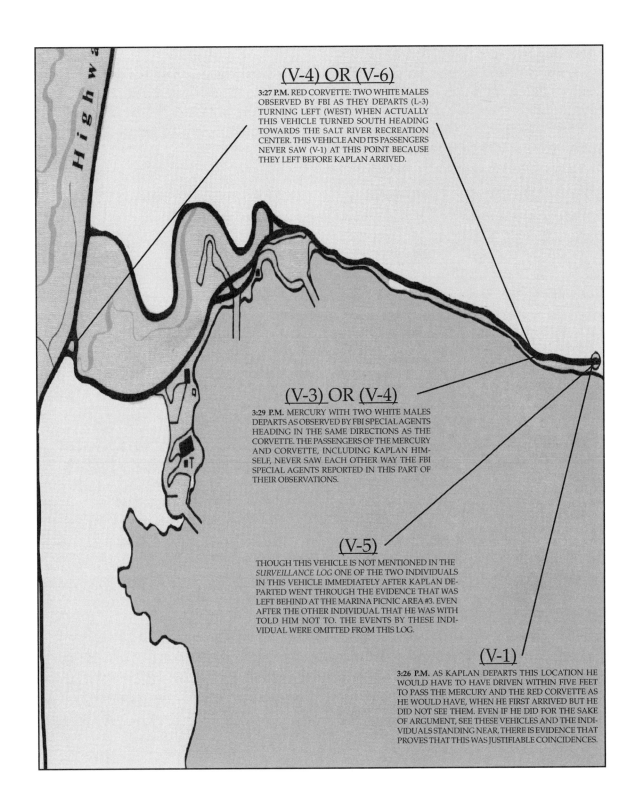

(V-4) OR (V-6)

3:27 P.M. RED CORVETTE: TWO WHITE MALES OBSERVED BY FBI AS THEY DEPARTS (L-3) TURNING LEFT (WEST) WHEN ACTUALLY THIS VEHICLE TURNED SOUTH HEADING TOWARDS THE SALT RIVER RECREATION CENTER. THIS VEHICLE AND ITS PASSENGERS NEVER SAW (V-1) AT THIS POINT BECAUSE THEY LEFT BEFORE KAPLAN ARRIVED.

(V-3) OR (V-4)

3:29 P.M. MERCURY WITH TWO WHITE MALES DEPARTS AS OBSERVED BY FBI SPECIAL AGENTS HEADING IN THE SAME DIRECTIONS AS THE CORVETTE. THE PASSENGERS OF THE MERCURY AND CORVETTE, INCLUDING KAPLAN HIMSELF, NEVER SAW EACH OTHER WAY THE FBI SPECIAL AGENTS REPORTED IN THIS PART OF THEIR OBSERVATIONS.

(V-5)

THOUGH THIS VEHICLE IS NOT MENTIONED IN THE *SURVEILLANCE LOG* ONE OF THE TWO INDIVIDUALS IN THIS VEHICLE IMMEDIATELY AFTER KAPLAN DEPARTED WENT THROUGH THE EVIDENCE THAT WAS LEFT BEHIND AT THE MARINA PICNIC AREA #3. EVEN AFTER THE OTHER INDIVIDUAL THAT HE WAS WITH TOLD HIM NOT TO. THE EVENTS BY THESE INDIVIDUAL WERE OMITTED FROM THIS LOG.

(V-1)

3:26 P.M. AS KAPLAN DEPARTS THIS LOCATION HE WOULD HAVE TO HAVE DRIVEN WITHIN FIVE FEET TO PASS THE MERCURY AND THE RED CORVETTE AS HE WOULD HAVE, WHEN HE FIRST ARRIVED BUT HE DID NOT SEE THEM. EVEN IF HE DID FOR THE SAKE OF ARGUMENT, SEE THESE VEHICLES AND THE INDIVIDUALS STANDING NEAR, THERE IS EVIDENCE THAT PROVES THAT THIS WAS JUSTIFIABLE COINCIDENCES.

Continued Surveillance
NEW FBI SPECIAL AGENTS

    3:40 P.M. FBI Special Agent Carl Henderson (10) discontinued his and seven other Special Agent's *Surveillance Log*.

    3:59 P.M. There was a new team of FBI Special Agents even though it has not been established, it will soon be. Where these Special Agents came from is a mystery and no one knows, because these Special Agents were not listed in the original *Surveillance Log*. Nevertheless, their reported observations will also lend credibility to the Conspiracy Theory and Cover Up.

-1-

FEDERAL BUREAU OF INVESTIGATION

Date of transcription   **2/17/92**

At 3:59 p.m., a radio transmission relayed, "A red corvette followed by a dark colored sedan left the area at a fast rate of speed. Anyone seeing, don't let it out of your sight."

    3:59 P.M. Special Agents R. Scott Rivas and Reno F. Walker reported on this investigation sheet (not a log) a radio transmission relayed "A red Corvette followed by a dark colored sedan left the are at a high rate of speed. Anyone seeing, don't let it out of your sight." The problem here again is, How did the FBI come to the time period listed above? Both of these vehicles left location (L-3) at approximately 3:15 P.M. before the FBI and Kaplan even arrived at this area. This information was clearly proven earlier on the examination of the discrepancies of the FBI's *Surveillance Log*. Additionally, the FBI reported that the Corvette followed Kaplan out of this area at 3:27 P.M. Not 3:59 P.M. ,and went opposite directions.

    However, this does give credibility to a Conspiracy Theory against the FBI, not the agency itself, some of the Special Agents involved investigating this case who actually lied to their bosses and the Federal Judicial System.

Location And Events Map

RED CORVETTE FOLLOWED BY SEDAN LEFT AREA AT FAST RATE OF SPEED
DON'T LET IT OUT OF YOUR SIGHT

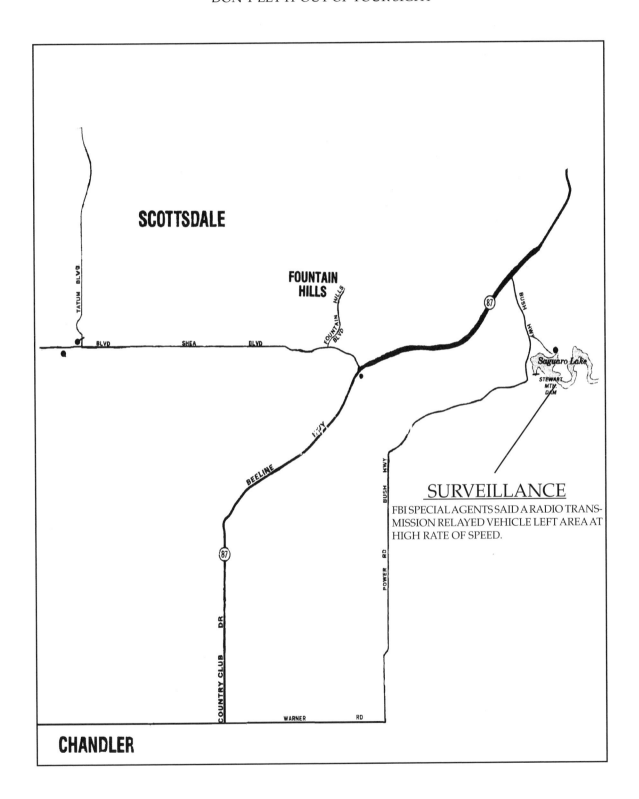

PAGE 1, SECOND HALF

At 4:00 p.m., a late model red Corvette was seen
driving west on Shea Boulevard through the intersection at
Saguaro Boulevard in Fountain Hills, Arizona, and backed into a
parking space on the south side of the MCDONALDS parking lot,
facing the building. A white male, late 20's, dark complexion,
black curly hair, 5'9", medium build, wearing faded blue jeans,
long sleeved black shirt, was seen leaving the passenger side of
Corvette and walking north across the parking lot. This unknown
individual was seen to be looking at Mr. MARC KAPLAN's vehicle
parked facing north on the north side of MCDONALDS parking lot.
Special Agents (SAs) RENO F. WALKER and R. SCOTT RIVAS then drove
by the MCDONALDS on Shea Boulevard and obtained the license plate
number of the red Corvette. The plate was Arizona EYV-571.

At approximately 4:20 p.m., red Corvette departed
MCDONALDS and proceeded to 6885 East Cochise, #116.

Investigation on __2/13/92__   at __Fountain Hills, Arizona__ File # __9A-PX-46497__

by __SAs R. Scott Rivas and Reno F. Walker/RFW__ Date dictated __2/17/92__

9/   (92)

This document contains neither recommendations nor conclusions of the FBI. It is the property of the FBI and is loaned to your agency;
it and its contents are not to be distributed outside your agency.   N000174

4:00 P.M. Special Agents R. Scott Rivas and Reno F. Walker reported they saw
the red Corvette and the PASSENGER, not the DRIVER, leaving the vehicle. They
also claimed that Kaplan's vehicle had already arrived.

4:20 P.M. These same Special Agents, reported the red Corvette departed
McDonalds and proceeded to 6885 E. Cochise. This report was investigated on February 13, 1992, but it was not transcribed until February 17, 1992, four days later.
Why?

Location And Events Map
RED CORVETTE ARRIVES AT *McDonalds* 4:00 P.M., DEPARTS AT 4:20 P.M.

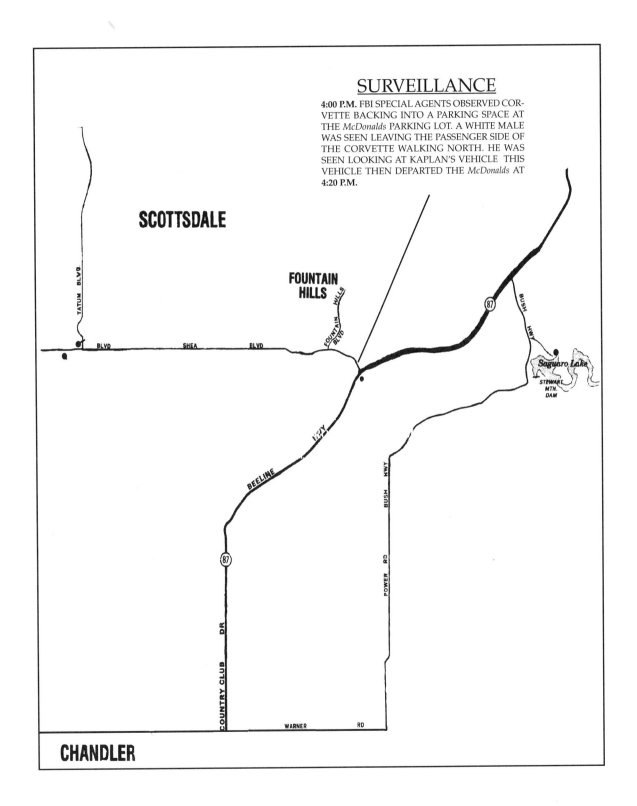

SURVEILLANCE

4:00 P.M. FBI SPECIAL AGENTS OBSERVED COR-
VETTE BACKING INTO A PARKING SPACE AT
THE *McDonalds* PARKING LOT. A WHITE MALE
WAS SEEN LEAVING THE PASSENGER SIDE OF
THE CORVETTE WALKING NORTH. HE WAS
SEEN LOOKING AT KAPLAN'S VEHICLE THIS
VEHICLE THEN DEPARTED THE *McDonalds* AT
4:20 P.M.

SCOTTSDALE

FOUNTAIN
HILLS

TATUM BLVD.

BLVD   SHEA   BLVD

FOUNTAIN BLVD

87   BUSH HWY

Saguaro Lake

STEWART
MTN.
DAM

HWY

BEELINE

BUSH HWY

87

POWER RD

COUNTRY CLUB DR

WARNER   RD

CHANDLER

Upon Information And Belief
THE TRUE ACCOUNT WAS THIS:

3:59 P.M. "A red Corvette followed by dark colored sedan left the area at a high rate of speed anyone seeing , don't let it out of your sight." The Special Agents at this time were following the victim, Kaplan. It is this time period Kaplan reported to the FBI Special Agents, "seeing the red Corvette just a few miles before the *McDonalds* and the driver and passenger appeared to be looking at him. Then drove away real fast passing him. Nelson did slow down to look at Mercedes, he loves that style of car (teal blue Mercedes Benz 500 Sl.). Note that the Corvette had to leave the lake and pass the car following the Mercedes which is believed to have been the FBI Special Agents, Rivas and Walker, then pass, slow down, and look at the Mercedes, 11.5 miles from the lake. It is here that these Special Agents actually radioed in seeing the Corvette, at the reported time of 3:59 P.M. These Special Agents observed through their rear view mirror a bright red Corvette moving very fast toward them, though these Special Agents omitted the actions of the Corvette slowing down looking at the Mercedes, from their report. The fact that the Corvette arrived at 4: 00 P.M. at the *McDonalds* and this vehicle traveled a total 13.5 miles. How fast would the Corvette have to travel 13.5 miles from the lake to the *McDonalds*, 2, stop signs and 1, traffic light, in 1 minute? "780.30 M.P.H.." This is equivalent of traveling 13.5 miles per one minute of time!

4:00 P.M. A red Corvette was seen backing into a parking space at the *McDonalds* Nelson the driver and Jeffrey M. Bonadonna, arrived first at the *McDonalds*. Bonadonna wanted to go to the bathroom and then get something to eat. Bonadonna went to the bathroom near the outside garbage bin then the two drove through the *McDonalds* drive-thru and ordered food. They pulled into a parking space and ate their food. Kaplan reported seeing the Corvette at the *McDonalds* when he was there, but he couldn't tell the FBI Special Agents when the car first arrived. The FBI Special Agent at the *McDonalds* did however know the truth and they did their best to change the facts to fit their motives. It's believed that the unidentified FBI Special Agent who apparently started to approach the passenger of the Corvette; who was supposably to be within ten feet of the Mercedes. Then he reentered the Corvette and departed the area immediately. This Special Agent knew in fact that the Corvette did arrive before Kaplan, because this Special Agent was there waiting for Kaplan to arrive, as earlier arranged by the FBI Special Agents. It's believed that this information was omitted from the report because this would have matched the truth of Nelson's alibi. The passenger, later identified as Jeff Bonadonna; who was reportedly looking at Mr. Kaplan, according to these same Special Agents. In fact, Jeff Bonadonna was as much as a suspect as Miller and Nelson based on his actions at the lake and at the *McDonalds*, according to the reporting Special Agents. This individual was not listed on the Criminal Complaint Affidavit, to be filed February 19, 1992. In fact, this was the individual who the FBI claimed made all initial contact with Miller and the passenger of his vehicle at *Saguaro Lake* and Marc Kaplan at the *McDonalds*.

4:05 P.M. After receiving their food Nelson and Bonadonna parked into a parking space to eat. They ate their food it took 20 minutes.

4:20 P.M. They departed *McDonalds*, then were followed by reporting FBI Special Agents. They drove to Nelson's home, at 70th street and Shea Boulevard in Scottsdale.

Miller, Barcon, Nelson, and Bonadonna had nothing to do with this heinous crime. They were living parallel lives, and happened to stumble upon a crime in progress. Nelson and Bonadonna did not know Kaplan or even if he shared with them, the same *McDonalds* parking lot at the same moment in time. They arrived before him and left before he left. This was enough cause for the FBI to began setting them up for the fall. Was the FBI after them? No, the FBI Special Agents in question were lazy and looking for a fall guy.

Location And Events Map

RED CORVETTE ARRIVES AT *McDONALDS* 4:00 P.M., AND DEPARTS AT 4:20 P.M.
ACCORDING TO FBI SPECIAL AGENTS.

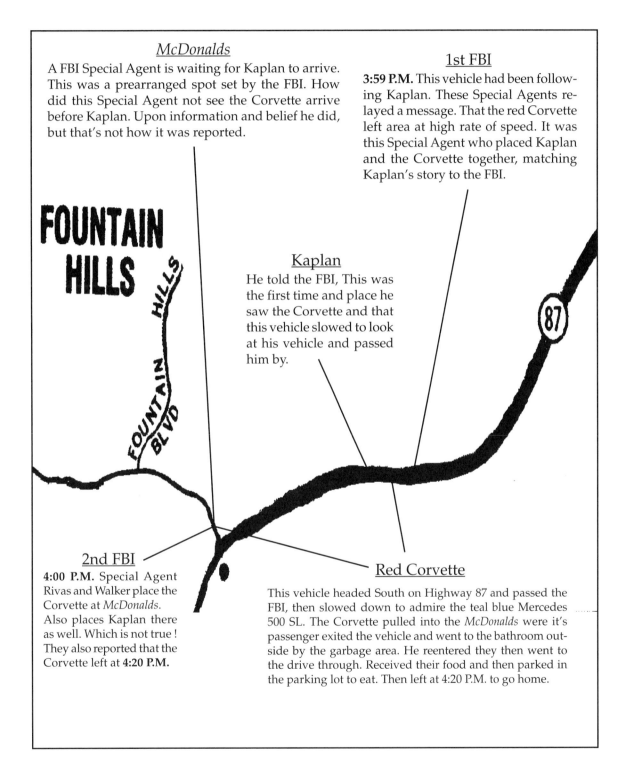

McDonalds

A FBI Special Agent is waiting for Kaplan to arrive. This was a prearranged spot set by the FBI. How did this Special Agent not see the Corvette arrive before Kaplan. Upon information and belief he did, but that's not how it was reported.

1st FBI

3:59 P.M. This vehicle had been following Kaplan. These Special Agents relayed a message. That the red Corvette left area at high rate of speed. It was this Special Agent who placed Kaplan and the Corvette together, matching Kaplan's story to the FBI.

FOUNTAIN HILLS

FOUNTAIN HILLS

FOUNTAIN BLVD

87

Kaplan

He told the FBI, This was the first time and place he saw the Corvette and that this vehicle slowed to look at his vehicle and passed him by.

2nd FBI

4:00 P.M. Special Agent Rivas and Walker place the Corvette at *McDonalds*. Also places Kaplan there as well. Which is not true ! They also reported that the Corvette left at **4:20 P.M.**

Red Corvette

This vehicle headed South on Highway 87 and passed the FBI, then slowed down to admire the teal blue Mercedes 500 SL. The Corvette pulled into the *McDonalds* were it's passenger exited the vehicle and went to the bathroom outside by the garbage area. He reentered they then went to the drive through. Received their food and then parked in the parking lot to eat. Then left at 4:20 P.M. to go home.

Continued Surveillance

```
                                    -1-

                    FEDERAL BUREAU OF INVESTIGATION


                                          Date of transcription   2/20/92


            At approximately 4:20 p.m., a red Corvette bearing
    Arizona license EYV-571 pulled out of the MCDONALDS parking lot
    located near the intersection of Shea Boulevard and Saguaro
    Boulevard in Fountain Hills, Arizona.  The Corvette was observed
    traveling westbound towards Scottsdale, Arizona.

            SA RIVAS followed the Corvette as it traveled westbound
    on Shea Boulevard and at numerous times observed the Corvette to
    change lanes quickly and frequently without using turn signals,
    which was perceived as a "washing" tactic by the driver.  As the
    Corvette approached 70th Street, the driver made a quick turn
    from the inside lane into the left turn lane at 70th Street.  SA
    RIVAS drove by the Corvette still westbound on Shea Boulevard and
    observed the Corvette to remain in the left turn lane even though
    there was no oncoming traffic on Shea.  When SA RIVAS was
    approximately 1/4 mile west of 70th Street, the Corvette was seen
    turning south onto 70th Street.

            At approximately 4:35 p.m., the red Corvette bearing
    Arizona license EYV-571 was located parked in a parking space at
    the apartment complex at 6885 E. Cochise, Scottsdale, Arizona.

    _____

    Investigation on   2/13/92        at  Fountain Hills, Arizona File #  PX 9A-PX-46497

    by   SA R. SCOTT RIVAS/jfb                      Date dictated  2/18/92
                                    92
    This document contains neither recommendations nor conclusions of the FBI. It is the property of the FBI and is loaned to your agency;
    it and its contents are not to be distributed outside your agency.                          N000182
```

4:20 P.M. Special Agent R. Scott Rivas reported the driver knew he was being followed and was using a washing tactic. The driver was not using this, "washing" tactic; in fact the traffic was slow, and the turn signal lever was broken. The Corvette was in the inside lane, closest to the left turn lane on 70th street because that was the entrance that lead to his home. There was heavy traffic flow due to the fact it was 4:30 PM., rush hour, on the busiest streets in North Scottsdale, at the time about 55,000 cars a day one way.

It was reported that the Corvette knew it was being followed. The Corvette and the registered owner, Mark A. Nelson were back at his place of residence, at 6885 E. Cochise #116, at 4:45 PM. Those are the chain of events that truly happened. (If the Corvette operator knew it was being followed, why did he lead the FBI to his home? The truth is "I did not know I was being followed, it was just time to go home, we had just eaten, *McDonalds*, drove around all day, and was very tired and just wanted to go to sleep!" Another further question is what happened to Special Agent Walker? He was in the FBI vehicle with Special Agent Rivas in their first investigated report.

Location And Events Map
RED CORVETTE ARRIVES AT *McDONALDS* AT 4:00 P.M., DEPARTS AT 4:20 P.M.

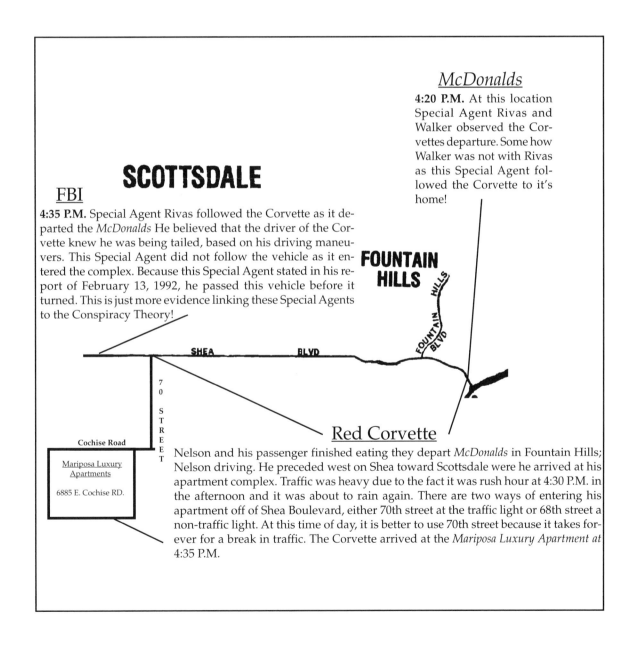

McDonalds

4:20 P.M. At this location Special Agent Rivas and Walker observed the Corvettes departure. Some how Walker was not with Rivas as this Special Agent followed the Corvette to it's home!

SCOTTSDALE

FBI

4:35 P.M. Special Agent Rivas followed the Corvette as it departed the *McDonalds* He believed that the driver of the Corvette knew he was being tailed, based on his driving maneuvers. This Special Agent did not follow the vehicle as it entered the complex. Because this Special Agent stated in his report of February 13, 1992, he passed this vehicle before it turned. This is just more evidence linking these Special Agents to the Conspiracy Theory!

FOUNTAIN HILLS

SHEA   BLVD

FOUNTAIN HILLS

FOUNTAIN BLVD

70 STREET

Cochise Road

Mariposa Luxury Apartments

6885 E. Cochise RD.

Red Corvette

Nelson and his passenger finished eating they depart *McDonalds* in Fountain Hills; Nelson driving. He preceded west on Shea toward Scottsdale were he arrived at his apartment complex. Traffic was heavy due to the fact it was rush hour at 4:30 P.M. in the afternoon and it was about to rain again. There are two ways of entering his apartment off of Shea Boulevard, either 70th street at the traffic light or 68th street a non-traffic light. At this time of day, it is better to use 70th street because it takes forever for a break in traffic. The Corvette arrived at the *Mariposa Luxury Apartment at* 4:35 P.M.

February 14, 15, 16
100 SPECIAL AGENTS

8:00 A.M. Special Agent Tolhurst is the Case Special Agent for this particular case and was busy assigning over 100 Special Agents to the required positions in the investigation of this case. The FBI knew that the safety of the victim, Kaplan, and his family, was in no immediate danger. Nevertheless, he took no chances in finding these suspects, who this FBI Special Agent as well as other Special Agents accused as being the actual individuals who conspired together to commit extortion; specifically, the possible overt action to kidnapping a young child and to sever its arms and legs. Indeed the FBI Special Agents involved were committing a conspiracy, not against the victim, but against two innocent men. Who truly had nothing to do with this crime.

The FBI was looking for three possible suspects; as listed in the actual extortion letter sent to Kaplan on February 7, 1992. These were a highly trained Special Forces Officers using the skills they learned from their government, and they were using black market high-tech government equipment during their supposed surveillance of Kaplan's home and business. The mortifying thing here is, the FBI believed this entirely fabricated story written in letter form, and made up by a distraught out - of - control individual by the name of *Frank Alber*. It was not until a few days later that information came fourth, linking *Alber* to this plot. Curiously Marc Kaplan, his wife and secretary told the FBI they suspected *Alber* to be the mastermind and even gave their reasons why. Even the Surveillance teams deployed by Special Agent Tolhurst at the $250,000 dollar drop off point, at *Estrella Mountain Park*, in their investigation reports told of observing *Alber* at this location. Special Agent Tolhurst still ignored the actual facts and proceeded forward with trying to link a Mercury and its two occupants, and the red Corvette and its two occupants to this extortion.

Additionally, Special Agent Tolhurst ordered the surveillance of Robert Smith and Bobby Smith (the two unidentified fisherman who should have been listed in the *Surveillance Log* written February 13, in vehicle (V-5). Michael Miller and Bennett Paul Barcon, (Miller being the registered owner and driver of the Mercury, Barcon his passenger.) Mark A. Nelson and Jeffrey Michael Bonadonna, (Nelson the registered owner and driver of the red Corvette, Bonadonna his passenger.) Cathy Blades, (Miller's girlfriend.) Lorenzo Arthur Gomez, (Miller's boss) Dawn Kaffman, (Nelson's ex-girlfriend) Nick Lees, (Nelson's boss) Steven Giancola, (Nelson's friend and possible nightclub employee). Tolhurst wanted to believe his own conspiracy and thought investigating these individuals would hide his falsehoods.

Special Agent Tolhurst ordered the telephone records of all individuals, under surveillance. And had his bosses pressing him for some kind of suspects. The media also wanted to break the story to the general public. They felt that the state of Arizona should be aware of the potential danger of this highly trained extortion ring. Tolhurst, asked if they (media), would hold up on the story until they made some arrest. The newspapers agreed and gave them a week, as did his bosses.

Monday, February 17
ENLIGHTENING INFORMATION

Johnson's Interrogation

The interviewing Special Agents were unknown because their names were omitted from the report. Mrs. Johnson was the sister of the intended victim, Marc Kaplan; she was also the secretary of Health Nutrition Laboratories, owned by her brother. Mrs. Johnson explained to the FBI that, *Alber* called into the business and spoke with Miles Gordon, an employee of the business. It seemed to Gordon that *Alber* called to learn the whereabouts of Kaplan. Mrs. Johnson also told the FBI she suspected *Frank Alber* of all the possible individuals. This information was ignored by the FBI Case Special Agent, Keith Tolhurst. *WHY?*

FEDERAL BUREAU OF INVESTIGATION

Date of transcription   **2/19/92**

MARLA JOHNSON, date of birth November 12, 1963, Social Security Account Number (SSAN)   16646 North 59th Place, Scottsdale, Arizona, was advised of the identity of the interviewing Agent and the purpose of the interview. She provided the following information:

PAGE 2 OR 5, NOT ALL REPORTS WERE PROVIDED BY FBI ONLY BITS AND PIECES

Continuation of FD-302 of __MARLA JOY JOHNSON__ , On __2/17/92__ , Page __5__

FRANK ALBER

FRANK ALBER did the computer programming at the KAPLAN business after MICHAEL EZELL left. He now does consultant work for their company. He is very smart and a "good guy." At the present time, he is experiencing financial problems. He is paying alimony to his ex-wife. His girlfriend became pregnant and refused to marry him after the birth of their baby. She did, however, take his car in exchange for support of their child. To further complicate matters, the child is very sick.

On Thursday, February 13, 1992, FRANK ALBER called into the business and spoke with MILES GORDON, an employee at the business. It seemed strange to GORDON that ALBER should be calling to learn the whereabouts of MARC KAPLAN.

On Friday, February 14, 1992, ALBER delivered his proposal to the office. He was very happy and bubbly. JOHNSON thought this strange since when she spoke to him he was experiencing so many problems with the child, the ex-wife and the girlfriend. JOHNSON avoided speaking to him inasmuch as he was a suspect. He remained for one hour before leaving. He has not returned.

Of all possible individuals, she suspects FRANK ALBER because of his background. He is intelligent, worked for a government agency in the past, has financial problems and is very detail-oriented because of the nature of computer programming.

JOHNSON was shown photographs of MICHAEL MILLER, MARK A. NELSON, DAWN KAUFMANN, JEFF (LNU) and unknown subject #2, seen with NELSON at Saguaro Lake on February 13, 1992. She did not recognize any.

February 18
ESTRELLA MOUNTAIN SURVEILLANCE OPERATION

9:30 A.M. Case Special Agent Keith Tolhurst ordered two separate teams with six Special Agents; at Estrella Mountain Park, observing a small suitcase, supposedly filled with $250,000.00 in cash! This was the money that was to be picked up by the supposed extorsion ring. This is five days after the February 13, call Kaplan received to go to the *Security Pacific Bank*, where Kaplan would find a note telling him to proceed to *Saguaro Lake*.

The FBI did note that there was a man at the drop-off sight. The Special Agents ran the plates of a blue convertible with a bicycle rack on back of the car. The FBI radio dispatcher recalled that the auto was registered to the owner *Frank Alber*.

This individual was named by Marc Kaplan and his secretary suspected that it was *Alber*, but said later on "It was not his voice on the tape that was on a recorded phone call made to Kaplan on February 13th from the *ABCO Supermarket*" The following page contains a copy of a Surveillance operation report that identifies *Frank Alber*, as a possible suspect in this case. Even though these three FBI Special Agents Gonzales, Garcia, and Myers were not close enough to positively identify the bike rider, Special Agent Meyers did obtain the license plate on the buick, which was called in by radio. A few minutes later, a response was received that this vehicle was registered to *Frank Alber*, 2747 South Santa Barbara, Mesa, Arizona. This was the Mastermind everyone told the FBI who they thought was the individual involved from the very beginning, and now the FBI knows. On the following two pages is the FBI account...

- 1 -

FEDERAL BUREAU OF INVESTIGATION

Date of transcription   3/16/92

Special Agents (SAs) RONALD HANSON MYERS, MARTIN A. GONZALES, and M. ANNETTE GARCIA were assigned as part of a surveillance team in the area of Estrella Park to assist in an extortion matter.

At approximately 9:30 a.m., on February 18, 1992, a 1986 Buick convertible, blue in color, with a white convertible top and a bicycle rack with bicycle on the trunk, pulled into the large parking lot at the private park near the lake at the intersection of Estrella Parkway and Elliott Road.

A White male was observed to exit the Buick and remove the bicycle from the rack on the trunk. This person put on a bike helmet and checked out his bicycle for a few minutes and then proceeded to ride toward Estrella Parkway until he was out of sight. He was wearing a helmet that was mostly red in color.

At the time this occurred, there were only four vehicles in the large parking lot, which were the above-described Buick and three Federal Bureau of Investigation (FBI) vehicles occupied by SAs MYERS, GONZALES, and GARCIA. The three FBI vehicles were parked at the far west end of the picnic and ramada areas. The driver appeared to take no notice of the FBI vehicles.

At approximately 10:00 a.m., the Agents in the lot overheard a radio conversation from Agents watching the location of the extortion package that they had observed a person riding a mountain bike near the drop location. The description provided over the radio seemed to closely match that of the person seen in the parking lot previously.

At this point, SA MYERS exited his FBI vehicle and walked across the lot to obtain the license plate on the Buick, which was called in by radio as Arizona license CRS 881. A few minutes later, a response was received that this vehicle was registered to a FRANK ALBER, 2747 South Santa Barbara, Mesa,

---

Investigation on   2/18/92   at Goodyear, Arizona   File # 9A-PX-46497

by SAs MARTIN A. GONZALES, M. ANNETTE GARCIA and
RONALD HANSON MYERS   RHM:jhf   Date dictated 2/25/92

154   80

This document contains neither recommendations nor conclusions of the FBI. It is the property of the FBI and is loaned to your agency; it and its contents are not to be distributed outside your agency.

Arizona. Upon hearing this registration, SA MYERS spoke with
SA GONZALES and both discussed why someone from Mesa would drive
all the way out to Estrella to ride his bike.

Approximately 15 minutes after hearing the radio call
of the bike rider near the drop location, the person who had been
seen previously to ride away from the park returned to his car.
The rider, who was a White male, approximately five feet ten
inches to six feet, 160 pounds, then returned to the car. At one
point, he took off his helmet and put on a soft cap. He sat in
the car for a few moments and then walked back to the rest room
area. Upon his return, he placed the bike on the rack and sat in
his car for a short time before departing.

Based on the distance involved, which was approximately
50 yards, it was not possible for any of the Agents to see this
person closely enough for a later identification.

Estrella Mountain Second Surveillance

10:00 A.M. Special Agents J. Antonio Falcon JR., Michael A. Behrends, and David Crawford all initialed their investigated report. This incriminating information was also ignored by the investigating Case Special Agent Keith Tolhurst. *Why?*

- 1 -

FEDERAL BUREAU OF INVESTIGATION

Date of transcription   4/21/92

      At approximately 10:00 a.m. the investigating agents were deployed as a team observing a site at which a package of money was to be retrieved by an unknown subject or subjects. At this time, an unidentified male riding a mountain style bicycle was observed to be moving toward the investigating agents from a position east of Estrella Parkway near the east end of Santa Elizabeth Drive. As one observation team was replaced and departing the observation point, the unidentified male riding the bicycle off of the paved road passed a point approximately thirty yards east of the observation point and came within five yards of the departing agents. The unidentified male on the bicycle continued in a northerly direction and then rode west toward Estrella Parkway before stopping at the top of a hill about one hundred yards north and west of the observation point. At the top of the hill, the unidentified male dismounted the bicycle and sat down. From this vantage point the unidentified male was able to observe the observation point, the observation team and the area of the package awaiting retrieval. The unidentified male remained at the top of the hill for approximately five minutes facing the observation team before departing toward the west on the bicycle out of vision of the investigating agents. About two minutes later, the unidentified male was again observed by the observation team riding his bicycle south on Estrella Parkway approximately one quarter mile south of Santa Elizabeth Drive before he crested a hill which obscured further view of him and Estrella Parkway.

      The unidentified male on the mountain style bicycle was described as follows:

Race:	White
Sex:	Male
Height:	5'10"-6'1"
Build:	Medium
Complexion:	Medium

Investigation on   2/18/92   at Goodyear, Arizona   File # 9A-PX-46497

by   SA J. ANTONIO FALCON, JR., SA MICHAEL A. BEHRENDS, and
   SA DAVID CRAWFORD/dms   Date dictated 4/21/92

Robert Smith's Interrogation
FIRST FISHERMAN AT (L-3), AT THE FBI HEADQUARTERS

The investigation sheet on the next page was a report filed by a FBI Special Agent Sherry L. Hancock. The man noted was one of the fishermen at *Saguaro Lake* on February 13, 1992, but his presence omitted from the FBI *Surveillance Log*. This witness's name was Robert Smith. FBI Case Special Agent Tolhurst used as his first witness (named only as fisherman at the lake) on the affidavit for the Criminal Complaint against and for Millers and Nelsons arrests. What you are about to read will astonish you because this person was *omitted* from the true facts of this case. The point alone brings attention to the Conspiracy Theory against Miller and Nelson. The confusing question is how many FBI Special Agents where in on the cover up? How many not only lied to their bosses, but the whole Federal Judicial System, the general public, family and friends!

This interrogation took place on February 18, at the offices of the Federal Bureau of Investigation. Robert Smith voluntarily and mysteriously came forward and confessed what he and his son seen. The evidence clearly shows beyond reasonable doubt that the *Surveillance Log* filed by the FBI on February 13, was falsely reported. For this witness to see vehicle (V-3), the Mercury, and observe the Corvette (V-4), as listed on this *Surveillance Log*. Yet, Smiths vehicle was omitted. *Why*?

This witnesses saw the Corvette back into a parking spot near the light colored vehicle. Smith told Special Agent Sherry L. Hancock; that an older man had been fishing and left in a blue truck. This individual was not listed on the FBI *Surveillance Log* of February 13, 1992. In fact, this older individual should have been listed as vehicle (V-3) instead of the Mercury because the blue truck was present first, then Miller arrived. The reason this individual was not observed and listed on the *Surveillance Log*, is because he left before the FBI arrived at the *Saguaro Lake* location (L-3). The FBI did not find out about this vehicle and its occupant until the investigation of Smith. Therefore, the FBI's *Surveillance Log* of February 13, 1992, Should have listed these observations. The older man in the blue truck would have been listed as vehicle (V-3), the Mercury would have been (V-4), Smith and his vehicle would have been (V-5). It is believed that after the red Corvette departed *Saguaro Lake*, an unidentified vehicle with two individuals pulled into the area. It is believed this was the FBI. That would have made the unidentified vehicle (V-7) and the red Corvette would have been listed as vehicle (V-6) not (V-4). This witness apparently did not see the other vehicle before the Corvette arrived, but his son did. Did this witness not see this other vehicle or was it just omitted or even altered to fit the investigation?

Smith told Special Agent Hancock that all of a sudden both vehicles were gone (Mercury and Corvette.) This information is the truth and the facts prove beyond reasonable doubt that a conspiracy of some kind took place by the powers of the Federal Bureau of Investigation's Field Special Agents, Reporting Special Agents, and Case Special Agent Keith Tolhurst. When one of the best trained law enforcement agencies in the world undermines facts so grossly, it's time to rebuild the machine. The machine who has enough power to convince the masses, these are the true criminals before you! With no remorse or a bit of care in their actions to pursue the innocent, this machine makes secret deals with criminals who will feed this machine anything they want, so they can get time off for his role by providing convicting information or made up the information. This style of investigating should be banned from the United States of America!

Special Agent Allan M. Davison during this same investigation with Smith displayed photographs to Smith wherein he identified Nelson and Miller. These pictures the FBI were showing to their witnesses were not photos of Miller and me at *Saguaro Lake* on February 13, 1992. There were pictures taken by Special Agent White (1) as listed on the FBI's *Surveillance Log* that same day and initialed in the photos attempted box. The pictures that were taken February 13, 1992, at the lake by this Special Agent did not contain either Miller, Nelson, nor any of their vehicles or the passengers. The reason they are excluded in these photos is because all of the events happened before the FBI arrived to take the photos. The photographs that were displayed to Smith where actual surveillance photos taken during the six days of surveillance of Miller and his family and friends, as well as Nelson's family and friends (including Bonadonna) and the places they visited. Why would this information be omitted from this investigation? How did these Special Agents keep this information from their bosses? The reason, trust, the *Federal Bureau of Investigation* that hired these Special Agents under strict guidelines. These Special Agents were supposed to set the Standards, "Truthfully, honestly and with the highest level of integrity" are just a few points listed in their "Sworn Oath to Serve." Therefore, there is no need to question their authority, until a precedent case like this investigation exposes FBI flaws by the facts of the evidence.

The *Surveillance Log* was maintained by Carl Henderson (10) he and seven

Special Agents: Bateman (4), Cowan (3), MacDonald (7), Beiter (8), Peterson (12), Ripley (PC), and White (10). Each of these Special Agents signed their name at the bottom of the *Surveillance Log* swearing to activities they observed to have actually happened of February 13, 1992. These events did not happen. Evidence proves otherwise.

The fact, that the mastermind suspect was already given to the FBI by Marc Kaplan, his wife and his secretary, (who is also Kaplan's sister, Marla Johnson) was ignored.

What about the two Surveillance Operation Teams, (assigned to this location by the Case Special Agent, Tolhurst) who observed *Frank Alber*, on February 18, 1992, at the money drop off point at *Estrella Mountain Park*. All of this exculpatory evidence was known to Case Special Agent Keith Tolhurst before he filed a Criminal Complaint Affidavit to his bosses one day before his bosses gave the "Okay" to file his (Tolhurst), affidavit with the U.S. Magistrate Judge Honorable Mortan Sitver. This judge ruled on the evidence listed on affidavit filed by Tolhurst, who sworn under penalty of perjury that the information was true and correct, for the arrest of two innocent men Miller and me.

The next witness to be interviewed by the FBI was Bobby Smith, Robert Smith's son (the two fisherman at the lake). Bobby, stated to his investigative Special Agent that Miller and me left before Kaplan arrived. Further, it was Bobby who actually contaminated the crime scene by going through the bag left by Kaplan. This information too was *omitted*...

On the following two pages Robert's interrogation went like this...

- 1 -

FEDERAL BUREAU OF INVESTIGATION

Date of transcription ____2/18/92____

        ROBERT THOMAS SMITH, 2853 North Flanwill Boulevard,
No. 16, Tucson, Arizona, telephone number (602) 325-3273
(recently disconnected, may be reconnected) or (602) 886-4412,
voluntarily appeared at the Phoenix Division of the Federal
Bureau of Investigation (FBI) and furnished the following
information regarding his February 13, 1992 visit to Saguaro
Lake:

        SMITH related that he presently resides in Tucson,
Arizona, and previously lived at 1514 Sheridan in Phoenix. SMITH
explained that he is a carpenter and previously worked at the
Palo Verde Power Plant (PVPP). SMITH explained that the general
contractor at PVPP was Bechtel.

        SMITH advised that on February 11, 1992, or
February 12, 1992, at approximately 4:00 p.m., he arrived in
Phoenix from Tucson. SMITH related that he came up to Phoenix to
visit his son, BOBBY SMITH, and his grandchildren.

        SMITH stated that on February 13, 1992, he and BOBBY
SMITH were "riding around that morning" and had gone out to
Fountain Hills. SMITH commented that they were looking at the
fountain and decided to go fishing. SMITH recalled that they
went to a Circle-K and BOBBY bought "worms and a couple of
things". SMITH related that he and his son discussed whether
they would go to the Verde River. SMITH stated that both he and
his son agreed to go fishing at Saguaro Lake. SMITH related that
when they left Fountain Hills, the clouds were breaking and it
was starting to clear.

        SMITH stated that when he and his son arrived at
Saguaro Lake, he noticed "loud rap music coming from a "bluish/
gray, a light colored", car. SMITH mentioned that he glanced at
the car and the occupants said hi. SMITH stated that a Corvette
came into the parking area and initially drove past. SMITH
advised that the Corvette returned and backed into a parking spot
near the "bluish/gray" vehicle. SMITH stated that the occupants

---

Investigation on ___2/18/92___ at _Phoenix, Arizona_____ File # _9A-PX-46497___

by _SA SHERRY L. HANCOCK/mbh_____ Date dictated _2/18/92_____

                                    75

N000175

in both vehicles started talking to each other. SMITH assumed
that the men in the "bluish/gray" vehicle were young, in view of
the music. SMITH stated that the driver of the Corvette had
"very long auburn hair pulled back in a pony tail.

SMITH advised that an older man, in his 60's who had
been fishing, left in a blue pickup truck.

SMITH related that when the Corvette backed into the
parking area, the other vehicle turned off the music. SMITH
stated that all of a sudden both vehicles were gone. SMITH
stated that he observed a Mercedes as he and his son parked
directly in back of it.

SMITH stated that his son, BOBBY SMITH, is nosey by
nature and was watching the man in the Mercedes. SMITH related
that they noticed the man in the Mercedes take a bag over to the
canopy area. SMITH advised that they also noticed that the man
from the Mercedes, wrapped the suitcase with tape, which he took
with him.

SMITH related that BOBBY walked up and said that the
man had left a case there. SMITH stated that he instructed his
son not to touch the bag. SMITH related that he walked over to
the area, but did not go over the fence. SMITH advised that he
noticed two identical pictures of a woman from the waist up,
which he described as a pretty blond lady. SMITH related that he
also observed a photograph of a younger girl and a photograph of
a man and a boy wearing Cleveland Indian baseball uniforms.
SMITH stated that he does not believe that he touched anything,
but that "it is possible". SMITH confirmed that BOBBY SMITH
touched everything as he was going through the bag.

SMITH advised that BOBBY SMITH has a landscaping
business with GLEN GROVE, who resides in Tucson. GROVE resides
with one of SMITH's daughters. SMITH stated that the landscaping
business is not licensed and that their business card read: R.K.
or R.J.S. Landscaping. SMITH was not certain about the name of
the landscaping business.

SMITH related that he has an arrest record, but no
convictions. SMITH advised that his most recent arrest was
before Christmas 1984. SMITH advised that the 1984 arrest
involved a domestic violence charge, which was dropped. SMITH

74

Continuation of FD-302 of ROBERT THOMAS SMITH   , On   2/18/92   , Page   3

advised that he is a union carpenter and has known and worked for PETER LICIVOLI in Tucson and Detroit for many years.

Special Agent (SA) ALLAN M. DAVISON displayed the following photographs to SMITH:

1. MARK ANDREW NELSON
2. BRET TAYLOR
3. Unknown Subject (UNSUB)
4. UNSUB
5. MICHAEL GRANT MILLER

SMITH identified the photographs of MARK ANDREW NELSON (No. 1) and MICHAEL GRANT MILLER (No. 5) as individuals he has seen before and believes that it was at Saguaro Lake on February 13, 1992.

The following is a description of ROBERT THOMAS SMITH obtained through interview and observation:

75   N000177

Sex:	Male
Race:	White
Weight:	220 pounds
Height:	5'9-1/2"
Hair:	Black with gray
Eyes:	Blue
Tattoos:	Eagle, left arm;
	Four leaf clover, left hand;
	Numerous
FBI Number:	809 435 F
Social Security Account Number:	
Date of Birth:	
Place of Birth:	Tucson, Arizona

Bobby Smith's Interrogation
AT THE FBI HEADQUARTERS

This report filed by the FBI, was investigated on February 18. The statements match the alibi that Miller gave the FBI on February 20, 1992. Bobby also stated he believed one of the two white male occupants of the Corvette, he was not sure, may have gotten out and left the Corvette for three to four minutes. Smith's first impression was to urinate. Later it was learned that no one got out of the Corvette at this location, even the FBI's *Surveillance Log* of February 13 doesn't list such an activity. *Why*?

One thing that stood out the most in Smiths, investigation was his sworn statement, that Miller and Nelson left before Kaplan arrived. It has been reported, that Kaplan never saw the red Corvette at the lake, nor did he see Miller and his car.

Kaplan stated he only saw Nelson and Bonadonna, on the freeway a few miles from *McDonalds*, who then looked at him briefly and sped off. It also was reported that Kaplan saw the Corvette at *McDonalds*.

The reason Kaplan and the FBI did not see the accused at *Saguaro Lake* is because they went in the opposite direction before Kaplan and the FBI even arrived, as it was reported by all witnesses, the accused Miller and Nelson, and even Kaplan himself! All of these witnesses' stories match. In fact, Smith admitted going through the crime scene and touching everything. These activities were omitted from the February 13, *Surveillance Log. Why*?

This interrogation was on February 18, 1992. At the offices of the Federal Bureau of Investigation. This volunteer witness, who somehow mysteriously came forward, and stated that he and his dad saw the vehicles the Mercury and Corvette. The witness is named Bobby Smith. He was one of the only two individuals the FBI had as witnesses, who saw Miller and me at *Saguaro Lake*. Smith states that Miller and his friend were drinking beer. As he and his father arrived an older man was just leaving. This confirms that the *Surveillance Log* of February 13, 1992, was fabricated, this older man an with his truck should have been listed in vehicle (V-3). Miller would have been vehicle (V-4), and Bobby and his father Robert Smith, would have been listed as vehicle (V-5), but they were not! *Why*?

Bobby observed a red Corvette that should have been listed as vehicle (V-6) come into location (L-3). He claimed the occupants left the car, but they did not. This information is believed to be paraphrased by the Investigating Special Agent. The Corvette did park three parking spaces down from the Mercury on the request of the passenger in the Corvette, who asked the driver me to pull in next to the guys in that car. The passenger wanted to ask them some questions about the lake. Smith also thought that these four individuals, including Miller and me, knew each other from their manner of behavior. The question here, is how are people, supposed to act when they meet someone for the first time, in a public place for leisure, and do these actions make you a criminal? Smith explained there was another vehicle that arrived shortly after the Corvette, and Mercury left. This unidentified vehicle should have been listed as (V-7) on the *Surveillance Log* of February 13, 1992. This vehicle was never mentioned because it's believed that this was the FBI Special Agents arriving at this location (L-3), once again these activities were not listed. This witness told the investigating Special Agents'; approximately five minutes later and a half hour to 45 minutes after they arrived (Smiths), a Mercedes pulled into the area. Bobby noted to his father that it seemed strange that the man was alone in the Mercedes. The problem with this statement is, Bobby's father told his Investigating Special Agent is that he and dad son parked behind the Mercedes. In fact, the Mercedes parked behind their vehicle. Why would Mr. Smith the first witness lie to his Investigating Special Agent?

These are the true accounts of the observations that the FBI didn't report. *Why*, was the activity of Kaplan removing his shirt and turning around slowly never mentioned by the Smiths or the FBI Special Agents. Because the note he retrieved from location (L-3) told him to do so, because he was being watched. The only individuals doing the watching was the FBI and Smiths. Because the red Corvette, and the Mercury left before Kaplan arrived.

Here is more damaging evidence, in support of the conspiracy taking place right before our eye's. The FBI took photographs of individuals at the lake as listed on the *Surveillance Log* of February 13, 1992. Bobby was shown a group of these photographs; he identified me as being one of the four males, talking prior to the arrival of the Mercedes. Bobby stated that I had my hair much longer and had it tied up in a pony tail when he observed me. This positive statement proves that the photographs of Nelson and his passenger were not taken at the *Saguaro Lake*, but in fact, are the surveillance photos taken the next day, after their visit to the lake on February 14. The photo he saw was one taken of me and Bonadonna exiting my apartment. The next morning at the Italian Deli, where Bonadonna and me were getting some food for Lacie's, birthday party that afternoon.

Bobby identified in other photographs; another individual he felt he observed at the lake. This individual was Brett Orville Taylor. The problem, again, is that Brett Orville Taylor was not the individual at the lake with Miller. The actual individual with Miller at the lake was Bennet Paul Barcon. Why, did the FBI report in their *Surveillance Log*, that pictures were taken. When in fact, not any of the possible four suspects at the lake on February 13, 1992? That is because by all accounts these possible suspects left before the FBI arrived at location (L-3) Marina Picnic Area at *Saguaro Lake*. This proves beyond reasonable doubt that if these FBI Special Agents where there as they reported on the *Surveillance Log* of February 13, 1992, they would have had pictures of the individual that was with Miller at *Saguaro Lake* on that day.

The interrogation report of Bobby Smith was accomplished on February 18, 1992, the date of dictation was February 18, 1992, the transcription date was February 19, 1992. This interviewing Special Agent Allan Davison, was the same individual who displayed the photos of Miller and me and the photos of the other two supposed suspects to Bobby Smith's father.

Smith stated he was certain he could identify me and Taylor as being at the lake if he could see us again. If only the pictures the FBI displayed for Smith were of the right individuals at the lake. This Orville Taylor was not the individual at the lake seen with Miller. That person was Paul Bennett Barcon. This indicates that Miller and Nelson left before the FBI and Kaplan arrived. Conspiracy?

On the following four pages is Smith's interrogation and it went like this...

- 1 -

FEDERAL BUREAU OF INVESTIGATION

Date of transcription   2/19/92

     BOBBY, no middle name (NMN) SMITH, 234 East Ruth
Street, Apartment #2, voluntary appeared at the Phoenix Office of
the FEDERAL BUREAU OF INVESTIGATION, at which time he was advised
of the identity of the interviewing Agent, and that he was to be
interviewed concerning his knowledge of events that transpired on
February 13, 1992, at the vicinity of the SAGUARO LAKE PARK,
northeast of Phoenix. He thereafter provided the following
information:

     ROBERT THOMAS SMITH, BOBBY SMITH's father, regularly
drives up from Tucson, Arizona, to Phoenix to visit BOBBY SMITH
and to visit SMITH's son. On February 13, 1992, ROBERT THOMAS
SMITH was in Phoenix and the SMITHs decided to ride around and
look at the Phoenix area. They drove to the vicinity of Fountain
Hills, Arizona, and watched the fountain display, and then
decided to do some fishing in the SAGUARO LAKE PARK. BOBBY SMITH
did not have his fishing pole, so he went to a CIRCLE K, bought
some fishing line, a couple of hooks, a bobber, and some weights
so that he could just fish from the side of the lake by hand.
ROBERT THOMAS SMITH, who is disabled, enjoys the beauty and
quietness of the SAGUARO LAKE area, so he regularly likes to
visit that recreation area.

     Upon their arrival at SAGUARO LAKE PARK, SMITH noticed
two white males standing by a "Grenada" type car, listening to
rap music from a boom box situated on top of the vehicle. They
were drinking Heinikens, or some type of import beer, laughing
and talking together. The SMITHs proceeded to go down the
embankment near the lake near the end of the road and close to a
cul-de-sac, where they began to fish by hand. As they were
arriving, an older man was just leaving and they briefly asked
this old man how the fishing was and received a negative
response.

     Sometime thereafter, a red Corvette came into the park
area driving very fast, and drove into the cul-de-sac, turned
around and stopped. SMITH believes one of the two white male

Investigation on   2/18/92   at Phoenix, Arizona   File # 9A-PX-46497

by   SA ALLAN M. DAVISON/jmd   Date dictated 2/18/92   N000178

                                      7b
                                              (20)

Continuation of FD-302 of ___BOBBY (NMN) SMITH_____ , On ___2/18/92___ , Page ___2___

occupants of the Corvette may have gotten out of the Corvette in
the cul-de-sac and left the vehicle for approximately three to
four minutes, while the car remained parked. His initial
impression was that the occupant who left the Corvette was
probably walking away from the area to urinate, but he did not
notice what this individual did. Thereafter, the Corvette drove
up and parked beside the Grenada type automobile and the two
initial individuals at the Grenada automobile and the two
occupants of the Corvette stood outside their vehicles talking
and laughing. It was apparent to SMITH that the four individuals
knew each other from their manner of behavior.

Thereafter, the two vehicles left the parking area
together, driving fast. Shortly thereafter, a vehicle with older
people in it arrived and drove through the area.

Approximately five minutes later, and about one-half
hour to 45 minutes since they originally arrived, a Mercedes
automobile pulled up in the area and SMITH commented to ROBERT
THOMAS SMITH that it was unusual that there was a lone white male
driving the vehicle with no woman with him. He said that because
it was such a beautiful day at the time and such a remote
location.

SMITH saw a white male with dark complexion and curly
hair get out of the Mercedes, take an attache case with him from
the car and go to a table and lay the attache case on the table.
He opened the attache case and was looking through it, and then
walked toward the water and thereafter, returned to the table.
This individual was very nervous and looking around, and this
caught SMITH's attention. The white male then walked to the
Mercedes, opened the trunk and got a suitcase out. SMITH
believed that he was getting some photographic equipment out,
such as tapes or a camcorder. The white male then returned to
the table and SMITH continued to fish.

Shortly thereafter, SMITH heard a ripping sound and
turned around and observed the white male wrapping the suitcase
with duct tape at both ends, but not ripping the tape and leaving
the rolls hanging on the suitcase. He was acting extremely
nervous, and appeared upset that SMITH was even looking at him.
The white male then took the case with the tape around it and
threw it in the trunk of the Mercedes, leaving the attache case
on the table. At this point, SMITH got up, walked up the

77

embankment and began to walk in the direction of the Mercedes, and the vehicle drove off. SMITH then walked to the table and looked in the open attache case, which had been left by the white male. In the suitcase he saw photographs of a blond lady, a young girl and the white male with a young white male wearing a Cleveland Indians baseball uniform. He picked these photographs up and looked at them. He probably handled other items in the case as he pushed things around. ROBERT THOMAS SMITH had told him not to touch the case, but SMITH stated that his curiosity was such that he wanted to see what was in the case that had been left by the white male.

SMITH then observed an envelope that was laying on the table which he looked at and noticed that it was open and empty. and he did not touch the envelope. He additionally recalled that when he had walked toward the area previously occupied by the Mercedes, he smelled something strange that he had never smelled before, perhaps that of the smell from the Mercedes catalytic converter. He stated that it was an odd lingering smell, and he though perhaps the white male had a dead body in the trunk of the Mercedes. He had this thought because of the strange actions of the white male.

SMITH was displayed a group of photographs and made the following observations concerning these photographs:

SMITH immediately identified a photograph of MARK NELSON, date of birth (DOB) June 12, 1960, as being one of the four individuals he observed talking prior to the arrival of the Mercedes. He stated that NELSON has his hair much longer and had it tied up in a ponytail when he observed him.

SMITH identified a photograph of BRET ORVILLE TAYLOR, DOB September 19, 1970, as being one of the two individuals who were standing by the Grenada type automobile, when the SMITHs first arrived at SAGUARO LAKE PARK.

SMITH stated that he believes that an individual wearing a yellow T-shirt with K.O. Kelly on the breast, and who is identified as Unknown Subject #1, is one of the individuals he associates with the red Corvette previously described.

SMITH selected a photograph of MICHAEL GRANT MILLER, DOB August 30, 1976, as being an individual he recognized as

78

having seen before, possibly one of the four individuals at the SAGUARO LAKE. SMITH stated that he is certain he could identify the individuals identified as NELSON and TAYLOR if he could see them again. He further stated that he has never observed any of these individuals before, to the best of his knowledge, and has had no personal contact with any of these individuals. He has never seen the white male in the Mercedes prior to February 13, 1992. He denies any involvement in any criminal activity on February 13, 1992, or any day in or around that date, and that his activities at the SAGUARO LAKE area as described by him are true and accurate to the best of his recollection as furnished during this interview.

The following biographical information was obtained concerning SMITH:

Name	BOBBY (NMN) SMITH
Date of birth	December 18, 1965
Place of birth	Tucson, Arizona
Social Security Account Number	
Residence	234 East Ruth, Apartment #2, Phoenix, Arizona
Will relocate on February 19, 1992, to	8801 East 3rd Street Phoenix, Arizona
Sex	Male
Race	White
Height	5'9"
Weight	180 pounds
Eyes	Blue
Hair	Blond
Tattoos	Rose tattoo on back; skull tattoo on back
Girlfriend	BRENDA KELLY
Date of birth	
Place of birth	Washington
Occupation	RJS Landscaping, self employed operating from his residence, works primarily on his own, occasionally hiring young kids for special jobs, has been

79

Nelson's Paralleling Life
AT THE MARIPOSA APARTMENTS

4:30 P.M. The Manager, Lynn and the maintenance man, Paul, told me that the FBI were looking for info on Richard Sollami, Jeff Bonadonna, and me. They wanted to see my lease and Richard Sollami's lease too. They also wanted to know if Bonadonna lived with me. I told these friends of almost two years that Bonadonna went home to Reseda, California. Paul told me that he'd told the FBI Bonadonna does not live with Nelson, but the FBI refused to believe Paul. The FBI asked the Manager if they could see my lease. She informed them that she couldn't do that unless they had a warrant. These FBI Special Agents told her they would be back, and not to say anything to me or to anyone else of this matter. Then both the manager and maintenance man asked the Special Agents "what did he do?" The Special Agents responded that it was none of their business and that they should just do what they are told. Paul told them that they must be mistaken about me being involved in any thing illegal, adding, he is too smart to be a criminal." Lynn agreed with Paul.

The unexplained thing here is that the FBI never came back with a search warrant to see my lease or to search my apartment. I immediately went over to Richard Sollami's apartment to tell him what had happened. He couldn't figure out why either. He told me that his buddy Ed Kahn, was contacted by the FBI.
He said "Ed is coming over and we all will talk."

Richard brought Ed over to my apartment. We could not figure out why the FBI was investigating us. We all knew that we did nothing wrong. We did come to the conclusion that it must have been something Bonadonna had done, and he bought it with him from California, and that the FBI had been following Bonadonna. FBI Special Agents followed everyone out of Richard's apartment on the day of his daughter Lacie's birthday on February 14, 1992. Ed Kahn had been apparently at this party. That's why he was contacted by the FBI. Ed Kahn had no connection whatsoever to this investigation. Later, it was learned that Mr. Kahn was fired by his employer, just because the FBI inquired about him. Apparently, Mr. Kahn was told by the investigating Special Agent to stay away from Nelson, and that he might be pulled into the case as 'guilty by association' and that he may be called as a witness against me.

The FBI Special Agents used these same scare tactics against all these potential witnesses who where either my friends, girlfriends, business associates, and even the general contractor Mr. Lees, who employed me as a painter and by whom I was to be promoted as estimator and Project Coordinator for this million dollar home builder. Mr. Cameron's house; where I painted, on the weekends so I could, have extra funds to invest into my *After the Gold Rush* nightclub proposal. Mr. Cameron was not necessarily considered a nightclub investor, but in I was going to ask him to be a board member...

Wednesday, February 19
CRIMINAL COMPLAINT

Moving Forward

CASE SPECIAL AGENT KEITH TOLHURST AT FBI HEADQUARTERS

The Case Special Agent Keith Tolhurst was having difficulties in making a case against Miller, and Nelson. Tolhurst knew beyond a reasonable doubt, upon the examination of the true facts pertaining to this investigation, he would never get an arrest warrant granted for any of these four suspects. Special Agent Tolhurst was under pressure from his bosses and the Media. He wanted so bad for these possible suspects to be involved. From February 19, 1992, to February 13, 1992, he altered and misconstrued all the information gathered by his fellow FBI Special Agents and, with help from these same Special Agents by signing their names on the *Surveillance Log* of February 13, 1992. It now is an apparent fact that this was the starting point for the Conspiracy Theory against four suspects.

Tolhurst knew that the finger print of Miller's on the pay phone at the *ABCO Supermarket* was not and could not have been made by Miller, because Miller could not have traveled from the *ABCO* to *Saguaro Lake* in less than 15 minutes. This too was a 60 minute travel time. Tolhurst also knew that Miller and Nelson had left the lake before the FBI even arrived, because there were no photos taken of either Miller, Nelson, their vehicles or their passengers. Tolhurst became so obsessed with his pursuit of the four possible suspects that he completely ignored the truth and any other possible suspects including the *Frank Alber*. This Case Special Agent pursued these for innocent men knowing that reliable evidence in his possession clearly indicated these individuals did not engage in any criminal activity!

On February 19, 1992, The Case Special Agent in charge of this investigation filed a six-page affidavit with the United States District Court of Arizona, the Honorable Mortan Sitver presiding.

The Federal Judicial System works like this: a Federal Law Enforcement Agency (e.g., The FBI has their Field Agents) gather as much information as possible to substantiate their claims, then file their reports to the Reporting Agents, these

Special Agents then they file their reports to the Case Special Agent in charge which was Case Special Agent Keith D. Tolhurst. This Case Special Agent, to the best of his knowledge and belief files a combined report to support his Affidavit. It was at this point, that he filed a false affidavit, on the paraphrased information against Miller and Nelson.

The Criminal Complaint on the following page will show you just how powerful these FBI Special Agents are, and the freedom they have to investigate their cases anyway they deem fit and necessary.

Sworn Criminal Complaint
FBI HEADQUARTERS

The affidavit on the second fallowing page is a sworn Criminal Complaint signed by Case Special Agent Keith Tolhurst for the arrests of Miller and Nelson.

The eighth paragraph is very interesting. In this report it says that an FBI Special Agent observed Miller at the *Saguaro Lake* picnic area. This is impossible. No witnesses reported seeing either Miller or Nelson around when Kaplan was at the lake. Robert Smith and Bobby Smith both said "Miller and Nelson left before Kaplan arrived." And there were no other witnesses to refute their statements, not even Case Special Agent Keith Tolhurst or any of his law enforcement group. In fact, the FBI Special Agents knew Bobby Smith went through that whole crime scene, as stated on his sworn testimony.

In the tenth paragraph, the FBI Special Agent noted that there were very few people at the lake and with only two real witnesses and the fact that Miller and Nelson left before Kaplan and the FBI arrived, that even makes it worse because it supports the fact Miller and Nelson left. As the FBI's false theory unfolds, these same FBI Special Agents claimed that Miller and Nelson were a quarter of a mile away from boat ramp #2 then it states, they were 100 feet from Kaplan! How could that be possible? No one saw Miller or Nelson during the time Kaplan was at the lake because Miller and Nelson left before Kaplan and the FBI arrived. Based on the fishermen's statements made to the FBI, and Kaplan not seeing Miller or Nelson either.

The eleventh paragraph, is the most shocking of them all. FBI Special Agents reported, according to SA Keith Tolhurst, that Miller and Nelson "soon thereafter fallowed Kaplan's vehicle out of the recreation area and went the other way opposite of Kaplan." So how is it that Nelson, going the opposite direction of Kaplan, arrived at the *McDonalds* at 4:00 PM., for, 17.8 miles, not including the other six miles Nelson drove with his friend, this is a total of 24.8 miles that Nelson traveled in one minute according to Special Agent Tolhurst. Which is totally impossible.

It is believed at 3:59 PM., when Kaplan saw Nelson pass him on the freeway traveling towards the *McDonalds*, that Nelson also passed the FBI Special Agent who said, "red Corvette just left the area at a high rate of speed, anyone seeing it, don't let it out of your sight!" Then at 4:00 PM., Nelson was at the *McDonalds* when Kaplan arrived! The truth of those FBI observations are very clear, if you can believe that the Corvette could cover 24.8 miles in one minute!

The twelfth paragraph is a real hard one to believe too! Here an FBI Special Agent observed a male passenger, not Nelson, get out of the car, walk to within approximately ten feet of Kaplan's vehicle. The FBI Special Agent said "the passenger looked briefly at Kaplan" and at the same time an FBI Special Agent began to walk toward Kaplan's vehicle. This passenger then walked back to and reentered the Corvette which immediately departed *McDonalds*! How long do you, think it would have taken someone to do this: immediately, 1 - 2 minutes?

FBI Special Agents reported that the Corvette left in 20 minutes, at 4:20, then followed the Corvette home. They failed to say what Nelson and his passenger were really doing at the *McDonalds*.... Eating!

The fifteenth paragraph is another stupid mistake. It says Miller was arrested in 1985 for possession of a dangerous weapon, for which the charge was reduced to a misdemeanor. That, when, in fact, it was Nelson who was arrested in 1985. (See appendix page 386 for the credibility of their Criminal Complaint.)

United States District Court

———————————————— DISTRICT OF —— ARIZONA ————————————————

UNITED STATES OF AMERICA
V.
Michael Grant Miller,
Mark Andrew Nelson

CRIMINAL COMPLAINT

CASE NUMBER: *92-5041 M*

(Name and Address of Defendant)

I, the undersigned complainant being duly sworn state the following is true and correct to the best of my

knowledge and belief. On or about ____February 6, 1992____ in ____Maricopa____ county, in the

_____ District of ____Arizona____ defendant(s) did, (Track Statutory Language of Offense)

knowingly and with the intent to extort money from Marc Kaplan, deposit in an authorized depository for mail matter to be sent and delivered by the Postal Service written communication postmarked February 6, 1992, addressed to Marc Kaplan and containing a threat to injure the son of Marc Kaplan that is his arm or leg would be removed, and aid and abet to the same.

in violation of Title ____18____ United States Code, Section(s) ____876 and 2____.

I further state that I am a(X) ____Special Agent of the FBI____ and that this complaint is based on the following
(Official Title)

facts:

See attached Statement of Probable Cause - Exhibit A.

Continued on the attached sheet and made a part hereof: ☒ Yes ☐ No

_____
Signature of Complainant

Sworn to before me and subscribed in my presence,

____February 19, 1992____   at ____Phoenix, Arizona____
Date   City and State

MORTON SITVER   N000137
United States Magistrate Judge
_____   _____
Name & Title of Judicial Officer   Signature of Judicial Officer

EXHIBIT A

92-5041m

<u>AFFIDAVIT</u>

1.   Your affiant, Keith D. Tolhurst, is a Special Agent
(SA) of the Federal Bureau of Investigation (FBI) currently
assigned to Phoenix, Arizona, and has been so employed for the
past 4 years. As such, your affiant is a federal law enforcement
officer within the meaning of Rule 41(a), Federal Rules of
Criminal Procedure.

2.   Since February 7, 1992, your affiant has been
participating with other SAs in an investigation involving a plot
to extort $250,000.00 from Marc Kaplan of Paradise Valley,
Arizona, under threat that physical injury would occur to his
son. As a result of your affiant's personal participation in
this investigation, and based on reports made to your affiant by
other FBI Agents, law enforcement officers, and witnesses
interviewed, your affiant is familiar with the facts and
circumstances set forth in this affidavit.

3.   On February 7, 1992, Marc Kaplan received in the
mail a computer generated letter, postmarked Phoenix, Arizona, on
February 6, 1992, wherein the sender demanded that Kaplan pay
$250,000.00 in cash in one week or his son's arm or leg would be
removed. This letter informed Kaplan that on Thursday,
February 13, 1992, he would receive a phone call at exactly 2:00
p.m. at his business office giving him further instructions.

4.   Based on this letter, FBI Agents obtained court
orders on February 11 and February 12, 1992, directing U.S. West
Communications and American Telephone and Telegraph to install

N000145

Trap and Trace devices on all the business phones of Marc Kaplan, who owns and operates Health and Nutrition Laboratories at 4545 East Shea Boulevard, Suite 160, Phoenix, Arizona. A Trap and Trace device captures the incoming electronic or other impulses which identify the originating number of a wire or electronic communication and the date, time, and duration of such incoming pulses.

     5. At approximately 2:17 p.m. on February 13, 1992, Marc Kaplan received a phone call at his business office. The male caller instructed Kaplan to immediately proceed to a closed Security Pacific Bank at Tatum and Shea Boulevards in Phoenix where he would find a note attached to a pole giving him further instructions. The caller then hung up. Shortly after this phone call was terminated, an employee of U.S. West Communications advised FBI Agents this call originated from a pay telephone located at ABCO Supermarkets, 1988 North Alma School Road, Chandler, Arizona. This pay telephone was located by FBI Agents and the receiver and telephone booth processed for fingerprints by officers of the Mesa Police Department.

     6. At approximatel 8:30 p.m. on February 13, 1992, a Fingerprint Examiner of the Mesa Police Department advised FBI Agents a fingerprint lifted from the telephone receiver removed from the telephone booth at ABCO Supermarkets matched the known fingerprints of Michael Grant Miller.

     7. At approximately 2:30 p.m. Marc Kaplan located the aforementioned note at the Security Pacific Bank, which

N000144

2

instructed him to immediately proceed to Saguaro Lake Boat Ramp #2, where he would find further instructions. Kaplan was followed and placed under surveillance by FBI Agents as he departed the bank and began driving to Saguaro Lake. The area surrounding Saguaro Lake was also placed under surveillance by FBI Agents.

8. Prior to Kaplan arriving at Saguaro Lake, FBI Agents observed a Mercury sedan, bearing Arizona license plate AWS-090 and registered to Michael G. Miller, at the Saguaro Lake picnic area, which had arrived before the agents arrived and which was approximately 1/4 mile from Boat Ramp #2 Shortly thereafter, and before Kaplan arrived, a red Corvette, bearing Arizona license plate EVY-571 and registered to Mark A. Nelson, arrived at the picnic area and parked next to the Mercury sedan.

9. At approximately 3:20 p.m. Kaplan arrived at Saguaro Lake and located a note containing additional instructions and a suitcase at the pre-designated location at the picnic area near Saguaro Lake Boat Ramp #2. The note stated in summary form: You are being watched - Take your shirt off and turn around slowly. The note also instructed him to place the money in the suitcase and then drive to the Estrella Development area west of Phoenix to a specified location, where he was to place the suitcase in a box in a hole and place dirt over it.

10. The FBI Agents noted that there were very few people at the Lake that day, but the agents did observe four males at the Corvette and the Mercury conversing with each other

3

at the Saguaro Lake picnic area, and approximately 100 feet from Kaplan. One of these four males was positively identified from his drivers license photograph as Mark A. Nelson by FBI Agents at the surveillance and one fisherman at Saguaro Lake that day. Another of the four males was tentatively identified, by one of *From a Drivers License Pic* the fishermen at Saguaro Lake that day as Michael G. Miller. Nelson was also observed by FBI Agents to be holding a hand-held mobile cellular telephone. Also one of the fishermen also identified Nelson as the driver of the Corvette.

11. As Kaplan departed the Saguaro Lake Boat Dock, FBI Agents observed the Corvette and Mercury soon thereafter follow Kaplan's vehicle out of the recreation area toward the highway. Kaplan went in one direction and the Corvette and Mercury then proceeded in another direction southbound on the Bush Highway at speeds estimated to be 85 miles per hour.

12. After Marc Kaplan departed Saguaro Lake en route to the Estrella Development, he stopped at a McDonald's Restaurant near the intersection of Highway 87 and Shea Boulevard. Either shortly before or after Kaplan arrived, Nelson's red Corvette also arrived at the McDonald's Restaurant and parked. An FBI Agent at this location observed a male passenger get out of the Corvette and walk within approximately ten feet of Kaplan's vehicle, and he looked briefly at Kaplan, who was sitting inside his car. At the same time, an FBI Agent began to walk towards Kaplan's vehicle. The male passenger then

4

N000146

walked back to and re-entered the Corvette, which immediately departed the McDonald's.

13.   After departing the McDonald's Restaurant, Nelson's red Corvette, still occupied by 2 males, was located by an FBI Agent as it proceeded into Phoenix on Shea Boulevard.   The Agent observing this vehicle noted the driver engaged in maneuvers which appeared to be attempts to prevent others from following him.   These maneuvers included changing lanes without signals, and delays in making a turn for no apparent reason, forcing others behind him to pass him.   This Corvette was followed by the FBI Agent until it entered an apartment complex at 6885 East Cochise in Scottsdale, Arizona. Agents learned from the apartment manager that Marc A. Nelson lives in this complex. Furthermore, agents observed Nelson at the complex on February 13, 1992.

14.   The 1982 Mercury bearing Arizona license AWS-090 was observed by FBI Agents at approximately 9:30 p.m. at 1653 South Harris, Mesa, Arizona. This address was reported as Michael G. Miller's address on a Mesa police report.

15.   A computerized criminal history information check on Michael Grant Miller and Mark A. Nelson reflected both had prior arrest histories for misdemeanor offenses. One of those offenses for Miller was for an arrest in 1985 for Possession of a Dangerous Weapon which was reduced to a misdemeanor.

N000147

5   *Subscribed and Sworn to before me this 19th day of February, 1992*

MORTON SITVER
United States Magistrate Judge

Nelson's Parallel Life
WITH THE WORLD AROUND HIM

Little was Nelson aware of it before hand on the day, the FBI received orders from Magistrate Judge Mortan Sitver for his arrest, based on the Criminal Complaint Affidavit filed on February 19, 1992, by FBI Case Special Agent Keith D. Tolhurst. Nelson's parallel life was this:

NELSON' DIARY: STAYED THE NIGHT AT NANCY'S HOUSE

7:00 A.M. I woke up took my dogs, Snuggles and Patches out back to do their thing. I said good bye to Nancy and gave her a kiss (she sure kisses good!). I got in my car and drove to my van, so I could go to work. I stopped over at Richard's apartment to see if any strange people had been around or anything happened. He told me nothing happened. He also told me he was sick and that he couldn't eat. He looked bad. I then went to work.

When I got off work I stopped over to see how Richard was feeling. He was still sick and pale. I felt bad for him.

I said, "don't worry, we've done nothing wrong, there is obviously some mistake!

He said, "I know, but my privacy has been violated for no reason."

"I know," I said. "I'll talk with you later. I'm going to Nancy's house." As I left for Nancy's house I drove to Gold Dust and Scottsdale Rd. I turned right on Scottsdale going south. I noticed a light colored van run a red light to make the same turn I did. At first I thought, "what an asshole." He risked getting into a accident just so he can make the light! I drove on, I watched the van, something inside told me I was being followed by the van.

I thought, I'll just turn left on Indian Bend Rd. heading east. I waited for the last safe minute before entering the left hand turn lane. I made the turn but so did the van I started to get worried. I had no idea why this van would be following me.

I decided to turn left at Pima, heading south. I used my hand signal to give the van, an idea where I was heading. The van was in the left lane, I was in the right lane - turning lane.

I made the turn but I looked over to my right, I noticed the van had gotten in the right lane and ran the red light to make the same turn I did. I didn't turn. The van, I could see was trying to slow down till I made the turn, but I didn't so the van had to keep heading south on Pima. I then made a right turn on Chaparral, then made a U-turn and went back onto Pima, heading south. I was three cars behind the van. The van came to the next street, I don't know the name, but he turned right. When I got to the intersection, I was going to turn left to, but figured maybe I was wrong. So I headed south on Pima. When I got through the intersection, I looked to the right, behind me, and saw the van make a U-turn, then I saw him make a right back on Pima, heading south. The van was about four cars, and 1/8 of a mile behind me. So I came to the next light. It was Indian Bend Road. I turned right and drove as fast as I could to make the first turn possible. It was left, heading south. I don't know the name of the street.

I waited a few minutes to see if the van was coming this way, but he didn't. So I got back on Indian Bend, heading east toward Pima. When I got up to Pima I noticed he was at Star Mart. I turned right on Pima. He saw me. I saw him. He pulled out of the Star Mart back on Indian Bend heading east real fast. The light had just turned red so he had to stop.

I then, pulled into the Star Mart off of Pima, and then went back to Indian Bend, heading west right behind the van. He had his turn signal on to turn left, the direction that I was heading at first.

But then, when I got behind him he turned off his turn signal. The light turned green and the van was driving west bound on Indian Bend.

That's when I called 911, told them I was being followed. They asked if there was a driving altercation between us. I said, "No." They asked for the license plate #. I gave it to them. They told me to pull of and don't follow. I said, "Okay." They said, they would have a police officer looking for him. As I was driving back to Nancy's house, the van pulled behind me again!

I called 911 again. They told me, "Keep driving!" I finally got to 74th Street and McDowell.

The 911 operator asked, if I could see van behind me.

I said, "Yes. I'm stopped at the traffic light on 74th Street and McDowell. I can see him! He's stopped down the street!" The 911 Operator told me to me to go ahead, go forward when the light turns green. I did. The van tried to make the light but didn't.

The 911 Operator said, "Pull over and wait." I did at 74th Street and Hubble.

The 911 Operator said, "The Scottsdale police pulled him over, stay at your location and a officer will be meeting with you. About 10-15 minutes later, one police car went by, then pulled into the parking lot across from where I was parked. Then another police officer pulled behind my car. I was out of my car across the street. I came over to the policeman who was behind my car.

He asked, "Are you the one being followed?"

I said, "Yes." I then looked at his badge. His name, I think, was Ryan, last name. It was real dark. Ryan told me that the guy in the van said he was not following a red, 1986 Corvette.

I said, "He was lying." Then Ryan told me, maybe he was trying to steal my car. He told me to keep it locked up. I said, "Okay." I then got in my car drove to Nancy's house. I asked Nancy if she would drive me by my apartment to see if the van might be in the area. She said, "Okay." We took her car. We didn't see any van.

We went back to her house. She made me the best dinner I even remember commenting, "how this is a meal fit for a king and it felt it was my last supper..."

Thursday, February 20

FBI Case Special Agent Tolhurst is preparing for the arrests of Miller and Nelson. Little did Special Agent Tolhurst realize, Nelson is going to call him first and ask why the FBI are following him and asking questions about him among his friends? Nelson still living parallel with the FBI investigation was this:

NELSON'S DIARY AWAKES FROM HIS FRIENDS HOUSE

7:00 A.M. I woke up to go to work. I asked Nancy if she would take me in her car, because if someone is going to steal my car I don't want it at my Apartment. She said, "Okay." But she asked if I could look at her car to see what the noise was. I did. I put soap on her belts, the loud, screeching noise was gone. I saved her lots of money. I told her if she'd taken it to a shop, they could have taken advantage of her, anywhere from $60-500.00 minium, "She was sooo happy!" As we were on our way to my apartment it dawned on me that last night officer Ryan told me the guy in the van wasn't following a red, 1986 Corvette.

I said, "Nancy, if the van wasn't following me, how did he know what year of car I was driving? And nobody can tell what year that car is. From 86 to 90. I didn't tell the 911 operator what I was driving. Maybe someone is after me and they know, but just don't know what." She said, "We'll just have to wait and see." She dropped me off at my van. I got into my van. When I did I noticed someone had been in it. I started the van. As it was warming up I heard this clicking, sound. I couldn't figure it out. As I looked up on the overhead consul, I noted someone had turned on my C.B., and also took my insurance papers out. I was really worried now. I went to work anyway. I was worried about a lot of things, just personal stuff, but with the

FBI and the van, I was about to collapse. What the hell was going on!

As I was trying to paint everything was going through my mind, even the love I still had for my ex-girlfriend, Dawn, and now my new friend, Nancy Kirkland, who I met on Valentine's Day.

So I started to work, then the FBI and the van started playing on my mind. I thought; fuck it, I'm going to call the FBI! I don't care what they think of me, but I need to know what's going on. So I called information. They gave me the FBI number and I called from my cellular phone. The first time I called, I hung up. I thought; I'm not calling them. If it was something serious they would tell me or come talk to me, then I went back to my work. My mind started dwelling on the van that followed me. Maybe it really has to do something with my car. Maybe the guys who sold it to me were trying to steal it back.

Then I started thinking about the night club. I've talked to so many people about the club. I thought maybe someone, made up stories about me and I was being investigated. I've worked so hard on this project, all my spare time went into this deal. But then I started thinking, why would a van with California plates be following me. At that time I said, "Fuck it, I'm calling the FBI" I did. I asked for an Inspector. They said, "they don't have one. We have Special Agents."

I said, "Okay, Special Agent." The first Special Agent I talked to was Special Agent Gross. I told him that the FBI was asking questions about me. And a van with California plates followed me, I wanted to know what was going on.

Gross said, "he didn't know what I was talking about." He said, "Slow down". He asked me my name, birth date, then told me to explain myself again. I told him about FBI at my apartment then the van following me.

He said, "Okay, But what's the point of calling?"

I said, "I was going to be opening a night club, and that I would be qualifying party for the Liquor Licence and I don't want to start on anything until I find out what's up with the FBI. I asked him if he knew Charlie Gross?

He said, "Who's that?"

"The one selling the club."

He said, "Hold on, a Special Agent just walked in." Then this Special Agent Keith, got on the phone. He asked why I called. I explained the same story I told Special Agent Gross.

This Special Agent Keith, first name I think, asked, why did I think the FBI was asking questions about me and my friends and how did I find out. I told then my friends at my apartment told me.

He said, "Some friends!" He said, "he didn't know what I was talking about. But if I could come into the office and talk about it, we could figure it out."

I told him, "Why do I need to come down there for? If you don't know what's going on, it doesn't matter if I'm there or not." I also told him I would go but I was working.

Special Agent Keith then said, "Okay, give me a phone number and I'll find out what's going on, and I'll call you back in a little while."

I said, "Okay!" I gave them my mobile number. I went back to work, then about 1/2 hour or so went by, no phone call from Special Agent Keith, so I called back, and left a message on his message machine.

I said, "I'm calling him back because sometimes, when you're calling me on my cellular phone, it doesn't go through. A few minutes later, eight Special Agents came walking onto the property where I was working, two Special Agents approached me and asked if I was Mark A. Nelson.

I said, "Yes."

They said, "You are under arrested, we have a warrant." They didn't even let me clean up. They left my client's home a mess and left my van blocking their garage door. They didn't care. Doug Cameron came out and asked if I could clean up the mess. They talked and then just walked away with me and that was the last I saw of my paint stuff.

Before they put me in the car one Special Agent, black short hair with sun glasses in white shirt and polyester pants, (the worst dressed of them all) asked me where Jeff Bonadonna was. I said, "at home."

He said, "Does he live with you?"

I said, "No, He lives in Los Angeles."

He said, "Are you sure he doesn't live with you?"

I said, "I told you that."

He said, "So if we get a search warrant and check your apartment he wouldn't be there."

I said, "I told you he doesn't live with me, he lives in Los Angeles."

He then said, "Okay, what's his phone number." They were looking through my computer address book like experts.

"He's not in here!" this Special Agent said. I told them Bonadonna's phone number in Reseda."

They said, "If he doesn't live with you, what's his address?"

I said, "In Los Angeles some where I don't know his actual address!"

He said, "We'll find him" Then the two Special Agents stuck me in the car, they took me to the *Federal Bureau of Investigation's Headquarters* in Phoenix, Arizona.

THE FEDERAL BUREAU OF INVESTIGATION HEADQUARTERS

Mark A. Nelson was immediately placed under arrest, but his Miranda Rights were not given to him though he was questioned by these Special Agents prior to his arrival at their headquarters. Nelson was escorted by these same FBI Special Agents, paraded around office to office, he was then lead into the office of head Special Agent Phoenix Division Larry McCormick. Nelson was still being questioned about his involvement to this case and yet he still was not read his Miranda Rights. Were

Nelson's Civil Rights violated by these FBI Special Agents? His meeting with Assistant Special Agent in Charge went like this:

NELSON IS INTRODUCED ASAC AGENT LARRY McCORMICK

I was introduced to the head FBI Special Agent McCormick. He told me that I was arrested for extortion of Marc Kaplan, along with some guy named Miller. He told me that if I would cooperate and tell what I know, then I could go.

I said, "I had nothing to hide and would cooperate."

He said, "Thank you," shook my hand, then introduced me to two Special Agents, one Doug and John. I can't remember last names. We shook hands and then they took me to an office, of their boss, Special Agent Hunt. I remember that because of all his awards on the wall. His nickname is Jack.

Special Agent Doug started asking questions but first they made me sign a paper stating that they read my rights and that I wasn't abused or coerced for the information I would give them. So I signed it. Special Agent Doug asked me the first questions: my name, address, birth date, family's names addresses, workplace, he asked where Bonadonna lived, how long I knew him, ask about Nick Lee's, asked me my background, asked if I knew anybody in these pictures (I was shown several photos), asked if I knew Marc Kaplan, etc. This went on for a few hours.

Doug asked if I would take a lie detector test. He said if I have nothing to hide then I should take the test and if it comes out clean I'm free, and they would call everyone and make amends.

I said, "Sure!"

Then Special Agent John, who was the best dressed of them all, dark pin-stripe suit with pink Polo shirt, a Paisley tie and penny loafer shoes and a real nice gold bracelet that he told me cost six months worth of wages.

He said, "he told his boss, Hunt, he had a gut feeling I was telling the truth. Special Agent John said, "Mark, don't make me look bad you've got to pass the lie detector test or his boss, Hunt, would be real pissed off at him. If you fail, you will be going to jail for a long time, and then I would have to deal with his pissed off boss."

I said, "not to count on me passing. I have this black cloud over me when it comes to pressure. I'd probably fail." I agreed to take the test. It was about 4:30 P.M.

Doug left the room and came back and said, "The guy that does the testing won't be here for a couple of hours. "At that time it was 5:00 P.M. Special Agent Hunt came into the office. I met him. He shook my hand. He told Special Agent Doug and John that they needed to go, something came up.

So they put another Special Agent on. I don't remember his name. They moved me to these other offices with cupboards I sat down and waited. I could see the clock. Doug had ordered me some food, *McDonalds*. But as I was waiting the Special

Agent that was assigned to baby sit me had a candy bar. He was a real nice guy. He split it with me. I was so hungry. That was nice of him. From this point on I will call him "Special Agent Baby-Sitter." We sat there and talked about his age, how he became an FBI Special Agent, and about the qualifications? As we were talking the food arrived, *McDonalds*. I had 1 cheeseburger, 1 regular fries, medium coke. It's not what I would have ordered but free food is always, okay. As I was eating Special Agent Baby Sitter asked me if I liked the food.

I said "Yes, I haven't eaten all day." It was now 6:00 P.M.

He asked, "how are you feeling?

I said, "Scared, and getting real tired. I was up at 7:00 A.M. this morning."

He said, "I can see you look tired." As we were talking I heard someone yelling. I could hear this guy saying, "I told you I just met the guy at the lake. He builds homes. I'm a framer!" I also heard him say that he just gave me his card then drove away. Then Special Agent Keith walked back into the office. I asked if I could use the phone to call my family and friends to tell them where I am.

Special Agent Keith Tolhurst replied, anyone that knows you, we've already told them what you did and what you've been arrested for. Then Tolhurst said, but go ahead and use your phone, but Special Agent Baby Sitter, has to listen on the phone with you. So they turned on my mobile phone and it was my ex-wife "Gina" calling, "we talked, she was worried."

I called Richard Sollami, Special Agent Baby Sitter listened to that phone call, too. Then when we got off the phone, Special Agent Hunt came back into the room and sat down. I looked at him and asked, "What's wrong?"

He said, "Well, even if you pass the test you still may have to go to jail."

"Have to go to jail? " Boy, my insides felt like someone just stabbed me. I was thinking these guys are fucking with my head!

Then Special Agent Hunt said, "I'll try the best I can for you. It's just that the warrant issued for your arrest demands that you go before the judge and that only the court judge, can lift." Then he got up, looked at me and said, "I can't promise you anything, but I'll try." Then he left.

I looked at Special Agent Baby Sitter and told him, "Great, that's just what I wanted to hear."

He replied, "Yea! That doesn't sound too good. Don't worry, he probably can do it. But we'll have to wait and see."

Boy, I was flipping' out on the inside of my mind. I didn't know what to believe any more, my God what is happening to me...?

I just asked God to look over me, and I'll just have to pass this test. I was thinking, well even if I pass, I still go to *jail*!"

Then I asked Special Agent Baby Sitter, where is the guy for the test? He replied, "Well, he wasn't called until 5:00 P.M., and he's coming from Flagstaff." Special Agent Keith walked back in and asked me more questions. Do I know Miller, Kaplan, etc. Asking the same questions over and over again and again. My mind was spinning, I need my medicine!

Then he told me I'll be taking the test soon. He left. I looked at Special Agent Baby Sitter and said, "They are going to make me take this test this late?"

He said, "I don't know, I just do what I'm told." It was now 9:00 P.M. He's just setting up. Special Agent Keith came back and said, "Be ready!"

Special Agent Keith led me to where the test was to be given. It was in Special Agent McCormick's office. It was now about 9:30 P.M. The person giving the test was an older man. I don't remember his name. I'll call him "Special Agent Lie Detector."

He went over the test, how it works, what the machine does, and went over the questions that are going to be asked. The test started. I guess, at about 10:00 P.M.

He hooked up the machine to my body. I was so tired, the lights in the office were so bright, they hurt my eyes, I could barely keep them open.

After the questions, Special Agent Lie Detector did the test questions three more times. At the end of the last test he took all the equipment off me. He said, "sit down I want to talk to you Mark." He told me that I was not telling the truth, that if I wanted to tell the truth now it the time to do it.

I said, "I was tired, that my head keeps spinning. I was thinking of all kinds of things, when I gave you my answers."

He said, "Now, Mark, I know you're trying to open a club, and you need money, so maybe you thought that is the best way for you." I told him that's not true and I didn't want to talk any more.

He said, "fine." Then Special Agent Lie Detector took me to the office where everyone was at. Special Agent Baby Sitter then took me to another room. We sat down. He asked what happened. I said, "I failed." I told Special Agent Baby Sitter that Special Agent Lie Detector was full of shit, and that I told everyone that the mind I had dwells on everything at one time. That's why I have ulcers and anxiety problems.

He replied, "Maybe they're going to give you the test again but ask different questions."

It doesn't matter. I'll fail it again. I'm too tired, my head is spinning. Special Agent Baby Sitter said, "Well let's see what happens?" He was right. They came back and took me back into Special Agent McCormick's office.

Special Agent Lie Detector said, "Mark, let's try this again." We sat down. He went over the questions that he was going to ask. He asked if I was ready for the test.

I said, "Yes." As I sat down, Mark Nuneez popped into my head. I thought, now I know what he went through with the "Temple Murders." (This guy was coerced to admitting he killed sever Buddhist monks, but they found the real killer later on.)

Anyway, as the Special Agent hooked up his machine to my body he asked if I was a Christian. I said, *Why?* He said, Because of the necklace you're wearing. I told him this, has nothing to do, with that.

Special Agent Lie Detector began his questions. He did this test three times again. My head was spinning and my stomach was bubbling. I was spitting up stomach acid and had to swallow it. My teeth felt gritty. I remember thinking; my God, these people are trying to frame me, but WHY?

His questioning all started to sound the same, I kept thinking of his last test questions compared to the ones he's asking me now. I was so tired. All I could think of was God and my two little dogs, Snuggles and Patches. That was the only thing that kept me from collapsing. I kept telling them I was tired. I told him he had the blood pressure on too tight. My hand and arm turned purple and red. But no one seemed to care! I never felt so helpless in my life.

At last, the test was over, he unplugged me from his **machine-god.**

He told me that he wanted to talk to me. He told me that he's been doing this for 3 years and had done over 300 of these tests and he was never wrong. When he made those statements I thought; "Oh fuck!" This guy thinks he's God...! I barely had the energy to listen to his shit, but kept face for my own respect.

He looked in my eyes and said, "even Christians lie, for reasons that not even God can control, due to money problems." He told me something is not right in my mind, that I was lying, and that I should save myself and tell the truth. I told him I was telling the truth.

He said, "Don't insult my intelligence."

I looked into his eyes and said, "Don't insult mine, you are full of shit, take me to jail! I'm too tired to listen to any more of your bullshit, and I am through!" I got up and walked out. As I walked out Special Agent Baby Sitter took me back in the office with all the NEC and laser printer boxes. I remember this because the first time I was in there, I noticed the big red boxes!

Anyway, Special Agent Doug came in and got me and took me back to Special Agent Hunt's office where Special Agent John was. They began to tell me, I'd better tell the truth. This was my last chance.

I said, "I was telling the truth." They did not believe me. Special Agent Doug went out of the room, then Special Agent John started drilling me.

He said, "Mark, you're lying. That machine is never wrong."

I said, "Fine, just take me to jail!"

"Is that what you really want?" he asked.

"Yes, because I'm telling the truth and you know it." I yelled!

Special Agent Doug came back in the room. Special Agent John asked, "Mark, do you remember when I told you that if you failed the test that you would be sorry?"

"Yes, but I was telling the truth." I told him sternly.

"Don't lie to my face," Special Agent John stood up and started to get angry. He was raising his voice and the veins in his skull were protruding through his skin. The saliva in his mouth squirted between his teeth like a mad animal! I told him in the most mild manner (yet inside, I wanted so bad to kick his ass to the floor and mess up his pretty little clothes) that he didn't need to get mad and talk to me that way!

"Don't tell him what to do and I'll do the telling, you just answer the questions!" he screamed. He was out of control he reminded me of my parents out of control; I think he tried to scare me he almost got his ass kicked instead. I couldn't even imagine what they would do to me if that was to happen, how's that for control?

"Yes sir!" I yelled.

He said, "I don't think so." Then he told Doug to leave the office. He (John) asked, Will you do something for me?

"What?" I said.

"Will you write something that I'll dictate to you?" Special Agent John then had me write stuff like, Marc Kaplan crossed the road for oranges and was late or something like that. Then Doug came back to the room. Special Agent John said, "Okay," that's good enough. He was reading from his note book. He closed it. Then he picked up the paper I wrote on, then he put it in his notebook. I asked what was that all about.

He (John) said, "Nothing. The truth will come out in the end."

I replied, "You're right, and you'll be apologizing to me!" There was no reply from either Special Agents.

Then Special Agent Keith and Special Agent Baby Sitter got me ready for jail. It was now 11:30 P.M., I was ready to collapse and they knew it...!

FBI HEADQUARTERS EVIDENCE SEIZED
FROM NELSON

When the FBI arrested me, the only evidence they had about me, as you can see, on the evidence sheet on the following page, was never linked, in anyway to their conspiracy claims against me. The FBI checked my cellular phone for any calls made in regards to this case, the FBI found no calls made to anyone in connection with this case. What they did find out was that I was telling the truth. The FBI also went through my electronic phone book the moment I was arrested at the house I was painting, it contained no names, addresses or phone numbers to anyone in connection with this case either.

Control of General/Drug/Valuable Evidence
FD-192 (Rev. 1-5-89)

Date 2/21/92

☑ General Evidence   ☐ Drug Evidence   ☐ Valuable Evidence

☐ Special Handling Requirement (i.e., FBI Lab Instructions Re Body Fluid Stains, Whole Blood, etc.)

Title and Character of Case
UNSUB;
MARK KAPLAN - VICTIM;
EXTORTION;
OO: PX

FILE NO. 9-PX-46497
OO: PX

Date Acquired	Acquired From:
2/20/92	MARK NELSON

To Be Returned	See Serial	Acquiring Agent	Case Agent
☐ Yes ☑ No		TOLHURST	TOLHURST

☐ Yes ☑ No   Grand Jury Material - Disseminate Only Pursuant to Rule 6(e), Federal Rules of Criminal Procedure

☐ Yes ☑ No   Property To Be Forfeited To The U.S. Government

Description of Property (Be Specific)

1) PR Shoes (HITOP)
2) BOOT STRAPS
3) 1 PAIR SweetPANTS
4) 1 Cellular Telephone, WITH CASE
5) 1 checkbook
6) 1 Electronic ADDRESS book

FOR DRUG AND/OR VALUABLE EVIDENCE ONLY - NAMES OF TWO AGENTS
INITIALLY VERIFYING AND SEALING:

_____   _____

For Use By ECT:

Location of Property: ECR/Shelf 1

BLOCKSTAMP
SEARCHED............ INDEXED............
.... FILED............

Control of General/Drug/Valuable Evidence
FD-192 (Rev. 1-5-89)

Date 2 20 92

☑ General Evidence   ☐ Drug Evidence   ☐ Valuable Evidence

☐ Special Handling Requirement (i.e., FBI Lab Instructions Re Body Fluid Stains, Whole Blood, etc.)

Title and Character of Case

UNSUBS:
MARC J KAPLAN - VICTIM;
EXTORTION A
OO: PX

FILE NO. 9A-PX-46497

OO: PX

Date Acquired	Acquired From: ~~MARC ARTHUR~~ NELSON ?
2 20 92	

To Be Returned ☑ Yes ☐ No	See Serial	Acquiring Agent STEPHEN T. GROSS	Case Agent KEITH TOLHURST

☐ Yes ☑ No   Grand Jury Material - Disseminate Only Pursuant to Rule 6(e), Federal Rules
of Criminal Procedure

☐ Yes ☑ No   Property To Be Forfeited To The U.S. Government

Description of Property (Be Specific)

SMITH & WESSON MODEL 422
22 LONG RIFLE WITH CLIP, ; 10 ROUNDS
AND HOLSTER

FOR DRUG AND/OR VALUABLE EVIDENCE ONLY - NAMES OF TWO AGENTS
INITIALLY VERIFYING AND SEALING:

_____   _____

For Use By ECT:
Location of Property: Gun CAB 3

Control Number: E0293538

(File Copy)

SEARCHED ___ BLOCKSTAMP ___
SERIALIZED ____ FILED ____

FBI - PHOENIX

9A-46497-1B(4)
N000372

326

Nelson's Interrogation
SPECIAL AGENTS DOUGLAS E. HOPINS, AND JOHN E. HAMILTON AT FBI HEADQUARTERS

2:15 P.M. Nelson was arrested on this date, his alibi was the truth and could not be proved otherwise. The blacked out marks that cover the lines on some of the following pages from the report were put there by the FBI so it was hard to read. Yet it turns out that he was telling the truth, he was not involved. The statements made by Nelson in these reports are not exactly what he said but was paraphrased with a negative overtone according to Nelson.

On the following four pages, is the report filed by these two Special Agents.

- 1 -

FEDERAL BUREAU OF INVESTIGATION

Date of transcription   2/21/92

MARK ANDREW NELSON, also known as (aka) Marcus Andrew
Giavani, was contacted at the FEDERAL BUREAU OF INVESTIGATION
(FBI) Office in Phoenix. NELSON was advised of the identity of
the interviewing agents and that he was going to be interviewed
regarding an extortion matter. Prior to the interview, NELSON
was advised of his constitutional rights by the reading of a
standard warning and waiver form. At the completion of the
reading of his rights, NELSON stated that he understood his
rights and was willing to be interviewed. Thereafter, MARK
ANDREW NELSON signed the standard warning and waiver form.
NELSON then provided the following information:

NELSON advised that he resides at 6885 East Cochise,
Apartment 116, Scottsdale, Arizona. He stated that his current
telephone number is (602) 377-8694, and previously he had
telephone number 991-4876. NELSON advised that he has resided in
Apartment 116 for approximately seven months. He stated he is a
painter and is employed by NICK LEES CUSTOM DEVELOPMENT COMPANY.
He stated he has worked for this company for approximately two
and one-half years, and he just recently got promoted to
estimator and project coordinator for remodeling jobs handled by
NICK LEES CUSTOM DEVELOPMENT. He stated that he has been working
at the house where he was arrested on this date for approximately
two months. He said that this is a job he obtained by himself
because he has been painting various other houses in that same
general vicinity. ████████████████████████████ly he has
been seeing a ███████████████████████████ He stated she
lives in an apartment at 92nd Street and Thunderbird and has home
telephone number (602) 451-0186. He stated that he has known her
for a while and has been dating her the past two months.
Regarding an individual by the name of JEFF, NELSON stated that a
friend of his by the name of JEFF BONADONA was recently visiting
with him from California. He stated that he has known JEFF
BONADONA since about 1985. At this point, NELSON was shown a
color photograph depicting an individual with dark hair. He
immediately identified this individual as JEFF BONADONA.

Investigation on 2/20/92   at Phoenix, Arizona   File # 9A-PX-46497

      SA DOUGLAS E. HOPKINS; and
by SA JOHN E. HAMILTON;   DEH/lpt   Date dictated 2/21/92

N000184 26

9A-PX-46497

Continuation of FD-302 of ___MARK ANDREW NELSON_____ , On ___2/20/92___ , Page ___2___

      NELSON indicated that on Friday, February 7, 1992, he
had traveled to California to visit a friend by the name of RAY
SHANK. He stated SHANK can be contacted at telephone number
(818) 609-9072. NELSON stated he drove his red Corvette to
California to visit his friend and while there, he met up with
JEFF BONADONA. He stated after hooking up with JEFF, they agreed
that JEFF would come back to Phoenix for a few days and help with
a painting project and then return to California. In that
regard, NELSON stated that he and JEFF BONADONA drove back to
Scottsdale, Arizona, on Tuesday, February 11, 1992. NELSON
advised on the next day, that being February 12, 1992, they went
sightseeing, and he recalls taking JEFF to various places around
the area. Specifically, he said that JEFF had inquired how
people managed to stay cool in this area during the heat. NELSON
stated he told JEFF there were many recreational areas in the
vicinity where you could go and stay cool.

      Regarding his activities on February 13, 1992, NELSON
stated that he recalls leaving his apartment at approximately
8:00 or 9:00 a.m. that morning to go see his friend, RICHARD
SOLAMI, a friend who lives in the same apartment complex. He
stated that it was his intention to try to do some painting on
that day but because it was raining, they were unable to do so.
NELSON stated he recalls they left in his Corvette at
approximately 1:00 p.m. on that date, ▮▮▮▮▮▮▮▮▮▮ the first
▮▮▮▮▮▮▮▮▮▮▮▮▮▮▮▮▮▮▮▮▮▮▮▮▮▮▮▮▮▮▮▮▮▮ that later
▮▮▮▮▮▮▮▮▮▮▮▮▮▮▮▮▮▮▮▮▮▮▮▮▮▮▮▮▮▮, they
arrived in the Sahuaro Lake area. He stated the reason they went
to this particular area was again because JEFF wanted to see some
places where you could go to cool off during the hot weather.
NELSON stated that he recalls that they parked near the bathrooms
located close to the lake. He said when they first drove up,
they noticed two other individuals parked in their car in the
same parking lot. He stated that these persons were unknown to
him, but JEFF walked over and began to visit with them. NELSON
said during the time they were at the lake, he had his radio on
loud playing music. He did this because he is somewhat hard of
hearing.

9A-PX-46497

Continuation of FD-302 of   MARK ANDREW NELSON _____ , On   2/20/92   , Page   3

He stated that they walked over and began to visit with
these two individuals who were drinking beer. ███████████ he
learned ████████████████████████████████ , and
he stated, inasmuch as he was always looking for subcontractors
to help with NICK LEES various jobs, ████████████████████████ In
████████████████████ the two individuals would be
described as a Caucasian male and a Mexican male. He stated he
did not know their names and does not recall being introduced to
them. NELSON described their car as an older, smaller car that
looked rather beat up. He stated it was somewhat of a grayish
color. NELSON estimated that he and JEFF were at the lake for
approximately 30 minutes.

NELSON said he recalls while they were at the lake
noticing a teal green Mercedes in the general vicinity. He said
he recalls that car particularly because that would be what he
would consider the ultimate automobile to own. He stated he
cannot be sure as to when he left the lake area in conjunction
with the Mercedes ██████████████████████████████████████
████ NELSON said that when he and JEFF drove away from the lake
area, they drove down toward the part of the recreation area
where the tubing activity begins. He stated that they then
returned to the normal exit to the lake and out on to the Beeline
Highway. He said as they progressed back down the road toward
Phoenix, they passed the teal green Mercedes. As he drove past,
he happened to look over at the individual, and he noticed that
the driver of the Mercedes was looking at him and had sort of a
strange look on his face. He stated that they then proceeded
down to the intersection of Shea Boulevard and the Beeline
Highway and at this point, JEFF indicated to him that he needed
to use the restroom. NELSON stated that he pulled up outside the
MCDONALDS, located near the intersection, and JEFF got out and
went in to use the restroom. NELSON said that after JEFF
returned to the car, JEFF asked him if he would buy him a
hamburger, and they then drove through the drive-thru and got
something to eat and t████████████████████████████████

NELSON said after that, they then drove back to
Scottsdale and directly to his apartment.

N000186

9A-PX-46497

Continuation of FD-302 of ___MARK ANDREW NELSON_____ , On ___2/20/92___ , Page __4__

        Regarding any telephone calls made on his mobile telephone during this time period, NELSON initially stated that he did not recall making any particular calls. NELSON did state, however, that all we had to do was check the toll records on his telephone and it would reflect exactly who he had called and when he had called them. ███████████████████████████████████ that ██ ████████████████████████████████████ NELSON stated that he does now recall making such calls, and the reason for them was that he had recommended the framers to NICK LEES, and he wanted to let NICK LEES know that these people may be calling in regards to doing some framing work for NICK LEES CONSTRUCTION COMPANY. Regarding telephone calls made to the SUBWAY Corporate Offices located in Scottsdale, NELSON stated the reason for these calls was that he had previously had contact with an individual by the name of RICHARD SCHREIBLER (phonetic), who is the Corporate President of the SUBWAY SANDWICH SHOP chain. He stated that SCHREIBLER had earlier indicated an interest in a home and that he (NELSON) was following up on the ███████████████████ ██ have ██████████████████████████████

        Regarding the individuals they had met at the lake, NELSON observed that those people seemed somewhat interested in who ███████ were and why ███████ had a telephone. ██ ███ █████████████████ NELSON described the individuals they had met at the lake as follows:

        Number One:

Race	White
Sex	Male
Age	Late 20s
Height	5'8"
Hair	Blond
Eyes	Brown

N000187

FBI Scrambling To Fit Innocent Bystanders
TO FBI VERSIONS OF THE CRIME ...

3:00 P.M. Nelson was taken to another office with FBI Special Agent Kaili. This Special Agent was to watch (baby-sit) Nelson and report everything Nelson said. Special Agent Kaili was then to file his report to the Case Special Agent Keith Tolhurst. The concerns here is that some of the information pertaining to Nelson by Special Agent Kaili was completely paraphrased, connecting Nelson to the intended victim Kaplan. In fact, Nelson and Kaplan never knew each other. The actions of this Special Agent would lend credibility to the Conspiracy Theory!

NELSON'S INTERROGATION

4:30 P.M. Special Agent Hugene H. Kaili in his investigation on the following page, that he too, was paraphrasing the conversation between him and me, in a very negative way, and not including the true facts as we know them now. No doubt this was done to tie me more into this case. Why would I lie to fit myself into this case, when evidence proves I was an innocent bystander, and had nothing at all to do with this case.? Was this Special Agent, too, part of the Conspiracy Theory against Miller and Me...?

On page one, in paragraph two of this interview: It turns out that; Nick Lees told the FBI That "Nelson never heard of Kaplan and he, (Nick) never brought up Kaplans name in front of Nelson because there was never a reason to. Kaplan's house was built years before Nelson started to paint for me, (Nick)." Even the Kaplan's never saw or heard of me before this case. The person I did tell this Special Agent about, who was having some warranty problems with a house Lees built, was Brian Holt's home. I never stated paragraphs 3, 4, 5. In paragraph 6 however, I did state I was going to open a nightclub. I told him it was Tempe, Arizona. Never did I say Mesa. This information was found on my electronic organizer. What's even worse, I told the FBI, all of this information the day I was arrested and it was all the truth. In paragraph seven what I really said was, "I had my gun because I was going to get it blued because it was rusty." I did not say to protect my girlfriend from people who might cause a problems with her outside the club. I could not have said that statement because my girlfriend, "Dawn" was not a topless dancer, and did not work at a club! "This Special Agent *lied!*"

On page two, paragraph six: I never told Miller not to sign on with Lee's. I would never use those terms! It wasn't Miller's who was going to bid on the work, but his boss, Gomez. It would have been Nick that was to pay this company for their work. Why would I say something that makes no sense at all! That's because this Special Agent Kaili, altered my statements to help frame me to this case! *Why?* Paragraph seven: I never told this Special Agent I saw Kaplan's scared face at the *McDonalds* parking lot...

- 1 -

FEDERAL BUREAU OF INVESTIGATION

Date of transcription   3/2/92

       MARK A. NELSON, a white male, date of birth June 12, 1960, was advised of the identity of the interviewing agent. NELSON had already been interviewed by Federal Bureau of Investigation (FBI) agents and agreed to take the polygraph examination. While awaiting the arrival of the polygraph examiners, NELSON provided the following information:

       NELSON stated he did not know MARC KAPLAN. He heard about KAPLAN through NICHOLAS LEES, who was building KAPLAN's house. NELSON said KAPLAN's house was not built well because of electrical and plumbing problems. KAPLAN and LEES had a dispute over fixing the problems with KAPLAN's new house. LEES refused to fix the electrical and plumbing systems so KAPLAN hired workers to fix his house, and paid out of his own pocket.

       NELSON advised LEES builds "shoddy" houses and "rips" people off. He said LEES uses cheap materials and non-specification materials to make a bigger profit.

       He said LEES ripped him off and owed him money. NELSON wanted to quit, but kept working after he talked to LEES and was told he would be given a better position in which he would be able to recruit workers and receive a commission.

       NELSON stated he is using LEES for his contractor's license to build homes from the ground up, from drawing board sketches, to frames, to the finished house. NELSON said he can build all aspects of a house.

       He is trying to open a night club in Mesa and has been talking to business people and investors for the capital. NELSON said he needed $1.5 million to open the club and has plans in his phone directory.

       He does carry a gun to protect his girlfriend from people that may cause a problem with her outside the club.

Investigation on __2/20/92__ at __Phoenix, Arizona__   File # __9A-PX-46497__

by __SA EUGENE K. KAILI/mbh__   Date dictated __2/28/92__

NJ000259

This document contains neither recommendations nor conclusions of the FBI. It is the property of the FBI and is _____ __ ____ _____.

9A-PX-46497

Continuation of FD-302 of   MARK A. NELSON _____ , On   2/20/92   , Page   2

        NELSON advised he does not have a lot of money and uses
his monthly income mainly for bills. He gets money from his
girlfriend and said it is a '90's kind of thing.

        He drives a Corvette as an image of a successful
businessman. NELSON also stated his car makes him an easy target
as a drug buyer and seller.

        NELSON stated this incident of being arrested by the
FBI is going to ruin his painting business which had taken a long
time to build up the trust of the richer people.

        NELSON has a brown belt in Tae Kwon Do.

        He went to Lake Saguaro to show JEFF BONADONNA where
NELSON cools off in the summer. NELSON did have his radio
"cranked" up due to his deafness in his ear.

        NELSON told MICHAEL G. MILLER at Saguaro Lake to give
him a call if MILLER wanted to work for LEES because NELSON would
receive a three percent commission for bringing in a worker.
NELSON also told MILLER not to sign on with LEES, but let NELSON
handle the schedule.

        NELSON stated the only thing he remembered about KAPLAN
is seeing his "scared" face in the McDonald's parking lot on Shea
Boulevard. He went to McDonalds because BONADONNA was insistent
on getting a hamburger to eat.

        NELSON advised he heard from his apartment manager the
FBI asked questions about him and wanted information on him.

        He also knew RICHARD SOLLAMI was questioned by FBI
agents. NELSON advised SOLLAMI would not be involved in anything
because SOLLAMI follows the same routine and schedule everyday.
He stated SOLLAMI is burnt-out from selling insurance. SOLLAMI
makes $3,000 - $4,000 a month from his insurance commissions.

                                                        MJ000260

FBI Special Agents At The Residence
OF MICHAEL GRANT MILLER

The arrest of Michael Grant Miller at his place of residence by Special Agents, Kenneth Allan Hancock, Anthony E. Oldham, Thomas G. Radke, Robert E. Casey, JR., Kevin E. Murphy, R. Scott Rivas, and Charles S. Kuchar.

THE ARREST OF MICHAEL GRANT MILLER

2:00 P.M. A total of seven FBI Special Agents arrested Michael Miller. This arrest was authorized by United States Magistrate Judge Mortan Sitver, based on the Criminal Complaint filed by Case Special Agent Keith Tolhurst, (United States vs. Miller and Nelson).

These Special Agents surrounded his apartment and made entrance and Made contact with Miller, with no confrontation. Miller's interview was this:

·1·

FEDERAL BUREAU OF INVESTIGATION

Date of transcription   2/21/92

On February 20, 1992, at 2:00 P.M., an arrest of
MICHAEL GRANT MILLER was conducted at 1653 South Harris Drive,
Apartment 2037, Mesa, Arizona. The following occurred:

At the time of MILLER's arrest, Special Agents THOMAS
G. RADKE, R. SCOTT RIVAS, KENNETH ALAN HANCOCK, KEVIN E. MURPHY,
CHARLES S. KUCHAR, and ROBERT E. CASEY, JR., approached MILLER's
apartment at 1653 South Harris Drive, #2037, Mesa, Arizona.
Agent RADKE knocked at MILLER's door, and a white male adult
matching the description of MICHAEL MILLER opened the door.
Immediately MILLER was advised that he was under arrest by Agents
of the Federal Bureau of Investigation (FBI) as an arrest warrant
had been issued in his name. MILLER was handcuffed, and the
immediate area surrounding him pursuant to his arrest was
searched.

MILLER was escorted while handcuffed to a
transportation vehicle and was driven to the FBI Office in
Phoenix, Arizona, for an interview and arrest processing. The
transportation and interview was conducted by Agents KUCHAR and
MURPHY.

Investigation on   2/20/92   at Phoenix, Arizona   File # PX 9A-PX-46497
      SAs THOMAS G. RADKE, R. SCOTT RIVAS, KENNETH ALAN HANCOCK,
      KEVIN E. MURPHY, ROBERT E. CASEY, JR., CHARLES S. KUCHAR,
by   and THOMAS G. RADKE   TGR:dpt   Date dictated   2/20/92   N000242
                                      74   (125)

This document contains neither recommendations nor conclusions of the FBI. It is the property of the FBI and is loaned to your agency;
· and its contents are not to be distributed outside your agency.

Miller's Arrival At FBI Headquarters
TO OFFICE ASSISTANT SPECIAL AGENT IN CHARGE McCORMICK

-1-

FEDERAL BUREAU OF INVESTIGATION

Date of transcription   2/27/92

MICHAEL G. MILLER was escorted into the office of ASAC LARRY J. MC CORMICK where he was requested to sit down and was left alone with ASAC MC CORMICK.

ASAC MC CORMICK advised MILLER of his identity and position with the FBI. He was requested not to make any statement at this time. He was notified that the FBI was currently conducting an extortion investigation with over 50 Agents presently conducting interviews of his employer, family and associates. He was advised this was the largest ongoing case for the FBI in Arizona. He was also advised that he had been arrested for Conspiracy and Extortion regarding a letter mailed to Mr. MARC KAPLAN demanding $250,000.00. The letter indicated if this money was not paid, Mr. KAPLAN's son would be abducted and his arm or leg removed. These charges were punishable for up to 25 years in jail.

MILLER was advised that this was his opportunity to cooperate with this investigation. He was advised that the FBI had evidence indicating that he had made the telephone call setting up the extortion and was observed at Saguaro Lake the same date. He immediately denied knowledge of the extortion, however stated that he had been at Saguaro Lake on February 13, 1992, with a friend. He denied any involvement in an extortion and stated that he may have been set up by someone else. He said he had "many friends".

MILLER was instructed to make no further comments to ASAC MC CORMICK, but to discuss this matter with the interviewing Agents, which he agreed to do. He was assured that his cooperation would be made known to the U.S. Attorney's Office. He was thereafter released to SAs KEVIN E. MURPHY and CHARLES S. KUCHAR.

Rigation on   2/20/92   at Phoenix, Arizona   File # 9A-PX-46497

ASAC LARRY J. MC CORMICK/jmc   Date dictated 2/24/92

000252

Special Agents Work For A Confession
WHICH THEY KNOW WILL NEVER MATERIALIZE

Michael Miller's interrogation by Special Agents Charles S. Kuchar (Field Special Agent), Anthony E. Oldham (Reporting Special Agent), Kevin E. Murphy (Reporting Special Agent). It was learned later, Case Special Agent Tolhurst was present off and on during this traumatic interview but that was omitted from this report. Miller was advised that he had been arrested based on a complaint authorized by a U.S. Magistrate in Phoenix, Arizona. Special Agent Murphy also advised Miller that the Special Agents were only seeking the entire truth of what happened in this extortion attempt, as known by Miller. Special Agent Murphy admonished Miller not to provide any false statements to the FBI, as such statements maybe construed as a separate crime by the government! Miller had no choice but to tell the truth which he did, he knew nothing of this crime and was not at all involved.

There is evidence here that was overlooked by all. That being that Miller was arrested based on the Criminal Complaint Affidavit filed by the Case Special Agent Tolhurst, which we now know was fabricated to implicate Miller and Nelson. This substantiates False Arrest and the Conspiracy Theory.

Miller's alibi, as ridiculous as it seemed by the FBI, it was in fact the *truth* even though he and his passenger, Barcon, were drinking different alcoholic beverages throughout the day. These individuals were observed at the lake drinking beer by the Smiths, the two witnesses the FBI used on the Criminal Complaint Affidavit. Miller went on to say he is being set up if his fingerprint was on the telephone that made the extortion call. And if someone was accusing him of being involved.

The FBI already knew that he had not made the call because the time the call was made and the time Miller arrived at the lake it was a travel time of 15 minutes. This, too, was an hour drive time from the *ABCO Supermarket* to *Saguaro Lake*, an impossibility to make in 15 minutes, though the FBI Special Agents involved at the time probably did not think anyone would figure that out. Even if Miller did use this pay telephone days prior and it happened to also be used by some unknown criminal, you will learn as this story unfolds that in fact Miller was telling the truth. That an informant was actually there at ABCO when the call was made February 13, 1992, implicating his buddy *Frank Alber*.

Miller even recalled seeing the fisherman at the lake, and the old man in the blue truck, who had been omitted, and the Smiths vehicle that drove passed Miller and his passenger. This information was also omitted from the FBI *Surveillance Log* of February 13, 1992. Is this more evidence to the actuality of the Conspiracy Theory?

On the following nine pages is Miller's interrogation and it went like this...

- 1 -

FEDERAL BUREAU OF INVESTIGATION

Date of transcription   2/26/92

      MICHAEL GRANT MILLER, white male, date of birth August 30, 1967, Social Security Account Number residence, 1653 South Harris Drive, Apartment 2037, Mesa, Arizona, telephone number (602) 926-0590, provided the following information to Special Agents (SAs) KEVIN E. MURPHY and CHARLES S. KUCHAR, who identified themselves as SAs of the FEDERAL BUREAU OF INVESTIGATION (FBI). This interview took place at the Phoenix Division FBI office, subsequent to MILLER being placed under arrest by the FBI.

      At the outset of this interview, SA MURPHY advised MILLER that he was arrested based on a complaint authorized by a U.S. Magistrate in Phoenix, Arizona, which charged him with Aiding and Abetting in mailing a threatening communication to MARC KAPLAN, to extort money from him, in order to prevent bodily harm to KAPLAN's son, BRIAN KAPLAN.

      Thereafter, SA MURPHY advised MILLER that prior to the Agents asking MILLER any questions concerning his involvement in this extortion matter, they were required to advise MILLER of his constitutional rights as indicated on an FD-395 form entitled "Interrogation: Advice of Rights". Thereafter, SA MURPHY read each of the rights listed on this form to MILLER. MILLER thereafter advised he understood his rights and was willing to talk to the Agents. MILLER then signed the waiver of rights on this form, which was witnessed by SAs MURPHY and KUCHAR.

      Additionally, SA MURPHY prior to the interview of MILLER, advised MILLER that the Agents were only seeking the entire truth of what happened in this extortion attempt, as known by MILLER. SA MURPHY admonished MILLER not to provide any false statements to the FBI during this interview, as such statements may be construed as a separate crime by the government.

      Thereafter, MILLER advised he knew he did not have to talk to the Agents, but wanted to tell them all he knew and to cooperate fully by telling the Agents the truth as he knew it. Thereafter, MILLER provided the following information:

Investigation on   2/20/92   at PHOENIX, ARIZONA   File # 9A-PX-46497

     SAs CHARLES S. KUCHAR, ANTHONY E. OLDHAM and
by   KEVIN E. MURPHY/KEM:mh:jla   Date dictated 2/25/92

4000243

Continuation of FD-302 of __MICHAEL GRANT MILLER_____ , On __2/20/92__ , Page __2__

    MILLER is a construction worker and specifically is a framer working for an individual named LOREN (phonetic) Last name unknown (LNU), who possibly works for ABIS CONSTRUCTION, Mesa, Arizona.

    MILLER's friend and work associate, BENNETT BARCON, who has a wife, CHRISTINA, resides in a brown two story house located on the east side of Arizona Avenue between Guadalupe and Elliott, just north of a canal, which might be located in Chandler, Arizona. BARCON's telephone number is (602) 892-9069.

    Approximately three weeks ago, MILLER, BARCON, and their boss, LOREN LNU, began framing a house in Carefree, Arizona, in a subdivision known as DESERT HILLS.

    During the week beginning February 10, 1992, because of numerous rain showers in the Phoenix metropolitan area, Tuesday, February 11, 1992, was the only day that week they worked on framing the house in Carefree.

    On Thursday, February 13, 1992, BARCON and MILLER went in MILLER's vehicle, a 1982 Mercury four door sedan, Arizona license plate number AWS-096, to the residence of their boss, LOREN LNU. MILLER does not know the specific address of LOREN LNU, but described it as being located in Mesa, near Center and University Streets.

    BARCON and MILLER arrived at LOREN LNU's residence at approximately between 7:30 a.m. and 8:00 a.m., in order to drive together to work on the framing job in Carefree. Another reason for BARCON and MILLER to go to LOREN LNU's residence was to be paid the money owed them for their framing work from LOREN LNU. Upon arrival at LOREN LNU's residence, LOREN advised them he thought it was too wet that day to work, and also that he had no money for them as the general contractor, HERB LNU, had not yet paid LOREN. MILLER believes that HERB possibly works for the aforementioned ABIS CONSTRUCTION COMPANY, address unknown.

    Thereafter, as these individuals did not go to work that day, they decided to remain at LOREN LNU's house and lift weights.

    Upon completing their weight lifting workout at LOREN LNU's house, BARCON suggested to MILLER that they go fishing.

N000244

Continuation of FD-302 of   MICHAEL GRANT MILLER _____, On __2/20/92__, Page __3__

    MILLER advised BARCON that he did not have any fishing equipment,
and therefore would have to borrow his parent's fishing equipment
in order for them to go.

    MILLER could not be certain if BARCON's suggestion
about fishing was made to MILLER at LOREN LNU's residence or
after departing LOREN LNU's residence, which occurred around
10:00 a.m. or 10:30 a.m.

    While driving around in Mesa, BARCON decided he needed
money for the day and asked MILLER to take him to his credit
union located near Center and 8th Street in Mesa. Thereafter,
BARCON withdrew approximately $75.00 from his account.

    Thereafter, MILLER and BARCON drove in Mesa and picked
up some beer at a convenience store and continued driving around
Mesa. MILLER believes he then told BARCON that he did not want
to go fishing as it was raining, and he did not want to get wet.

    Thereafter, BARCON said to MILLER "That's cool", after
which time MILLER suggested that they go to a bar known as
JARAMILLIOS (phonetic), located near Mesa Drive and Southern in
Mesa.

    MILLER and BARCON remained at this bar for
approximately two hours where they played pool and drank beer.

    During approximately the early afternoon, on this day,
upon departure from JARAMILLIOS (phonetic), MILLER and BARCON
continued driving around Mesa to look for another bar in which to
drink and play pool. MILLER drove west on Southern to Dobson, as
he was thinking about drinking at a bar known as PINKY'S
(phonetic), located at approximately Southern and Mill Avenues,
Mesa. Upon approaching this location, MILLER and BARCON decided
that PINKY'S was a little too expensive and decided to continue
driving around, with no destination in mind.

    Thereafter, MILLER advised he saw a dark, heavy rain
cloud east of them and decided it would be fun to chase this rain
cloud to see if they could get underneath it. BARCON also
thought it would be fun to attempt to chase this rain cloud.

    MILLER advised that although this does sound ridiculous
about chasing the rain cloud, it was the total truth of the

Continuation of FD-302 of __MICHAEL GRANT MILLER_____, On __2/20/92___, Page __4__

reasons why in part they were inspired to drive later to SAGUARO LAKE, located near Fountain Hills, Arizona.

MILLER continued that their driving route took them south on Dobson Road all the way to approximately Guadalupe Avenue or Warner Avenue. Upon reaching one of these streets, MILLER turned left and headed east.

As they continued attempting to follow the rain cloud, and as they approached Arizona Avenue, BARCON asked MILLER if MILLER was taking BARCON home as they were getting fairly close to BARCON's house. MILLER said no, and BARCON acknowledged he was glad, as he did not want to return home at that time.

Eventually, MILLER began driving east on Baseline Avenue heading toward Gilbert Road, which was near the location of where his girlfriend, KATHY BLADES, works at a JACK IN THE BOX.

MILLER thought about stopping at the JACK IN THE BOX to see his girlfriend, but decided against it as he felt she probably would be too busy to visit with him. BLADES has a home telephone number of (602) 497-1646.

As MILLER continued driving east, BARCON asked MILLER if MILLER wanted to go fishing. MILLER replied "No".

Because MILLER noticed that the rain cloud seemed to be moving toward the vicinity of SAGUARO LAKE, and as he knew BARCON wanted to go the lake, he decided to get on the Superstition Highway at the Val Vista entrance and head east to Power Road. MILLER then headed north on Power Road, at which time he believes they stopped at a CIRCLE K, located at Power Road and McKellips in order for BARCON to use the telephone to call his wife, CHRISTINA, who was working that day. MILLER advised that he believes CHRISTINA is employed as a manicurist for a beautician in possibly the Mesa area. MILLER does not recall if he used the phone at that CIRCLE K to call anyone, including his girlfriend, KATHY BLADES.

SA MURPHY asked MILLER if he had placed a call that day from a telephone booth located at Alma School and Warner Roads. MILLER advised that he could not recall making a phone call that day from that location, but believes he has been to the ABCO

Supermarket, located in that vicinity and possibly had used the telephone in the past.

SA MURPHY displayed to MILLER copies of five photographs depicting telephones located at that intersection next to the ABCO Supermarket bearing telephone number (602) 899-6475. Upon examining these photographs, MILLER again advised that he may have in the past used one of these telephones depicted, but does not recall using this telephone on February 13, 1992.

SA MURPHY asked MILLER if he had ever telephoned MARC KAPLAN from this telephone booth or if not, did he know who had done so. Additionally, MILLER was asked if he in any way took part in calling an individual by the name of MARC KAPLAN and giving KAPLAN instructions as to where to find written instructions which KAPLAN had to follow in order to deliver money as noted in the extortion letter mailed to KAPLAN the week before.

MILLER again emphatically denied any involvement or knowledge in any plot to extort from MARC KAPLAN or anyone else.

SA MURPHY played for MILLER a tape of a telephone call received by MARC KAPLAN from telephone number 899-6475, which bore a thumb print belonging to MICHAEL MILLER.

Upon listening to this voice, MILLER advised that was not his voice on the tape and it was not the voice of his friend, BENNETT BARCON. Additionally, MILLER emphasized that he has no idea whose voice it was and had no role in any way of extorting money from MARC KAPLAN.

MILLER stated to the Agent's that he felt he was being set up if his fingerprint was on that telephone and someone was accusing him of being involved in an extortion involving MARC KAPLAN.

SA MURPHY asked MILLER if anyone had recently asked MILLER to make a telephone call or to receive a telephone call at the previously described telephone booth located at Warner and Alma School Roads. MILLER advised that he recalls no one ever advising him to use that particular telephone booth, in order to set him up, by leaving his fingerprints behind.

Continuation of FD-302 of __MICHAEL GRANT MILLER__ , On __2/20/92__ , Page __6__

SA MURPHY displayed to MILLER copies of an envelope addressed to MARC KAPLAN marked "Confidential" as well as three typed letters which provided instructions to KAPLAN as to extortion demands, as well as instructions on where to take the bag of the demanded $250,000 cash, which included a trip to SAGUARO LAKE by KAPLAN during the afternoon of February 13, 1992.

Upon examining these letters, MILLER denied authoring any of these letters and advised not only did he not author such letters, he was not capable of authoring such letters, as he did not have the educational background or the equipment to do so. Additionally, MILLER again emphasized he has no knowledge of anyone authoring such letters and that MILLER's trip to SAGUARO LAKE was purely coincidence and he and BARCON only went to SAGUARO LAKE to drink beer and nothing more.

Upon departure from the previously noted CIRCLE K, located at Power Road and McKellips, MILLER and BARCON went down Usery Pass to Ellsworth, crossed the Salt River and then continued to SAGUARO LAKE.

Neither MILLER nor BARCON went to the lake for any reason other than to b.s. with each other and drink beer. They did not go there to observe anybody, including anyone by the name of MARC KAPLAN. They parked in a parking lot located near the water and MILLER recalls he parked very casually and took up several parking spaces, as he was feeling very relaxed.

MILLER recalls observing an individual fishing in the lake. Approximately 10 minutes after parking near the lake, a red Corvette parked several spaces from them and parked very methodically into the empty parking lot into a space near MILLER and BARCON.

The occupants of this red Corvette were two white males, and after MILLER and BARCON observed them for a few minutes, they suspected these individuals were gay.

Eventually, MILLER went down to the lake to feel how cold the water was. Again, MILLER observed an individual fishing, but observed no unusual happenings and does not recall seeing anyone drive up, get out of his vehicle, and carry a bag or suitcase.

Continuation of FD-302 of ___MICHAEL GRANT MILLER_____ , On __2/20/92__ , Page __7__

Upon MILLER's return to his vehicle, MILLER and BARCON struck up a conversation with the occupants with the red Corvette. The driver of the red Corvette stated he was into real estate sales and was in the business of building custom homes. MILLER advised the driver that he and BARCON also were in the construction business and were framers. The driver then introduced himself as MARK Last name unrecalled by MILLER, and handed MILLER a business card with the name LEES CONSTRUCTION on it. This business card was blue and white and MILLER believes this card since then was taken by him to LOREN's house in Mesa.

MILLER advised that prior to this occasion, he had never before met the occupants of this red Corvette. MILLER advised that he recalls the driver, MARK, making reference to the other occupant of the red Corvette to be from Los Angeles, California.

During this casual conversation, MARK advised MILLER and BARCON that he was into big money and that he eventually was soon to buy a bar in Phoenix known as the GOLD RUSH.

Several minutes later, MARK and his friend left in the red Corvette and MILLER has never heard or seen these individuals again.

MILLER advised the Agents that he is not a co-conspirator in any way to any attempt to extort money from MARC KAPLAN or the KAPLAN family. MILLER has never heard or met the following individuals: MARC KAPLAN, LEE KAPLAN, MARCI KAPLAN, FRANK ALBER, NICHOLAS LEE, MIKE EZELL, GARY HALPERT, and MIRIAM (phonetic) OGLE (phonetic).

MILLER has never worked or visited ESTRELLA PARK, located off of Interstate 10, on the west side of Phoenix.

Concerning topless bars, for the first time in approximately one year, approximately two weeks ago, MILLER, BARCON, and LOREN LNU, went to BABE'S in Scottsdale, Arizona.

MILLER advised that he leads a very simple life and has no reason whatsoever to get involved in an extortion attempt, as he has no urgent need for money for any reason, due to a drug habit, being blackmailed, and so forth.

N000249

Upon MILLER's return to his vehicle, MILLER and BARCON struck up a conversation with the occupants with the red Corvette. The driver of the red Corvette stated he was into real estate sales and was in the business of building custom homes. MILLER advised the driver that he and BARCON also were in the construction business and were framers. The driver then introduced himself as MARK Last name unrecalled by MILLER, and handed MILLER a business card with the name LEES CONSTRUCTION on it. This business card was blue and white and MILLER believes this card since then was taken by him to LOREN's house in Mesa.

MILLER advised that prior to this occasion, he had never before met the occupants of this red Corvette. MILLER advised that he recalls the driver, MARK, making reference to the other occupant of the red Corvette to be from Los Angeles, California.

During this casual conversation, MARK advised MILLER and BARCON that he was into big money and that he eventually was soon to buy a bar in Phoenix known as the GOLD RUSH.

Several minutes later, MARK and his friend left in the red Corvette and MILLER has never heard or seen these individuals again.

MILLER advised the Agents that he is not a co-conspirator in any way to any attempt to extort money from MARC KAPLAN or the KAPLAN family. MILLER has never heard or met the following individuals: MARC KAPLAN, LEE KAPLAN, MARCI KAPLAN, FRANK ALBER, NICHOLAS LEE, MIKE EZELL, GARY HALPERT, and MIRIAM (phonetic) OGLE (phonetic).

MILLER has never worked or visited ESTRELLA PARK, located off of Interstate 10, on the west side of Phoenix.

Concerning topless bars, for the first time in approximately one year, approximately two weeks ago, MILLER, BARCON, and LOREN LNU, went to BABE'S in Scottsdale, Arizona.

MILLER advised that he leads a very simple life and has no reason whatsoever to get involved in an extortion attempt, as he has no urgent need for money for any reason, due to a drug habit, being blackmailed, and so forth.

Continuation of FD-302 of __MICHAEL GRANT MILLER_____, On __2/20/92__, Page __8__

SA MURPHY displayed additional photos to MILLER after which time MILLER identified the following individuals:

1. MARK NELSON (Last name unrecalled by MILLER. This individual was the driver of the red Corvette).

2. JEFF Last name unknown (LNU). This individual was the occupant in the red Corvette driven by MARK.

3. KATHY BLADES (girlfriend of MILLER).

4. BRETT TAYLOR (roommate of MILLER).

MILLER was unable to identify the individuals depicted in photographs of NICHOLAS LEE, FRANK ALBER, LEE KAPLAN, DAWN KAUFMAN, and PENNYE WITUCKI.

MILLER advised that all that he told the Agents was the complete truth and that he is totally willing to take a polygraph to clear his name from the extortion charges being levied against him.

While being fingerprinted by SA ANTHONY E. OLDHAM, SA MURPHY asked MILLER if he took part or had any knowledge of anyone holding up a recording device and playing a recorded voice of instructions to MARC KAPLAN from a telephone booth on February 13, 1992. MILLER again denied having any knowledge or involvement in any manner pertaining to the extortion attempt against MARC KAPLAN, including taking part in or having any knowledge of playing a recorded message from a telephone booth to MARC KAPLAN.

The following descriptive and background information was obtained through interview and observation:

Name	MICHAEL GRANT MILLER
Sex	Male
Race	White
Date of birth	
Place of birth	Mesa, Arizona
Height	5'8"
Weight	180 pounds
Hair	Blond
Eyes	Brown

Continuation of FD-302 of   MICHAEL GRANT MILLER   , On   2/20/92   , Page   9

Age	24 years
Social Security Number	
Occupation	Framer/Carpenter
Current residence	1653 South Harris Drive
	Apartment 2037, Mesa
Telephone number	
Tattoos	Dagger and flower located
	on left back shoulder; skull
	located right side of chest.
Criminal history	Disorderly conduct; sale of
	marijuana; assault, Mesa.

MJ000251

<u>Cathy Blades Interrogation</u>
FBI SPECIAL AGENTS AT LOCATION 2251 E. JEROME AVENUE

Cathy Blades, Interrogation by Special Agents Kenneth J. Williams, James H. Hauswirth, And Linda G. Bateman at FBI Headquarters. Cathy Blades is the girl-friend of Miller. She told FBI she met Miller in 1990, at a river near *Saguaro Lake*. She could not offer any information supporting the FBI. In fact, she said, "Miller was not smart enough to do this crime or any crime."

On the following two pages is Blades interrogation and it went like this...

- 1 -

FEDERAL BUREAU OF INVESTIGATION

Date of transcription   2/28/92

       CATHY LYNN BLADES, date of birth November 21, 1971, was located at 2251 East Jerome Avenue, Mesa, Arizona, where she resides with her parents. BLADES was advised by the interviewing agents that MICHAEL MILLER had just been placed under arrest by the FBI for an extortion violation. She was further advised that the interviewing agents would like to talk to her concerning information about MILLER and his associates. BLADES stated that she would cooperate with the interviewing agents, but preferred to be interviewed at a location other than her parents' home. The interviewing agents agreed and at 2:25 p.m., BLADES, along with the interviewing agents, traveled via Bureau vehicle to JB's Restaurant located at 1809 East Baseline. They arrived at the restaurant at approximately 2:30 p.m. All three individuals proceeded inside the restaurant at which time BLADES provided the following information:

       BLADES advised that she is currently MILLER's girlfriend. They met on May 6, 1990, at the river near Saguaro Lake. During the summer, they usually go up to the river every other weekend.

       Currently, MILLER is employed by ROY REDDING in Scottsdale framing houses. Prior to that job, MILLER worked for LOREN (LNU). The job for LOREN is located in Carefree. BLADES advised that MILLER completed that job but was only paid $50 out of $300 or more. BLADES believes there were only three men on the crew working for LOREN. These people were MILLER, BENNETT BARCON, and LOREN. BLADES stated that MILLER had previously worked with TERRY PETTIJOHN and that PETTIJOHN was the one who told him (MILLER) about LOREN and his work. BLADES added that BENNETT BARCON's wife is CHRISTINA BARCON.

       BLADES then advised that two friends of MILLER are PAT MERTEN and KEVIN DOHERTY. In addition to those friends, MILLER's current roommate is BRET TAYLOR. BLADES stated that TAYLOR currently works with GRAHAM (LNU) in a gold mine. BLADES described GRAHAM as being a white male, 5'7", medium build, older

---

Investigation on   2/20/92   at Mesa, Arizona   File #   9A-PX-46497

    SA JAMES H. HAUSWIRTH and
by   SA LINDA GRAHAM BATEMAN/LGB/jla   Date dictated   2/25/92
                                126

N000257

with children, usually wears cowboy boots and levis. BLADES
added that TAYLOR moved in with MILLER about the end of 1991
toward the early part of December.

BLADES advised that although MILLER is currently
working in the Scottsdale area, he has worked all over in the
greater Phoenix area. MILLER's trade is the house framing
business.

When asked what after work places MILLER might attend,
BLADES stated that MILLER took her to a Mr. B's Deli Shack. She
added that MILLER may go with TAYLOR and DOHERTY to Pinky's.
BLADES advised that that is the only club that she is aware of
MILLER attending. BLADES added that MILLER got sick over the
last weekend and then BLADES became sick. In view of the fact
they were both ill, they stayed at each other's home and watched
videos.

BLADES was then asked to recount last Thursday,
February 13, 1992. BLADES stated that early in the morning
between approximately 6:30 a.m. and 7:00 a.m., MILLER telephoned
BLADES at her residence. MILLER woke up BLADES' twin sister,
CARLA. CARLA and MILLER got in an argument and later BLADES and
MILLER exchanged cross words. The phone call was then
terminated. BLADES stated that on Thursdays, she and her sister
usually attend class at Chandler/Gilbert Community College
(CGCC), but they were not going to attend that day. BLADES does
recall that it was raining very heavily on Thursday,
February 13, 1992. BLADES attempted to telephone MILLER between
7:30 a.m. and 8:30 a.m., but the call was not answered at
MILLER's residence. BLADES then proceeded to go over to MILLER's
residence, but he did not answer the door and she noticed that
MILLER's car was not parked at the apartment complex. BLADES
then proceeded to MILLER's parents' home on Catalina Street to
look for MILLER, but did not locate him there. When BLADES got
to MILLER's parents' house, it was still before 9:00 a.m. BLADES
stated that since she was unable to locate MILLER, she went on to
her 9:00 class at CGCC. BLADES went on to advise that when her
class finished at approximately 10:00 a.m., she met with her
Spanish tutor for the first time. CARLA went with her to her
Spanish tutor where they remained until 11:30 a.m. BLADES
advised that she followed CARLA home since it had been raining
very hard and then went to the bank and then McDonald's

127

Bennett Barcon's Interrogation

Bennett Paul Barcon was interrogated by Special Agents Kenneth J. Williams, (Reporting Special Agent), James H. Hauswirth (Reporting Special Agent), Linda G. Bateman (Reporting Special Agent), and even the Case Special Agent Keith Tolhurst at FBI Headquarters. These are the same Special Agents that interviewed Miller's girlfriend Cathy Blades.

Bennett Paul Barcon was the unknown individual with Miller, at *Saguaro Lake* on February 13, 1992. If you remember Special Agent Allan M. Davison displayed photos of who they suspected was Miller's passenger, Brett Orville Taylor, to the two fisherman at the lake, Robert and his son Bobby Smith on February 18, 1992. This proves that the FBI was not at the lake as they reported in their *Surveillance Log* of February 13, 1992. Additionally, Barcon told these Special Agents that another individual was also at the lake when the Smiths drove up. This now substantiates the fact there were other vehicles at the lake that were omitted from all reports. *Why*?

Barcon admitted to drinking seven to eight beers and Miller to drinking a few more than him. Barcon stated to these Special Agents, that the short - haired individual with Nelson; "initiated the conversation with them." He added that he did not believe that Miller had the education to write an extortion note. This was the same response given about Miller, by everyone of his family and friends.

Barcon's alibi matched Miller's alibi, yet, the FBI still pressed on that Miller was involved. He also stated he did not know anyone involved in this investigation.

Furthermore, to prove conspiracy by preponderance by the FBI Special Agents, this individual was never mentioned to any prior witnesses already interviewed. In fact, the Special Agents advised Barcon that the FBI had information that he was with Miller the day at the lake. You see, Miller was the individual that told the FBI the identity of Barcon and that he was with him at the Saguaro Lake.

That is why Miller's girlfriend Blades, was never told of Barcon's identity, Nelson was never told of Barcon's identity, and the fishermen at the lake, when shown pictures, picked Brett Orville Taylor; not Barcon. Because there were no pictures of him at the lake, because the FBI had not yet arrived at this location. As they previously stated in their Surveillance Log of February 13. Conspiracy? So therefore, If it wasn't for Miller to tell the FBI Special Agents on this day of February 20, about the identity of Barcon, the unknown individual with him at the lake. You probably would be reading about Brett Orville Taylor in this book, instead of Miller.

On this page and the following three pages is Barcon's interrogation and it went like this...

- 1 -

FEDERAL BUREAU OF INVESTIGATION

Date of transcription _____2/27/92_____

BENNETT PAUL BARCON, date of birth January 22, 1968, was interviewed where he resides at 200 East Campbell, Chandler, Arizona. BARCON was advised that his friend, MICHAEL MILLER, had been arrested earlier that day on an extortion charge. BARCON was further advised that the FBI had received information that BARCON was with MILLER on the day the extortion drop was made, February 13, 1992. BARCON was then asked to provide us information concerning his association with MILLER and the events that occurred on February 13, 1992. BARCON agreed and provided the following information:

BARCON stated that he has known MILLER for a very long time. He stated that they both attended Gilbert High School, but neither one of them graduated. BARCON added that he has received his GED. He went on to state that he was currently working with MILLER for LOREN (LNU) at Abe's Construction.

BARCON was then asked by interviewing agents whether or not he could remember the events that occurred last Thursday which was February 13, 1992. BARCON advised that he could not remember. BARCON was then advised that on that date it had rained extremely heavily which was unusual in the Valley. BARCON stated that he did recall that he and MILLER were trying to get money from LOREN. He went on to say that he usually goes over to MILLER's in the morning to lift weights. He believes that MILLER and he went to LOREN's that day and drank beer. BARCON then said after drinking beer they went out to Saguaro Lake. BARCON stated that LOREN lives somewhere in the area of Center and Eighth Streets.

BARCON was then asked why he and MILLER had gone to Saguaro Lake on a rainy day. BARCON stated that it was MILLER's idea to follow a rain cloud out to the lake. BARCON stated that they were at the lake from about noon to 4:00 p.m. that day. He advised that he and MILLER parked a ways down from the marina, between the guard shack and where the road turns around. He advised that when they got to the lake, he saw two fishermen in

---

Investigation on ___2/20/92___ at ___Chandler, Arizona___ File # ___9A-PX-46497___

by ___SA KENNETH J. WILLIAMS, SA JAMES H. HAUSWIRTH___
___and SA LINDA G. BATEMAN/LGB/jla___ Date dictated ___2/25/92___

NJ000253

86

(126)

Continuation of FD-302 of   BENNETT PAUL BARCON _____ . On __2/20/92__ . Page __2__

the area where they parked their car. He stated that while at
the lake, he and MILLER met a framing contractor who was driving
a nice looking Corvette. He stated that this individual had long
hair, pulled back in a ponytail. He stated that this individual
was also with another guy. BARCON went on to state that he and
MILLER talked to the two men in the Corvette for approximately 30
to 40 minutes. He went on to advise that the Corvette took off
from the area after which he and MILLER remained at the lake for
approximately 20 more minutes. BARCON was then advised by
interviewing agents that he and MILLER had both been observed by
FBI Agents at the lake. He was further advised that there had
not been a 20 minutes lapse of time between the Corvette taking
off from the lake and MILLER's car leaving the lake area. BARCON
then stated that, "No, we followed the Corvette to the bridge
where they stayed and MILLER and I went on from that area".

At this point in the interview, BARCON's wife,
CHRISTINA BARCON, appeared at the door of the room in which the
interview was being conducted.

BARCON stated that he believed he and MILLER tried to
call LOREN from MILLER's house before going over to LOREN's. He
stated that the route they would have taken from MILLER's to
LOREN's house would have been south on Harris to Southern to Mesa
to University, and then to Center. He added that he remembered
that he had to pick up his children at 4:30 p.m. on that Thursday
at McKellips and Country Club which was his aunt's house.
CHRISTINA then spoke up and advised that she had had their car
last Thursday, so BARCON could not have driven it over to
MILLER's. BARCON then advised that he goes over almost every
morning to MILLER's, but does not remember if on Thursday,
February 13, 1992, whether MILLER picked him up at his residence
or whether his wife, CHRISTINA, dropped him off at MILLER's
residence.

At this point in the interview, CHRISTINA BARCON left
the room where the interview was taking place.

BARCON stated that basically he remembers that one day
last week (the week prior to this interview) he and MILLER went
to Saguaro Lake in MILLER's car where they met two guys. BARCON
was then shown a color photograph of MARK NELSON and JEFF (LNU).
BARCON positively identified the two individuals as the same two

87

that he and MILLER met at Saguaro Lake on February 13, 1992. He
stated that the short haired individual initiated the
conversation which took place between the four of them. The long
haired guy told MILLER and BARCON that he was building a house
and that his business was located in Scottsdale, Arizona. This
individual then gave MILLER a business card.

BARCON stated that during the course of Thursday,
February 13, 1992, he did not notice MILLER acting any way out of
the ordinary. He does not remember MILLER making a call at any
pay phone during that day. He recalls buying beer at a Circle K
and a Quick Stop. He added that during the course of the day, he
consumed seven to eight beers and also some coolers. He stated
that MILLER had a few more beers than he had consumed.

BARCON was then asked whether or not he knew
individuals by the name of NICK LEES or LEE KAPLAN. BARCON
stated that he did not know either individual. BARCON was then
shown a photograph of LEE KAPLAN and advised that he did not
recognize the individual depicted in the photograph. He was then
shown a photograph of FRANK ALBER after which he advised that he
did not recognize the person depicted in that photograph.

BARCON was then, again, asked if he left the lake area
immediately following the Corvette to which he responded that he
thinks he and MILLER left at least five minutes after the
Corvette left the lake. He stated that he and MILLER proceeded
toward the bridge area where they spotted the Corvette. He
stated that he believes that the people driving the Corvette had
been hanging out at the bridge for awhile looking for girls.

BARCON was asked whether or not he observed anything
unusual or people acting in an unusual manner while at Saguaro
Lake. BARCON stated he did not pay any attention to anyone at
the ramada area near where MILLER's vehicle was parked. He
stated he had noticed an older guy fishing in the lake. He went
on to state that two other guys in a truck pulled up to the area
of the fisherman and started talking to him.

BARCON was asked whether or not any drug transactions
had occurred while they were at the lake to which he stated that
he was not involved in any drug exchange at Saguaro Lake. BARCON

FD-302a (Rev. 11-15-83)

9A-PX-46497

Continuation of FD-302 of ___BENNETT PAUL BARCON_____ . On ___2/20/92___ . Page ___4___

      added that he did not believe that MILLER had the education to
write an extortion note.

         The interview was terminated at this time.

         The photograph of the two individuals who were
positively identified by BARCON as being at Saguaro Lake on
Thursday, February 13, 1992, was dated and initialed by SA LINDA
G. BATEMAN and the photograph has been placed, along with the
original notes of this interview, in an FD-340 and filed in case
9A-PX-46497.

89

Friday, February 21
FBI MAKE ARRESTS

FBI Headquarters
SPECIAL AGENTS PREPARE FOR THE TRANSPORT OF NELSON

12:30 A.M. FBI Case Special Agent Keith D. Tolhurst had a real problem, the investigation was not matching his Criminal Complaint Affidavit. You see, this affidavit was used by the investigating Special Agents who interviewed Miller and Nelson from the time of their arrest to this date. Each of these Special Agents had no reason to question the authenticity of this affidavit. Or the Special Agents who signed their name to the *Surveillance Log* of February 13, 1992. These Special Agents had also taken a sworn oath to uphold the truth and dignity, of the Federal Bureau Of Investigation. Is this more evidence to the Conspiracy Theory?

Mark A. Nelson was escorted by the Case Special Agent Keith Tolhurst and Reporting Special Agent Eugene K. Kaili, to the *Madison Street Jail Annex* in Phoenix, Arizona. Now let's visit the trip to jail from portions of Nelson's diary; the events are documented as this:

Nelson's Diary:
ARRIVAL MADISON STREET JAIL

1:00 A.M. I arrived at the Madison jail, where I was to be held in a holding cell with more guys than this cell could hold, until tomorrow at 8:30 A.M., when I would have pretrial. The last thing I remember was them closing the door on me in jail.

When I got into the "tank" I went right for the phone. I called Nancy and then my father. All of a sudden I noticed this blonde haired guy looking at me and talking to this Mexican guy. He looked at me as if he recognized me, he stood up and walked over to me.

He said, "Hey, they told me I was extorting money from you."

I said, "What the fuck are you talking about? If you were extorting me, why would I be in jail?"

He didn't answer. He then said, "Hey man, you're the guy that drove the red Corvette."

"Yea."

He said, "You gave me your business card."

"Yea!"

He said, "I never saw you before in my life until the day at the lake."

"That's right!"

"Do you even know my name?"

"No."

He said, "he was Miller."

"Great, so you're the one in the picture I saw."

He said, "Yep."

I said, "What did you tell the FBI?"

"I told them I've never seen you before and that you gave me your card, and that you had property and you are going to be buying a night club and that you needed a framer. I told the FBI that I gave your card to my boss. My boss didn't want the business." Miller said.

I asked Miller, "Did you tell the FBI that?"

He said, "I sure did." Then all of a sudden they called me out of the "tank" and put me into another "tank" that was the last time I saw him that night. This was strange, I was getting scared, I just knew that something was wrong, with this whole investigation. I was tired, I tried hard to keep my cool, I hate jail, everyone has to prove they're tough, someone that looks like me, is either going to fight or get fucked!

I remember, when I first walked in jail, and there was this trusty, who told me I was "dead, mother fucker, when you get into general!"

"Fuck You!" I said, "You don't know... a mother fuckin' thing!" I walked away as he mumbled more crap. As I looked up, I saw myself on the news. It was late night news. I knew my life was over and that someone was responsible for this devastation! I will make who did this to me responsible for their actions. I would have to stop, and assure myself no, not the FBI, this is one of the best trained, investigating services in the United States and even quite possible the World. My head was just spinning out of control now as I lay on the cell's floor with no blanket, no pillow, no rights! I wanted and needed to fall asleep so bad, but I couldn't go to sleep. I was scared something would happen, so I would lay on the smelly ground of urine and vomit. It was bad, but I still lay there with my eyes closed oh-so lightly to keep watch for danger...!

Media Blitz
THE ARIZONA REPUBLIC

The Arizona Republic. It was reported that two men were arrested for extortion. This article goes a long way exploiting the guilty, according to the FBI. It tells of using about 100 Special Agents; they brought in technical experts from across the United States. They used some sophisticated electronic equipment during the investigation. It even went so far to say, they lifted the finger prints of one of the suspects, Michael Miller.

This was a very serious crime, what's worse is the chilling fact they arrested the wrong men, 100 percent not involved! Instead, Miller and Nelson were victims of tunnel-visioned FBI Special Agents with overactive imaginations, who pursued false arrest charges and false indictments knowing that the truth and reliable evidence in their possession clearly indicate that Miller and Nelson, did not engage in any criminal activity, as they were charged for at all.

What you, will read in the next few chapters of this book will not only open your eyes, but show you just how out of control some of our employees of the United States Government really are...!

FINAL EDITION

THE ARIZONA REPUBLIC

35¢

ª Copyright 1992, The Arizona Republic

Friday, February 21, 1992   ★★★   Phoenix, Arizona   G   102nd year, No. 279

2 held in kidnap-maiming plot

Ring threatened to cut off boy's arms — more arrests likely

By Randy Collier, Charles Kelly and Eric Miller
The Arizona Republic

The FBI arrested two men Thursday in a bizarre $250,000 extortion scheme that involved a threat to kidnap and chop off the arms of the 12-year-old son of Marc Kaplan, owner of the now-defunct Sun City Rays senior-league baseball team.

The boy was allowed to continue to attend school under the watchful eye of FBI agents after the agency was notified Feb. 8 of the threat. No attempt was made to kidnap him.

It wasn't clear why Kaplan was targeted in the extortion.

Kaplan, a Paradise Valley businessman, owned the Sun City Rays team of the Senior Professional Baseball Association before the league folded in December 1990.

Kaplan was running Health and Nutrition Laboratories of Phoenix, a multiproduct mail-order marketing firm, when it was investigated in 1989 for what some consumers claimed was a misleading diet-plan mail campaign.

The company later agreed to drop the campaign.

The two men arrested Thursday on warrants accusing them of extortion are Mark A. Nelson, 31, of the 6800 block of East Cochise Road, Scottsdale, and Michael Miller, 24, of the 1600 block of South Harris Drive, Mesa, the FBI said.

They were taken in handcuffs to FBI headquarters at 201 E. Indianola about 2:45 p.m. Thursday and were booked into a Maricopa County jail. They will appear before a federal commissioner today.

More arrests are expected, said James Ahearn, special agent in charge of the FBI office in Phoenix.

— See 2 ARRESTED, page A8

2 arrested in extortion plot

— 2 ARRESTED, from page A1

The Arizona Republic learned of the extortion investigation more than a week ago but waited until now to write about it, at the request of Ahearn.

"The FBI is grateful to *The Arizona Republic* for holding off on this story," Ahearn said. "If a story had been written before now, it would have blown the case."

The extortion attempt began Feb. 7, when Kaplan received a detailed four-page letter directing him to get $250,000 and follow a series of instructions to deliver the money to a team of extortionists.

Kaplan was told that if he did not comply with the demand, his son, Brian, would be kidnapped, and his arms would be cut off.

Kaplan reported the threat to the Phoenix Police Department and U.S. postal inspectors, then contacted the FBI the next day.

The FBI assembled a large task force to keep the family under surveillance and to track efforts by the extortionists to collect the money, Ahearn said.

The first letter and a series of notes and phone calls from the extortionists led Kaplan from place to place in Maricopa County, including Saguaro Lake, as he attempted to comply with their directions. FBI agents staked out his movements and the drop point for

FBI agents usher Michael Miller into bureau headquarters in Phoenix. The Mesa resident was arrested Thursday in a $250,000 extortion plot. Mark A. Nelson of Scottsdale also was arrested.

John Samora/The Arizona Republic

the money, which was never picked up.

"We've used about 100 agents on this assignment," Ahearn said. "We brought in technical experts from other bureau offices, and we used some sophisticated electronic equipment during the investigation."

He said teams of agents have been at the Kaplan home since the FBI entered the case. Kaplan's children, Brian and Lauren, 7, were monitored by agents as they attended school. The principal of the school was told of the extortion attempt.

The arrests were made after the

Mesa Police Department lifted Miller's fingerprints from a pay phone used to contact Kaplan, authorities said.

Equipment installed on Kaplan's telephone enabled agents to discover the origin of all calls made to the Kaplan home.

Nelson's Diary
THE UNITED STATES DISTRICT COURT OF ARIZONA

8:30 A.M. Special Agent Baby Sitter and a female Special Agent came and got me. I was tired and stunk real bad, but I made it without showing fear, and did not have to fight in this place. Defend yourself from rape, death or just an ass beating from nothing to lose prisoners!

They took me to the Federal Court. There I was detained in a cell. They brought in Miller and put him in a cell next to me. I couldn't see him, but I could hear him talking about the case with other prisoners. He was telling them he's being framed by the government, and that they've got nothing on him! He went on to say he was at the lake just drinking beer with a friend, and that he just met some dude, at the lake, and he's got a bitch'en Corvette and that, this is all bullshit...!

Then this jailer came and got me and put me into this cell with a probation officer. Her name was Mrs. Stewart she was very attractive, and she smelled so pretty. When that was over they put me back into the "tank." Then the jailer came back and got me to see this lawyer. That's when I met Jeffrey D. Ross. He introduced himself to me then gave me his card. I just read his name, then he started asking questions.

He first said, "I don't know much about the case only what the newspaper said, and what the complaint states."

I said, "Newspaper?"

He said, "Yes, front page." Then he started with the questions, but all I could think of was what did the papers say? Front page even, there goes the knife of destruction on my life!

Mr. Ross asked me to give my version. "We didn't have much time, and don't worry. From what I can see, you've got nothing to worry about, but Jeff Bonadonna is a very important witness."

I gave him the information on Bonadonna, then we had to go to court. I went back to my cell then Special Agent Keith and Special Agent Baby Sitter came and got both myself and Miller. I did not like the way they brought us out together, like we were buddies. I was so fuckin pissed off, but who cared?

They were doing exactly what they wanted and knew by bringing us in together and sitting us next to each other. I came to see why the news media made it look like we were pals. That is bullshit, but what could I do?

Then we went in front of the judge together. I thought, shit, they're really making this look like we're pals, which is furthest from the truth! I have never met Miller until the day at the lake, and the FBI knew it.

I was before the judge the government prosecutors didn't want to release me because I was a threat to the community. Boy, there goes the knife of destruction to my life! The judge asked my dad if he would take third party custody if the court granted so. He said he would not. I remember looking over at my ex-wife, Gina. She came all the way from California to stand up for me. She was sitting next to my ex-girlfriend Dawn, Lea and also Nancy Kirkland, a girl I met on Valentines Day of this year. I could not believe they were all sitting next to each other I knew Gina, Dawn, and Lea all loved me, because they told me so, and we all shared something special. Nancy, I had just met and she seemed to like me too. When the Court took a small break, one of the sheriffs told me he never seen so many girls one man dated to be all in one court room. He said "I must be a neat guy to have all those girls sitting next to each other crying for me." I thought if I was so great why is there no one except the girls in my life sticking up for me? The court resumed and the judge ordered me detained, and pretrial was set for Wednesday, February 26, 1991, at 1:30 P.M.

Then, as I was standing there, I looked behind me and saw Marlene Galan, the brown eyed news caster for Channel 12, she's married to the (Arizona) Attorney General, Grant Wood. I always thought she was pretty when I saw her on the news and I used to tell Richard, "I bet she's prettier in real life." Boy, was that an understatement, her eyes are big and brown. That was the best part of this whole bad dream. I also saw newsman Larry Martel of KPHO channel 5.

Then we were put back in our cells. I was so hurt that this is what my life had finally come to. And the thought that bothered me the most was I'm not guilty. But the way the system is today, I'm guilty until proven innocent. And if nobody believes that then why am I in jail, why am I a threat to the public? No one can answer these questions.

My mind sat with despair and frustration. God, did I hurt inside...

Steven John Giancola's Interrogation
UNDISCLOSED LOCATION

Steven John Giancola was interrogated in a undisclosed location, by Special Agents Melvin O. Cervantes (Field Special Agent), and Charles S. Kuchar (Field Special Agent). Special Agent Kuchar was also present at Michael Miller's interview.

Giancola first befriended Nelson, in August 1991, working on the same job sight for Nick Lees. He described his friend as a wheeler dealer, always trying to make money legitimately.

Giancola informed these Special Agents that Nelson was talking about putting together a business plan to buy a nightclub called "After the Gold Rush", and Nelson had asked him if he would like to manage the club; because of his trustworthiness. It was later learned that Giancola told these Special Agents that he had asked Nelson, where he was getting the 1.5 million dollars to open the club. Nelsons response was he put ads in the classified sections of the "*Chicago Tribune*" and the "*New York Times*" for investors. This information was not quite written that way. This was the same information Nelson gave to the Special Agents conducting his interrogation. But that fact was omitted from Nelson's report. Why?

Giancola reportedly told the FBI about Brian Holt, this was the individual that Nelson went to California to visit and look at the boat and receive a payment of three hundred dollars for touch-up painting on his house. This information was also *omitted* from Nelson's report filed by the interviewing Special Agents Douglas E. Hopins (Reporting Special Agent), John E. Hamilton (Reporting Special Agent), and Eugene K. Kalili (Reporting Special Agent). As of February 21, 1991, Nelson was painting the home of Zoe, Doug Cameron's wife. Cameron's were the individuals Nelson was painting their $900,000.00 home, when the FBI kicked opened the gate and arrested Nelson while they (Camerons) were eating brunch. Giancola also saw an unknown individual, (Bonadonna) that was with Nelson observing the job sight. However, this individual was never observed doing any work on this job site.

Giancola explained to these Special Agents that he believed that during the week of February 9-15, 1992, Nelson was having a feud with his girlfriend before Nelson left to Los Angles on February 7, 1992, This is not how these FBI Special Agents reported their interviews. They're all written in a paraphrased manner to implicate two innocent men. The fact that Nelson told the FBI that he and Bonadonna were going to paint but could not is because it was raining; this is more proof to substantiate the Conspiracy Theory that Nelson was telling the truth! How could Nelson and Bonadonna paint at this job site when it been raining and was scheduled to rain more that late afternoon and evening...? On the following two pages is Giancola's interrogation and it went like this:

- 1 -

FEDERAL BUREAU OF INVESTIGATION

Date of transcription   2/24/92

        STEVEN JOHN GIANCOLA, born August 18, 1958, Social
Security Account Number (SSAN)
                         was advised of the identities of the
interviewing agents as well as the purpose of the interview. He
thereafter furnished the following information:

        GIANCOLA is a licensed contractor doing business as
VINTAGE DOOR & TRIM. He is currently doing subcontract work for
NICHOLAS LEES CUSTOM DEVELOPMENT.

        GIANCOLA first befriended MARK NELSON in approximately
August, 1991, as he was working on the same job site and
eventually on job sites which were next to each other. He
described MARK NELSON as an individual who is a wheeler-dealer
who is always trying to find new ways of making money and and who
has recently placed ads in the "Chicago Tribune" and "New York
Times" newspapers for investors in "After the Gold Rush" bar
located on the river bottom around McClintock and Hayden in
Tempe, Arizona. MARK NELSON was trying to buy this bar and at
various times suggested that GIANCOLA could manage this bar as
NELSON felt GIANCOLA was trustworthy. The purchase price for
this particular bar was $1.5 million.

        MARK NELSON had befriended a BRIAN HOLDT whose house
was built by NICHOLAS LEES CUSTOM DEVELOPMENT and subsequently
painted by MARK NELSON. BRIAN HOLDT apparently would be a
primary investor in this bar.

        MARK NELSON always mentioned legitimate ways of making
money including painting, selling custom lot job sites as he
would earn monies for bringing new customers to NICHOLAS LEES
CUSTOM DEVELOPMENT, and obtaining investors for different
money-making ideas.

        MARK NELSON had purchased a brand new red Corvette
claiming to have put no money down as he had a friend in either
the car or finance business which enabled him to qualify for this

---

Investigation on   2/21/92   at Mesa, Arizona   File # PX 91A-PX-46497

     SA CHARLES S. KUCHAR and
by   SA MELVIN O. CERVANTES   MOC:dpt   Date dictated   2/24/92
                               140

Continuation of FD-302 of   STEVEN JOHN GIANCOLA   , On   2/21/92   ., Page   2

vehicle. As of February 21, 1991, MARK NELSON was painting the
home of a ZOE and was seen with a second individual on two
different days driving his Corvette looking at the job site.
GIANCOLA could not name this second individual, however, was able
to identify a picture of this unknown individual.

MARK NELSON never mentioned drugs at all and never used
drugs in GIANCOLA's presence. NELSON usually dated dancers who
made easy money and "put him up."

During the week of February 9 through 15, 1992, MARCUS
NELSON was acting strange; however, GIANCOLA believed this was as
a result of NELSON having a feud with his girlfriend.

NELSON does not have many friends. The unknown
individual seen with NELSON observing the job site was the first
male friend GIANCOLA ever saw with NELSON. However, this
individual was never observed doing any work on this job site.

141

Lorenzo Gomez' Interrogation
AT A UNDISCLOSED LOCATION

The interesting part of this individuals interview is the fact that Miller's boss; no relation to Marc Kaplan's maid. Not only told the same story that Miller did. He also mentioned to the Special Agents during his interview that Miller arrived at his home around 4:00 P.M. from the lake.

This evidence means, we know Miller made a couple of stops. But his estimated time of departure at about 3:15 P.M. Right after the red Corvette departed, and definitely before the FBI Special Agents and Kaplan's Arrival...

```
                              - 1 -
                 FEDERAL BUREAU OF INVESTIGATION


                                   Date of transcription   2/24/92


         LORENZO ARTHUR GOMEZ, date of birth (DOB) December 15,
    1961, residing at 36 West 8th Street, Mesa, Arizona, telephone
    number (602) 461-8357, provided the following information:

         GOMEZ advised he has known MICHAEL MILLER and BENNETT
    BARCON for approximately one month.  GOMEZ said both men work for
    him as framers in the building of new homes.  GOMEZ said he is a
    sub-contractor for ABE'S CONSTRUCTION, telephone (602) 237-3121
    and that HERB LAST NAME UNKNOWN (LNU) is his contact at ABE'S.

         GOMEZ recalled certain events that occurred on
    Thursday, February 13, 1992, a day that he didn't work because of
    rain.  GOMEZ believed that BENNETT BARCON may have called him
    prior to coming to his (GOMEZ) home in Mesa around 9:00 A.M.
    GOMEZ said he owed BARCON and MILLER some money and that they
    wanted to collect from him.  GOMEZ said he hadn't received any
    money for a certain job from ABE'S CONSTRUCTION so he couldn't
    pay MILLER and BARCON.  GOMEZ estimated that MILLER and BARCON
    remained at his home from 9:00 A.M. to 9:30 A.M. before
    departing.  GOMEZ stated they all lifted weights during this one-
    half hour period.  GOMEZ stated MILLER and BARCON made no mention
    of their plans for the rest of the day from his recollection.

         GOMEZ said around 4:00 P.M. on February 13, 1992,
    MILLER and BARCON returned to his home, staying for about one-
    half hour.  GOMEZ said the two men had been drinking and they
    mentioned they had been to the "lake".  GOMEZ assumed they meant
    SAGUARO LAKE as it is the closest lake.  GOMEZ said MICHAEL
    MILLER had mentioned he and BARCON met two gay males who
    allegedly were contractors while at the lake.  GOMEZ said MILLER
    told him one of the two men at the lake showed him and BARCON a
    photo of an expensive home in Scottsdale they had built.  GOMEZ
    said he wasn't sure why MILLER and BARCON stopped by his home in
    the afternoon, nor did he have any idea where they went upon
    departing.


    _____

    Investigation on  2/21/92      at Mesa, Arizona       File #  9A-PX-46497

    by   SA JAMES H. HAUSWIRTH:bbb          Date dictated  2/24/92      N000268
                                      124                        36
    This document contains neither recommendations nor conclusions of the FBI. It is the property of the FBI and is loaned to your agency;
```

Continuation of FD-302 of   LORENZO ARTHUR GOMEZ   , On   2/21/92   ; Page   2

     GOMEZ said BENNETT BARCON called him earlier on this
date advising MICHAEL MILLER and another man had been arrested
for extortion. GOMEZ said he wasn't sure what extortion was, but
that it must be a serious offense as BARCON said MILLER was in a
"lot of trouble". GOMEZ said MILLER has a big mouth, but doubted
that he would carry out any threats such as were made to the
victim of the extortion.

     GOMEZ said he owes MILLER and BARCON less than $400.00
for their services, and that he had no reason to believe they
were planning any type of criminal activity from their comments
or demeanor on February 13, 1992.

     GOMEZ said he is not aware of any drug trafficking
being carried out by either MILLER or BARCON, but that both of
the men have smoked marijuana in his presence after work in the
past month.

     GOMEZ identified a photograph of MICHAEL GRANT MILLER,
DOB August 30, 1967 as the MICHAEL MILLER who has worked for him
the past month. GOMEZ also identified a photograph of
CATHY L. BLADES as being MILLER's girlfriend. GOMEZ viewed
photographs of MARK ANDREW NELSON, DOB July 12, 1960, FRANK
ALBER, LEE KAPLAN, BRETT TAYLOR and NELSON LEE advising he is not
acquainted with any of those individuals.

/25

Miller's Resident: Second Search
BY THE FBI

The FBI Special Agents' wanted badly for Miller to be involved with this crime. The FBI asked if they could search his apartment. During his interrogation it's believed the FBI said, "if you did not do any thing wrong, then you wouldn't mind us searching your home." Miller authorized a search of his home. The FBI Special Agents had him sign Consent to Search form. As these Special Agents searched, they gathered as much information they believed linked Miller to this crime, but to no avail. All evidence seised did not link Miller to any suspects or to this crime, whatsoever!

- 1 -

FEDERAL BUREAU OF INVESTIGATION

Date of transcription _____3/3/92_____

On February 21, 1992, at approximately 12:30 p.m., the residence of MICHAEL GRANT MILLER, 1653 South Harris, Apartment #2037, Mesa, Arizona, was searched for evidence relating to an extortion investigation. Prior to the search, MILLER signed an FD-26 (Consent to Search) authorizing a search of his apartment. Present during the search were Special Agents (SAs) of the Federal Bureau of Investigation (FBI) ROBERT W. CALDWELL, IV, and MIRELLA NAVA.

RENEE COOK, Apartment Manager, Trails East Apartments, 1653 South Harris, Mesa, Arizona, released to SA CALDWELL a copy of MILLER's apartment contract. Prior to initiating the search of MILLER's apartment, SA CALDWELL observed trash was spread all over the floor of the apartment and a black cat was digging in the trash in the kitchen.

Found in MILLER's living room was a gray 1991 daily planner. Within the daily planner, the following names and phone numbers were listed:

TYLER, 229-3600 and 752-2167

J. W., 482-3715

JEFF, 497-6075

PAT, 827-0972

TIFFANY, 275-3095

BIG MILL B.R., 926-8829

NATE, 389-7881

PAT, 389-1969

MATT, 649-3904

Investigation on __2/21/92__ at __Mesa, Arizona__ File # __9A-PX-46497__

SA MIRELLA NAVA and
by __SA ROBERT W. CALDWELL, IV/RWC/jla__ Date dictated __2/26/92__ N000263

96

68

This document contains neither recommendations nor conclusions of the FBI. It is the property of the FBI and is loaned to your agency; it and its contents are not to be distributed outside your agency.

Continuation of FD-302 of ___RESIDENCE OF MILLER_____, On __2/21/92__ , Page __2__

TIFFANY, 801/266-0560

DAN, 396-4219

WADE, 969-7704

HICKEY, 839-1344 and 450-2902

BLOTTO, 921-3011

BRIAN, 649-0117 and 238-5241

A.M., 545-7135

A.B., 890-2632 and 969-9028

TOMMY, 943-2426

MICHELLE HOWLEY, 4536 North 105th Avenue, Phoenix, Arizona, work 978-8669, home 877-8560

VICTOR JOHNSON, 483-6353

RICKY, 496-6832

BAKERSFIELD, 805/331-9850

EXPRESSIONS, 213/854-6655

MON, 678-7545

TY, 678-7897

ANTHONY, 503/686-8436

MICHELLE, 213/384-9098

JEFF STUMP, 242-5963

WILLIE FORD, 801/292-4433 and 298-4432

CHARLIE, 978-2197

97

MARK, 892-2656

KENT, 940-1414

DAVE KOSH, 963-9081

BREWNERS, 619/352-6431

TRENT, 801/298-3575

Also found within the daily planner was a book of
checks with the following address: BRETT TAYLOR, 8250 South
Hardy Drive, #3052, Tempe, Arizona. The daily planner was not
seized as evidence due to a discrepancy as to who owned the daily
planner. Within the daily planner, nothing was recorded on any
of the dates. Next to the daily planner was a letter from Public
Storage, 1964 East University Drive, Tempe, Arizona, telephone
number 602/966-9071. The letter was in reference to a delinquent
rental payment on Space #G-660 and the letter was addressed to
BRETT TAYLOR. The letter was not seized as evidence.

On the coffee table in the living room, a brown leather
wallet was found containing a drivers license of MICHAEL GRANT
MILLER. Also in the wallet a Price Savers card was observed
with bar code number 41400086440. The Price Savers card had the
names CAROLYN MILLER, DON MILLER, Pioneer Builder, printed on it.
The resale number on the card was 07-331289-T and the card was
dated September 19, 1992.

The following items were seized as evidence by SA
CALDWELL:

Item Description	Location of Item
One piece of small paper with Palo Verde printed on it along with a telephone number	On TV stand in living room
One Candy Land Bar advertisement	On TV stand in living room

98

4000265

Continuation of FD-302 of RESIDENCE OF MILLER   , On   2/21/92   . Page   4

One piece of notebook paper with names and telephone numbers written on it	On TV stand in living room
One piece of notebook paper with names and telephone number	In kitchen drawer
One notebook with cover torn off	In kitchen dining room
One torn out page from address book	In kitchen drawer
One red address book	In bedroom
One small possible marijuana plant	In bedroom window sill
One small plastic bag with a white powder inside	In small metal box sitting on top of dresser in bedroom

The residence was unoccupied during the search. The interior of the residence consisted of a living room, dining room, kitchen, one bedroom and one bathroom. The bedroom had one large closet and the hallway in the apartment also contained a storage closet. A copy of the property receipt listing the items seized was left in plain view in the residence.

The search of the apartment was concluded at approximately 2:30 p.m. The above seized items were appropriately marked and placed into evidence facilities at the Phoenix Office of the FBI.

99

Miller's Car Searched

At approximately 2:30 P.M., FBI Special Agents by Miller's permission, also searched his Mercury. It took only a half hour to complete and the FBI confiscated a circular saw, a row of nails bound together, and a sample of nails found in the trunk.

These Special Agents believed these items were used to build the box the $250,000 was to be placed in at Estrella Park. Once again all three pieces of evidence gathered proved to be worthless and therefore could not be used to link Miller to this case. It did, however, prove he was a carpenter!

```
                              -1-

              FEDERAL BUREAU OF INVESTIGATION


                                    Date of transcription   3/3/92


          On February 21, 1992, at approximately 2:30 p.m., the
     vehicle of MICHAEL GRANT MILLER, a 1982 Mercury, Arizona license
     plate AWS-096, was searched for evidence relating to an extortion
     investigation.  Prior to the search, MILLER signed an FD-26
     (Consent to Search) authorizing a search of his vehicle.  Present
     during the search of the vehicle were Special Agents (SAs) of the
     Federal Bureau of Investigation (FBI) ROBERT W. CALDWELL, IV, and
     MIRELLA NAVA.

          MILLER's vehicle was parked in front of his residence
     at 1653 South Harris, Apartment #2037, Mesa, Arizona.  Taken
     during the search were the following items which were found in
     the trunk:

          1.  A circular saw, silver in color.

          2.  One row of nails bound together.

          3.  A sample of assorted nails found in the trunk.

          The search of the vehicle concluded at approximately
     3:00 p.m.   A receipt for the items taken from the vehicle was
     placed in MILLER's residence, 1653 South Harris, Apartment #2037,
     Mesa, Arizona.  These items of evidence have been placed in
     evidence storage at the Phoenix Office of the FBI.


Investigation on  2/21/92        at Mesa, Arizona        File #  9A-PX-46497

     SA MIRELLA NAVA and
by   SA ROBERT W. CALDWELL, IV/RWC/jla        Date dictated  2/28/92    N000267
This document contains neither recommendations nor conclusions of the FBI. It is the property of the FBI and is loaned to your agency;
it and its contents are not to be distributed outside your agency.
```

Nelson's Diary:

ARRIVAL MADISON STREET JAIL

12:00 P.M. I was taken back to the Madison Jail. As we were leaving (the Federal Building) they opened the doors and there was the media, like a bunch of rabid infested wolves that haven't eaten in days. Their cameras, like huge eyes, let the world see an innocent man's life crumble before his own eyes!

I just put my head down with shame, knowing that the knife of destruction had struck again. My stomach was bubbling with acids that I would throw up and have to swallow. It tasted bad and my teeth felt gritty. I needed my medication but still no one cared. As we got back to Madison, I was led back to my cell with Miller. They were going to put us together. I told Officer Lombardo that he wasn't going to put me in the cell with "Fuckhead." Lombardo looked at me, then looked at Miller. Then Miller looked back at me. I looked at Miller and said, "Yes, Fuckhead, they're not putting me in the same cell with you! Got it!" Lombardo said, "Okay" and put us into separate cells.

The cell I was in everyone knew who I was, they saw me on the news. Then this black guy started fucking with me. I told him to, "Fuck off, and get out of my face!" He was looking at his bros for back up. No one would say anything. I felt good but still worried. Finally, Lombardo came back with his sergeant because this same black guy was giving him trouble, too. I didn't hear what the Sergeant said, but it didn't matter he still had a problem.

I walked up to talk to Lombardo to see if I could use the phone, to call my lawyer it was about 1:30 P.M. When I walked up, " I bumped into the black guy by accident. He turned around and said, "Hey..., Mother, Fucker!" Watch who you're bum-pin!"

"Fuck off!" I said. This statement was made to step down from the confrontation. It's a respect thing!

Meanwhile, Lombardo opened the cell and let me out to use the phone. He was so cool to me, he made me feel he really cared! That might sound funny, but having any enemies in a place like this, could be fatal! I went to his desk and he signed me in. He told me that he had long hair before he went into the service.

I said, "Really?" Then one of his buddies, also a corrections officer, said, "Really? You had long hair?"

He said, "Yeah." His buddy looked like James Dean. What was funny, his name was J. Dean

Lombardo said, "Yea, he does look like James Dean." Then Dean left. Before he left he looked at me and said, "I would be in the movies but never got there, Good luck." I thought he was cool.

Then another buddy of Lombardo's was talking to me. He was getting ready to escort prisoners somewhere. He was chewing tobacco. I told him my grandfather-in-law died of cancer, and that they removed part of his jaw, then it spread into his body. It was sad for me to watch my wife and her family go through such sorrow, watching a loved one slowly die before their eyes... I felt helpless! He was the best!"

I told the guard, he really could get cancer!

He said, "Really?" Then he spit into a garbage can. "Thanks, I'm going to quit." Then he left.

Lombardo was talking to me about his life, that he was single, that when he gets off this job he goes to a second job as a waiter at *Perishing* restaurant. He told me he makes more money waiting on tables than he does being a jail guard.

I said, "That's good then."

"I'll put you in another cell so that black guy won't bother you." Lombardo said.

"Yeah, he was trying to pick a fight," I told him.

He said, "That would be a bad mistake on his part. We would fuck him up, and he wouldn't like where we would put him!"

Then he walked me to my cell. I said to him, "my ex-wife's grandpa; my grandpa in-law, also happened to be a Lombardo, too."

He turned to me before we arrived at my holding tank, he opened the door and said. "That's wired man, I heard you telling Dean. I'm sorry to hear he passed away, and hey, don't worry! Everything will be Okay. You'll get off. I heard they arrested the wrong guys, just hang in there. I'm going to tell the guy that relieves me not to put you in with Miller or the black guy."

I said, "Thanks." I stepped inside the cell, a few minutes later they called my name. I was getting 'rated' or something. I met this lady in this very small office cell, she was nice. She told me, "Don't worry. Everything will work out, I heard that this is a bizarre case!"

I thought, shit, everyone seems to think I'm innocent. I started to feel good again. She also said, "I should be in protective custody due to the crime against a child!"

"Crime against a child?" I said.

She explained to me that certain prisoners, don't care if you're guilty or not, they would try to hurt me badly. I took the protective custody, thinking to myself, "If I get into a fight, I will defend myself till-death!" I was on total alert now, knowing someone is going to hurt me bad!

As she finished she said, "Don't worry. I'll have them put you in protective custody now, since you're already getting into problems with the inmates."

"It's not me causing problems, I just won't bow-down!" I told her.

"Good luck, Mr. Nelson," she said. When she said that, I felt good. I was getting sicker, But I could not show pain or weakness.

They put me into this little cell next to the officers' desk (Lombardo's). After a while, this lady sergeant was sitting at the desk of the guy who took Lombardo's watch, I heard them talking.

She said, "He's got hair better than me and most women."

He said, "That's Mark Nelson." She looked at me and they started talking about my case. I tapped on the window. They both looked at me. I said, "I'm innocent."

The man said, "What?"

"I'm innocent," I repeated.

"What?" He came over and opened up my cell door and said, "We couldn't hear you."

"I'm innocent." I said.

He replied, "Hey, we weren't talking about you. We're just discussing your case."

"Well, I'm innocent," I said.

He replied, "Hey, don't worry. Before I even read the paper I came to work and heard you're innocent. So don't worry, everything will be all right. Then the female guard said, "you have nice hair, be careful in here!"

A little while later they came and got me to take me to my cell. As I was leaving, the officer at the desk with the female officer opened my cell door to let them strip search and then I was issued a bed blanket and one towel.

I was walking to my cell I had to wait. There was a guy mopping the floor. He asked me what I was in for.

"I'm innocent!"

He said, "That's what they all say."

I said, "But I really am."

"They all say that too!"

He then told me, "Hey, let me give you some advice. Don't tell anyone why you're here. If someone asks, you don't know. Don't talk to any one. There are a lot of bad people in here that will turn you in just to get a reduced sentence. I saw you on the news. Your a marked guy, make sure you stay out of the general population! Be careful and Good luck! If you're innocent don't worry, and stick to the truth."

I was brought to 64 B-8, that was my new living area. This, is where I was to spend my 23 hours a day, locked in a white cell with white light, with 1 hour to get out and watch TV or shower. I go to pretrial on February 26, 1992, seven days from now.

What the fuck, am I, going to do now? Can I go to jail for something I know nothing about? My mind was spinning. I was so tired, my eyes so dry from not allowing myself to cry. Was the fear of showing weakness through those tears worth hiding the mental pain of trying to compose physical strength?

So I sat in my cell. It was 2:30 A.M. As I lay about my bed, the cell very bright, my eyes teared like a baby. I prayed to my God for help and thought about my poor little animals, my best friends! Good Night...

Miller's Car Searched

At approximately 2:30 P.M., FBI Special Agents by Miller's permission, also searched his Mercury. It took only a half hour to complete and the FBI confiscated a circular saw, a row of nails bound together, and a sample of nails found in the trunk.

These Special Agents believed these items were used to build the box the $250,000 was to be placed in at Estrella Park. Once again all three pieces of evidence gathered proved to be worthless and therefore could not be used to link Miller to this case. It did, however, prove he was a carpenter!

-1-

FEDERAL BUREAU OF INVESTIGATION

Date of transcription   3/3/92

On February 21, 1992, at approximately 2:30 p.m., the vehicle of MICHAEL GRANT MILLER, a 1982 Mercury, Arizona license plate AWS-096, was searched for evidence relating to an extortion investigation. Prior to the search, MILLER signed an FD-26 (Consent to Search) authorizing a search of his vehicle. Present during the search of the vehicle were Special Agents (SAs) of the Federal Bureau of Investigation (FBI) ROBERT W. CALDWELL, IV, and MIRELLA NAVA.

MILLER's vehicle was parked in front of his residence at 1653 South Harris, Apartment #2037, Mesa, Arizona. Taken during the search were the following items which were found in the trunk:

1. A circular saw, silver in color.

2. One row of nails bound together.

3. A sample of assorted nails found in the trunk.

The search of the vehicle concluded at approximately 3:00 p.m. A receipt for the items taken from the vehicle was placed in MILLER's residence, 1653 South Harris, Apartment #2037, Mesa, Arizona. These items of evidence have been placed in evidence storage at the Phoenix Office of the FBI.

Investigation on   2/21/92   at Mesa, Arizona   File #   9A-PX-46497

         SA MIRELLA NAVA and
by   SA ROBERT W. CALDWELL, IV/RWC/jla   Date dictated 2/28/92
                                            /oo   (74)   N000267
This document contains neither recommendations nor conclusions of the FBI. It is the property of the FBI and is loaned to your agency:
it and its contents are not to be distributed outside your agency.

Saturday, February 22
MEDIA FRENZY OF THE INDICTMENTS

Early Edition

THE ARIZONA REPUBLIC

Web of directions helped to snare extortion suspects

Businessman aided FBI's plan

**Randy Collier
and Charles Kelly**
The Arizona Republic

Extortionists threatening to cut a limb off a Paradise Valley businessman's son forced the man to follow a complex series of directions and to bury $250,000 in a suitcase, according to a federal affidavit released Friday.

As Marc Kaplan was led from place to place around Maricopa County on Feb. 13, FBI agents kept him under watch and identified suspects in the case, the affidavit says.

The affidavit was released Friday in connection with the initial appearance of two men arrested on one count each of using the mail to extort money.

Appearing before U.S. Magistrate Morton Sitver were Michael Grant Miller, 24, of the 1600 block of South Harris Drive, Mesa, and Mark Andrew Nelson, 31, of the 6800 block of East Cochise Road, Scottsdale.

A preliminary hearing for both men is scheduled for 1:30 p.m. Wednesday before Sitver.

James Ahearn, special agent in charge of the Phoenix FBI office, said more arrests are expected.

The affidavit gave this account of events:

On Feb. 7, Kaplan, who owns Health and Nutrition Laboratories, 4545 E. Shea Blvd., got a letter that had been written on a computer and postmarked in Phoenix the day before.

The letter demanded that Kaplan pay $250,000 in one week or his 12-year-old son's arm or leg would be removed.

The letter told Kaplan that he would receive further instructions in a phone call at 2 p.m. Feb. 13 at his office.

Kaplan notified the FBI, and agents got court orders to install tracing devices on his business phones.

Kaplan got a call from one of the extortionists at 2:17 p.m. Feb. 13, and was told to go immediately to a closed Security Pacific Bank branch at Tatum and Shea boulevards, where, on a pole, he would find a note with further instructions.

FBI agents traced the call to a pay telephone at a supermarket in Chandler. A fingerprint taken from the phone by Mesa police later was matched to Miller.

Kaplan went to the bank and found a note telling him to go to Saguaro Lake Boat Ramp No. 2 for further instructions. Before he arrived, FBI agents monitoring his movements spotted cars owned by Miller and Nelson near the ramp.

Nelson and Miller were among four males seen near the cars, Nelson holding a mobile cellular telephone.

At a picnic area near the ramp, Kaplan found a suitcase and another note. In summary, the note said, "You are being watched. Take your shirt off and turn around slowly."

The note also told Kaplan to put the $250,000 in the suitcase and drive to the mostly vacant Estrella development 20 miles west of Phoenix, then bury it at a certain spot.

After the lake, Kaplan stopped at the McDonald's restaurant at Arizona 87 and Shea Boulevard. Nelson's car arrived shortly thereafter, and a passenger who got out of the car appeared to be observing Kaplan. As an FBI agent approached Kaplan's car, the passenger returned to Nelson's car, which left immediately and drove to the apartment complex on Shea Boulevard where Nelson lives.

Kaplan drove to Estrella and buried the suitcase as directed, but the money never was picked up.

Nelson's Diary:
MADISON STREET JAIL

8:00 A.M. I just woke up. They let me out of my cell or pod for one hour. It was 8:00 A.M. I went and called Nancy, my father, and Richard Sollami. They were all worried. They told me I was on the news, every station ABC, CBS, NBC, even KPHO and all the newspapers, *The Arizona Republic*, *Phoenix Gazette*, *Scottsdale Progress*, and *Tempe Tribune* even some national newspapers. I was devastated all over again. My father said, I'll come and visit you." I really could see you! I told him. He said "No problem." I remember thinking, that he might have changed and I hope so. My hour was up and I had to go to my cell. It (the hour) went by too fast. My stomach started to bubble again but I had a toilet to throw up in. I don't think I could have taken another swallow of that acid-bile shit.

4:00 P.M. My father came and visited me around. He said, "I needed a haircut and he read in the newspaper today that Kaplan was at the *McDonalds* and shortly thereafter your Corvette arrived, and the passenger then got out of your car and was looking at Kaplan. That's when an FBI Special Agent approached Kaplan and your passenger got back in your car and immediately left the area to your apartment. "That knife of destruction stabbed me again. I was so pissed. My father said, "Don't worry, your attorney said you have nothing to worry about."

"Tell that to the newspapers." I said. Then the officer came and told my father my visiting right don't start until six o'clock. So he had to leave. I almost got into another fight with an inmate. A he, who thought he was a she, did not want me to eat at the same table as the rest of the freaks. She told me that I did not ask for permission to sit at her table. This was a very big dude, and he was a transvestite prostitute, this individual was 6'4" and about 300 pounds. I did not care how big this person was. I did call it dude a couple of times. That's when it got bad, I told him he was an asshole, and if he did not stop bothering me. I would kick him in the balls so hard, they will come out of his mouth. The rest of the freaks all started to laugh, and he stormed off just like a girl. I have to go...

An Accomplice: Rick Fair Comes Forward
CALLS FBI HEADQUARTERS AND SPEAKS TO SPECIAL AGENT KEITH D. TOLHURST

A man came forward early morning. His name is *Richard Fair*, (*Rick Fair*) He called the FBI and informed them he had information pertaining to this extortion case. This phone call was immediately transferred to Case Special Agent Keith Tolhurst. *Fair* said to Case Special Agent Tolhurst "the FBI arrested the wrong men and he knew who really made the phone call to Marc Kaplan's office, from the *ABCO Supermarket* in Chandler, Arizona. And that this call was made at about 2:15 P.M." He went on to implicate *Frank Alber* as the individual, along with himself that made the actual phone call."

It was reported that *Fair* told his story to an unbelieving Special Agent Tolhurst whom asked him again, are you sure of the information you are telling me is true and correct. *Fair* again said to Case Special Agent Tolhurst "the individuals you arrested and accused of making the phone call, was not at the *ABCO*, when the call was made and did not know either of these two individual you arrested, period." *Fair* also mentioned he could lead them Frank Alber, who made him make the call for him, because he was standing right next to him."

Tolhurst asked, "Who is this man you are referring too and how did you know about the arrest?"

Fair said, "I saw it on all the TV news stations and the individual you really want is *Frank Alber.*" *Fair,* assured he would help the FBI in their investigation but he wanted protection, and did not want to go to jail.

Case Special Agent Tolhurst asked *Fair*, if he would come forward to the FBI headquarters to help implicate his friend, *Frank Alber*. Tolhurst told *Fair,* to show up Sunday 23, 1992 and he would do what he could to keep him from jail, and the Media.

Nelson's Diary:
MADISON STREET JAIL

6:00 P.M. I received visitors. It was Dawn and Lea. I really didn't feel so hot but I went down anyway. They told me that everyone couldn't believe what's happening. Lea said, "Richard doesn't want you to call any more because the neighbors keep talking." They won't let Lacie, play with any of her friends and some of Richard's friends called and said, "You'd better stay away from him. The FBI will drag you in too." Lea was in tears. I said, "Don't worry Lea. This is just the beginning for me. A lot of people aren't going to want me around even if I'm found innocent. So tell Richard, I'll never call him again and that I'll pay him his forty - seven dollars, and he can fuck off!" She started crying.

Even Dawn told me some of her friends told her to stay away from me because I must be 'bad news' because the FBI and the newspapers said so.

I was so hurt. I felt that fucking knife again, but this time it went through my heart and hit my soul. I felt a burning sensation I have never felt before in my life. It felt as if something inside died... But I don't know what. I just knew that this was just the beginning for me! An officer took me back to my cell. As I walked through the halls I felt cold and lonely. I was bleeding on the inside. This was the first time I wanted to kill myself, and also trying to figure out how!

I walked through the halls they seemed so long. I could hear nothing, but the echo of my thoughts in my mind. I couldn't wait to get back to my cell. I thought I was going to pass out. I was throwing up and swallowing faster than I could breath. But I could not let anyone see my face or tears, for fear that the other inmates might think I'm weak and can be toyed with, and walked on like a spineless creature that has no backbone. I called upon God in my mind and asked for strength! I can't let these evil doers have their way with my mind body and soul. I made it to my cell but my stomach burst into pain and I threw up. Then an officer came to my cell and asked if I was "Okay."

I said, "I need my Zantac and Valium #10."

"He would see what he could do." he said, Then as I was laying on my bed crying because my stomach was in such pain, I felt I was going to have an anxiety attack. The guard came back and opened my cell and said, "Here, I can give you Malox." He poured it into a glass. Then he asked me if I wanted to talk. Which I could barely talk. I told him what my father told me about the news stations and being exploited in all the newspapers! I also told him, "I'm innocent."

He said, "that it takes a lot more than what they've got on you to convict you. So just hang in there. Everything will be "Okay." He really helped me. I don't know if he knows it or not, but it helped me. I need to sleep now...

Sunday, February 23

Rick Fair Signs Waiver Agreement
WITH FBI SPECIAL AGENTS

This page is a Waiver Agreement between the FBI and *Rick Fair,* the man along with *Frank Alber*, who made the advisory call February 13, 1992. This is the telephone that the FBI and the Mesa Police added in their reports, they lifted the fingerprints of the defendant Miller off the telephone from which the call to Kaplan was made.

Fair reportedly told Special Agent Tolhurst he did not know how Miller's fingerprints got onto the phone, because Miller or Nelson were not around! He has never seen them until he saw the news on television and *The Arizona Republic . Fair* reportedly told Case Special Agent Keith Tolhurst he would cooperate with the Government if they protect his identity, and from going to jail!

Fair signed the waiver February 23, 1992. Along with This was two days after the arrest of the defendants Miller and Nelson.

WAIVER

I RICHARD C. FAIR understand this:

1. I have voluntairly chosen to come to the FEDERAL BUREAU OF INVEST-IGATION (FBI) office and talk with FBI agents concerning MARC KAPLAN, FRANK ALBER, MICHAEL MILLER, MARK NELSON, and any other persons information and evidence and concerning the MARC KAPLAN extortion investigation/prosecution.

2. These voluntary discussions with the FBI began on Feb. 22, 1992 and will continue until I choose to terminate them.

3. It has been explained to me by SPECIAL AGENT KEITH D. TOLHURST that I had in my conversation with him on Feb. 22, 1992 implicated myself or indicated possible criminal responsibility.

4. I have the complete right to terminate these meetings at any time.

5. This waiver is not the result of any force, threat, assurance or promise and not at the direction of or because of the recomendation of any person.

6. I am not now on or under the influence of any drug, medication, liquor or other intoxicant or depressant which would impair my ability to fully understand the content of this waiver.

SIGNATURE LINE _____

DATE   2/23/92

RICHARD C. FAIR   *Richard C. Fair*

WITNESS _____ SA FBI Px Az 4:16 PM
        _____ SA FBI Px Az 4:16 PM

Nelson's Diary
MADISON STREET JAIL

11:30 P.M. I felt much better. I met that guy who told me not to say anything to anybody, the one who mopped the floor. He said he saw me on the phone early morning yesterday and tried to get my attention but couldn't.

But his name was Harvey. His real name was Javier Quezada. He gave me this note pad, pencil and pen. I asked, "Why are you helping me?" He replied, "I've been in here for two years. You can tell who's criminal and who's not. You're definitely not criminal, and I believe you're not guilty. And you can probably use a friend right now." He's lent me magazines, gave me bars of soap (*Dial*), and a pack of cigarettes Marlboros even though I don't smoke. He even gave me some notebook paper. I started writing this account of unjust, cruel and unusual punishment without cause!

Everyone was quiet, as the echo's of uncertainties ran wildly through my mind, and the tears ran down my face, as I prayed to my God, I sure miss my dogs, bird and Dawn, Nancy, Lea, my father, my painting, even the outside air. I hope to God everything comes out right...

Monday, February 24

Media Frenzy
"FBI TO THE RESCUE"

The Editorial on the next page was published in *The Arizona Republic* on February 24, 1992. Just eighteen days after the crime date of February 7, 1992, and just four days after the arrest of the defendants Miller and Nelson!

FBI Special Agent in charge, James Ahearn, did his job correctly. He spent thousands of dollars without question from the American tax payers, and ordered protection for the Kaplans, and he called in FBI Special Agents and Specialist from various parts of the United States! They put, Case Special Agent Keith Tolhurst, in charge of 100 FBI Special Agents and their reports. Tolhurst was also to gather information with other law enforcement agencies and then file his report to his superiors. This is were the deception started.

The FBI and the Mesa police working together did not lift the finger prints of two of two suspects, as it was reported. In fact, supposably they only lifted defendant Miller's fingerprints. This was still never really proven in court if these were actually Miller's prints. Defendant Nelson's fingerprints where not lifted from anything, as reported in the TV and radio especially the daily papers and it was this editorial, "FBI to the Rescue" that brought question towards the FBI's Case Special Agent Keith Tolhurst, and the U. S. Attorney Chuck Hyder for actions in their team work style of conspiracy, to bring false prosecution towards the defendants Miller and Nelson!

MONEY WELL SPENT

FBI to the rescue

Back in the days when J. Edgar Hoover was at the helm, the FBI was often in the news, but the recent trend has been for the G-Men, as the Prohibition mobsters called them, not to hog the

limelight. It is only when a dramatic crime is revealed that we are reminded once again that one of the best-trained police agencies in the world is quietly doing its job.

How the FBI performs on a regular basis came to light Friday when *The Republic* revealed an attempt to extort money from a prominent Paradise Valley businessman, Marc J. Kaplan. Mr. Kaplan was warned in a four-page letter that kidnappers would grab his 12-year-old son and amputate the boy's arms unless Mr. Kaplan handed over $250,000.

FBI Special Agent in Charge James Ahearn took the threat seriously. He removed agents from less urgent assignments and called in specialists from FBI bureaus in various parts of the United States. For two weeks agents worked around the clock, guarding the Kaplan family, keeping watch on several suspects and observing a small suitcase full of money that had been placed at the pickup spot named by the extortionist. Working together, the FBI and Mesa police quickly lifted the fingerprints of two suspects, who were arrested Thursday.

With good reason, Americans sometimes question how their federal tax dollars are spent. In this instance, Agent Ahearn spent thousands of dollars assuring the safety of Brian Kaplan and his family, while simultaneously pursuing the extortionists who had threatened a young boy. No will argue that this was not money well spent.

Fortunately for the Kaplans and other potential victims, the FBI was there when a family needed help.

Cooperation Agreement
BETWEEN RICHARD FAIR AND CASE AGENT TOLHURST

The FBI Special Agents were now caught by a media frenzy brought on by their actions, and now they had to stick to the story. The Case Special Agent Keith Tolhurst reported, to Special Agent Ahearn and U.S. Attorney Chuck Hyder, to build the government case against defendants Miller and Nelson. Special Agent Tolhurst and the FBI Special Agents under his direction, commenced deceptive investigations! Only 11 days into the case, it is clear that Tolhurst had given false reports and had falsely reported information to his superiors and Attorney Chuck Hyder condoned this activity as will be proved beyond a reasonable doubt, as you will see later on in this book.

On February 24, 1992, two days after Miller and Nelson's arrests the government was working hard to making the case fit the "Headlines"!

So a Cooperation Agreement (copy on next page), was drawn up between *Rick Fair* and the FBI, this was on February 24, 1992 .

This was the man who made the advisory phone call on February 13, 1992, from the *ABCO Supermarket* to Marc Kaplan; to go to the *Security Pacific Bank* for further instructions, which then lead him to *Saguaro Lake*!

On the following four pages is the actual agreement, between two rats...

<u>COOPERATION AGREEMENT</u>

The Federal Bureau of Investigation (hereinafter sometimes referred to as the "FBI") through their authorized representative and Richard C. Fair agree:

1.   WHEREAS, the purpose of this agreement is to record the respective responsibilities and rights of the parties regarding and participation of Richard C. Fair in the investigation and prosecution by the FBI of the Marc Kaplan extortion.

<u>RESPONSIBILITIES OF RICHARD C. FAIR</u>

2.   Richard C. Fair, will truthfully and honestly with no knowing misstatements or omissions, assist and cooperate with the FBI in any manner designated by the FBI in identifying and investigating persons who are engaged in or suspected of engaging in extortion; that assistance will include but not be limited to:

a.   At the direction of and under the supervision of the FBI introducing agents of the United States government acting in an undercover capacity to individuals engaged in or who are suspected of engaging in illegal activities;

b.   At the direction of and under the supervision of the FBI, engaging in consensual visual, oral, and wire recordings of meeting and telephone communications relating to this agreement and its purposes. Richard C. Fair will provide written authorization to the FBI to monitor such meetings and communications prior to such monitoring/recordings.

c.   Testifying truthfully before any grand or petit jury or court;

d.   Furnishing all information relating to any investigation which is the subject of this agreement, in his possession, custody, and control, truthfully and honestly with no knowing misstatements or omissions;

e.   Submitting to a polygraph examination at the sole discretion of the FBI with respect to any statement made by him pursuant to this agreement. Such examination will be conducted by a polygrapher chosen by and conducted in a manner determined in the sole discretion of the FBI. The examination shall not be the exclusive means of determining the truthfulness of Richard C. Fair's statements and shall in no manner limit the FBI's methods of verifying the truthfulness of Richard C. Fair's statements.

3.   Richard C. Fair is not an employee, partner, member of a joint venture, associate, or agent of the United States

government and, in particular, the FBI. Richard C. Fair has no authority to obligate and/or bind the FBI to any contractual or other obligations. Richard C. Fair will never assert, identify, or hold himself out to be an employee, partner, member of a joint venture, associate, or agent of the FBI, or the United States government.

4. Richard C. Fair will not participate in the violation of any federal, state, or local laws. However, and only insofar as the FBI authorizes in writing, Richard C. Fair will engage as directed and supervised by the FBI in criminal activities necessary and in furtherance of the FBI's investigation of crime. Richard C. Fair understands that he is not by this agreement and never will be authorized to commit perjury, give false statements, commit any act of contempt or obstruct justice. He also understands that the United States will prosecute him for any such offense and any unauthorized federal criminal activity and the United States will be permitted to use against him, directly or indirectly, any sworn or unsworn statements he has made or provided to the United States during the investigation. Further, Richard C. Fair also understands that if he violates any state or local law not within the terms of this agreement, the government will furnish the state or local authorities with any information or evidence in its possession to assist in such prosecution.

5. Richard C. Fair is not permitted to possess contraband without prior authorization from the FBI.

6. Richard C. Fair is not permitted to possess a firearm.

7. Richard C. Fair will not entrap any individual or business entity. Hence, he will not implant in the mind of any innocent person the diposition to commit a criminal offense. Specifically, Richard C. Fair will not enduce a person to commit a crime by persuasion, trickery, fraud or any other means when such person was not otherwise predisposed to commit the crime.

8. Richard C. Fair will not use this contractual relationship with the FBI to resolve personal matters, or for his personal gain in any respect.

9. Richard C. Fair will not reveal or disclose to anyone, including family members, the fact or nature of this agreement, the investigation, or any part of it conducted pursuant to this agreement and the identity of individuals participating in and/or connected with this investigation. Further, Richard C. Fair will not undertake any publication or dissemination of any information or material that results from this investigation or related prosecution without the prior written authority of the FBI.

10. Richard C. Fair is responsible for FBI property loaned to him or of which he comes into possession and control during the term of this agreement. Richard C. Fair will reimburse the

FBI for the replacement value of any such property which is lost, damaged or destroyed by him.

RESPONSIBILITIES OF THE FBI

11. At the conclusion of Richard C. Fair's cooperation, completed pursuant to requirements of this agreement, the FBI will bring to the attention of the United States Attorney the nature, extent and quality of Richard C. Fair's cooperation.

12. Richard C. Fair understands that his cooperation with the United States pursuant to this agreement will not ensure Richard C. Fair any type of leniency from the United States regarding its decision to seek prosecution against Richard C. Fair if such prosecution would be warranted.

BREACH

13. If Richard C. Fair should fail in any way to fulfill completely each and every one of his obligations under this agreement, the FBI:

a. may in its sole discretion declare any provision of this agreement null and void, including paragraphs 11 and 12 above;

b. Seek an indicment and prosecute Richard C. Fair for any offenses for which he may be responsible.

c. use against Richard C. Fair, in any prosecution, the information, testimony, and documents that he provided to the FBI both before and after this agreement.

14. Nothing in this agreement shall be construed to protect Richard C. Fair in any way from prosecution from perjury, false declaration or false statement. Any information, testimony, and documents which Richard C. Fair provides to the United States pursuant to this agreement may be used against him in any such prosecutions.

GENERAL PROVISIONS

15. This agreement shall commence on the date of acceptance by the parties as signified by their dated signature below and shall continue for a period of 1 year, unless earlier terminated

by the FBI. Richard C. Fair's obligations in this agreement as
set forth in paragraph 2, subparts c,d and e above, shall survive
the completion of or termination of this agreement.

    16. The foregoing represents the entirety of the agreement
between Richard C. Fair and the FBI.

    By their signatures below, the parties herewith acknowledge
they understand, completely agree with, and will abide by this
agreement.

February 24, 1992
DATE

_____
RICHARD C. FAIR

_2/27/92_
DATE

_____
SA KEITH D. TOLHURST, FBI

Entrapment Of _Alber_
WITH SPECIAL AGENTS

6:40 A.M. This was a consensually monitored nagra recording between Richard Fair and _Frank Alber_. It was filed by Case Special Agent Keith Tolhurst after the cooperation agreement was made between _Rick Fair_ and the FBI. On this same day, the FBI placed a tap recording device on _Rick Fair_ to entrap _Alber_, the man who actually planned this crime all by himself.

In this tape _Alber_ is heard saying, "He made the phone call with Fair at the shopping center." It also states he, _Alber_, never heard of Miller or Nelson.

This tape clearly shows the innocence of the defendants Miller and Nelson, plus all the witnesses's reports. There is no conflicting evidence anywhere period! Why then, did Special Agent Tolhurst keep pursuing Miller and Nelson?

Here is a man; _Rick Fair_ who did do the crime, and struck a deal so he would not get prosecuted. While Miller and Nelson awaited indictment for something, they were truly not involved with!

8:00 A.M. As _Rick Fair_, the FBI's informant/witness, departs _Frank Alber's_ house, he walks to a vehicle, opens the door, and you can here the beeping sound from the vehicle. He closed the door. _Fair_ was greeted by FBI Case Special Agent

Keith Tolhurst, who told Fair he did real good. *Fair* responded, "Well Thank You!" Special Agent R. Scott Rivas who was the known male saying "Real Good!" As Tolhurst took the stuff from an agreeable Fair. There were some unidentified noises and conversation going on between these three individuals. As Fair unzipped his pants, laughing about dropping his drawers in front of them. The rest of the conversation becomes unidentified. FBI Special Agent R. Scott Rivas, not sure of the time, signs off... (See appendix page 405 for transcript of tape)

Jeffrey Bonadonna's Interrogation
IN RESEDA, CALIFORNIA

On this page and the following two, is a report filed by the FBI Special Agents. Bonadonna was the passenger of the Corvette and who made first contact with Miller, and asked Nelson to go to *McDonalds* before and after *Saguaro Lake*. The question here is, "why didn't this man get arrested?" He had more contact than Nelson and according to the FBI. In fact, Bonadonna was telling the truth and his story matched Nelson's.

- 1 -

FEDERAL BUREAU OF INVESTIGATION

Date of transcription ___2/25/92___

On February 24, 1992, JEFFREY MICHAEL BONADONNA, 18900 Ledan Street, Northridge, California, was interviewed at his residence concerning an attempted extortion of MARK KAPLAN. After having been advised of the official identities of the interviewing Agents and the nature of the interview, BONADONNA provided the following information.

BONADONNA stated on or about February 8, 1992 he ran into an acquaintance, MARK NELSON. He stated he had last seen NELSON about two years ago and had seen NELSON only once in the past four years. NELSON spent two or three days at BONADONNA's house and on the evening of February 11, 1992, the two of them left California and drove to Phoenix, Arizona in NELSON's Corvette. They arrived in Phoenix in the early morning hours of February 12, 1992. BONADONNA related that he is a self employed sound engineer and NELSON wanted him to come to Phoenix to consider helping NELSON open a night club. BONADONNA stated he had never visited Phoenix and was not busy at the time. It gave him an opportunity to have a short vacation and explore a business opportunity.

BONADONNA had difficulty recalling specific activities on specific days, but had a general recollection of their activities from Wednesday to Saturday, at which time BONADONNA flew back to California. BONADONNA stated they slept until around noon every day. Almost every day they would go by NICHOLAS LEES' office, where NELSON was employed, to check on any work. They would then spend the afternoon driving around the Phoenix area where Nelson showed BONADONNA various points of interest. They would then go back to NELSON's apartment, take a nap, and NELSON's girlfriend, DAWN, would come over and cook dinner. After dinner, they would go out to various topless bars and nightclubs. They usually stayed out until the early morning hours, and would then repeat the routine of sleeping until noon.

---

ration on ___2/24/92___ at Northridge, California File # ___9A-PX-46497___

SA JOHN E. HAMILTON
SA JACQUELINE J. FELTON _____ Date dictated ___2/25/92___

82   (70)

cument contains neither recommendations nor conclusions of the FBI. It is the property of the FBI and is loaned to your agency; s contents are not to be distributed outside your agency.

4000270

BONADONNA remembered going to Saguaro Lake, but could not recall the specific day. He remembered sleeping until around noon on that day. He and NELSON went to a job site where NELSON was painting a house. It was their intention to paint that day, but because the weather looked like it was going to rain, NELSON decided not to paint. They went by NICHOLAS LEES' and then drove around in NELSON's Corvette. BONADONNA remembered arriving at Saguaro Lake mid to late afternoon. He stated there was no prior conversation concerning Saguaro Lake. He remembers NELSON pointing out various sites and eventually they just "arrived" at Saguaro Lake. He repeated that there had been no prior conversation whatsoever concerning going to Saguaro Lake. He stated this was consistent with other days activities where they just got in the car and drove.

BONADONNA stated when they arrived at Saguaro Lake there were two other individuals at the lake drinking beer. They were driving an old car but he does not recall the make or model. NELSON struck up a conversation with the two and found out they were construction framers. After that, NELSON and the two spent the entire time talking about construction and building homes. He remembers that NELSON gave them his business card. He is positive that NELSON had never met either of the two before. BONADONNA viewed a photographic spread and positively identified MICHAEL GRANT MILLER as one of the two individuals at the lake. He stated the other individual looked Hispanic. BONADONNA stated they were at the lake for twenty or thirty minutes and then left and went to McDonalds, where they got a hamburger. They then returned to NELSON's apartment where they took naps. Later, NELSON's girlfriend, DAWN, came over and cooked dinner. He is not positive, but he does not believe they went out that night.

BONADONNA could not recall seeing anyone at the lake in a Mercedes, and did not recall passing anyone in a Mercedes or seeing anyone at McDonalds in a Mercedes. He further does not recall having any conversation with NELSON about anyone in a Mercedes. BONADONNA stated that NELSON talks all the time and is "into" cars. He stated NELSON's Corvette is an extension of NELSON's persona. He stated it is entirely possible NELSON made comments about someone in a Mercedes that BONADONNA just ignored. BONADONNA is certain he did not see anyone at the lake in a Mercedes.

83

Continuation of FD-302 of   JEFFREY MICHAEL BONADONNA   , On   2/24/92   , Page   3

          BONADONNA further advised he does not specifically
recall NELSON making any telephone calls while at the lake. He
stated NELSON has a cellular telephone which he uses all the time
and BONADONNA did not associate any particular calls with any
particular times or locations.

          BONADONNA stated Friday was not unlike any of the other
days in that they slept late, went to NICHOLAS LEES, drove around
and saw the sites, took naps, and went out to bars that night.
He did not recall specific places and pointed out that was his
first visit to Phoenix. BONADONNA stated on Saturday afternoon
they grilled hotdogs and hamburgers at NELSON's neighbor, RICH
SALAMI (phonetic). SALAMI then drove BONADONNA to the airport
and he flew back to Los Angeles at 7:30 p.m.

          BONADONNA stated he is not familiar with the names,
MARC KAPLAN, FRANK ALBER, and MICHAEL MILLER. BONADONNA was
further unable to identify any individuals depicted in a
photographic spread, other than his previous identification of
MICHAEL MILLER. BONADONNA denied any knowledge whatsoever
regarding an extortion attempt directed at MARC KAPLAN.

          The following descriptive information was obtained
through observation and interview:

          NAME   JEFFREY MICHAEL BONADONNA
          SEX   MALE
          RACE   WHITE
          DOB
          POB   BROOKLYN, NEW YORK
          HEIGHT   5'11"
          WEIGHT   165
          HAIR   BROWN
          EYES   GREEN
          RESIDENCE   18900 LEDAN STREET
                            NORTHRIDGE, CALIFORNIA

          TELEPHONE

84

N000272

Inadvertently Omitted Information
FROM JEFFREY BONADONNA'S INTERROGATION

Bonadonna advised FBI Special Agents Hamilton and Felton, upon his arrival at the *McDonalds* on February 13, 1992. That he exited the Corvette and went to the bathroom outside, which is still not mentioned in this report. Where he returned to the car and he and Nelson went through the drive-thru and ordered food.

On April 3, 1992, over a month after the fact a report was filed that information was inadvertently omitted from the reporting interview of February 24, 1992. What was omitted was the fact that Bonadonna did go to the bathroom outside *McDonalds*, and did get something to eat. Nothing like the story, the Criminal Complaint filed February 19, 1992, by Case Special Agent Keith Tolhurst. The question is *"why* ,was this key evidence omitted, then remitted?"

FD-302 (Rev. 3-10-82)

- 1 -

FEDERAL BUREAU OF INVESTIGATION

Date of transcription   4/3/92

The following information is set forth to supplement a Report of Interview of JEFFREY MICHAEL BONADONNA dated February 24, 1992, to include information inadvertently omitted from that Report of Interview.

BONADONNA stated he and MARK NELSON left Saguaro Lake and went to McDonalds where they got a hamburger. Omitted from the Report of Interview was the fact that BONADONNA advised upon arriving at McDonalds, he got out of the car and went to the bathroom. He then returned to the car and he and Nelson drove through the drive-in and ordered a hamburger.

Investigation on   2/24/92   at Northridge, California File # 9A-PX-46497

SA JOHN E. HAMILTON
by   SA JACQUELINE J. FELTON   Date dictated   4/3/92

This document contains neither recommendations nor conclusions of the FBI. It is the property of the FBI and is loaned to your agency; it and its contents are not to be distributed outside your agency.

N000273

<u>Tuesday, February 25</u>

Arrest And Search
BY FBI SPECIAL AGENTS

During his arrest, *Frank Alber*s was searched. Recovered in this search were copies of the extortion letter and the computer it was written on, and various receipts and submissible evidence implicating *Alber*. No information was found or obtained linking Miller or Nelson to this crime or any connection with *Alber* whatsoever.

In fact, the FBI discovered a cancelled check made payable to a Michael Miller. It turns out, it was Alber's divorce attorney not the Mike Miller in custody. *Alber* admitted this in an interview with the investigating Special Agents on February 25, 1992. This was more circumstantial evidence to be used by FBI Case Special Agent Keith Tolhurst to fool everyone, linking Miller further to the crime...

On this page and the following page are a few pages from the report...

Control of General/Drug/Valuable Evidence
FD-192 (Rev. 1-5-89)

Date: 2/25/92

☒ General Evidence   ☐ Drug Evidence   ☐ Valuable Evidence

☐ Special Handling Requirement (i.e., FBI Lab Instructions Re Body Fluid Stains, Whole Blood, etc.)

Title and Character of Case

UNSUB;
MARC KAPLAN-VITIM
EXTORTION

FILE NO. 9A-PX-46497
OO: PHOENIX

Date Acquired	Acquired From:		
2/25/92	2747 S. SANTA BARBARA, MESA AZ		

To Be Returned	See Serial	Acquiring Agent	Case Agent
☒ Yes ☐ No		SA ROBT CASEY/KLIMAS	SA KEITH TOLHURST

☐ Yes ☒ No   Grand Jury Material — Disseminate Only Pursuant to Rule 6(e), Federal Rules of Criminal Procedure

☐ Yes ☒ No   Property To Be Forfeited To The U.S. Government

Description of Property (Be Specific)

Item # 106 - Six (6) Carbon receipt check books, American Natnl Bank, name of Frank Alber.

Item # 114 - Original ANB check #1659, name of Frank Alber, payable to Price Club

Item # 125 - 3 Original ANB checks, name of Frank Alber, 0 #1619 to Price Club; #1622 to Price Club, #1623 to Michael Miller

FOR DRUG AND/OR VALUABLE EVIDENCE ONLY - NAMES OF TWO AGENTS INITIALLY VERIFYING AND SEALING:

For Use By ECT:

Location of Property: Shelf 2

Control Number: EO293957

(File Copy)

SEARCHED ___ BLOCK STAMP
SERIALIZED ___ FILED ___
FEB 25 1992
FBI — PHOENIX

9PX-46497-7B(22)

340   N000386

```
Control of General/Drug/Valuable Evidence                                                    DPS
FD-192 (Rev. 1-5-89)
                                                              Date
                                                                      2/25/92

☒ General Evidence        ☐ Drug Evidence        ☐ Valuable Evidence

☐ Special Handling Requirement (i.e., FBI Lab Instructions Re Body Fluid Stains, Whole Blood, etc.)

Title and Character of Case
   UNSUB:                                           FILE NO. __9A-PX-46497__
   MARC KAPLAN - VICTIM
   EXTORTION                                        OO: _____PHOENIX_____
```

Date Acquired	Acquired From:		
2/25/92	2747 S. SANTA BARBARA, MESA AZ		

To Be Returned	See Serial	Acquiring Agent	Case Agent
☐ Yes ☒ No		SA ROBT. CASEY/KLIMAS	SA KEITH TOLHURST

☐ Yes ☒ No   Grand Jury Material - Disseminate Only Pursuant to Rule 6(e), Federal Rules of Criminal Procedure

☐ Yes ☒ No   Property To Be Forfeited To The U.S. Government

Description of Property (Be Specific)

Item #109 - Blue ring binder containing printed extortion letter with handwritten notations to "Lennon Leadbetter" (4 pgs.); printed paper with related procedures (1 pg.); 2 pink message slips with notations,

Item #112 - Printed extortion letter with handwritten notations (4 pgs).

FOR DRUG AND/OR VALUABLE EVIDENCE ONLY - NAMES OF TWO AGENTS INITIALLY VERIFYING AND SEALING:

For Use By ECT:

Location of Property: _Shelf 2_

Control Number: _EO293960_

(File Copy)

```
BLOCKSTAMP
SEARCHED............INDEXED..........
SERIALIZED..........FILED............
       FEB 25 1992
   FBI - PHOENIX
```

9-PX-46497-1B(25)

343   4000389

Frank Alber's Interrogation
AT THE FBI HEADQUARTERS

Frank Alber was arrested by the FBI and transported to the Phoenix FBI office he was advised of his rights. *Alber* understood his rights and agreed to be interviewed. *Alber* initially indicated that he was aware of the extortion of Marc Kaplan to the extent that it was in the paper. He used to do consulting work for Kaplan 4-5 years ago. *Alber* was terminated from his position with Kaplan's company.

Alber went to see Kaplan at his business and drop off a "mailing piece." This occurred about the week of Feb. 9-15. *Alber* also on February 13, 1992, appeared again at Kaplans business to talk to an employee named Miles.

Alber was currently unemployed and helps his brother by working nights at his brother's 7-11 store. He was also attempting to put a business package together with *Rick Fair*.

Alber told FBI Case Special Agent Tolhurst and Special Agent Oldham, (remember, the Special Agents that secretly taped the conversation between *Fair* and *Alber*.) He did not know Michael Miller or Mark Nelson. It was at this point *Alber* preferred not to comment about anyone's involvement in the extortion, according to the FBI. *Alber* was advised that the FBI was already aware of *Rick Fair* and that Fair's voice had been recorded making the extortion call, actually it was not a extortion call but a call to give Kaplan further instruction on what to do next. *Alber* indicated to these interviewing Special Agents this is what he has been waiting to hear and admitted asking *Fair* to make the advisory phone call February 13, 1992.

Alber said "he could one-hundred percent absolutely guarantee *Fair* had no knowledge of what the call was about." *Alber* started to tell his tall tales when he interrupted his own interview and requested to speak with an attorney.

On the following three pages is Alber's interrogation and it went like this...

FD-302 (Rev. 3-10-82)

- 1 -

FEDERAL BUREAU OF INVESTIGATION

Date of transcription   3/2/92

FRANK ROBERT ALBER, a white male, date of birth
4/12/55, social security number 114-46-7837, residing at 2747
South Santa Barbara, Mesa was arrested by the Federal Bureau of
Investigation (FBI) and transported to the Phoenix FBI office.
ALBER was advised of his rights from an FD-395 interrogation;
advise of rights form. ABLER indicated he understood his rights
and agreed to be interviewed. ALBER provided the following:

ALBER initially indicated that he was aware of the
extortion of MARC KAPLAN to the extent that it was in the paper.
He used to do consulting work for KAPLAN 4-5 years ago.
Approximately three years ago, KAPLAN named ALBER as President of
Health and Nutrition Laboratories. At the end of 1991, KAPLAN
"let (ALBER) go" meaning his employment had been terminated.
ALBER felt he had "not great feelings, but no major hard
feelings" toward Kaplan. ALBER would often stop in at KAPLAN's
business because he had dealings with MILES GORDON, another of
KAPLAN's employees. ALBER would hardly ever go to see KAPLAN.

About "6-7 months ago" he went to see KAPLAN to try and
get another business going with KAPLAN. KAPLAN told him the
"diet business" was not a good area to get into at the time and
explained to ALBER why it was a bad idea. Alber decided not to
pursue the idea further based on KAPLAN's advise.

ALBER went to see KAPLAN at his business and drop off a
"mailing piece" for MARC to see to get MARC's opinion/advise on
it. This occurred about two weeks ago (the week of Feb. 9-15).
ALBER also needed a report from MILES GORDON and GORDON gave him
some "floppys". GORDON may also get involved in a current San
Diego business venture of ALBER's .

ALBER has never called KAPLAN at home with the
exception of calling him 2-3 years ago for directions to KAPLAN's
New Years party. He hasn't called KAPLAN's business asking to
speak with KAPLAN in the last few months.

Investigation on   2/25/92   at Phoenix, Arizona   File # 9A-PX-46497

ANTHONY E. OLDHAM
by   KEITH D. TOLHURST/kdt   Date dictated 3/2/92

This document contains neither recommendations nor conclusions of the FBI. It is the property of the FBI and is loaned to your agency;
it and its contents are not to be distributed outside your agency.

KAPLAN owns at least one or two houses, and owns a BMW, a Mercedes in Cleveland, and a new Mercedes. ALBER indicated the new Mercedes was "green" and commented he didn't know why anyone would "spend $90,000 dollars on a new car" and get the color green. KAPLAN also used to have a corvette 2-3 years ago.

ALBER is currently on unemployment, however, he helps his brother by working nights at one of his brothers three 7-11 stores. ALBER is also attempting to put a business package together with RICK FAIR.

ALBER stated he did not know MICHAEL MILLER or MARK NELSON although he did have a divorce attorney named MICHAEL MILLER. He preferred not to comment about anyones involvement in the extortion. He was advised that the FBI was already aware of RICK FAIR, and that FAIRs voice had been recorded making the extortion call. ALBER indicated that was what he had been waiting to hear and admitted asking FAIR to make the telephone call.

ALBER said he could "100%, absolutely, guarantee he (FAIR) had no knowledge of what the call was about". ALBER was afraid that someone would recognize his voice so he asked FAIR to make the call. ALBER and FAIR were together at the time of the call which was made outside Walgreens at Alma School and Warner. ALBER stated "what I was doing I didn't think was 100% legal". He and FAIR were drinking at GALLAGHERS restaurant and when they left he gave FAIR a handwritten note to read over the telephone. He told FAIR the call was the start of a car rally. The call was placed at approximately 2:00 PM.

ALBER wrote the handwritten note at the direction of an individual by the name of RICHARD WOOLRIDGE (phonetic). ALBER said WOOLRIDGE was from California and in the "international mailing" business, however, he was again reluctant to discuss anyone elses involvement in the extortion, or any further specific implications of his involvement other than the telephone call. ALBER was advised that a letter similar to the extortion letter received by KAPLAN was found in his home while the search warrant was being executed. ALBER said he "did not send the extortion letter" and had no idea how it could have gotten into his home.

ALBER obtained the information to use on the extortion call from WOOLRIDGE after he was contacted by WOLLRIDGE by

telephone.   ALBER did not know WOOLRIDGE and his total
association to him was two telephone calls. During the first
call, WOOLRIDGE gave ALBER the "general idea" of what was to take
place. The second call instructed ALBER what to say on the
telephone. ALBER was told that KAPLAN owed WOOLRIDGE
approximately $42,000 dollars and some people wanted a chance to
get even. Also mentioned were an individual named GARY, STU, and
an "actor". ALBER was told he would receive $500 dollars to make
the call. He thought WOOLRIDGE was "going for $50,000 dollars".

        ALBER later attempted to contact WOOLRIDGE after the
call had been placed and determined that WOOLRIDGE did not exist.
ALBER could only recall the area code 714 as belonging to
WOOLRIDGE.

        KAPLAN was described as not being one of ALBER's "top
ten" friends. When asked if he would fit as one of his "top ten"
enemies, ALBER indicated he did not have that many enemies but
considered KAPLAN to be "one of my highly dissatisfied people".

        ALBER stated he had no connection to Saguaro Lake.
ALBER indicated he did like to do a lot of bicycle riding in the
Estrella Parkway area. He was asked by WOOLRIDGE to suggest a
remote location and he suggested the Estrella area. ALBER did
not know how individuals from California would be able to direct
KAPLAN to remote areas of the Arizona.

        The interview was ceased upon Alber's request to speak
with an attorney.

<u>Nelson's Diary:</u>
MADISON STREET JAIL TO UNITED STATES DISTRICT COURT OF ARIZONA

I was not scheduled for court until tomorrow morning, I heard the judge tell me the 26th of February. But why am I going now, the 25th of February. I really could not understand, I thought I was going to get jumped and killed. I was so scared I tried to tell the corrections officer I wasn't suppose to go. He yelled, "get ready anyway!"

I was shackled by my ankles, my wrists, and waist. There was a man in front of me and in back of me. I thought there would be no way for someone to get me while I was secured with other inmates. I just kept my eyes and ears open for any danger that may lie ahead for me.

When I arrived I kept telling the fingerprint processor that I was not scheduled for court. He said he did not know anything. I just sat there all day. Then all of a sudden at about mid-afternoon, there was a lot of commotion going on. I saw FBI Special Agent Tolhurst and one I did not know his name, all of a sudden put this guy into the cell that I was in. I was laying down with my arm over my head. I could still see everything that was going on. As I looked at the man sitting next to my feet, I heard them call his name, *Frank Alber*. I was so mad, my heart started beating really fast. I thought I was going to have an anxiety attack. This was the man that the FBI said I was helping. I wanted so bad to kick his ass! Then all of a sudden as I was looking through my arms, covering my face, I could see a camera with a red light on it. Someone was watching us. I decided to just lay there as though I was sleeping. Then the fingerprint processor came by the cell and yelled my name. I had no choice but to answer. I looked up at him. He asked me "have you had been to court?"

I said to him, "you know I have not, and I'm not scheduled to go until tomorrow. He told me not to get smart and just answer the question. I said, "no" then went and laid back down. A few minutes later, they came and took *Frank Alber* away, I never saw him again. I think if I would have seen him I would have smashed his head to the ground.

I never did go to court these clowns are so sneaky. I'm back in my new cell with a freak that is 40 years old and has a thirteen-year-old girlfriend. He told me he likes them young. I'll just kept one eye open. Please watch over me, God! Good Night...

Wednesday, February 26

Media Frenzy
CONTINUES IN *THE ARIZONA REPUBLIC*

Information provided by the FBI and certain witnesses pertaining to the Kaplan's extortion plot revealed these interesting points: Kaplan suspected *Frank Alber* earlier to be involved in the extortion plot against him. Marc Kaplan's sister, Marla Joy Johnson reported to the FBI on February 17, 1992, that she suspected *Alber* too! Additionally, the two Surveillance Teams at *Estrella Park* observed *Alber* and his blue Buick on February 18, 1992.

Alber's former wife, Mary Ann *Alber*, said Frank once worked with Michael Grant Miller. This is not the Michael Miller who was being framed in this extortion case, but actually Alber's divorce attorney. This was just more circumstantial evidence used to link the innocent to the FBI's crimes.

The person who contacted the FBI and said, *"Alber* was the letter writer." *Rick Fair*, the one who signed the Cooperation Agreement on February 24, 1992, with the FBI, but there was never any mention that he knew that *Alber* was the actual letter writer. Other information on *Alber* was not released because U.S. Attorney Linda Akers asked a federal court official to keep sealed an affidavit filed in support of the arrest of *Alber* and to protect *Rick Fair*.

This article claims that after Kaplan received the phone call from the extortionist February 13, 1992 he went to the *Security Pacific Bank* branch as directed and found a note that sent him to *Saguaro Lake* boat ramp #2, to get further instruction. This is not a true, Kaplan was not sent to boat ramp #2, but Marina Covered Picnic area #3, over a half-a-mile away...

Would this information substantiate the Conspiracy Theory or just bad investigative reporting by the FBI?

3rd man held in maim plot

Threat to harm child alleged

By Randy Collier and Charles Kelly
The Arizona Republic

A Mesa man who neighbors said was deeply in debt and desperate for money was arrested by FBI agents Tuesday and charged with masterminding an extortion scheme in which he threatened to maim the child of a Paradise Valley man.

Frank R. Alber, 36, was arrested Tuesday morning when he arrived at his home in the 2700 block of South Santa Barbara. Agents had put Alber under surveillance for the past few days, the FBI said.

Alber was whisked away to FBI headquarters in Phoenix while agents searched his house. They removed several items, including a personal computer that agents believe was used to write an extortion letter to Paradise Valley businessman Marc J. Kaplan.

Kaplan said he was relieved by the arrest of Alber on Tuesday and of two other men picked up in the plot last week.

Kaplan said Alber had worked for him as a computer

— See **3RD MAN**, *page A2*

3rd man held over threat to maim boy

— 3RD MAN, *from page A1*

programmer in direct-mail marketing operations for three or four years until about a year ago, when Alber no longer was needed as a full-time worker but continued to work for him as a consultant.

"There certainly was never animosity between him and anybody in our operation," Kaplan said. "He's obviously a desperate individual."

Kaplan said that in the past year, he had advised Alber on possible business projects but declined Alber's requests to invest in the projects.

Kaplan said he had suspected early that Alber might be involved in the extortion plot.

Two clues, he said, were that the extortion letter was written on a computer and that it was packaged distinctively, as if by someone familiar with direct-mail marketing techniques.

Neighbors who watched agents arrest Alber said that during the four years Alber has lived in the neighborhood, he has suffered several financial losses.

Rich Brown, who lives across the street, said Alber once drove a Mercedes-Benz and a Chevrolet Corvette but was forced to sell both cars.

"Now he's driving an old Buick," said Brown, pointing to a blue-and-white convertible with a massive oil leak under it. "He definitely had a champagne appetite."

Marion Minchuk, a Mesa real-estate agent and a longtime friend of Alber, said his friend "had been under a lot of stress. You'd be under a lot of stress, too, if you had two kids and were out of work and couldn't find a job."

Alber's former wife, Mary Ann Alber, who has custody of their 8-year-old daughter and lives in Chandler, said Alber worked at one time with Michael Grant Miller, 24, of the 1600 block of South Mesa Drive, Mesa, who along with Mark Andrew Nelson, 31, of the 6800 block of East Cochise Road, Scottsdale, was arrested last week on suspicion of extortion.

In the course of investigating the extortion plot, FBI agents traced one call made to Kaplan's office to a pay telephone at an ABCO supermarket at 1988 Alma School Road, Chandler. A

fingerprint taken from the phone by the Mesa police was matched to Miller.

At the time Miller and Nelson were arrested, the FBI said that on Feb. 7, Kaplan, who owns Health and Nutrition Laboratories, 4545 E. Shea Boulevard, got a letter that had been written on a computer and postmarked in Phoenix the day before.

"The sender demanded that Kaplan pay $250,000 in one week or his son's arm or leg would be removed, according to an FBI affidavit released last week.

The threat was directed against Kaplan's son Brian, 12. Kaplan also has a daughter, Lauren, 7.

The FBI said Thursday that it thought the two men who were arrested were minor players in the scheme. James Ahearn, special agent in charge of the Phoenix FBI office, said agents still were searching for the person who wrote the letter on a computer.

After a story in Friday's *Arizona Republic*, a person contacted the FBI and said Alber was the letter writer, it was learned Tuesday.

Other information on Alber was not released, because U.S. Attorney Linda Akers asked a federal-court official to keep sealed an affidavit filed in support of the arrest of Alber.

After getting a phone call from the extortionists Feb. 13, Kaplan went to a Security Pacific Bank branch as directed and found a note that sent him to Saguaro Lake boat ramp No. 2 to get further instructions. Before he arrived, FBI agents monitoring him saw cars owned by Miller and Nelson a quarter-mile from the ramp.

Nelson and Miller were among four males seen near the cars, and Nelson was holding a mobile telephone, the affidavit released last week says.

Both Mary Ann Alber, the former wife, and Michelle Fritz of Glendale, Alber's girlfriend and the mother of his 7-month-old son, said they were shocked by his arrest.

"I've known him for 10 years, and there is not a mean bone in his body," his former wife said.

Fritz called the arrest "preposterous" and said, "He wouldn't do anything like that."

Contributing to this article was Pamela Manson of The Arizona Republic.

Grand Jury Testimony
FBI SPECIAL AGENT KEITH D. TOLHURST

9:40 A.M. Before the Federal Grand Jury for the District of Arizona in Phoenix, at the grand jury testimony of Case Special Agent Keith D. Tolhurst in regards to the Kaplan extortion plot. Information here was from the reporter's transcripts of proceedings that were provided by Assistant U.S. Attorney Charles F. Hyder to Mark A. Nelson's Defense Team, Johnston, Maynard, Grant and Parker: Only eleven pages numbering from 11-12, 14-16, 19-20, 23-24 and 29-30. These pages also contained deleted information that the prosecutor withheld from Nelson's defense team.

The Federal Grand Jury in this instance will be given information regarding facts they feel implicate who they contend is responsible for this crime, there is no defense for these individuals being sought. Only the witnesses for the prosecution are present and the facts they determine as the truth, to warrant such indictments. Clearly, one sided testimony! This is what happened as the prosecutor presented his claims and his witnesses to 12 people who then decided the fate of innocent individuals.

A juror asked on line 7, was there any relationship between *Mr. Alber* and Bonadonna? Case Special Agent Tolhurst, on line 10 answered, *Mr. Alber* indicated individuals from California maybe involved, on sample extortion letters, there was a mention of San Diego and Orange County areas, the connection in California with *Alber*, which is where Mr. Bonadonna lives and there is nothing really concrete between the two. Here again, if an individual lives in the same area as a suspected criminal, maybe used in a court of law.

Bonadonna is the individual that made first contact to strangers of the Mercury and according to the FBI walked within 10 feet of Kaplan's vehicle at the *McDonalds* parking lot. A FBI Special Agent, (who was there waiting for Kaplan to arrive) started to approach this individual as listed on the Criminal Complaint Affidavit filed on Feb. 19, by Case Special Agent Tolhurst, Bonadonna got back into the Corvette and immediately left the area. This is why Bonadonna was not arrested, because it did not happen the way the FBI reported it. Lines 19-25 omitted. This is the end of testimony, there were more pages, but they were not given to Nelson's Defence Team. *Why* not? (See appendix page 442 for the actual transcript)

Nelson's Diary:

8:00 A.M. Today is real bad day, I go back to court to see what fate lies ahead for me. These people are crazy if they think I had some thing to do with a crime. One day I will find out why this happened to me. I have some uncertainties, my dad does not want to help me, I don't blame him or his wife. I really don't talk much to them they don't even know me. Well they're here to get me for Federal Court appearance today I'd better go.

11:00 A.M. I'm sitting in a jail cell in the *Federal Court Building* awaiting my trial. I haven't spoken to my parents or anyone today, I was not sure what my dad was going to do about me being placed under his custody. Should he decline I will have to go to jail. I'm so scared, I wish I knew who was behind this plot against me.

I don't know what time it is. I just got back from court. It was not like the court filled room I saw a few days ago. There was nobody except my dad, all my friends did not want anything to do with me. I was hurt! Gina had to go back to her home in Los Angeles. If it wasn't for her I would be going to jail. I love her so much.

I was very proud of my dad for coming forward although his wife declined my staying with them at first, she some how changed her mind. I'm glad she did. I would not last long in jail without some serious life threatening situation to happen against me. I knew I 'd *die* before I would ever bow down or submit to anyone, under these unwilling conditions. I don't like that I was forced to live again with my father after 13 years. I remember what he was like to live with then, and just from idle talk between the two of us, he's still the same. What bothers me is I, too have not changed and will not take any verbal abuse or violence. I'm no longer that little helpless boy. I will fight back. I hope it won't go there, I would rather go to jail than to be pushed into a corner and have to fight my way out. My dad is not that 200 plus pound *United States Air Force* boxer any more. In fact, he has became very lazy and weak looking, the odds definitely are in my favor not in my wishes. He is the only father I know!

They're coming to get me and transport me to Madison. I'm not looking forward to this trip, for a trip means strip when you go back to the pit. Some of these prisoners are very dirty and smell of shit or alcohol. Some even have dried blood and vomit on their clothes. My nose is so sensitive to smell, but I won't complain or get sick and that is a sign of weakness, and there will be none of that from me...

Thursday, February 27

Media Clarification
IN THE ARIZONA REPUBLIC

In this clarification published in *The Arizona Republic*, Mary Ann Alber, Frank's wife said she realized she made a mistake after seeing a photo of Miller that he is not the Miller she reported to the FBI and the newspapers with whom her ex-husband had worked. That the Michael Miller she was talking about was her and her husband's divorce attorney! How can you make a mistake like that?

This reference is to the original American National check # 1623 made payable to, Michael Miller and found by the FBI February 25, 1992, at the residence of *Frank Alber* during the search of his home. It was believed by the FBI to be written to the codefendant, Michael Miller, when in fact, it was written to Alber's divorce attorney with the same name. "<u>What a coincident</u>."

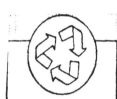

Thirty-nine percent of the newsprint used by Phoenix Newspapers, Inc. contains recycled paper fiber. Please recycle *The Arizona Republic*. Call 256-5626 for the recycling center nearest you or 257-2372 for a free state recycling directory.

TODAY'S CHUCKLE
When the spirit moves you: drunks who dance.

TODAY'S PRAYER
Lord, help us to deal with life's tragedies. Amen.

CORRECTIONS
An incorrect caption was placed under a car-review photo on Page CL1 of Sunday's Wheels section. It should have referred to the Subaru SVX below the photo.

A story on Page B8 Wednesday said Republican Richard Kyle of Phoenix is running for the U.S. House in the new 6th Congressional District. Kyle is a candidate for the Arizona House in the Legislature's new District 6.

CLARIFICATIONS
In a Page A1 story Wednesday about the arrest of Frank R. Alber on a warrant accusing him of extortion, Alber's former wife, Mary Ann, said he had once worked with Michael Miller, another defendant in the case. Mary Ann Alber said after the story was published that she realized she had made a mistake after seeing a photo of Miller. She said her ex-husband had worked with another "Michael."

Media Frenzy
MAIMING-PLOT SUSPECT DETAINED

The article on the following page was published in *The Arizona Republic*. In the early morning edition just hours before indictment charges are sought against Miller and Nelson. In this trial it states that *Frank Alber* was ordered detained. This was 14 days after Kaplan retrieved the note on February 13, 1992.

The supposed codefendant Miller was released on a $5,000 bail, but the article does not also state that Miller was placed under house arrest at his parent's house. Miller's mother and father were devastated by what was happening to their son. His parents by the way, put their house up for collateral for her son's bail.

The supposed codefendant Nelson was released without bail, but the article also fails to state Nelson was placed under house arrest with his dad and his dad's wife. Nelson's father at first declined to accept responsibility for his son's custody due to the fact that his wife, Carol was extremely scared. Nelson's ex-wife Gina flew in from California to aid her ex-husband against these false claims!

Gina told her ex father-in-law, "How dare you turn your back on your son, he needs you more than ever. You need to let him stay with you. Do you even have a clue what is in store for your son if he goes to prison. Possible *death,* and not necessarily his! I came out from California to aid my ex-husband, I know my ex-husband, he is not guilty!"

Gina also told him, "I know your wife is scared, but she has no reason to be, and you adopted Mark, before you met her!" So with that he changed his mind. Boy was I *lucky*?

The article also stated that before Kaplan arrived at *Saguaro Lake*, FBI monitoring him said they saw cars owned by Miller and Nelson a quarter-mile from ramp #2. The question here is how did the FBI Special Agents monitoring Kaplan arrive before Kaplan did at the lake, to see the cars of codefendants Miller and Nelson when witnesses have stated That Miller and Nelson left before Kaplan arrived!

Maiming-plot suspect detained

By Pamela Manson
The Arizona Republic

A man accused of masterminding an extortion scheme in which he threatened to maim a child was ordered detained Thursday by a federal magistrate.

Frank R. Alber, 36, of Mesa, was ordered held by Magistrate Morton Silver of U.S. District Court in Phoenix after a detention hearing Thursday.

Two co-defendants were released from custody Thursday. Silver earlier in the day set bail of $5,000 for Michael Grant Miller, 24, of Mesa, and ruled that Mark Andrew Nelson, 31, of Scottsdale, could be released without bail.

The three are accused of plotting to extort money from Paradise Valley businessman Marc J. Kaplan, who received a letter on Feb. 7 demanding that he pay $250,000 or his son's arm or leg would be removed, according to an FBI affidavit released last week.

Kaplan owns Health and Nutrition Laboratories, 4545 E. Shea Boulevard. The threat was directed against his son Brian, 12. Kaplan also has a daughter, Lauren, 7.

After getting a phone call from the extortionists Feb. 13, Kaplan went to a Security Pacific Bank branch as directed and found a note that sent him to a Saguaro Lake boat ramp to get further instructions. Before he arrived, FBI agents monitoring him said they saw cars owned by Miller and Nelson a quarter-mile from the ramp.

The two were arrested last week. Alber was picked up Tuesday.

Kaplan said Alber had worked for him as a computer programmer in direct-mail marketing operations for three or four years until about a year ago, when Alber no longer was needed as a full-time worker but continued to work for him as a consultant.

Neighbors of Alber say he was deeply in debt and desperate for money.

Carmen Anna Gomez Interrogation
AT KAPLAN'S RESIDENCE

The report on the very next page was from a witness by the name of Carmen Anna Gomez, (no relation to Miller's boss), the housekeeper for the Kaplans for, four years. She never observed a red Corvette which belonged to Nelson.

Gomez was totally unaware of any threatening phone calls to the Kaplan home, and she had not seen any strangers in, around or near the Kaplan home. Marcie Kaplan called Gomez, February 25, 1992, to tell her that *Alber* had once worked for the Kaplans, Gomez did not remember him. Gomez was then shown some photographs of some people, but in order to understand clearly we have to break them down to three groups:

1. *Frank Alber*, "the Mastermind."

2. Michael Miller "the falsely accused" and Bennet Barcon "the passenger at *Saguaro Lake* with Miller."

3. Mark Nelson "the falsely accused" and Jeff Bonadonna, "the passenger at *Saguaro Lake* with Nelson, and Dawn Kauffman, "Nelson's girlfriend" and "Nick Lees."

- 1 -

FEDERAL BUREAU OF INVESTIGATION

Date of transcription   **3/2/92**

CARMEN ANNA GOMEZ, 2930 East Osborn Street, Apartment #460, Phoenix, Arizona, telephone number 957-6780, provided the following information to SA ALICE D. DAYS:

GOMEZ has worked for MARC and MARCIE KAPLAN for approximately 4 years as a housekeeper. In addition to cleaning the house, she watches their home when the KAPLANs are on a trip. She oftentimes acts as a babysitter when the KAPLANs are away. She works six days a week.

9A-PX-46497

continuation of FD-302 of   CARMEN ANNA GOMEZ   , On   2/27/92   , Page   2

          GOMEZ was told by MARCIE that the family had received
threats which explained the presence of strangers in the home.
It was not until an unidentified vehicle slowly drove past their
home and everyone was told to get down on the floor that she was
told the "strangers" were FBI.

          From then on, the family was concerned about slow
moving vehicles driving past their home. GOMEZ only recalls a
white car driven by a white female. However, she attributed the
slowness of the vehicles to the attempted sale of the home. Many
slowly drove past the home. She never observed a red Corvette.

          GOMEZ was made aware of the nature of the threats
alluded to by MARCIE when the two men were arrested and the
article appeared in the newspaper. The day FRANK ALBER was
arrested, MARCIE called GOMEZ at home to tell her that he had
once worked for the KAPLANs, and to ask if GOMEZ remembered him.
She did not recognize ALBER and did not know him.

          GOMEZ is unaware of any threatening phone calls to the
KAPLAN home. Although she monitors the calls through the
answering machine, she never answers the phone.

          GOMEZ has seen no strangers in, around, or near the
KAPLAN home.

          Photographs of FRANK ALBER, MARK NELSON, DAWN LEIGH
KAUFFMAN, NICHOLAS LEES, MICHAEL MILLER, BRET TAYLOR, JEFF
BONADANNA, and LEE KAPLAN were shown to GOMEZ. None were
recognizable to her except LEE KAPLAN.

U.S.A. vs Defendants

REDACTED INDICTMENT MICHAEL MILLER, MARK A. NELSON AND *FRANK ALBER*

On this day of February 27th 1992. The defendants are now officaly charged by the grand jury of their crimes. On this page and the following two is the actual indictment...

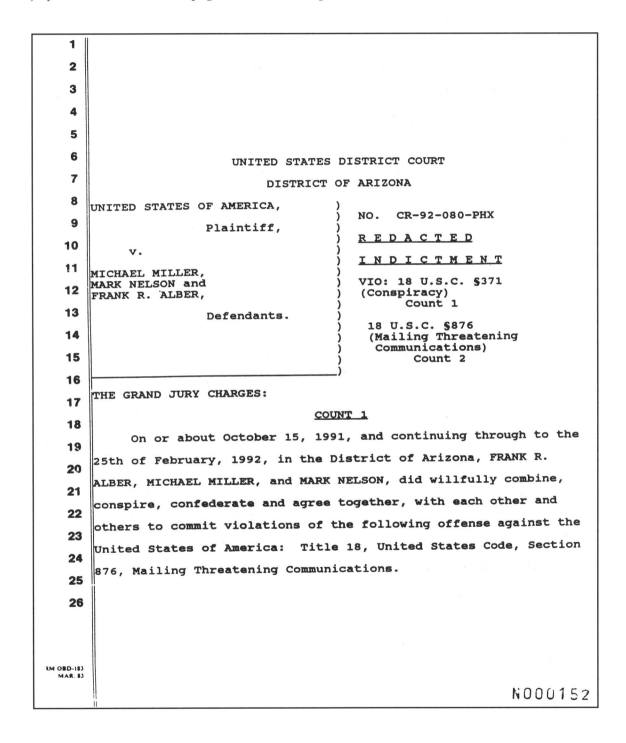

```
 1
 2
 3
 4
 5
 6                    UNITED STATES DISTRICT COURT
 7                       DISTRICT OF ARIZONA
 8   UNITED STATES OF AMERICA,    )
 9              Plaintiff,        )    NO.   CR-92-080-PHX
                                  )
10        v.                      )    R E D A C T E D
                                  )
11   MICHAEL MILLER,              )    I N D I C T M E N T
     MARK NELSON and             )
12   FRANK R. ALBER,             )    VIO: 18 U.S.C. §371
                                  )    (Conspiracy)
13              Defendants.       )         Count 1
                                  )
14                                )    18 U.S.C. §876
                                  )    (Mailing Threatening
15                                )     Communications)
                                  )         Count 2
16                                )
17   THE GRAND JURY CHARGES:

18                            COUNT 1

19        On or about October 15, 1991, and continuing through to the

20   25th of February, 1992, in the District of Arizona, FRANK R.

21   ALBER, MICHAEL MILLER, and MARK NELSON, did willfully combine,

22   conspire, confederate and agree together, with each other and

23   others to commit violations of the following offense against the

24   United States of America:  Title 18, United States Code, Section

25   876, Mailing Threatening Communications.

26
```

LM OBD-183
MAR. 83

N000152

OVERT ACT

In furtherance of the conspiracy and to effect the objectives thereof, the defendants performed the following overt act, among others, within the District of Arizona, and elsewhere:

On February 7, 1992, a computer generated letter was sent through the United States mail to Marc Kaplan demanding that Kaplan pay $250,000.00 in cash in one week or that JOHN DOE'S arm or leg would be removed by a group of individuals who described themselves as former officers in the "Special Forces" who had committed such violent acts of extortion before. The letter was postmarked Phoenix, Arizona, on February 6, 1992.

All in violation of Title 18, United States Code, Section 371.

COUNT 2

On or about February 6, 1992, in the District of Arizona, FRANK R. ALBER, MICHAEL MILLER and MARK NELSON, did knowingly deposit in an authorized depository for mail matter to be sent and delivered by the United States Postal Service a threatening communication postmarked February 6, 1992, addressed to Marc Kaplan, 4545 E. Shea Boulevard, Suite 160, Phoenix, Arizona 85028, and containing a threat to injure JOHN DOE, the said threat being substantially as follows: That if Marc Kaplan did not pay $250,000.00 in one week, as instructed, to a group described as former officers in the "Special Forces" who had committed such violent acts of extortion before, that JOHN DOE would meet with violence by having an arm or leg removed.

OBD-183
MAR. 83

N000153

1   In violation of Title 18, United States Code, Section 876.

2   A TRUE BILL

3

4   LEWIS A. EVANS
5   FOREMAN OF THE GRAND JURY
                                     DATE:
6
     LINDA A. AKERS
7   United States Attorney
     District of Arizona
8

9

10   Charles F. Hyder
     Assistant U.S. Attorney
11

12

13

14

15

16

17

18

19

20

21

22

23

24

25

26

OBD-183
MAR. 83

N000154

<u>Nelson's Diary:</u>
HIS RELEASE FROM MADISON STREET JAIL

6:00 P.M. I'm about to be released into my dad's custody and I hope this is a good idea. I'm thinking maybe staying in this hell will get me released earlier, everyone now seems to think this is a cake walk. They don't know my dad. Maybe I'm wrong, Diary? I hope that I am!

8:00 P.M. At my dad's house when my dad picked me up from the Madison Street Jail it was a sure sign of the things to come. His car was filled with cigarette smoke and his ashtray so full ashes that the cigarette butts where spilling and falling all over the carpet of his vehicle. The very first thing out of his mouth was "You'd better do as your told and what ever Carol, wants you to do, you do it. You also better thank her for her helping you because if you don't I will kick your ass!" These orders were stern and to the point, he made me feel like I was 13 years old, the same age I was 18 years ago. Things were different, I'm 31 years old and 180 pounds. Trained in street fighting and Martial Arts. I no longer weighed 100 pound I would rather go back to jail then beat on him like he did me and not just with his hands but his verbal attacks as well, but out of respect and the love for my dad I will heed his demands.

I am writing from my living quarters until I'm found innocent of the crimes I stand accused of. It's a small room, it has a big desk that takes up about 1/4 of the room. The single bed that takes up the other 1/4 and all their bookcases and a chair, I only had enough room to stretch out on the floor in one direction. I have no clothes not even socks or underwear. I just had the clothes from the time of my arrest on February 20. Dawn said she would go to my apartment and get some clothes for me. I'm not allowed to leave this place or I will go to jail and my dad would also have a possible Criminal Complaint filed against him since I was placed in his custody, he is held liable in the rules of home arrest. I will follow the rules!

I was just called for dinner, Carol is a very good cook and she is nice. She is far more pleasant than my dad.

9:00 P.M. I just got through with dinner and already got into it with my dad. Boy, is he an asshole. He started smoking at dinner, and I asked if he could please wait until I was finished. He yelled at me "go outside and eat with the dog if I don't like the smoke. Remember, you are not here for vacation and we will not compromise our living habits for you. It's bad enough that someone has to stay home here and watch to make sure you don't leave."

Carol was telling me the story of their dog "Zoro" named after the football player Zorich of Notre Dame. She was telling me Zoro bit the little girl next door and have seven stitches. I was so mad. I said, "if some dog bit my little girl. I would hunt it down and kill it. I don't care who's dog it belonged to. I couldn't even own a dog I couldn't let my grand kids socialize around, without the fear of getting bitten."

My dad got so mad he told me I was excused and to go to my room and if I ever lay a hand on his dog, I would see who would get killed. And he said to me "keep your stupid, God dammed opinion to yourself." I just walked out. I think he needs help. I wanted so bad to push his big ass off the chair. I knew I would hurt him. I can remember all those beatings and the verbal borage of madness this man would put me through my whole life. I remember wishing, thinking that when I got older, bigger, and stronger, I would treat him the same way. Now not excepting the reality that my once get-even dreams have materialized in front of me. I no longer want to hurt the only dad I know, a man who took me in from being an orphan, knowing I'm a far better man by just walking away then punching around a foolish, old frail man, who at this point couldn't even run around the block. But in his head he acted as though he still had the power and force as he once used on me. I see a man struggling with his age and this is his final chance to be a dad.

Well Diary, it's time to go to sleep, tomorrow I see Dawn. I love her so much. She is still an escort but she's still the only person sticking around. It shows me she is a good person. This morning's newspaper article confused the hell out of me. How could a lady not know who her husband's divorce attorney is? Something is wrong with this whole stupid case. When are they going to get it right? Good Night...

Friday, February 28
HOUSE ARREST

Nelson's Diary:
DAD'S HOUSE FIRST MORNING OF HOME ARREST

8:00 A.M. My dad woke me up yelling it's time to wake up. I asked him why did he have to yell for, and why couldn't he knock. He told me that I've got to be kidding, this is his house and there is no way he's going to knock on the doors of his own home. He said "why in the hell are you sleeping on the floor." The bed was too soft and it would hurt my back, I explained. He told me that I was full of shit, and to sleep on the bed next time. I was getting mad at this old man and his ignorance towards me. He told me if I did not like these arrangements, I could just go back to jail and see if I would like that better. I just agreed to shut his bullshit up.

When I went out for breakfast he was smoking at the breakfast table. I asked my dad if he would wait to smoke because I'm to sensitive to cigarettes. They bother my breathing and I don't enjoy it near my food either. He wanted to know if I was going to start that crap again and if I was I can go outside and eat or go back to jail.

This man bothers the shit out of me. He is trying so bad to get his ass beat. I refuse to let this man, I call dad, get the best of me. Between him, and his dumb ass dog, I would rather be in jail. At least if one of those prisoners gave me shit, I can say what's on my mind and not be afraid to beat some ass. Here I can't say or do anything, why does he have to be so damned mean. I came back into the room, I now call home.

I have nothing of mine in this room or my animals. I'm starting to want to *die* again. These sick feelings of suicide are boiling in my thoughts once again. The whole seven days I was in jail it took everything I had not to take my life, for me the easy way out of a bad situation. "Please, God help me, I really don't want to *die!*"

Dawn is coming over today I can't wait to see her. I love her more now then I ever did before. She is going to be my only friend and she will come visit me and I will hold her and kiss her. I miss her pretty face and even her braces on her teeth. I think I'll lose her in time. She is young though she acts older she, still a little girl of innocence locked inside. I wish she would quit her escort job, with that kind of money she lives a disillusioned life with outrageous cash and an extremely fast paced night life. One even I don't understand.

10:00 P.M. Dawn just left, she stayed nine hours with me. We made love. It was great. She told me how sorry she was that this was happening to me. She promised me she would stick with me because she loved me. Good Night, Diary...

MARCH 6 - 20
SEARCH FOR ADDITIONAL INFORMATION FROM ALBER'S HOME

The FBI searched additional computer disks and computers that they retrieved from the *Frank Alber's* home. At this point, Special Agents Karen Hajek and Robert J. Klimas found no further evidence to link Miller and Nelson to the extortion plot. In fact, they found no evidence to implicate anyone else to this crime as well. This proves that *Frank Alber* fooled everyone, including one of the best trained investigative services in America. The Case Special Agent Keith Tolhurst, knew by the evidence he had access to that Miller and Nelson had nothing to do with this crime.

Special Agent Tolhurst for some unknown reason chose to mislead the whole investigation and, with help of a few Special Agents falsely filed a Criminal Complaint against the defendants, Miller and Nelson. These seem to be very harsh words against the FBI, but in fact it's not towards them at all as far as a whole organization. It was the few Special Agents who handled this particular case who are the true criminals of this administrative crime, lead by the mastermind Case Special Agent Keith Tolhurst.

On or about February 14, 1992, Special Agent Tolhurst also ordered the toll records of everyone he thought or tried to place as potential individuals in the supposed extortion ring. He assigned Special Agent Jack Cusack to gather information regarding the same. The toll records are kept by the phone company for 90 days. These toll records are then erased so that the new toll records can be stored. The phone company can trace every call whether long distance or local. They can tell whom and when, calls are placed from a certain phone. On Friday, March 27, 1992, the conclusions of these toll records were made available and the results were as follows...

Friday, March 27
TOLL RECORDS FROM ALL THE SUSPECTS PHONES
FBI HEADQUARTERS

Case Special Agent Tolhurst ordered a toll record search. The phone company provided to Special Agent Jack Cusack, the toll records from November, 1992, through March, 1992. Once again, there was no evidence linking anyone Case Special Agent Tolhurst thought or tried to place as, the potential individuals in the supposed extortion ring. That's 90 days of toll records on all home, business, and cellular phones.

All of the toll records searched were concluded, before the actual indictments of the defendants Miller, Nelson, and *Frank Alber*. Still with this evidence, Miller and Nelson were brought up on false charges stemming back to the Criminal Complaint filed by the Case Special Agent of February 19, 1992. Even Nelsons's cellular phone toll records proved to be worthless and did not contain any information linking him to the crime.

No further evidence was known, that would lead a reasonable person to believe that Miller or Nelson was involved in any activity related to the extortion against Kaplan. In fact to the contrary, all of the evidence gathered by FBI Special Agents to be used against Miller and Nelson, proved to match both of these individual interviews, not to mention all of these individual, families and friends who were also interviewed by the same Special Agents.

How could a reasonable person (Tolhurst), at this point of his investigation still find probable cause to pursue prosecution, and defamation of the characters of Miller and Nelson to their peers? FBI Case Special Agent Keith Tolhurst's conduct was so extreme and outrageous that it would be shocking to a person of ordinary senses.

Special Agent Tolhurst desecrated his oath as a servant to the Federal Bureau of Investigations. His falsifying of records, as with the other Special Agents involved, wrongfully and improperly lead to arresting, indicting and imprisoning Michael Miller and Mark A. Nelson. All of these Special Agents were employees of the United States of America and fell below the standard of care of a reasonable person under the same circumstances. They were causing physical, psychological, and emotional turmoil for Miller and Nelson. One day these Special Agents will have to answer to these monstrosities which by the powers of will, They deemed fit and necessary!

Wednesday, April 1
NELSON'S DIARY FROM HOME ARREST

9:00 P.M. Hello, Diary, I'm so stressed out! I was allowed to go back to work in the forbidden zone in Scottsdale, back to the house were it all started. I was only allowed to finish if my dad went as guard. I was so embarrassed, that my dad had to escort me to the job and stay there until I was finished. Mr. Cameron did tell us that the FBI had not talked to them and that they called the FBI because of the legitimate concerns they had in regards to my involvement. Cameron told me that he told the FBI Case Special Agent, I could not be involved with this crime that I was too bright a young man to be involved with such stupid nonsense. I was thankful to hear that he stuck up for me. I had to ask him though why is the government still holding me, if everyone I know, including myself, has told the truth. Mr. Cameron stated back to me, "They must obviously know something we don't know or they wouldn't be holding you like they are, just stick to the truth and everything will work out fine."

For some reason, when he told me that I knew that this was only a beginning to the destruction of my life, not by the powers of my will, but the wills and hands of the government, the United States of America. One of the most powerful nations in the world, in this democratic society where we as Americans have the power to vote this imbalance out of our society. These individuals who have the power to lead or persuade any investigation anyway they deem fit and necessary will continually to do so. But I stand alone in my fight to prove my innocence. I stand a chance of being a victim in an investigation where I'm not involved. They will do whatever they feel is necessary to paraphrase information so that the prosecutor can then see what laws had been broken. No one will ever know what it truly feels like to stand accused of being a part of an extortion ring and to threaten to sever the arms off a young boy. To be compared with the Jeffrey Daumar, he killed his victims and cut them in pieces and ate their remains. These where just some of the remarks I heard from certain individuals. I'm trying to understand their ignorance towards me! I feel deep rage and with me writing to you Diary, I get relief!

Today, when I got home. The finance company for my Corvette called, and told me they had received information that I was going to jail for a long time. I asked them who they heard it from. They said, "the FBI." I didn't believe them. Someone told them about my arrest. Who? It has been almost 40 days since the last news report on this case. These people did not have the right to take my car I have made all my payments and my insurance was up to date so by law they could not repossess my car, but they did! I called my attorney, Jeffrey Ross. He was an asshole to me, everyone would say how lucky I was to be issued a court appointed attorney with Board Certification in Criminal Law. He stated to me that he was not my baby sitter and that he had more important things to worry about and that I need to be a man and face the reality. That I may be put in jail for 50 years. He said, "there was nothing he could do." I'm going to call the Attorney General in California tomorrow.

Let me assure you people in the American Judicial System, if someone comes before you and he does not fit the normal clean cut all-American white individual, with blue eyes, no tattoos or body piercing or long or short wild hair or even bald and no matter what color you are in America, you'll always be perceived as potential criminal to every Law Enforcement Agency in America. Even the clean cut white individuals, now must worry about false Criminal Complaints filed against them or someone they know. Each and every deviation from this form of repression in judgement toward first impression of a certain individual could be used to connect them to a crime. That's why it's important to look at the real evidence to what actually happened, not to what certain investigators who thinks because of an individual's aura, they are now considered potential suspects to these Special Agents and no matter how positive and how true a individual tells the truth. These Special Agents ignore the facts because they have a feeling based on an individuals' look.

The individuals who work in the Judicial System come from all walks of life, and are of different colors, creeds, and religion. These individuals only see one particular look for a criminal which is me and others like me. That's why when a person becomes the target of any investigation and the allocation of evidence federal law enforcement officers present to their superiors, to support Criminal Activity, in this case they had the means to manipulate their facts to support a more positive prosecution in their favor. They had to have altered the true facts in order to substantiate their false claims towards me.

Diary, I know in my heart that something is wrong with this case. I don't know who is behind these allegations of this heinous crime. I just want my life back and my car too! Good Night...

Thursday, April 2
NELSON'S DIARY HOME ARREST

10:00 A.M. I called my finance company, they explained that in order for me to get my Corvette. I would need to pay off the loan of $16,000 dollars. I tried to explain that I did not have the money, but they would not listen. I told them I would call the Attorney General in South Dakota where their main headquarters are located and tell them you falsely impounded my car. This jerk laughed at me what an asshole! I hung up and called the Attorney General for South Dakota. He explained to me that if my car payments and my insurance are up to date no one can legally impound my car, just because I stand accused of a crime, it does not grant automatic repossession. I told this man that the finance company told me it was their right to protect the collateral to the loan. This Attorney General assured me that if I called my finance company and tell them that I have spoken to this attorney general and that if I do not get my car back within the end of today's business day, I am supposed to call him back and he will take care of the matter.

I can't believe that it can work! I called my finance company and told them who I talked to and that you must give me back my car or you'll have to deal with some serious consequences according to the Attorney General. They told me they would call me back. I'll let you know what happened later.

9:30 P.M. Hello Diary, I have good news, I've got my Corvette back! That Attorney General was so cool. He needs to be the Attorney General here in Arizona! I'm so stressed out and the best thing is that I did not give up! Chalk one up for determination. The finance company was not too happy. They could not believe I went so far in my quest for what was right. I told them I was the wrong person to try

Thursday, May 13
NELSON'S DIARY OF HOME ARREST

A month after Mark Nelson and his girlfriend, Dawn, found out she was pregnant everything was going as well as it could be. She would visit him every day. This could not have happened if Nelson was in jail. She was adamant about seeing Nelson as much as she could. Though her mother and friends were getting upset with Dawn for allowing herself to get pregnant and not knowing the uncertainties that lay ahead for her and Mark. Dawn would tell them she loved Mark and that she knows in her heart that he did not do anything wrong and that she knew everything that he was involved with and these charges are not going to stick. She was very positive that any day the government would drop the case against her boyfriend and the soon to be father of her child would be together to raise their baby.

There were people excited about the news about the baby to come. One of these individuals was Mark's probation officer, Ms. Stewart. She allowed Mark to go to the doctors with Dawn. Mark was so grateful Ms. Stewart allowed him to go. He believed too, the government would soon drop the case any day, but that did not happen. The pressure on Dawn to reconsider having Mark's baby by her mother and friends starting to get to Dawn. She started to withdraw from Mark. She stopped coming to see him and stopped calling him on the phone. Mark would try calling her at work and her friends told Mark to leave Dawn alone, she did not want to see him any more. Mark would call her house and her mother would lie and say she was not home. Mark knew she was lying because he would have his friend call, that Dawn's mother would not know, and she would then put Dawn on the phone. This did not last long because they became aware of this tactic, plus the friend of Mark's was told by her husband that she was no longer allowed to talk to Mark because the FBI said, "they may be called as witnesses against Mark and that they were to stay away." They were also told by the FBI that they could be implicated for the same crimes due to guilt by association.

This caused Mark great pain. Incarcerated at his father's house, and here is what he wrote in his Diary:

9:30 P.M. My God, please help me understand why these people won't leave Dawn alone! Why can't these people understand that the government has made a mistake. My heart hurts, I have no friends, and the soon mother of my child is being persuaded by her mother and friends to have nothing to do with me. Dawn told me the other day that the FBI told friends of hers at work that my charges will not allow him to see the bright of day for fifty years! Fuck those mother fuckers...! I told Dawn. But she said, "they must know something, it has been over three months and they still haven't let you go. And who is going to take care of the baby, I want my child to have a father, and the way it looks you won't be there." I got so mad at her I called her a loser and asked if she was going to have an abortion. She became furious and called me an asshole, then hung up. All I could do is cry right now, this feeling of lifelessness is getting to me. I don't want to live any more. I must think of a way to depart this fucked-up situation. I can't let the government beat me, but I'm weak and I have no one to talk to. I just tried to talk to my dad and he gave his usual dumb ass comment of "You don't need to be thinking about some girl having your baby, you need to hope the government doesn't find anything that would make these charges stick!" I told him that I was innocent, my dad's response was, "If you're so innocent why is the government still holding you!" I felt this rage of anger so bad that I wanted to slap my father around like he did me when I was a kid. I just walked away. I finally realized that I was on my own that nobody really gave a fuck about me.

My adopted dad, big man, he had no clue how close he came to see how much hurt I could have done to him. Please, God, forgive me, you are my only hope I have to survive this plot against me. The ignorance of the people around me is, far less of a concern than the will for me to stay alive. Please, make the pain in my heart go away, let me see my dogs, my bird, my belongings. It's now been three months and I have lost 15 pounds. I really am scared and there are no more tears to cry, I'm drying out from the inside. Only the echoes of the negative thoughts running wildly in my mind are trying to take hold of my soul! Good night...

Thursday, May 14
NELSON'S DIARY OF HOME ARREST

11:00 A.M. Dawn just called me and asked if she could come over and talk I was so happy, I haven't seen her over a week. I remember when I first met her, she was working at a restaurant as a waitress. She waited on me she was wearing my favorite perfume that woman could wear "*Bijon*!" Dawn told me that she worked at the restaurant part-time and answered phones for a company part-time at night. Everything seemed perfect, we hit it off real well! Then one day after a few weeks passed, I found out through a mistake on Dawn's part, that the phones she answered at this office was an escort service. I was so disappointed but she assured me that she just answered the phones. All I could think was that she was a prostitute, based on all the negative media reports. Maybe I'm wrong. I will find out just what she does then I'll figure out what to do then. She is so pretty and her eyes are like gems and she treats me like a king. A few more weeks went by and I found out that she was actually an escort, at this time of the relationship I was very much attached to this girl. The fact she had been lying to me and that she was an escort flipped me out. She was lying to everyone, even her mother. Boy, how do I get involved with such fucked-up situations?

As the relationship went on things got out of control I wanted her to stop living a lie, and become a normal person. This was out of the question for Dawn. She liked the money and she swore that she never did anything with her clients this made me sick to my stomach. I knew that it would only be a matter of time before we would no longer be a couple. Every time I would try to break things off she would cry. I then would change my mind and stay with her. I thought maybe I could convince her to quit her job and just be my girlfriend the waitress, and when the night club would open she could work there. We did end up breaking up, but just like my ex-wife who flew in from Los Angeles to save me from going to jail Dawn came back to be with me during these troubled times and that's how she got pregnant. My dad said to me a very dumb-ass question "You better make sure you're the father!" I just blew it off and considered the source.

8:30 P.M. Dawn just left after a few hours, things though were not the same. She was telling me she was having cramps and that she needed to go to the doctor. I told her I would call Ms. Stewart and ask if I could take her. She said, "she would rather wait a few days to see what happens." I thought that to be strange but I could not convince her otherwise. I couldn't believe she did not want to go to the doctors. That's my baby too, I thought, "don't I have any rights to this child?" Dawn just told me that she is going away for a day with her mother to Flagstaff, Arizona. And that she would be gone all day, and that there would be no way to contact her. I got mad at her, I asked her if she was so sick, why was she going to Flagstaff. She told me that she needed to get away for a while and that all she is going to do is sleep in the back of the car. She insisted that her mother wanted her to go too. Dawn also told me not to call her mother's house, the restaurant or the escort service they are getting tired of my phone calls and that if I was to persist on calling they will call the police and file harassment charges on me. "Those fucking assholes, I hate them all!" I 'm so confused, Diary but what can I do or say? Well I'm going to sleep, watch over me God! Good Night...

Saturday, May 16
NELSON'S DIARY OF HOME ARREST

4:30 A.M. I just awoke from a bad dream I have to write it down because I can not sleep. I 'm dripping wet with sweat and my heart is beating fast and my eyes are full with tears. I saw Dawn at a clinic, I was looking through a hole in the ceiling. Dawn was crying and her mother was comforting her. I could not believe what was about to happen and in a few minutes it did. They killed my baby! I knew I was dreaming and I tried to wake up but I could not. As Dawn lay there with her mother after the operation, I too could only lay there in disbelief! I wanted to cry out to them all and say, how could you do this to me and my child, is it only you that has choice to choice from life or death? Where are my rights as a father? Though I believe in freedom of choice and that an individual has the right to decide right or wrong for themselves, I do not believe that if two individuals create life that only one individual (mother), can decide on death! I don't believe Dawn would do such a thing and I'm glad it was only a dream! I want to call Dawn and tell her of my dream. I can't or they will call the police! God, I hurt inside! Good Night...

7:00 P.M. I have not heard from Dawn, I have had a real tough day, not to mention the dog bite to my leg from my dad's dog (Zoro) the other day. It was hurting real bad, dad asked what I did to make his dog bite me. What an asshole! He didn't even ask if I was okay. He is so very lucky I walked away, for I'm not that little boy that this one time 6′ 3,″ 200 plus pound, golden gloves boxer used to beat on like one of his opponents. I did not need any trouble. I just realized the truth about this old man I called dad. I'm sorry I have to be so hateful diary, but what can I do? I'm about to lose my mind and nobody fuckin cares! Talk to you tomorrow.

9:00 P.M. I just heard from Dawn I asked her how was her trip? She got upset with me and said, "you don't believe I went to Flagstaff?" I didn't even ask her if she had gone. Boy, I didn't know what to think. She hung up on me, I didn't dare call her back! I was feeling sick, something was not right. I just can't figure it out. I'm too tired I must go to sleep! Good Night...

Wednesday, May 20
NELSON'S DIARY OF HOME ARREST

10:30 P.M. I can't handle it any more. I haven't heard from Dawn for four days. I'm going to call her at work I don't care at this point if they call the police on me or not! She is carrying my child, too, and I want to know how she is feeling or if she is even alive. I'll let you know what happened Diary. Oh, I passed my drug test!

11:00 P.M. I finally reached Dawn. The people at her work at first would not let me talk to her, but she did finally get on the phone after I begged. Dawn told me that things are not going to work out with us any more and that nobody wants you around, especially here! "Fuck those people at your work" I said, "they are the lowest form of human existence, doing the work they do." Dawn got very mad! "Fuck you asshole" she said, "then you are calling me that too." I said, "if the shoe fits, then so be it!" I tried to calm her down for our child's sake. She started to listen to the dream I had almost a week ago. She stopped me and said, "how dare you, think I would have an abortion." The names she called me, then her friends at work started calling me names too! One of Dawn's body guards/driver even threatened to come over and kick my ass, telling me how big he was. Dawn knew better than that, she told him she didn't think that would be a good idea, that I would definitely hurt him more than he could even try to imagine. I heard that dumb-ass say, "Really you think he could kick my ass?" Dawn's reply was definitely, at this moment, he is threatening to come over here and kick the fuck out of everyone in here. I wanted so bad to let out these built up frustrations on all those losers at the escort service. But there was no way I would let those low-life fucks get the best of me. Sorry again,

Diary, I'm just about to go insane, but I'm sane enough to realize my self-destructive ways.

Dawn then informed me that the reason she has not talked to me was because she suffered a miscarriage and on Monday, May 18, she had a DNC, at her mothers doctors office. I had asked her why she did not go to her doctor, the one we both went to see when we first found out she was pregnant; I did get permission from Ms. Stewart.

Dawn started coming up with all these lame excuses. I knew she was lying. I told her that she really had an abortion and that I being the father, by her words (no DNA test was done). I had a right to know the truth. Dawn became very belligerent, "How dare you say I had an abortion, and call my fucken mother and ask her if she was with me at her doctors on Monday." Dawns last words to me: "Fuck You, you mother fucker, I hope you rot in jail for 50 years, for what you have caused me... Don't ever call me again or I will personally call the police and tell them of your threatening me! She then hung-up the phone!"

I could not believe my ears, my heart was broken, and now stepped on like a piece of shit. My poor little baby, I tried to help you, and I just want you to know that I will do whatever I can, to not let your life be taken in vain! My eyes and face covered with tears. My hand shaking, I can barely write. I love you my child, and I'm so very   sorry   that   you   are, *DEACD*..!

Thursday, May 21
NELSON'S DIARY OF HOME ARREST

10:30 P.M. I'm not feeling well. Last night was a spinning carousel out of control. I don't believe Dawn had a miscarriage. I believe she had an abortion. I called the doctor, Dawn told me she went to on Monday, May 18; her mother's doctor. But when I called the office to confirm that Dawn had actually went to this doctor. They told me that Dawn's mother was a patient, but they did not perform any DNC on Dawn Kauffman, because they are not opened on Mondays. I can't believe what is happening, this bitch is lying to me. *Why?* I called Planned Parenthood too! To find out if Dawn went there to get a possible abortion. The clinic told me they do abortions every other Saturday. I asked them if it was this Saturday the 23 of May, They would be performing abortions? The lady on the phone told me no, but last Saturday the 16, was the scheduled abortions. I asked her how long does an abortion take. She said, "a little while, the longest part of the procedures is waiting for the anesthesia to wear off and to make sure everything is okay, which takes all day."

I had asked if Dawn might have been a patient with them. They told me that I was not entitled to that information. "How can I not be allowed to know if the mother of my child put our child to death?" I said. Her answer was really shocking, she told me, "You have no rights to this child in this day and age."

How can you say this, "it took the two of us, to make this child, and only Dawn has the power to take away our baby's life? I replied.

She said, "I'm sorry sir, but we do not make the laws, we just enforce them. The majority of the mothers that come in here have a choice, "life or death." We carry out their wishes and protect their identity. Here the father has no rights, whether married or not." I hung up on her, I am so fuckin mad right now!!!

I called Dawn's mother. She was mean to me, and she said, "leave my daughter alone. That you have no right asking anyone about Dawn's personal decision on her own well being, and that you are being selfish. Do not to call any more and to move on with your life." I asked her if she could please tell me if Dawn had an abortion? She insisted that it was none of my business. I asked her if she took her daughter to her, doctor on Monday 18. She said, "yes." Then hung-up the phone. I hurt inside, please make the hurt go away. I don't know what to do with myself any more. I just want to *die...* these thoughts are getting closer and closer to becoming a reality. I must be strong and work this out. I 'm tired, I don't know what is happening to my life or my court case.

It's been four month know and I still sleep on the floor, because the single bed that is in the office of my father's house were I sleep is too soft. All the car accidents I have been in have taken their toll on my body. My dad's big screen television is too loud. I try to ask if he could turn down the volume. The television sits on the other side of the wall less than two feet from my head. Dad sits about fifteen feet away, and his hearing is going out. He does not give a rat's ass about me! Yes, I'm here at his house and he has told me numerous times, that it could be worse. I would always tell him, that at least in jail, lights and televisions are out by 10:00 P.M. He is so ignorant. Zoro his dog tried to bite me again, if his dog bites me one more time.. I will kill it!... All I do is sit in this room on the floor wishing, for my freedom and now, wanting to *die*... God watch over me and keep me strong! Good Night...

Saturday, May 23
NELSON'S DIARY OF HOME ARREST

8:00 P.M. It's been a few days since I have heard from Dawn. I wish this court shit was out of my life! I really don't understand why and how this could of happened to me. I'm innocent but these people are treating me like I was guilty. I am so confused. Maybe one day I will learn why this has happened. This morning around 10:00 A.M., I went to Dawn's work at the Italian restaurant; this area was the forbidden zone I was not allowed to travel in. I can't explain it, Diary. I did not plan to go to this forbidden zone. I just arrived, nobody believed me though, but what did I expect? I subconsciously just wanted to know the truth about the death of our child. I really don't give a damn what people think. I believed that this was my child and I did not whatsoever give permission to abort my child. These people have turned on me. They don't believe that I have nothing to do with this extortion case. Dawn was very upset that I showed up to her work. That stupid bitch was just getting out of the passenger side of car, driven by a guy, she kissed him good bye! I was pissed! She told me it was a friend. She did admit she stayed the night at his house, but insisted it was platonic; the only reason she told me was the fact she was unaware of my arrival. When I first arrived, I checked her car motor's hood to see if it was warm from driving. It was not and the restaurant was not opened yet. When Dawn arrived the restaurant had just opened, so she was kind of busted if you know what I mean? She told me she was going to call the police if I did not leave. I confronted her on the facts about her telling me of her miscarriage. She was pissed, she said, "You had no right to call my mother or doctor. You are a piece of shit, I hope you rot in jail."

I did leave immediately. When I got home, my dad was very pissed off. He said, I'm going to call my probation officer and tell her you went into the forbidden zone." He had a right to be mad because he was basically the bail that was put up so that I could be released into his custody. If I broke probation, he would have to go to jail, too. What I did was wrong but when it comes to life or death situations (my child), I would probably do it again. Boy, I'm at the lowest point of my life and my God, show me who my friends really are. I thank you. I'm scared, I have to call my probation officer. I'll probably have to go to jail now! I figured my child is worth any punishment given. Good Night...

Monday, May 25
NELSON'S DIARY OF HOME ARREST

9:00 A.M. I called my probation officer, Ms. Stewart, and told her I broke the conditions of my release. She was sorry for my loss of my child, but had me understand the severities of my actions. She was sure the U. S. Attorney Chuck Hyder, would have the courts revoke my probation, and I would have to surrender to the courts to be placed in jail. (I really don't understand why I have a probation officer, it is completely mind boggling. I didn't do anything wrong but I have to submit urine tests. These people all treat me like I really am a criminal).

Mrs. Stewart was right, before she could even write her recommendations, the U.S. Attorney and FBI had already been notified by Dawn's mother. I won't find out what's going to happen until this afternoon. I should have never left I can't believe I was so out of control. The reasons behind my actions to me were family related, so I took the route my subconscious mind guided me. I know this is hard to believe, Diary, but I really loved the child that was growing in Dawn's body. I was drawn to it's existence. It would have been the first blood relation I would have experienced, but not any more. I'm trying to limit my foul language, sometimes it helps to release these negative words, built up from this negative energy inside me.

4:30 P.M. I just got off the phone with Mrs. Stewart. She informed me that the prosecutor is filing a motion to have my probation revoked (this means I 'm going to jail). Why, goddamn it? Doesn't this prosecutor have any feelings towards my loss? I don't see why he should, nobody else has. My head is spinning and my stomach is killing me. I'd guess I'd rather be in jail that way I can't act on my desires. Mrs. Stewart told me she would not recommend jail for me. She would rather push for me to wear an electronic device around my ankle. I won't know for a few days. I did not want to tell her I'd rather go to jail, because my dad's wife is an excellent cook! Speaking of food, it's time for dinner! Thanks for listening!

10:00 P.M. I can't sleep my dad's TV is so loud, every time I ask him to please turn it down he gets mad. Why does he have to be so selfish. I wish I could tell him what he is doing to me. I love my dad yet, I want to kick his ass. I wonder what my biological parents would do if they knew what was happening to their son.

"Oh, God, do I hurt inside." There is nowhere I can go to escape the pain and confusion that constantly runs rapid in my mind. The thought of death seems a pleasant desire, though I still have the ability to know right from wrong. Taking my own life will not satisfy the stone throwing in my life. The only way I will win the true victory of life, is to live out the good and bad of my trials and tribulations, because life is now, and death is forever, in my present state of existence. Good Night, Diary...

Tuesday, May 26
NELSON'S DIARY OF HOME ARREST

8:30 P.M. This was a very scary day I had to go to court and I am now required to wear an electronic monitoring bracelet on my ankle which will monitor my location at all times. The U.S. Attorney Chuck Hyder wanted me to go to jail. This man is a zealot. He has no compassion. I can see why, he's over weight and seems to have a wooden leg or something is wrong with it. I believe there is something wrong with this whole case. One day, I will find out the truth behind the prosecution. When I do these people better watch out. I'll take my findings to the highest level, maybe to the President of the U.S.A. I'll take it to Capital Hill in Washington D.C. if I have to. I just don't know what to believe in any more.

This bracelet, I'm to wear is the closet thing to the mark of the beast explained in the book of Revelations, in my *Roman Catholic Bible.* What this device is supposed to do is between the hours of 8:00 P.M. to 5:00 A.M. The federal monitoring computer will call my dad's house any time throughout this time period. I 'm supposed to answer the phone and listen to a few seconds of instructions on what I'm to do next. Then I place this long rectangle shaped box which is connected to a cord which is plugged into the phone jack. I place this unit to the device on my ankle. I then hear a series of tones, and the computer asks for a voice verification of my name then it tells me a connection has been made and that I may hang up. This process takes about five minutes.

10:30 P.M. Dawn just called me a few minutes ago. She told me that the FBI wants to ask her questions about me. I asked her what she expected, she and her mother turned me in. The phone call they made to my father wasn't good enough for them, they called my probation officer.

I asked her again about our child. She got upset with me again. She told me to fuck off and that she hopes they put me in jail and throw away the key. She went on to say that she was going tell the FBI whatever they want to know. I told her go ahead, she knew damned well I had nothing to do with this crime. She said, that if I didn't why were they still holding me and that she doesn't know why the government would *lie*! I told her to go do what she has to do and one day she will be sorry for the death of our child. She said, "fuck off" and then hung up on me. What a loser, I should have known the cowardliness that dwelled in her character, look what she did for a job. All those times she lied to me and her mother. I'm better off without these people who turned their backs on me! I have a great hate and the anxiety in my body. I can't believe I have allowed myself to be eaten away by the ignorance of others. What do I expect, when the *Federal Bureau of Investigation* and the U.S.A. attorney tells everyone that I was part of an extortion ring, and threatening to kidnap a young child and cut off his arms and legs; if their demands were not met. These assholes are destroying my life.

Diary, God showed me who was real and who was a coward, but I still don't know who is behind this conspiracy against me. I'm not feeling too well I have to go to sleep. Dad's television is so loud. I'm starting to hate this man all over again. I feel that these feelings building up between us are not his fault. I haven't lived with him permanently, since I was tossed out of his home, when I was eighteen. He was persuaded by my ex-wife Gina to help me. If only he could have helped me because I was his son and not the adopted reject that I have felt all my life. Good Night...

Wednesday, May 27
DAWN KAUFFMAN'S SECOND INTERROGATION

This interview reported by Case Special Agent Keith Tolhurst was the second interview with Nelson's ex-girlfriend, Dawn Kauffman although the first interview was never filed with the attorneys that represented Nelson. But then again, neither were other interviews by the FBI concerning the alibis of Mark Nelson. (Nick Lees, Brian Holt, Doug and Zoe Cameron, The managers of the apartments where Nelson lived for almost 2 years). Because of the fact that these other interviews proved positive that Nelson was telling the truth. During this interview, Dawn told Tolhurst that Nelson was looking for her and knew to go look at the restaurant she frequented. This information was incorrect, Dawn actually worked at this restaurant. This was the restaurant where Nelson met Dawn. For some unknown reason, someone misconstrued this statement. *Why?*

Dawn also reiterated in this interview that she was convinced that Nelson was not guilty of the crimes he had been charged with, and that any connection that may suggest he had anything to do with this extortion plot was coincidental. She did give this Special Agent information about some friends of Nelson's that had a friend whose sister was very good friends with the supposed victim, Marc Kaplan's wife, Marci. Though this information was checked out, there was still no connection between the intended victim or his friends of friends to or of someone who might know someone who knew something, that could shed light on this case. Clearly, Case Special Agent Keith Tolhurst and his merry men conspired together to implicate Miller and Nelson to this crime. These Special Agents were just trying to create evidence to fool everyone. When in fact, they only fooled themselves.

Dawn stated that she would be happy to cooperate with authorities and would provide any information they requested. Case Special Agent Tolhurst told Dawn to stay away from Nelson, because she may be called as a witness to testify against Nelson. Dawn agreed to his request. Dawn Kauffman's interview went like this:

FEDERAL BUREAU OF INVESTIGATION

Date of transcription   6/9/92

        DAWN KAUFFMAN, a white female, date of birth November 9, 1970, was interviewed related to the fact that MARK A. NELSON had violated the restrictions of his release pending trial. KAUFFMAN stated that she did meet MARK NELSON "out of bounds" at an ABCO Supermarket on the corner of Scottsdale Road and Shea. She stated that NELSON had been looking for her and knew to look there since she frequented a restaurant in that shopping center.

        KAUFFMAN reiterated that she was convinced that NELSON was not guilty of the crimes he had been charged with and stated that any connection it may appear he has to this extortion was probably coincidence. KAUFFMAN further stated that Scottsdale is a small city and there were numerous coincidences continually popping up between individuals. KAUFFMAN stated that just recently she found out that a friend of MARK NELSON's, RICHARD SOLOMI, and his wife, LEA SOLOMI, commented that a friend of theirs, TONY (LNU), had a sister who was very good friends with MARCI KAPLAN.

        KAUFFMAN stated she would be more than happy to cooperate with authorities and provide them any information they requested. KAUFFMAN further advised that she felt it necessary to notify her mother who in turn notified MARK NELSON's father that he violated his restrictions by going "out of bounds".

stigation on   5/27/92   at Phoenix, Arizona   File #   9A-PX-46497

by   SA KEITH D. TOLHURST/jla   Date dictated   6/2/92

This document contains neither recommendations nor conclusions of the FBI. It is the property of the FBI and is loaned to your agency; it and its contents are not to be distributed outside your agency.

June 12, 1992
NELSON'S BIRTHDAY

9:00 P.M. Today is my birthday, I'm 32 years old. I never thought I would ever be in a situation like this. I stand accused of extortion, with the overt act of kidnaping and threatening to cut the arms off of a young child. How could anyone ever think I could do such a thing?

My dad's wife, Carol, cooked a dinner for me. Nobody called to wish me a happy birthday. I did receive a card, it wasn't very nice. The coward who sent it to me did not sign a name. I was not shocked, I can only imagine who the sender was. I figured at least this person went out of their way to send it to me; any acknowledgment at this point, whether good or bad means at least I got a card.

My adopted brothers and sisters never called, what did I expect. These people blame me for the breakup of our adopted parents and family. They all live in a glass house, my dad having the biggest. To this day, my family still believes I'm the deceiver to the facts of my mom's promiscuous ways. She never fooled me; that's why I was always in trouble with her because she could not get me to admit to her lies as being the truth. I would rather take her beating, which then lead to my father's inability to accept the truth that his wife was fucking his best friend, the sheriff! I'm sorry, Diary, for being so blatant, but I've carried this burden around for almost 28 years. These people can all kiss my ass. I called my mom, why, I didn't know? I guess I wanted to know if she had changed, as people do as they get older. I found out that she really believes her own lies. I haven't talked to her in six years. The first thing out of her foul mouth was, "now you know what its like to be accused of something you didn't do." I asked if she meant what happened between her and dad? She said, "that I knew damn well what she was talking about!" I now know why, I haven't spoken to her.

She has convinced everyone that I'm some kind of animal to spread such lies. I know this to be fact based on all their actions towards me my whole life. My dad's wife did tell me eight years back that while she moved into my dad's house, she found love letters to my mom from the sheriff. My dad never told anyone of their findings. I think That's pretty low of him not to say anything to exonerate me with my family. At this point, I just want to forget. But it's very hard I can not leave, I'm a prisoner of the courts and my dad is ordered to watch me. It's almost like I was adopted all over again. The only difference is I'm 32 years old now.

Boy this electronic device on my ankle is starting to drive me crazy! The home monitoring system is suppose to call me 2-3 times a night from 8:00 P.M. to 5:00 A.M. This would drive anyone crazy knowing that if you did not answer the call you would go to jail. I'm a very heavy sleeper and to make things worst, this system has called me almost 7-12 times a night. I don't know what to do any more, every time I complain the calls increase. Not only does this effect me, but also my dad and his wife. I'm starting to see spots I'm very tired. I haven't had a good full night's sleep in the last three weeks, I've lost another 5 pounds I'm down to 157 pounds. Boy, I don't look to good any more. I've noticed the hair on my body has grown faster and the hair on my head is getting grey.

These mother fuckers are trying to keep me from sleeping and it's starting to affect my body. It's been almost four months that I've been under house arrest. I've lost my job, friends, and I'm starting to lose my mind. I went to the doctors, they gave me Prosaic, Buspar, and Zoloft. The drugs gave me severe headaches and made me feel like a robot without any programing. I would just sit in my room. I want to *die...* I don't care about my life any more! No one believes that I had nothing to do with this crime. Who are the masterminds behind this conspiracy against me and why are they getting away with these actions against me? The phone is ringing it's the computer monitoring system. I have to go. Good Night...

Tuesday, August 4
JOHN R. HANNAH ASSISTANT FEDERAL PUBLIC DEFENDER
WRITES A LETTER TO JEFF ROSS, ATTORNEY FOR NELSON

Assistant Federal Public Defender John R. Hannah was the court-appointed attorney for Michael Miller. He contacted Jeffrey Ross, the attorney for Nelson. Hannah was distraught over the evidence sent to him by U. S. Attorney Chuck Hyder. He admitted to Ross that he received FBI reports and material that apparently Ross did not receive. He further stated that he did not receive certain FBI reports or material that Ross had received from the FBI and wanted Ross to send what he does not have to him. It was apparent that Hannah knew that something was wrong with the way all of the FBI reports and materials were distributed. Hannah did tell Ross, that this trading of information should never be revealed to Hyder.

Mr. Hannah, knew that the case was weak against his client and Nelson, he just could not figure out why nothing matched to the claims of the FBI toward these two defendants. He was contacted by Mr. Black, the *Frank Alber*'s attorney. Mr. Black notified him that the FBI and the U.S. Attorney's office were trying to make a deal with *Alber*. They wanted him to admit that Miller and Nelson really had something to do with this case. Mr. Black assured the FBI and the U.S. Attorney office that *Alber* could not make a deal with them to these regards because Miller and Nelson had nothing to do with this case and he was not about to commit perjury.

Mr. Hannah and Mr. Black, even though they to are employed by the government, knew that the government had made a mistake. They had sworn to uphold the law not worrying about the consequences later with their peers. These two men should be rewarded for their commitment to the truth. Little did they know, it was no mistake. It was actually a Government Conspiracy, not by our actual government, but by employees of our government. The prosecution against Miller and Nelson was furthered by the commission of fraud, perjury, and the misrepresentation or falsification of evidence presented to Magistrate Judge Sitver on the Criminal Complaint Affidavit filed February 19, 1992 by FBI Case Special Agent Keith Tolhurst.

Furthermore, these same actions were carried out and presented to the grand jury by Tolhurst and Hyder for the indictment against Miller and Nelson. These individuals clearly conspired not just against the two defendants, but against their superiors as well. These kinds of actions are the reason our American Judicial System is out of control, out of balance, and a mockery of law. This should in no way be tolerated in any system that boasts justice for all...!

FEDERAL PUBLIC DEFENDER

District of Arizona

320 North Central Avenue, Suite 200

PHOENIX, ARIZONA 85004

FREDRIC F. KAY   (602) 379-3290
Federal Public Defender   (FTS) (602) 379-3290
                                                                        (FAX) 602-379-4300

August 4, 1992   AUG   5 1992

                                        BUDOFF & ROSS, P.C.

Jeff Ross
BUDOFF & ROSS, P.C.
111 W. Monroe, Ste. 1212
Phoenix, AZ 85003

RE: United States v. Michael Miller

Dear Jeff:

Enclosed are the FBI reports and materials that Hyder appears to have sent to me but not to you. It looks like the only materials that you received but I didn't are FBI pages 82-85 (report of SAs Hamilton and Felton) and pages 91-92 (report of SAs Rivas and Walker). Please shoot some copies my way.

Remember, this exchange of information should not ever be revealed to Hyder.

Very truly yours,

JOHN R. HANNAH
Asst. Federal Public Defender

JRH:cfc
C2146LJRH

Enclosure

September 10
NELSON'S DIARY OF HOME ARREST

9:00 P.M. Today was a very bad day even though I'm painting and making enough to pay my car insurance and my probation officer. Just these three items combined are a total of $800. The problem I have is no one would give me a job through a company. I was forced to seek work on my own. I make about $200 a week; I'm 32 years old and have painted for over 14 years and I'm making less than if I worked at *McDonalds*. If I don't pay my probation officer I go back to jail. My father assured me that he would never make my payments so I'd better do what I had to do to keep the payments up. The hate I have for these people not so much my dad but the Federal Judicial System! I will not let them beat me!

To make things worse, when I came home from work my dad said he wanted to talk to me. He did not look too happy. He told me that my probation officer called and said, "I did not answer the phone last night." I tried to tell him I was home, he wouldn't listen, he started to yell at me. I was just about to knock him on his fat ass, when Carol stepped in, and told my father to calm down. I mentioned that if I was not here to answer the phone I looked at Carol and said, "you would have had to gotten up to answer the phone, because dad's lazy ass, would have made you get up to answer the phone late at night." My dad about hit the roof, but for some reason he agreed with me.

He couldn't believe this was happening to us. This was almost the end of my home arrest, my dad was about to call this whole thing off and tell them to put me into jail. I did everything I could to keep this man happy for the last seven months of home arrest, I cannot believe these stupid asses, were still holding me. Why, am I not going to court? What happened to my speedy trail, and who's in charge of these kangaroo courts anyway? My head is spinning, I just want to *die*! I don't know how much more I can take of this bullshit.

The other day, I filled the bathtub up with water, got inside and I had an electrical appliance to drop into the water. Everything was set. As I was laying there inside the tub, my mind, flopping back and fourth with the true uncertainties of my planned death. I was so scared. I was sweating. I never felt so alone in my life. There was no one to call, no one to tell of my suicidal wish, no one to care for my existence.

I was so scared of death and the permanent outcome it reveals, and the fact my dad's wife, Carol, would have to bare the reality of my death in her home. I got out of the tub and went into the room in which I sleep. I closed the door and cried. The tears poured from my eyes like a bad storm. I wish there was someone I could hold and to tell me everything was going to be "Okay." I knew it was close to the end of my life.

I'm so tired, I'm going to go to sleep if I can. My dad is watching a war movie and the speakers on his big screen are right behind the wall on the floor were I sleep.

The phone will ring again tonight, I don't know when. I don't know a damn thing any more. Good Night, Diary...

November 13
NELSON'S DIARY OF HOME ARREST

6:00 P.M. I just got off the phone with an ex-girlfriend of mine named Connie South. She told me I was a father of twins. I can't believe it. Death of one child, and now I have two. I have to tell you Diary, this girl was strange but I was so attracted to her it did not matter. I met her almost a year ago at the night club *After the Gold Rush*. I was there with a different girl. Connie came up to me and told me, that I was a very sexy guy. I had this shirt on that exposed my chest a little, Connie put her hands under my shirt and told me I had a nice chest, as well. I couldn't believe this girl I wanted her real bad. She turned me on with her excitement over me! She asked me for my phone number. I gave it to her and the next day she called me. We dated for a few weeks She was on probation for something but she wouldn't tell me, even though I paid her probation officer a few times during our short courtship. I never found out what she was on probation for. Connie always told me it was really none of my business, and in time she would let me know what she was on probation for. I just blew it off, she was so beautiful to me and I wanted to stay with her as long as possible.

We made love on Halloween night, I knew that we conceived a child, but I never told her about my feelings she would have thought I was crazy! We did however break up a few weeks later. She had a boyfriend named Brad. (I knew this guy during the night club business days). Brad came over to her house while I was there, he had been out of town for a few weeks. He was furious, I did not feel right leaving her alone with this guy, but I too was mad at Connie for lying to me. She told me she had no boyfriend, (men are always the ones being accused of cheating, but when a girl does it, it seems to be "okay.") Brad ended up beating her up pretty bad, he even slammed her head into his vehicle. I received a phone call from her roommate when I got home, that she needed me to come back to her. I did go back to see her, she was in bad shape. When I saw her there crying to the police looking for sympathy, it was then I realized there was no room in my life for a girl like this. I left and we never saw each other again. However, I did receive a phone call from her a few weeks later informing me she might be pregnant. I was happy, I told her I would do what ever it took to make her happy and that I would like to get back with her. She told me she did not want to be in a relationship based on children alone. She wasn't sure if she was pregnant and she would let me know. Connie did call me back but she informed me she was not pregnant. I did not believe her but I just accepted her words as truth. From that point until today I have not heard form Connie South.

Connie wanted to know if I would like to meet my daughters, and that I had nothing to worry about she wasn't looking for money and I wasn't even on the birth certificate. I thought this was strange she would be telling me this information. I do know these are my two daughters, why did she leave me off my childrens' birth certificate. What gives her that right to keep from me, something I had a part of creating. I will find out soon she is coming over tonight! "Damn," I'm so scared. I still love this girl and she doesn't even realize, I always did! Now she is the mother of my children that has to mean something. I hope we can work it out so my children will enjoy *Biological Parenting*. I will know when I see her, If I get those feelings like I did before, then it would be up to her if she thinks of me the same way and not just someone night stand! I'll talk to you later, Diary!

11:00 P.M. "Oh my God!" My children looked like me! I could see me in them! Connie was so pretty I could not believe my eye's I wanted to cry so bad. If I was not accused of this crime, chances are I would not ever have found out that I have two daughters, and they are twins... Connie told me she saw me on the TV news and in *The Arizona Republic*. She wanted me to know I had children and that the reason she told me she wasn't pregnant, was that she was just going to have an abortion. And knew if she had told me, I would of try to change her mind or talk her into staying together because of the children. "I thought about it" she said. Then decided to keep them, I didn't know I was going to have twins!

When she told me that I was flipping pissed off! Boy I wanted to tell her how selfish that was. To think someone has the power to destroy a living human being growing and living inside, now comes another woman, who gave birth to these children also has the power to exclude me from their life. What is happening here? I'm so glad she changed her mind. As these children grow up, she will think to herself; "I almost killed these two little girls!"

I did have a problem with my dad, he did not like Connie's tattoos. It really upset him he kept asking about her tatoos. I had to walk away, and then he started to tell me I'd better have a paternity test done to make sure these are your kids. He is so fucked up sometimes. Why can't he talk to me instead of at me? I don't take this shit from anyone but for him I will.

Well I'm getting tired I sure miss my dogs I haven't seen them for a while. I have no personality left. These children are my hope of a new life when this is all over. I will have to wait and see. I just thank you, "God," I'm alive to see these children and for the children to see their father! She said she will let me see them but I detect a negative uncertainty in her voice and mannerisms. I want to believe in her so bad so why would she come around me knowing I'm looking at 50 years. Is this her way to clear her conscience? I hope not, with my predicaments I don't know what is going on with my life. I do know, I want these children in my life. Good Night, Diary...

November 23

AFFIDAVIT OF PRIVATE INVESTIGATOR & PLANNING
AND ZONING COMMISSIONER JONATHAN COLVIN

Mr. Colvin agreed to submit an affidavit concerning his involvement with, Nelson. This was the individual who had dinner with an executive of a bank and told him of this bizarre story. This executive then told Dan Maynard about the story and asked Maynard if he would look into the case for him. Nelson was never told who this vice-president of this bank was, who had asked Maynard to examine it more closely.

A F F I D A V I T

STATE OF ARIZONA   )
) ss.
COUNTY OF MARICOPA   )

Jonathan Colvin, being duly sworn, deposes and says:

1. I, Jonathan Colvin, am self employed and a resident of Glendale, Arizona. I am a private investigator and I am 44 years old. I am also a Planning and Zoning commissioner for the City of Glendale.

2. In May of 1992, I saw a sign in the yard of a freshly painted home on the way home from playing golf with my son. It was on a Sunday evening, and as I had wanted my home painted, I called Mark Nelson. Previsouly, I had experienced problems with painters showing up even for an estimate, so when Mark Nelson said he would come over late on a Sunday afternoon, I was surprised but pleased. He arrived promptly, was very business-like, and said he would prepare an estimate for me. He returned the next day, on time as scheduled with a very reasonable estimate. I was hesitant to hire Mark Nelson based on his appearance. He did not look like a painter. He was very clean, had long hair, wore gold jewelry, and drove a flashy car. After a conversation with my wife, a former art teacher, and Mark, we decided that Mark had been punctual, reliable and was an experienced house painter. He also was very sincere and knowledgable. He assured us that he would perform the work himself and therefore guarantee it.

N000163

Mark Nelson proved to be very reliable and trustworthy. He
kept all scheduled appointments, and always arrived as per
his word, or would call to let us know he could not make the
appointment.

    3. Mark Nelson has told me about his arrest and the
circumstances surrounding his release and his ankle device.
He has experienced a great deal of emotional distress over
the calls in the middle of the night and also over the
impending trial. He has been upset that he has been unable
to participate in family outings or even go to a movie. He
has virtually no social life. He has also confided that the
circumstances of living with his parents are difficult for
both Mark and his parents.

    4. I do not believe that Mark Nelson is a flight
risk. He is a very hard and conscientious worker and is a
person that would benefit greatly from reduced supervision
and a return to a normal emotional and social life.

            FURTHER, AFFIANT SAYETH NOT.

                                JONATHAN COLVIN

SUBSCRIBED AND SWORN to before me this 23RD day of November,
1992, by JONATHAN COLVIN.

                                Notary Public

My Commission Expires Nov. 3, 1995
my commission expires

                                              N000164

"New Years Eve 1993 "
NELSON'S DIARY OF HOME ARREST

I 'm facing a new year, I never thought I would ever be were I am today. I was supposed to have "my night club opened" and I was going to be in the band that would have performed that night. This was my night to celebrate all the hard work I did for this project. It would have been great, maybe I'll get out of this crazy mess and everyone will be my friend again, and I'll get my job back and everything will be cool.

Now almost 11 months under house arrest, few days ago Connie told me that she can no longer live with the uncertainties of my legal battle. She said, "my parents, family, and friends didn't think that I should come around any more." Connie explained to me that she did not want our children to even know what their father was accused of. I can't believe this selfish girl. Who does she think she is keeping me from my children? There is really nothing I can do about it now and she knows it! I feel so sick, when in the hell is this nightmare going to be over? All my belongings were boxed up and locked away in storage, and not having my dogs, Snuggles and Patches does not help the situation. Losing my job I worked so hard for; my night club I worked so hard to open and all the money I had going toward my businesses. All the business associates and friends who gave up on me. Standing accused of being a highly trained mercenary trained by his government to be a part of an extortion ring who, according to the grand jury, FBI, and the United States Attorney's Office, Threatened a man (who I never meet in my life) and told him "His child would be kidnapped and I would have his arms and legs cut off if the demands of $250,000 were not paid!" I don't understand why this happened to me, but I will try one day to explain the situation and make us all understand.

My attorney, Dan Maynard, told me he was going to make the prosecutor take it to court. The end is near for this court case; I can feel it, and my God tells me so. I just have to keep the faith. I will not let this destroy me. I stand alone to fight this demon whose presence I can now recognize, and it's slowly killing me. Pushing my buttons for a reaction that would lead me to further destruction of my life through myself! Though this entity I have exposed; no one can see it but me, right now...!

One day, I will show the world this negative energy; that sucks and feeds off ignorance, greed, and false persecution for self worth. It is within the vortex of this sightless hole, all things will gather. I have now figured out my life and the purpose of my being in it. For it's not about life, but death and where you were before you were born. Life is a time period that all humans experience on this planet, and it's through these experiences, no matter what nationality, religion or language, one individual happens to be, they will have to choose; *Heaven or Hell*... Good Night... Diary...

Thursday, January 7
STATEMENT OF UNDERSTANDING AND STIPULATION
BETWEEN THE UNITED STATES OF AMERICA AND *FRANK ALBER*

On this day a statement of understanding and stipulation between the United States of America and *Frank Alber*, the proven mastermind behind this extortion attempt.

STATEMENT OF UNDERSTANDING AND STIPULATION BETWEEN THE UNITED STATES AND FRANK ALBER

The United States and Frank Alber agree that the mutual understanding between them is as follows:

1. Frank Alber, a defendant in United States v. Alber, et al., CR-92-080-PHX-RCB, agrees to truthfully and honestly with no knowing misstatements or omissions, assist and cooperate with the United States by providing the United States with a sworn statement designated to identifying and investigating persons who are engaged in or suspected of engaging in the extortion of Marc Kaplan.

2. The defendant Frank Alber agrees to submit to a polygraph examination or examinations at the sole discretion of the United States with respect to any statement by him pursuant to this agreement. Such examination will be conducted by a polygrapher chosen by and conducted in a manner determined in the sole discretion of the Federal Bureau of Investigation. The examination shall not be the exclusive means of determining the truthfulness of Frank Alber's statements and shall in no manner limit the United States' methods of verifying the truthfulness of Frank Alber's statements.

3. If Frank Alber should fail in any way to fulfill completely each and every one of the obligations he has agreed to under this Statement of Understanding and Stipulation, the Federal Government:

    a. May seek an indictment and prosecute Frank Alber for the offense of perjury for any false material statements for which he may be responsible;

b. Use against Frank Alber, in any prosecution, the information, testimony and documents that he has provided to the Federal Government during and subsequent to his giving his sworn statement and in the verifying polygraph examinations.

4. Should Frank Alber fail to pass any polygraph test, he agrees and stipulates herein that the Federal Government may use that information against Frank Alber should he testify for the defendants Mark Nelson and Michael Miller or on his own behalf in the subsequent prosecution of them for the extortion of Marc Kaplan.

5. Frank Alber understands and agrees that it will be in the sole discretion of the United States to determine whether or not Frank Alber has breached this Statement of Understanding and Stipulation.

6. Frank Alber understands and agrees that if in the sole discretion of the United States by and through the persons of Charles F. Hyder and Harriet M. Zeitzer, Assistant United States Attorneys, that they are satisfied with the truthfulness of his statements and elect not to prosecute Michael Miller and Mark Nelson in the belief that, based upon the representations of Frank Alber, they were not involved in any way in the extortion of Marc Kaplan that they will so notify the court of the defendant Alber's cooperation, and the extent of his cooperation.

7. The foregoing represents the entirety of the Statement of Understanding and Stipulation between Frank Alber and the United States.

8. By the signatures below, the parties herewith acknowledge they understand and completely agree with and will abide by this Agreement.

1-7-93
_____
Date

(signature)
_____
FRANK R. ALBER
Defendant

1-7-93
_____
Date

(signature)
_____
MICHAEL V. BLACK, Esq.
Counsel for Defendant Alber

1-7-93
_____
Date

(signature)
_____
HARRIET M. ZEITZER, Esq.
Assistant U.S. Attorney

1/7/93
_____
Date

(signature)
_____
CHARLES F. HYDER, Esq.
Assistant U.S. Attorney

Thursday, January 14
MOTION TO DISMISS WITHOUT PREJUDICE
THE UNITED STATES OF AMERICA vs MILLER AND NELSON

Exactly seven days after the Statement of Understanding and Stipulation between the United States of America and *Frank Alber*, the United States of America
respectfully requested that the Honorable Court dismiss without prejudice the indictment Against Michael G. Miller and Mark A. Nelson, the defendants. It gives,
"Reason For Dismissal" and "Reason To Grant" the Government's Motion to Dismiss.

1 LINDA A. AKERS
   United States Attorney
2 District of Arizona

3 CHARLES F. HYDER
   Assistant United States Attorney
4 Arizona State Bar No. 001967
   4000 United States Courthouse
5 230 North First Avenue
   Phoenix, Arizona 85025
6 Telephone: (602) 514-7500

7

8   UNITED STATES DISTRICT COURT

9   DISTRICT OF ARIZONA

   UNITED STATES OF AMERICA,   )
10   )
                Plaintiff,   )   NO. CR-92-080-PHX-RCB
11   )
        v.   )   MOTION TO DISMISS WITHOUT
12   )   PREJUDICE
   MICHAEL G. MILLER and   )
13 MARK NELSON,   )
)
14   Defendants.   )
   _____)

15
        The United States of America, pursuant to Rule 48(a) Fed. R.
16
   Crim. P., respectfully requests this Honorable Court to dismiss
17
   without prejudice, the indictment in this matter.
18
        The reason for this motion is set forth in the accompanying
19
   Memorandum of Points and Authorities.
20
        It is expected that excludable delay pursuant to Title 18,
21
   United States Code, § 3161(h)(1)(a) may occur as a result of this
22
   motion or from an order entered pursuant thereto.
23
        Respectfully submitted this _14th_ day of January, 1993.
24
                                LINDA A. AKERS
25   United States Attorney
                                District of Arizona
26

                                CHARLES F. HYDER
                                Assistant U.S. Attorney

FILED   LODGED
RECEIVED   COPY

JAN 1 4 1993

CLERK U S DISTRICT COURT
DISTRICT OF ARIZONA
BY_____ B DEPUTY

1   <u>MEMORANDUM OF POINTS AND AUTHORITIES</u>

2   I.   <u>REASON FOR DISMISSAL</u>

3   The government, in a review of the evidence in this matter, is

4 faced with a question as to whether the government has accurately

5 determined the scope of the criminal activity in this case by the

6 defendants MILLER and NELSON and possibly others. The government

7 submits that it's in the public's interest to insure the government

8 investigates this matter more thoroughly before proceeding further

9 with this prosecution. Due to the recent development in this

10 matter regarding the defendant ALBER and the speedy trial issue

11 raised by the defendants MILLER and NELSON, and the Court's ruling

12 today, the government believes it is in the best interest of

13 justice to request this dismissal without prejudice.

14   If the government decides it was correct in its original

15 assessment of the case and seeks to refile the case it will have to

16 do so by seeking a new indictment. Accordingly, in that situation,

17 the defendants will be in the same position they are presently --

18 the defendants will not be harmed or prejudiced by a dismissal

19 without prejudice.

20   II.   <u>THIS COURT SHOULD GRANT THE GOVERNMENT'S MOTION TO DISMISS
        WITHOUT PREJUDICE IN ITS INDICTMENT OF MICHAEL G. MILLER AND</u>

21   <u>MARK NELSON.</u>

22   Rule 48(a) of the Federal Rules of Criminal Procedure

23 provides, in part, that ". . . the United States Attorney may by

24 leave of court file a dismissal of an indictment . . . and the

25 prosecution shall thereupon terminate." <u>See</u> Fed R. Crim. P. 48(a).

26 As a general proposition, a Rule 48(a) dismissal is without

1   prejudice, and, assuming that the applicable statutes of limitation

2   are not violated, a second indictment may be brought on the same

3   charge. United States v. Mendenhall, 597 F.2d 639, 641 (8th Cir.),

4   cert. denied, 444 U.S. 855, 100 S. Ct. 113 (1979); DeMarrias v.

5   United States, 487 F.2d 19, 21 (8th Cir. 1973), cert. denied, 415

6   U.S. 980, 94 S. Ct. 1579 (1974).

7   The district court has discretion to determine if the

8   Government's motion to dismiss an indictment should be granted, but

9   if the government can show that dismissal is sought for bono fide

10 reasons that are not clearly contrary to manifest public interest,

11 then the court must grant the motion to dismiss. United States v.

12 Weber, 721 F.2d 266, 268 (9th Cir. 1983) (because the Government's

13 reason for seeking the Rule 48(a) motion to dismiss was not clearly

14 contrary to the public interest, it was error for the trial court

15 to deny that motion); United States v. Perate, 719 F.2d 706, 710

16 (trial court must grant Government's motion to dismiss made

17 pursuant to Rule 48(a) absent finding of bad faith or disservice of

18 public interest); United States v. Hamm, 659 F.2d 624, 629 (5th

19 Cir. 1981) (district court may not deny Government's motion to

20 dismiss under Rule 48(a), except where it appears prosecutor is

21 motivated by considerations clearly contrary to manifest public

22 opinion).

23 ///

24 ///

25 ///

26 ///

1   For the reasons set forth above, the Government moves this

2 Court to grant its motion to dismiss without prejudice its

3 indictment of MICHAEL MILLER and MARK NELSON under Rule 48(a) of

4 the Federal Rules of Criminal Procedure.

5   Respectfully submitted this 14ᵗʰ day of January, 1993.

6   LINDA A. AKERS
                               United States Attorney
7   District of Arizona

8

9   CHARLES F. HYDER
                               Assistant U.S. Attorney
10
Copy of the foregoing mailed this
11 14ᵗʰ day of January, 1993, to:

12 John R. Hannah
    Assistant Federal Public Defender
13 320 North Central, Suite 200
    Phoenix, Arizona 85004
14 Attorney for Defendant Miller

15 Daniel D. Maynard, Esq.
    JOHNSTON MAYNARD GRANT & PARKER
16 2300 Great American Tower
    3200 North Central Avenue
17 Phoenix, Arizona 85012
    Attorney for Defendant Nelson
18
    Michael V. Black
19 3101 N. Central Avenue, Suite 530
    Phoenix, Arizona 85012
20 Attorney for Defendant Alber

21

22

23

24

25

26

                              4

Tuesday, January 19
NELSON'S DIARY: THE NIGHT BEFORE FREEDOM

10:21 P.M. One more day of incarceration of the worst kind. For almost eleven months, I almost *died*! After eight months being awakened two to three, sometimes even four times, a night by the ring of the telephone. I remember the first three and a half weeks, the telephone rang six to seven times a night, but guess what, I'm still here! Those individuals behind the orders, I'll find you next!

As for me, I am in tears, and I can't believe it's over! I love you, God, for showing me who was the force behind my life. I don't have much of a life, and my health well that's not too good either, especially my *mind*! This is were I start my new life and the uncertainties that may follow me. I will go find my children, move from my dad's (I don't know were I'll go, my credit is ruined, I had just signed a six-month lease at my apartment in Scottsdale the week before my arrest.) I'll be lucky if I get section eight housing. I do still have my Corvette! Good Night, Diary... I'll write back when I settle in...

Sunday, February 19, 1994
JOHN HANNAH ASST. FEDERAL PUBLIC DEFENDER

John Hannah informed Dan Maynard; Nelson's defence attorney. He suspects FBI Case Special Agent Keith Tolhurst lied to the grand jury, and Hyder condoned it. Mr. Hannah also noted, Hyder told him; "He did not know about the *Fair* and *Alber* conversation when they went before the grand jury." Mr. Hannah uncovered that the tape was transcribed on the day of the conversation.

Even though Mr. Hannah lists Saturday, as the day in question when it actually was Monday, February 24, 1992. His theory seems to be on the right track on the following page is his letter.

FEDERAL PUBLIC DEFENDER
District of Arizona
320 North Central Avenue, Suite 200
PHOENIX, ARIZONA 85004

FREDRIC F. KAY
Federal Public Defender

(602) 379-3668
1-800-758-7053
(FAX) 602-379-4300

February 9, 1994

HAND DELIVERED

Dan Maynard
Johnston, Maynard, Grant and Parker
Phoenix, AZ

Dear Dan:

What I have is Hyder's disclosure of the "exculpatory" part of the grand jury testimony. Tohlhurst did testify that an unnamed individual, and not Mike Miller, had made the phone call to Kaplan. But Tohlhurst and Hyder did not disclose the later recorded conversation between Fair and Alber, from which its absolutely clear that neither Fair nor Alber knows who Miller or Nelson is. That conversation is "evidence . . . with regard to Mr. Miller and Mr. Nelson and Mr. Alber and their connection with each other." Transcript at 20. It unravels their whole theory, because it shows that Miller had <u>no connection at all</u> with the phone call. The failure to disclose this evidence in response to Hyder's question was a lie, in my view; and Hyder obviously condoned it.

It is also worth noting that, during the litigation, Hyder told me that he did not know about the Fair/Alber conversation when they went before the grand jury. I find that incredible, especially since the FBI 302 reflects that the tape was transcribed on the day of the conversation -- Saturday, February 24.

Please let me know if I can help in any other way. You are welcome to review any non-privileged information in my file, e.g. correspondence between me and Hyder.

Very Truly Yours,

JOHN R. HANNAH
Asst. Federal Public Defender

JRH/st

Friday, March 25, 1994

MARK A. NELSON FILES COMPLAINT WITH
THE UNITED STATES OF AMERICA

On this day I filed a complaint against the United States of America, the FBI, and the United States Attorney's Office for the District of Arizona, Chuck Hyder and Keith D. Tolhurst. I alleged malicious prosecution, negligence, and intentional infliction of emotional distress, pursuant to the Federal Tort Claims Act ("FTCA"). My attorney Dan Maynard contends that Tolhurst intentionally misled the grand jury to issue the indictment, and Hyder condoned Tolhurst actions. When in fact, my contentions are that the actual Criminal Complaint Affidavit filed by Special Agent Tolhurst was misleading and full of misconstrued information. But no one wanted to listen to me, not even Dan Maynard my own attorney.

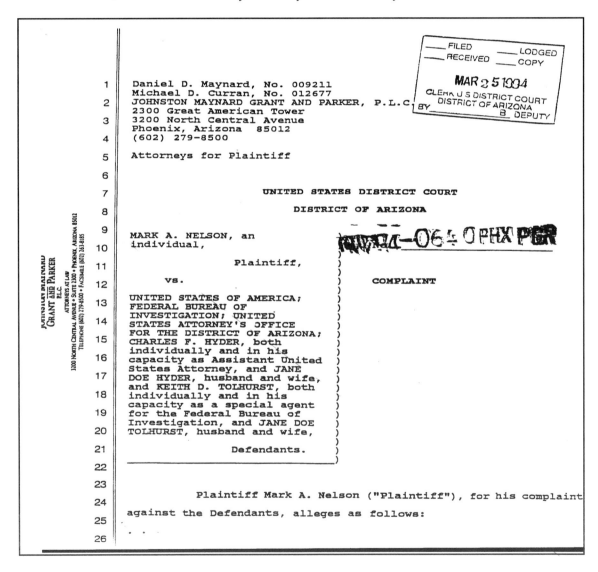

Wednesday, March 31
NELSON'S DIARY: LETTER TO ATTORNEY GENERAL
OF THE UNITED STATES OF AMERICA TO HONORABLE JANET RENO

10:00 P.M. Hello, Diary! It has been over two months since I have written. I'm no longer under house arrest with my dad, he and my little brother lent me enough money to get an apartment in section eight housing; this area is so bad that neither *Pizza Hut* nor *Domino's* will deliver here! I am having a hard time dealing with my freedom, all I seem to do is explain my innocence to people. My head still spins out of control, I want to *die*! I have no credit for housing, but I drive a Corvette? I can't live like this, I can't even get a job. How do I explain where I have been the last eleven months.

I tried to find my twin daughters and their mother, but to no avail; they are gone. I wrote them a letter at their last known address but it came back return to sender, address unknown. I am very sad and alone, something is wrong with my mind and body. I feel as though I am a walking corpse. The life I lived is now but a dream. I am a stranger to this new way of life. I live in a drug-infested neighborhood and my neighbors are the underbelly of society. I have to make a change, I don't know what to do. Please, God, show me the way.

There is a bright side to my writing you. I have a friend named Lynn, she helped me through a lot of turmoil. This was my last attempt to notify someone in my government that a conspiracy of some kind had taken place with a few employees of our government. I saw the Honorable Janet Reno during her conformation hearings. I believe she will make a difference if she is given a chance. I will send this letter to her and see if she was what she said she was. I hope she's not lip service. Good Night...

March 31, 1993

Janet Reno, Attorney General of the United States
Constitution Avenue, 10th St. NW
Washington, D.C. 20530

Honorable Janet Reno,

I am writing to you because I was intrigued by some of
the statements you made during your confirmation
hearing for the Office of United States Attorney
General. In particular, I was interested in your
clear dedication to "cleaning up the system" by
eliminating corruption in publicly held offices.

In my opinion, corruption can take many forms, from
officials in government that use political power to
gain personal profit, to officials that make errors in
judgement due to professional "burnout" or personal
problems which effect their ability to carry out their
jobs effectively. Sometimes these judgmental errors
can cause irreversible damage to innocent tax payors
lives.

You called yourself the "peoples lawyer" and mentioned
that you have a listed telephone number so that anyone
needing your assistance may get in contact with you. I
have taken it upon myself to send you several newspaper
articles and a copy of the claim my attorney recently
filed against the U.S. Government. I hope that you
will take a moment to review my case and not let it get
lost in the bureaucratic process.

I was wrongly accused of a heinous crime, charges were
eventually dropped; however, I have suffered
tremendously in the process, as has my family and
friends. I have been labeled a criminal and find it
difficult to find employment. In addition, I would like
to get counseling to help heal some of the emotional
and psychological damage I have suffered but am unable
to obtain these services financially. I believe when

Janet Reno, Attorney General of the United States
March 31, 1993
Page 2

you review this case and scrutinize the way it was
handled by the F.B.I. and U.S. Attorney for the State
of Arizona you will agree that the charges they sought
were unsubstantiated by any evidence and their decision
to continue to pursue me was an abuse of power and poor
judgement. I didn't think these individuals would ever
be held liable for the damage and pain they have caused
in my life, until I heard you talk about making a
difference in government. I have suffered greatly and
feel that as a U.S. Citizen it is my right to notify
you, perhaps justice will truly prevail in America!

I believe the road to righteousness starts with the
actions we do, not the words we speak. You have a
tremendous responsibility to the people of this great
Nation that I think you will not take lightly.

Good Luck during your incumbency and many prayers along
the way.

                         Sincerely,

                         Mark A. Nelson

MN:11

ATTACHMENT

<u>Monday, April 12</u>
TRANSCRIPT OF SENTENCING FOR *FRANK ALBER*
CLOSING ARGUMENTS FOR USA; CHUCK HYDER AND MICHAEL BLACK; DEFENDER

Before the Honorable Robert C. Bloomfield, a United States District Judge, stands the defendant, *Frank R. Alber,* for his sentencing to the crimes he committed. Appearances for the plaintiff; Charles Hyder, U.S. Attorney's Office. Appearance for the defendant; Michael Black, attorney.

9:31 A.M. Hyder and Black are arguing to the court: To see if *Alber* was to receive credit or acceptance of responsibility, which the government has argued against. Hyder wants an upward departure (maximum penalty), and Black wants a downward departure (minimum penalty).

Hyder explains to the court: "By mere fortunate circumstances was *Mr. Alber* even caught in this particular matter. Had not *Mr. Fair* come forward, it's doubtful whether *Mr. Alber* would have been caught. Thank you your honor." (If this is how Hyder felt, can you imagine if *Fair* did not come forward, Miller and Nelson would have been prosecuted for something they were not involved with!).

Black explained to the court: "The Government simply cannot accept the fact that they made a mistake and that there are no other people involved but *Alber.* The Government along with the FBI simply cannot accept the fact that they made a mistake with regards to Mr. Miller and Mr. Nelson; and now they think that because they made this mistake, a fact they cannot accept, that *Mr. Alber* was perpetuating a lie, that others were involved. So that two genuinely innocent folks wouldn't stand the possibility of getting convicted for something they genuinely did not do. *Mr. Alber's* clear guilt and his acknowledgment of guilt, who stood the chance of getting convicted and going to prison for an equally long period of time. And in *Mr. Alber's* letter to you, your Honor, he indicates that the reason he didn't come forward was because he could not conceive of the government continuing a prosecution against those two individuals. It was almost ineffable to him. Thank you your honor."

Honorable Robert C. Bloomfield; I'll make certain findings: "First, I find by a preponderance of the evidence that there is sufficient evidence of a conspiracy without designating the partners or coconspirators, but to include at least *Mr. Alber* and one or more other individuals. The letter itself is evidence of conspiratorial conduct, to be sure. One acting by himself or herself in a letter could appear to involve others, when in fact they are not, but it is evidence of a conspiracy. As far as the polygraph evidence, it would not be something that I would rely upon. But more important to me, that it would be difficult, but certainly not impossible, for a single individual to hatch, plan, carry out the conspiracy that occurred in this instance. Also, it just is too coincidental for this court to accept that Mr. Miller and Mr. Nelson just happened to be at *Saguaro Lake* and left *Saguaro Lake* at the same time they did, immediately after Mr. Kaplan did, (We know now this did not happen, the only problem the judge does not). And that at least one of them, perhaps both--it's unclear--stopped at the same place where Mr. Kaplan stopped to make a telephone call at the *McDonalds.* The fact that Mr.--I don't recall whether it's Miller's fingerprint or Nelson's fingerprint was on the telephone where the threatening call was made (this was not a threatening call, it was an advisory call no threats were made at all on this call). Probably is coincidence, although in fact it could be further evidence to show that there was a conspiracy. I do find the conspiracy, by a preponderance." (How can a judge give facts or findings, if he cannot recall the right facts, plus the facts he was trying to recall are all misconstrued information and the true conspiracy lies with the Government's employees)!

(See Appendix on page 453 for the transcript of sentencing for *Frank Alber* before the Honorable Robert C. Bloomfield United states District Judge; *omitted* are the pages due to irrelevance or not pertaining to Miller and Nelson.)

June 1994
THE AMERICAN LAWYER OPINION OF ROGER PARLOFF

Roger Parloff wrote a four page opinion that was published in *The American Lawyer* titled: "Whitewash" It first starts out as a letter to the Honorable Janet Napolitano, the United States Attorney for the District of Arizona. He then tells her why he wrote her; asking her to explain why Chuck Hyder is still with the U. S. Attorney's Office.

Parloff wrote that "Hyder, who maybe the only active federal prosecutor today who himself attempted to commit a capitol crime. I maybe wrong about that, and, if so, I would like some dispassionate Arizona lawyer to explain to me in writing why I'm wrong. At this point, you are the only reasonable candidate."

Mr. Parloff was referring to the possible prosecutoreial misconduct of Chuck Hyder, for the John Knapp case. John Knapp, was accused of setting fire to his home and killing his two little girls, one almost four, and the other almost three. Chuck

Hyder was the Maricopa County Attorney prosecuting John Knapp for murder.

Mr. Parloff also wrote that "A judge who might have explained it to me, Superior Court judge Frederick Martone--who has been elevated to the Arizona Supreme Court--chose not to do so for good reason after holding a misconduct hearing in July 1991." Martone was then presiding over the retrial of John Knapp. Martone wrote that "There was substantial evidence in this case in connection with withheld evidence, the destruction of evidence, and inaccurate representation." Martone withheld his decision on whether Hyder was actually guilty of misconduct because as he read the law, he was not legally empowered to do anything even if Hyder was guilty of such conduct. "The remedy for professional misconduct lies with another body," Martone wrote, alluding to the *State Bar of Arizona*.

Parloff also mentioned in his opinion, that a civil rights suit brought on by Mark A. Nelson, accusing Chuck Hyder of concealing exonerating evidence from his federal grand jury in February 1992; Hyder has previously denied wrong doing.

Parloff wrote asking Napolitano "Why federal prosecutor Hyder is going unprosecuted, unpunished, unsanctioned, unchided, and un-wrist-slapped for conduct that looks to me like the most heinous crime any lawyer can commit."

Roger Parloff, a senior reporter at *The American Lawyer*, wrote a book about the John Knapp case, Published jointly by *American Lawyer Media, L. P.*, and *Little, Brown & Company*. The book is based on a prosector named Chuck Hyder titled: *Triple Jeopardy*. (See Appendix page 465 for Roger Parloff's four page opinion as published in *The American Lawyer* in June 1994.)

Wednesday, October 5
DECLARATION OF ASAC LARRY J. McCORMICK

FBI Assistant Special Agent in Charge (ASAC), Larry McCormick, was ordered by the United States Attorney's Office to declare and state all the facts pertaining to this case and his involvement. Under the penalty of perjury that his declaration are true and correct to the best of his knowledge.

Larry McCormick said he supervised approximately one hundred and forty Special Agents. He went on to say that the public and social policy consideration of the FBI, include the safety of the public, the deterrence of crime, and, as well, the rights of the accused. Yet, Special Agents have the discretion of determining how best to conduct an investigation, and therefore, investigative behavior is not mandated by the FBI. But provide that Special Agent the option of using discretion and judgment while conducting extortions investigations. (I, (author) feel that this book will help change the investigative policies of the FBI. Special Agents are promoted from position to position based on their investigative, and administrative skills, and their ability to supervise other Special Agents. It is here any Special Agent hired by his superiors, without any mediated investigative behavior by his superiors, can mislead, fabricate, and paraphrase any and all information he deems fit and necessary to substantiate his case against the accused. McCormick had no reason to question his Special Agents based on the policies of the FBI during this investigation, and the oath every Special Agent swears to before becoming an FBI Special Agent. In short; for Honesty, Truth, and Dignity. And with that McCormick believed his reporting Case Special Agent, and his Special Agents under his supervision and why should he not?

On the next page is the Declaration of Assistant Special Agent in Charge Larry McCormick.

JANET NAPOLITANO
United States Attorney
District of Arizona

RICHARD G. PATRICK   Arizona Bar No. 5148
Assistant United States Attorney
4000 United States Courthouse
230 North First Avenue
Phoenix, Arizona 85025
Telephone: (602) 514-7500

UNITED STATES DISTRICT COURT
DISTRICT OF ARIZONA

MARK A. NELSON,	)	
	)	
Plaintiff,	)	CIV-94-640-PHX-PGR
	)	
v.	)	DECLARATION OF LARRY J.
	)	McCORMICK
UNITED STATES OF AMERICA,	)	
	)	
Defendant.	)	
	)	
_____	)	

I, Larry McCormick, do declare and state as follows:

1. I have been a Special Agent for the Federal Bureau of Investigation (FBI) since April 4, 1971.

2. I am currently assigned as an Assistant Special Agent in Charge (ASAC) in the Phoenix Office of the FBI and supervise approximately four Supervisory Special Agents.

3. At the time of the incident that forms the basis of this lawsuit, I was assigned as the ASAC in the Phoenix Office of the FBI and supervised approximately one hundred forty (140) Special Agents.

4. I am familiar with the rules, regulations, statutes, directives and guidelines which pertain to the activities of FBI Agents.

5. These rules, regulations, statutes, directives and guidelines of the FBI do not mandate investigative behavior, but provide the investigating Agent the option of using discretion and judgment while conducting extortion investigations.

6. Agents are left with the discretion of determining how best to conduct an investigation in fulfillment of the policies of the FBI while taking into account the delicate balance between the public, social and economic policies of the FBI and the safety of the public.

7. The public and social policy considerations of the FBI, in situations such as the one involved in this case, include the safety of the public, the deterrence of crime, and, as well, the rights of the accused.

I declare under penalty of perjury that the foregoing is true and correct to the best of my knowledge.

Executed this 5th day of October, 1994.

_____
LARRY J. McCORMICK, Special Agent
Federal Bureau of Investigation

Thursday, October 13, 1994
DECLARATION'S OF THE GOVERNMENT'S EMPLOYEES

Declaration Of Keith D. Tolhurst
SPECIAL AGENT FOR THE FEDERAL BUREAU OF INVESTIGATION

Case Special Agent Keith D. Tolhurst was ordered by the United States Attorney's Office to declare and state all the facts pertaining to this case and his involvement, and under the penalty of perjury. That his declaration is true and correct to the best of his knowledge.

Tolhurst stated based on Nelson's activities at *Saguaro Lake* prior to and after Kaplan departed, his appearance at the *McDonalds* and his appearance of being surveillance conscious on route back from the lake, supported his view that Nelson was involved in the Kaplan extortion. (You, as the reader, know that the information that he has now given under oath, is not true information. In fact, much is information he and his Special Agents misconstrued to fit their claims.)

He further stated that Nelson was employed by the construction company that built the Kaplan's house. Tolhurst also said that Nelson did not work for the company at the time the victim's house was built, but Nelson was working during the time repairs were made under warranty of the builder. (These statements are also incorrect. Kaplan's house was actually built years before Nelson worked for Nick Lees, the contractor that built his house. And as far as the warranty for the house, Nick told Special Agent Tolhurst: "That he only gives a one year warranty to all of his clients, and that warranty had expired years before Nelson started to paint his clients house's. That the very first job Nelson painted for me was Brian Holt, a client of mine who owns a few drug stores in Las Angeles and Las Vegas").

In addition, Tolhurst sated once again that Nelson told FBI Special Agents he did not know Kaplan, however, the secretary of Nick Lees advised Special Agents that Mark Nelson spoke with her one week prior to the extortion and identified the Kaplans by name. During that same conversation, Nelson stated that someone in the vitamin business (Kaplan's business) "owed him big". (Here is more misconstrued information given by Tolhurst. Nelson, did however tell the Special Agents he did not know Kaplan! In fact, the secretary actually told Tolhurst "That a week before the extortion Nelson was in the office to talk to Nick about an estimate for a new paint job, and told her he was going to Los Angles in his new Corvette to visit some friends he has not seen in a few years. And to see Brian Holt. Mr. Holt owed him $300 for some touch up painting on his house.")

Therefore, when Case Special Agent Tolhurst took the case to AUSA Roslyn Moore -Silver, he did so with the belief that probable cause existed to implicate Nelson in the Kaplan extortion. Tolhurst's purpose in bringing this matter to the attention of the United States Attorney's Office and initiating a prosecution request; was to bring an offender to justice. (The only reason probable existed was because Case Special Agent Tolhurst perjured himself and his misconstrued information of facts!

On the next page is the Declaration of FBI Case Special Agent Keith D. Tolhurst.

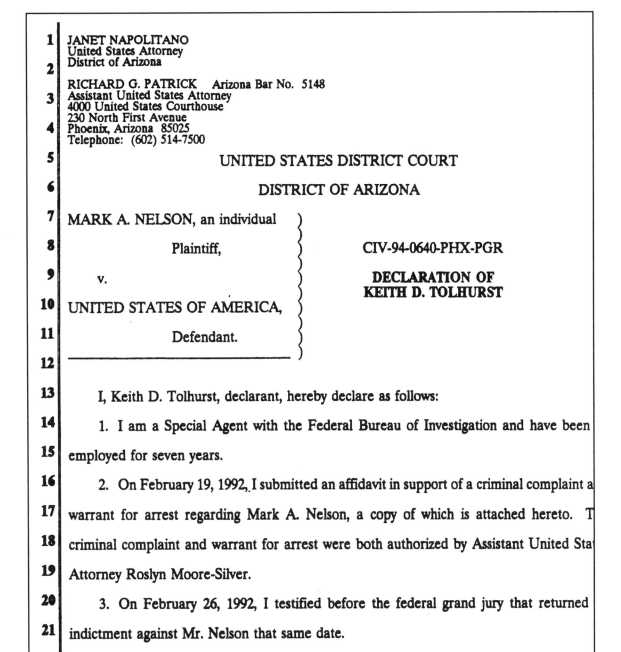

1 JANET NAPOLITANO
   United States Attorney
2 District of Arizona

   RICHARD G. PATRICK   Arizona Bar No. 5148
3 Assistant United States Attorney
   4000 United States Courthouse
   230 North First Avenue
4 Phoenix, Arizona 85025
   Telephone: (602) 514-7500

5   UNITED STATES DISTRICT COURT

6   DISTRICT OF ARIZONA

7 MARK A. NELSON, an individual   )

8   Plaintiff,   )   CIV-94-0640-PHX-PGR

9   v.   )   DECLARATION OF
)   KEITH D. TOLHURST
10 UNITED STATES OF AMERICA,   )

11   Defendant.   )

12 _____

13   I, Keith D. Tolhurst, declarant, hereby declare as follows:

14   1. I am a Special Agent with the Federal Bureau of Investigation and have been

15 employed for seven years.

16   2. On February 19, 1992, I submitted an affidavit in support of a criminal complaint a

17 warrant for arrest regarding Mark A. Nelson, a copy of which is attached hereto. T

18 criminal complaint and warrant for arrest were both authorized by Assistant United Sta

19 Attorney Roslyn Moore-Silver.

20   3. On February 26, 1992, I testified before the federal grand jury that returned

21 indictment against Mr. Nelson that same date.

22   4. In Mr. Nelson's complaint (¶ 37), he alleges that I was involved in the commissi

23 of "fraud, perjury and/or the misrepresentation or falsification of evidence that was present

24 to the grand jury." Since the filing of Mr. Nelson's complaint, I have reviewed a transcript

25 my grand jury testimony and said testimony was truthful.

26

5. In Mr. Nelson's complaint (¶ 18, 19), he asserts that based upon the Alber-Fair recorded conversation of February 24, 1992, any reasonable person would conclude that Nelson had no involvement in the Kaplan extortion. While Alber did make exculpatory statements regarding Nelson in that conversation, other statements made by Alber to Fair at this time were known to be false, (lies I believed were perpetrated by Alber in an attempt to calm Fair's fears of being involved in criminal activity). For example, Alber told Fair that he did not know who wrote the extortion letter received by Kaplan and that he did not have anything to do with it. During the search of Alber's house on February 25, 1992, (prior to my Grand Jury testimony) however, Agents seized a computer-generated letter, mailing envelopes and mailing labels similar to those received by Kaplan. Alber also told Fair that his involvement in the extortion was limited to making a telephone call at the request of an individual living in California named Richard Woolridge, who allegedly was "ripped off" for $40,000.00 by Kaplan. When Kaplan was interviewed by Agents on February 25, 1992, concerning this information, however, Kaplan advised he did not know a Richard Woolridge nor had he had any dealings with a person in California to whom he owed $40,000.00. Thus, I did not believe Alber's attempt to exonerate Nelson.

6. In addition, Nelson activities at Saguaro Lake prior to and after Kaplan departed, his appearance at McDonald's Restaurant and his appearance of being surveillance conscious on the route back from the lake supported my view that Nelson was involved in the Kaplan extortion. Mark Nelson was employed by the construction company that built the Kaplan's house. Although he did not work for the company at the time the victim's house was built, he did work during the time repairs were made under warranty of the builder. Nelson told FBI agents that he did not know the victims (Kaplans), however, the secretary of the construction company advised agents that Mark Nelson spoke with her one week prior to the extortion and identified the Kaplans by name. During that same conversation, Nelson stated

1   that someone in the vitamin business (Kaplan's business) "owed him big". Therefore, when

2   I took the Nelson case to AUSA Roslyn Moore-Silver, I did so with the belief that probable

3   cause existed to implicate Nelson in the Kaplan extortion.

4   7. My purpose in bringing this matter to the attention of the United States Attorney's

5   Office and initiating a prosecution request was to bring an offender to justice.

6   8. In initiating a prosecution request of Mr. Nelson on behalf of the FBI, I exerted no

7   pressure on Assistant United States Attorney Moore-Silver or Hyder to prosecute Mr. Nelson.

8   I presented the information I had and left the decision to prosecute or not to prosecute to the

9   prosecutors.

10   I declare under penalty of perjury that the foregoing is true and correct. Executed on

11   October ____, 1994.

12

13   KEITH D. TOLHURST

14

15

16

17

18

19

20

21

22

23

24

25

26

3

Declaration Of Chuck Hyder
ASSISTANT ATTORNEY FOR THE UNITED STATES OF AMERICA

Assistant United States Attorney Chuck Hyder was ordered by the United States Attorney's Office to declare and state all the facts pertaining to this case and his movement and that under the penalty of perjury. His declaration is true and correct to the best of his knowledge.

Chuck Hyder interviewed FBI Case Special Agent Tolhurst regarding the Kaplan extortion investigation, and Nelson's suspected involvement. During this lengthy interview, Tolhurst fully advised Hyder of the status of the investigation and the reasons for Nelson's suspected involvement. Based on the truthful disclosures, Hyder decided that the government had sufficient grounds to believe that a federal crime had been committed and that Nelson was a culpable participant in that crime. (Hyder believed all the misconstrued information Special Agent Tolhurst told him. Not to mention the fact 14 years ago; Hyder was trying to implicate me on my 65 keg party, when he was Maricopa County Attorney. Could this be motive enough for a conspiracy against me, by Hyder?)

Hyder recalls a monitored conversation with *Rick Fair*, (informant) and *Alber* stating he did not know Miller or Nelson. (Hyder in the beginning told everyone, he was unfamiliar with this secretly taped conversation recorded by FBI Case Special Agent Tolhurst. That is why they had to move fast for the indictment) Hyder felt that Nelson's activities at the *McDonalds Restaurant* thereafter and his apparent attempt to evade the FBI's surveillance strongly suggested *Alber* lied during his conversation with *Fair*. (Therefore the misconstrued information Tolhurst gave in his Criminal Complaint was believed by the prosecution.)

Hyder, also declared that Nelson lied to the FBI regarding his knowledge of Kaplans based on Tolhurst's declaration at paragraph 6. (No matter how much evidence proves I did not know these individuals, and if an FBI Special Agent says that I did, and the evidence proves otherwise, I now am a culpable participant in that crime or investigation according to Hyder.) Additionally, Hyder was influenced by the fact that Nelson failed two polygraph examinations on the evening of his arrest. (In fact, the FBI never proved I failed their test and it doesn't matter what their machines say anyway, Nelson was 100% not involved.)

On the next page is the Declaration of United States Attorney Chuck Hyder.

1   JANET NAPOLITANO
    United States Attorney
    District of Arizona
2
    RICHARD G. PATRICK   Arizona Bar No. 5148
3   Assistant United States Attorney
    4000 United States Courthouse
    230 North First Avenue
4   Phoenix, Arizona 85025
    Telephone: (602) 514-7500

5   UNITED STATES DISTRICT COURT

6   DISTRICT OF ARIZONA

7   MARK A. NELSON, an individual   )

8   Plaintiff,   )   CIV-94-0640-PHX-PGR

9   v.   )   **DECLARATION OF**
)   **CHARLES F. HYDER**
10 UNITED STATES OF AMERICA,   )

11   Defendant.   )

12 _____)

13   I, Charles F. Hyder, declare as follows:

14   1. I am an Assistant United States Attorney for the District of Arizona in the Criminal

15 Division and was so employed in 1992. I have been a criminal prosecutor with the U.S.

16 Attorney's Office since August, 1988. Prior to that date, I was a criminal prosecutor with the

17 Maricopa County Attorney's Office for 11 years.

18   2. Following Nelson's arrest on February 20, 1992 and before his scheduled preliminary

19 hearing on February 26, 1992, the Alber/Miller/Nelson criminal case was assigned to me by

20 Roslyn Moore-Silver, Chief of the Criminal Division, because Ms. Moore-Silver, who initially

21 was involved with the case, was to be in Washington D.C. on February 25-26, 1992.

22   3. On February 25, 1992, prior to Nelson's February 26, 1992 scheduled preliminary

23 hearing, I extensively interviewed FBI Agent Tolhurst regarding the Kaplan extortion

24 investigation and Nelson's suspected involvement therein. During that lengthy interview,

25 Tolhurst fully advised me of the status of the investigation and reasons for Nelson's suspected

26 involvement. On the basis of Tolhurst's complete and, in my view, truthful disclosures, I made

1   the independent prosecutorial decision that the government had sufficient grounds to believe

2   that a federal crime had been committed and Nelson was a culpable participant in that crime.

3   4. On February 26, 1992, without pressure from Tolhurst or anyone else at the FBI, I

4   made the decision to bring the matter before a federal grand jury which returned an

5   indictment against Mr. Nelson.

6   5. Despite the fact that on or about February 24, 1992, Alber stated in a monitored

7   conversation with Richard Fair that he did not know Michael Miller or Mark Nelson, I felt

8   that Nelson's activities at Saguaro Lake, his activities at the McDonald's restaurant thereafter

9   and his apparent attempt to evade the FBI's surveillance strongly suggested that Alber lied

10 during his conversation with Fair. Other statements made by Alber during that monitored

11 conversation (Tolhurst Declaration, ¶ 5) were believed to be false and Nelson himself

12 appeared to have lied to the FBI regarding his knowledge of the Kaplans (Tolhurst

13 Declaration, ¶ 6). Additionally, I was influenced by the fact that Nelson failed two polygraph

14 examinations on the evening of his arrest.

15   6. On January 14, 1993, I filed the United States' Motion to Dismiss Without Prejudice

16 in CR-92-080-PHX-RCB. A copy of that motion is attached to the United States' Statement

17 of Facts at Ex D.

18   I declare under penalty of perjury that the foregoing is true and correct. Executed on

19 October 13th, 1994.

20
                                            CHARLES F. HYDER
21   Assistant United States Attorney

22

23

24

25

26

                                            2

Declaration Of Roslyn Moore-Silver
CHIEF OF THE CRIMINAL DIVISION OF THE U. .S ATTORNEY'S OFFICE

Chief of the Criminal Division of the United States of America for the District of Arizona Roslyn Moore-Silver. She states that she authorized Case Special Agent Keith Tolhurst to contact Magistrate Judge Morton Sitver, for the purpose of seeking an arrest warrant for Nelson. Prior to Tolhurst's contacting the judge, she interviewed Tolhurst and reviewed his Criminal Complaint Affidavit, the one to be filed with the court. Having worked with Tolhurst before, she knew him to be reliable and truthful.

Based on that interview and review she made the decision that a federal crime had been committed and that Nelson was a participant in that criminal activity. She then authorized the Criminal Complaint and the application for the arrest warrant of Nelson. (Moore-Silver based her independent prosecutorial decision, based only upon the Criminal Complaint Affidavit, and believing Case Special Agent Keith Tolhurst to be reliable and truthful, until now?)

Roslyn Moore-Silver, believed independent evidence provided by the FBI of Nelson's activities at *Saguaro Lake, McDonalds* and his actions to avoid surveillance, provided probable cause to believe that he was involved in the Kaplan extortion. (You, as the reader now knows; I left the lake before Kaplan and even the FBI arrived, and I arrived at the *McDonalds* first; before Kaplan, per the request of Bonadonna, so that he could use the bathroom then get something to eat. As Bonadonna returned to the Corvette from relieving himself outside, Kaplans vehicle was parked in front of the Subway sandwich shop next to the *McDonalds*. Remember, Kaplan was only two miles or so back from this location and the Special Agents awaiting him should have known these true facts, not the facts they claimed to be the actual events as they happened. As far as Nelson knowing he was being followed. His turn signal bracket was broken and his Corvette sits only 8 inches from the ground, and is a very low profile vehicle, and it only appeared to be driving mysteriously. When in fact, that's just the way the Corvette looks going down the road.)

Her belief was reinforced by the fact that Nelson supposedly failed two polygraph examinations, (provided by the FBI ,and those test were never actually proven to be accurate only by the FBI. Furthermore, even if Nelson did fail; he had no involvement with this crime. But after nine hours of interrogation and Special Agent after Special Agent telling me, "you were involved," and that you should confess now while you still had a chance. Who really knows what was going on in the accused's head at the time, in their desperate attempt to implicate me to this case.)

She stated the extortion letter Kaplan received indicated that at least three people were criminally involved. (Here again the extortion letter did mention three individuals, and she suspected *Alber*, Miller, and me. But what she failed to disclose is the full descriptions of these individuals as stated in the letter; three officers of the special forces. Miller and Nelson had no military background at all.

The fact, Miller and Nelson were implicated because half of what the extortion letter describing, three individuals involved. The truth in fact, is this was an untrue story made-up by a desperate man named *Frank Alber,* who was once employed at the victim's business. Along with *Rick Fair*, (informant, the individual who talked to Kaplan, while *Alber* held the phone informing Kaplan to go to the *Security Pacific Bank*.)

She further declared that Nelson had previously worked for Kaplan. (This is the most disturbing of all. I never worked for Kaplan, and never met him. The *Million Dollar* question we would like to know. Where did Roslyn Moore-Silver get this perjurious information? Did she not review the reports as I did? Or did she completely take for granted the truths of her reporting FBI Special Agents'?)

A conclusion might be this: "The next time she becomes involved in a particular case like this one, let me investigate the interviewing Special Agents reports and I will be able to tell her my opinion of the Special Agents reports, and if their using discretion and judgment while conducting their investigations." With this case you decide.

On the next page is the Declaration of Chief of the Criminal Division of the United States Attorneys Office Roslyn Moore-Silver.

1 | JANET NAPOLITANO
United States Attorney
District of Arizona
2 |
RICHARD G. PATRICK   Arizona Bar No. 5148
3 | Assistant United States Attorney
4000 United States Courthouse
230 North First Avenue
4 | Phoenix, Arizona 85025
Telephone: (602) 514-7500
5 | UNITED STATES DISTRICT COURT
6 | DISTRICT OF ARIZONA
7 | MARK A. NELSON, an individual   )
8 | Plaintiff,   )   CIV-94-0640-PHX-PGR
9 | v.   )   **DECLARATION OF**
)   **ROSLYN MOORE-SILVER**
10 | UNITED STATES OF AMERICA,   )
11 | Defendant.   )
12 | _____   )

13 | I, Roslyn Moore-Silver, declare as follows:

14 | 1. I am the Chief of the Criminal Division of the United States Attorneys Office for the

15 | District of Arizona and was so employed in 1992. I have been a criminal prosecutor with the

16 | U.S. Attorney's Office for 14 years.

17 | 2. In mid February 1992, I was contacted by the FBI regarding their investigation of the

18 | Kaplan extortion. I received periodic reports from the FBI during that investigation and, on

19 | February 20, 1992 authorized Special Agent Keith D. Tolhurst to contact Magistrate Judge

20 | Morton Sitver late that evening for the purposes of filing a criminal complaint against Mark

21 | A. Nelson and to seek a warrant for Nelson's arrest. I had worked with Agent Tolhurst on

22 | the Earth First criminal cases during 1990 and 1991. On the basis of that relationship, I knew

23 | Tolhurst to be reliable and truthful. Prior to Tolhurst's contact with the Magistrate Judge,

24 | I interviewed Tolhurst and reviewed his affidavit that was to be used in support of the criminal

25 | complaint and the arrest warrant. On the basis of that interview and review, I made the

26 | independent prosecutorial decision that a federal crime had been committed and that Nelson

1 was a participant in that criminal activity. In making my decision to authorize the criminal

2 complaint and the application for the arrest warrant, I was not pressured by Tolhurst nor

3 anyone else at the FBI.

4   3. Because I was to be in Washington D.C. on February 26, 1994, I reassigned the

5 Alber/Miller/Nelson case to AUSA Charles F. Hyder to handle Nelson's preliminary hearing.

6 At that time, I was aware of Alber's February 24, 1992 monitored statement that he did not

7 know Miller or Nelson; nevertheless, I believed that the independent evidence of Nelson's

8 activities at Saguaro Lake and at McDonalds and his actions to avoid surveillance provided

9 probable cause to believe his involvement in the Kaplan extortion. My belief was reinforced

10 by the fact that Nelson failed two polygraph examinations on February 20, 1992, that the

11 extortion letter indicated that at least three people were criminally involved and that Nelson

12 had previously worked for Kaplan.

13   I declare under penalty of perjury that the foregoing is true and correct. Executed on

14 October 13, 1994.

15

16   ROSLYN MOORE-SILVER
                                                Chief, Criminal Division
17

18

19

20

21

22

23

24

25

26

                                           2

December 1995
REFLECTING BACK

I haven't heard any more about my law suit with the United States Government, since the declarations. I now live in Virginia Beach, Virginia. It's been a long while since I had to move away from my home state of Arizona; about two years ago since Thanksgiving of 1993.

When I first came to Virginia, I lived in the city of Poquoson, with my girl-friend Danya, who I met in Phoenix. She agreed I could not live in Arizona any more and said her mother wanted us to come live with her, and start a new life where no one would know anything about me.

I could not find my twin daughters, nor could I find employment. I became suicidal again just a few months from being released. Stripped of all credit, no place to live and no one wanting me around because of not knowing if what the Government said about me was true or not. These people were truly scared and there was nothing I could do or tell of my innocence, because if the FBI says you did something wrong, these thoughts are permanently downloaded into peoples' subconscious minds.

Feeling very alone I meet Danya, she was beautiful girl, I met her during a paint job at a Topless bar in Phoenix, called "Baby Dolls". I was painting the exterior of the building. This paint job was my big chance to start over. I was to use this money for a better place to live (if I could find a co-signer). Danya was very special, and she had her problems too! But she really liked me, and did not care what had happened to me, she still wanted to go out. I did not like the fact she was a topless dancer, I needed someone to care about me again. She helped me through a lot of post traumatic stress. I realized Danya was right, this place I called my home state of Arizona no longer made me feel like it's home. I sold everything, loaded up my red

Corvette and moved with Danya, and my two dogs Snuggles and Patches.

When I first got to her town we just relaxed and went sight seeing. After a few weeks I went looking for a job. The only problem was when I went to fill out my application I had no current work history because from now to the time I was released from house arrest, it was 21 months. Also me pulling up in a bright red Corvette doesn't help prevent concerns of who I am and what they thought I was running from. My answer to all the questions from my possible employers, was the truth and what had happened to me. As soon as extortion; with the overt act of cutting the arm or leg off a young child was mentioned I can tell you this, I did not get the jobs. Being frustrated, I told Danya why I was not getting work and she told me not to tell anyone what happened and just tell them it was personal and you do not want to talk about it, and just hire you for your experience."

I agreed. I called a painting company called *McDougals Painting*, the owner Jim McDougal asked if I would come in and talk fill out an application and talk to him about my experience. I said, "Okay." When I went to meet with him, he was very over bearing. He would not take my reason for where I have been, for the last year, for an answer. I broke down in tears telling him my story. Afterwards he hired me and said he would be keeping an eye on me. If there was room for me in the company, I will have to prove it but based on my experience both in application of paint, and supervisorial skills I should be supervising my own work in no time. I assured him I would not let him down.

As time went on I started to take notice how prejudiced he was towards the Blacks and Hispanics, but to his peers he seemed to be noble for his hires of minorities.

I started to complain about the way things are handled and the dirty equipment. I approached McDougal and he said he would take care of it and for me not to worry. The next day at one of his morning meetings he told everyone what I had said to him, about the equipment and that he was disappointed with his supervisor Jim. I can assure you, Jim (supervisor), pulled me to the side and told me; "I had no business going behind his back and if I did that again he would fire me!"

I told him, "Your full of shit, and Mr. McDougal, told me to tell him, if I saw any problems. I did just that.. If you don't like those arrangements talk to your boss and leave me alone. By the way, you did not hire me, Mr. McDougal did and he'll have to be the one to fire me."

"Fuck you!" he shouted. "I'll see you down the road, in your pretty little red Corvette unemployed, and you're right, if I fire you McDougal, will have to pay Unemployment Insurance, and he will take it out of my bonus pay. But I can sure make it quite miserable for your working conditions. We will see how long you last, Punk...!"

I just ignored him...

The next few weeks of work was hell, he did make it very difficult. I was getting nowhere with their way of business, I was shorted on my overtime pay. I started to ask the supervisor Jim, why, I was not paid the correct overtime pay?

"We don't owe you shit!" he said. "Take a look at your employment contract that you signed. We have been doing this for years, and you know you can't change that!" I ended up quitting my badly needed job. I did however file a complaint against the company, for my back overtime pay, (I did get my back pay.) and the other employee's too. They received their money as well, especially the ones that had been with *McDougal* for years.

As far as the home front, Danya and me broke up. I loved her, but she had some problems and my problems seemed to never go away. The paranoia, the panic attics when the telephone rings, never really able to relax in public or private not knowing if there was a crime in progress at the location, and if there was you can be considered a culpable participant in that crime. There is no true escape from this madness of thoughts running wildly through my mind. I have tried everything and I felt I was complete failure, I met a few people along the way that helped me, but their family or friends became extremely jealous. They also made it extremely hard to be their friend.

This brings me to a sad story about the day my dog cried. I was living in a bad roommate situation that I found in the paper. I had to move out. I still had my two dogs Snuggles and Patches. They were Shih ztu dogs, and they were of champion blood line. Snuggles, was named because when we first got her all she wanted was to snuggle close to whoever pick her up, and she had tremendous energy. Patches, on the other hand, had a #5 heart murmur, blind in one eye, and was 80% deaf. It was a challenge to raise her with Snuggles because I would always scold Snuggles because Patches could not hear me. Unless I would whistle real load, then she would look around the room not knowing were it came from. Even if I did it directly in front of her.

Anyway, I was packing all my stuff in my Corvette, I did not have much, I became very ashamed. Here I was almost 35 years-old. I can't believe I have no home again! I'm about to give my dogs away. I knew this black guy that always inquired about my dogs, and how much he would love to have couple of dogs like mine. He just did not have the money to purchase such fine looking animals. We would never really talk much he would just repeat the same phrase. I would just walk away.

On this particular day I was forced out of the home early, the son of this family, called the cops and told them I was staying at their house and that he thought I was a fugitive from the FBI. The FBI told them "I was not being sought and that I do currently have a law suit filed against them. But at this point he's legal." This information this son gathered on me, was not good enough. He created a untrue story and called the police, and tried to have me arrested.

The police did not believe the story that this individual was telling them. This officer, pulled me to the side and told me "You should find yourself a new place to live this guy thinks you're hiding, and doesn't want you around, his family really seems to like you, but they are in a choosing situation between you, and their son. You have 30 days legally, but he did say he would make it difficult for you to live there within legal limits... So you may leave sooner the better, you are too good for this treatment. I just met you, and you seem pretty nice to me, but I'm not the one with the problem with you, it's that little man over there; pointing to the son. Move on to the next level of your life. Things will be better if you make it."

Two weeks later I had to move out I could not stand this guy's attitude any longer. I decided to move. I went over to that black guys house, and asked if he would like to keep my dogs. He could not believe I was giving him my dogs, he looked as if he was going to cry. He told me "He would be honored." I gave him my address and he came over. As I was loading his car with the dogs beds and their toys. Snuggles, was running back and forth from this individuals car and the house. Her tail was like a gyro helping her with balance as she snoops from place to place. I could actually feel her uncertainties. She was so distraught, Patches she was never sad. Every day was play time for her. I think she was a little mentally challenged as well.

Snuggles, was almost uncontrollably out of control. She would not listen, she was in her own world. I never seen her like this before. She usually does everything I say. But this time she was deliberately ignoring my commands. I finally got the leash on her and gave it to the new owner of my dogs, to me they were like my family and it was very hard to just give what I loved so much away. It was just a couple of *dogs* right? Let me tell you this: When I finally handed over the leash to the dogs I tried so hard for Snuggles to look at me but she would have nothing to do with me. I yelled out her name, Snuggles! She looked up at me; as I was down on one knee. Her eye's were full of tears, they flooded full and with a blink of her big eyes the tears broke, falling to her fury little face..., her mouth twitching back--and--forth as though she was trying to tell me something. I started to cry myself, but knew there was no other way but let them both go...

A few weeks went by things for me were getting worse. I have a new room-mate, and his telephone always rings and it was driving me crazy. I had met this girlfriend she was so beautiful. Her name was Safire, (Matel, the company that makes Barbi Dolls, would hire her and she would dress up like Barbi, and go to malls for promotions for the doll.) She was also a female dancer, and I had fallen in love with her beauty. I was not stable enough and my mental behavior, I wanted to *die...*

I finally moved out from the incontrollable rings of the telephone. I was about to move in with my friend Ron, and my head was hurting so bad from a migraine I was having. I could not even think straight. I went to the bar that she worked at and told her of my migraine and she was so distant to me, One of her good clients was there and she did not want me there when he was there. I got mad and left. As I was sitting in my Corvette my head was about to explode, I had some Demerol pain killers left over from the dentist. I opened my bag and took the bottle of pills, and opened them I could barely open the bottle. As it finally opened I poured the whole bottle into my hand, I could see eight pills just before my eyes. But the pain was so severe I could only think about getting this anxiety migraine to go away and shoved all the Demerol into my awaiting mouth. I drank it down with a few hour-old can of Coke.

I drove around the streets crying for relief and that my head get better. I was about half way through my tears when I finally realized what I did. I pulled my car over behind a building off Military Highway, I started to become nauseous and vomited. I thought I was going to die. I called Safire's second job, the club was busy and the manager said he would go get her. When she got to the phone I told her what I did. She became very worried for me. I never thought she would ever really care about someone else, except for herself. I was wrong. She came and picked me up. She was crying, her tears filled her pretty blue eyes. She told me that I needed to go to hospital, and that she loved me but she needed some time alone.

It was this night on April 27, 1994, at 12:24 A.M. She took me to the Virginia Beach General Hospital's Emergency Room. For possible overdose. I was so scared and I really was tired of where I am in life and I really need some help. I was too afraid to ask for help so when the time came to admitting that I had a mental stability problem, I was in complete denial, due to what people might think of me. What's funny, they already thought I was going crazy, and that I was too paranoid about my surroundings. But I could not tell these doctors that I had suicidal thoughts before this incident, (Under house arrest.) Because they would not have believed me. Plus I didn't want to be locked away. I had no other choice I really did want to *die* but for some reason I didn't.

On the next page is the report filed by the Emergency Attending Physician, Dr. Kardon.

VIRGINIA BEACH GENERAL HOSPITAL
EMERGENCY PHYSICIANS OF TIDEWATER

PATIENT NAME: NELSON, MARK   **BED #:**   **SSN:** 527 69 5601
Time Seen:

CHIEF COMPLAINT: Possible overdose.

HISTORY OF PRESENT ILLNESS: The patient is a 33-year-old male who states that he was having a severe episode of anxiety due to multiple domestic concerns. The patient states that he started to develop a headache which is typical of him when he develops anxiety. The patient states that out of a fit of desperation, he took eight of his Demerol tablets because he wanted to overcome the pain. The patient states that at approximately twenty minutes later he felt nauseous and vomited. He states that he counted all eight pill fragments in an emesis that appeared relatively intact. The patient denies any other significant influence from the medication. The patient states that he told his girlfriend who then advised him to call poison control and then advised him to seek medical evaluation. The patient states that his headache has since resolved. The patient denies any other influence currently. He denies any problems. He states that he feels fine. The patient states that his headache was typical of his anxiety spells. He denies any new weakness on any one side of his body, any visual changes, or any syncope with this headache. He denies any fevers, chills, or neck pain with this headache as well. The patient states that he is not suicidal nor homicidal. The patient states that he has underlying anxiety but not severe depression. The patient states that he has initiated help with anxiety. The patient specifically and repeatedly denies that this was an attempt to harm itself.

PAST MEDICAL HISTORY: The patient has a history of anxiety. The patient denies any previous suicidal attempts.

FAMILY HISTORY:

SOCIAL HISTORY:

PHYSICAL EXAM: **VITAL SIGNS:**   Temperature 98.6, pulse 90, respirations 18, blood pressure 153/80. In general, he is alert, oriented, and in no apparent distress. Examination of his head reveal the pupils to be equal, round, and reactive to light. The extraocular movements are intact.   The oropharynx is benign. The TMs are normal bilaterally. NECK: Supple with no meningeal signs. LUNGS: Clear to auscultation. HEART: Regular rate and rhythm. ABDOMEN: Soft and nontender.   EXTREMITIES: No clubbing, cyanosis, or edema. Neurologically, the patient was fully alert, oriented, and did not appear to be under the influence of any type of drug.   Cranial nerves II-XII are intact.   The patient has good strength and sensation in all four extremities. The patient is able to ambulate without difficulty. He was Romberg negative.

IMPRESSION/DIFFERENTIAL DIAGNOSIS: This is a 33-year-old male who apparently had a nontoxic overdose of Demerol without any apparent side affects. This does not appear to be a suicidal gesture. We will get a pulse oximeter to confirm that there is no respiratory depression before discharge.

ANCILLARY SERVICES:

EMERGENCY DEPARTMENT COURSE AND TREATMENT: The patient was discussed with and evaluated by the Emergency Attending Physician, Dr. Kardon.

PROCEDURE LIST:

DISCHARGE/DISPOSITION: We will confirm that there is no respiratory depression before discharge.

CONDITION ON DISCHARGE: Satisfactory.

FINAL DIAGNOSIS: 1.   Nontoxic overdose.
                  2.   Anxiety.

MATTHEW L. EMERICK, M.D./\ERIC M. KARDON, M.D.

MLE/ald
DD:DT:JOB: 042694:042794:8133

N000449

A couple of months went by and I was becoming more depressed. I had no girlfriend and could not handle my now suicidal thoughts, after her taking me to the hospital things were never the same again.

Then one night on June 28, 1994, I could not take life any more I was so alone and I could not deal with my mental state of mind. I drove to a place called Mount Trash Moore, (it used to be a garbage dump, that was redeveloped into a huge park.) I climbed to the top were an American flag was sailing gracefully in the wind. As I got to the top I looked around I felt this was the end of my life and dreams. I pulled out of my pocket the note I wrote to the people who find me, explaining why this dead man lays about them. I had all my newspaper clippings. I was set but for one thing I had no way of killing myself. I became very afraid and frustrated that I looked down on the ground franticly hoping to find a sharp object so that it can penetrate my skin.

I found a piece of thick glass and went back to the flagpole. I sat down and prayed forgiveness then I proceeded to cut into my wrist. It did not cut it scraped my skin. I tried so hard to make that perfect incision for death, but it would not do it. I saw blood dripping from my wrist, and the pain was making the reality of how foolish and cowardly, this act of physical violence to myself really was. I panic, crying allowed like a baby I did not really want to *die!* I ran down the hill to my Corvette to wrap my wrist with something. When I got to my car I became incoherent and decided I would go to the pay phone down the street and call 911 for help.

I first called Jay and told him what I did. He was pissed off at me and told me he was going to call the police. I told him I would then I hung-up on him. After a few minutes I called 911.

"911, what's the emergency?"

"I need to be taken to the hospital. I tried to kill myself!'

The operator asked, "Where are you located?"

I told them, "you know damn well where I'm located, and take a look on your computer screen."

"Sir help is on it's way just relax and talk to me for a minute and tell me your name." she asked.

"Marcus Nelson-Giavanni" I told her.

"Are you driving a red Corvette?" she questioned.

"How do you know that, have the police been following me?" I really flipped out I could understand what was going on how did they know I was driving a red Corvette.

"I don't know how you found out my vehicle but I'm going to hang-up now!" I told them.

The operator said, "Your friend called us, he was really worried about you. Is that the emergency medical team sirens I here?"

"Yes it is! But they're not approaching me they're just sitting in the their vehicle." I answered.

"They are waiting for the police to arrive." she said.

"The police!" I yelled.

"It's the law if someone is suicidal and tries to go through with the act, it is illegal and the police are always called in and you could be arrested." she said.

"Arrested for what? You will never catch me!" I told her. I started to run I saw the police coming down the street their sirens were blasting in the air waves like trumpeters at a chariot race in the roman Empire days. I was frantic I ran and ran as fast as I could. I ran behind this building and I became so tired and sick and my arms started to hurt too. I hid under some bushes hoping the police would not find me. But to no avail..

"Hey come out from under the bushes it's all over and you are okay. No one is going to hurt you. We are here to help!"

"Please don't hurt me! I don't want to go to jail! I told them. I gave them my suicide letter and all the newspaper clippings about my predicaments. These officers were so nice to me. They placed me in the back of the car with no handcuffs and let the EMT unit attend to my wrist. As I was waiting I saw about three plain clothes officers talking to the uninformed officers. They were discussing my newspaper articles. Then this black four door sedan with blackened windows and many antennas pulled up to the scene. One of the plain clothes officers got into this vehicle about fifteen minutes went by and the plain clothes officer exited the car. The Black sedan then drove off I was really petrified. I could not see who those individuals were in that car. They did seem very official and whoever they were, could have took advantage of this fallen citizen. But they chose to proceed forward. The officer that departed the car and started to walk over to the squad car that I was sitting in. He asked the EMT person "if I was going to be all right!" And he assured him I would be.

This officer got into the vehicle and asked everyone to give him a few minutes with me.

"I'm really sorry about what had happened to you in the past and from what I read and just found out you are telling the truth. But I want to assure you that not all law enforcement is bad. If you were to *die* then your fight for the truth will no longer be valid. You must stay on the right track, and stick to what you believe is true. But with that, this is a very cruel world, and not everything is just and pure, as you have found out, one must fight for justice." he told me.

"Right!" I said.

"I had a friend in the department that took his life he had some false things said about him. He could not take it either and he killed himself. It was very hard on everyone. His world had collapsed around him and he was never able to pull himself out. If you were he and I had the chance to give him the advice I just gave you. He might still be alive" he said.

"Thank you! I will not ever do this again, and I will fight for justice and the time you spent and the advice you gave me will not be in vain"

"I hope so, you seem to be a bright young man that just needs some help. You are going to be taken to the Virginia Beach Psychiatric Center, for a evaluation," and

"Good luck." he said.

I arrived at the center. There I was evaluated by Dr. Amar Singh and he had ordered me to stay for a three days of observations. While I was there I saw individuals that were worse than I mentally. I thought if I did not get the help I would end up in a place like this for a long time. These individuals scared me they had thought patterns that they exposed to everyone. These same individuals would come into my room and say and do things that made me realize I was not as sick as these patients were and I will not give into the request of being sent to *Eastern State Mental Hospital*. It would be there I was told that I would be given drugs and I would never be the same again. I called an Attorney named John "Duke" Brickhouse I painted his law office. He knew I had no money But he liked like me as a person and told me not to worry about the money and that I should just get help on an outpatient basis.

I went before the court and the judge asked me "if I wanted to go to the hospital or was I able to care for myself?"

I told him that "I was fine and that outpatient care is what I need." But the court's doctor wanted me to be sent to the mental hospital and my attorney, as well as my Attending Physician Dr. Singh argued against such a place, and that it would destroy me and is not the best interest for him. The judge agreed and I was released from the Psychiatric Unit.

On the next two pages are the reports of Dr. Amar Singh, M.D. and his evaluation of me on that day of June 28, 1994.

VIRGINIA BEACH PSYCHIATRIC CENTER
Virginia Beach, Virginia

ADMISSION NOTE ADDENDUM
TEMPORARY DETENTION ORDER

Patient: Mark A. Nelson
Medical Record #: 54345-1
Date of Admission: 6-28-94
Attending Physician: Amar Singh, M.D.
Unit: CIE
Age: 34

Patient was seen on 6-28-94 and complete psychiatric evaluation dictated. Patient was since detained after verbalized that he feels people are after him and he is not sure he wants to live. The patient is very suicidal. The patient was prescreened and according to the detention papers patient is mentally ill and unable to care for himself.

Today mental status examination revealed an alert, oriented, cooperative, still severe depressed, episodically suspicious and paranoid young man. Somewhat delusional thinking, but no evidence of hallucinations. Patient is not homicidal. Concentration is somewhat better. The patient understands that he needs to seek help.   The patient remains severely suicidal, but has not verbalized a plan.

In my opinion, the patient may need to be hospitalized for approximately 2 to 3 days to be stabilized on medication and then be discharged to outpatient care. The patient is willing to do so.

The patient is cooperative. He knows right from wrong and knows the consequences of not receiving treatment, that is, his not being able to function. The patient stated that he currently has a job painting and he will return to the job upon discharge. I will be willing to treat the patient while in the hospital. The patient may voluntarily be admitted into the hospital for further stabilization.

Amar Singh

AS/

6-29-94

ADMISSION NOTE ADDENDUM

4000458

VIRGINIA BEACH PSYCHIATRIC CENTER
Virginia Beach, Virginia

Patient: Mark Nelson
Medical Record #: 54345-1
Date of Admission: 6-28-94   4/30
Attending Physician: R. Jeremy A. Stowell, M.D., F.A.P.A.
Date of Exam: 6-28-94
Exam Performed by: Joseph F. Killen, Jr., M.D., A.B.F.P.
Unit: CER
Age: 37 years old

HISTORY OF PRESENT ILLNESS:

This patient is a 37-year-old white male. He is admitted currently
for evaluation and treatment of severe depression and suicidal
ideations.

PAST MEDICAL HISTORY:

SURGERIES:

1. Removal of right rib secondary to a thoracic outlet syndrome in
    1985.

2. Chest tube placement on the right chest secondary to auto
    accident in 1985.

3. Reattachment of right middle finger as a child.

SERIOUS ILLNESSES: None.

HOSPITALIZATIONS: For the above noted surgeries.

CURRENT MEDICATIONS:

None.

ALLERGIES:

None.

HISTORY AND PHYSICAL EXAMINATION

N000459

Boy, I really hate remembering the past; so now I will bring you back to the present December 1995.

Like I was saying, I was doing a lot better by this time and now I have some really good friends, Carr and Katherine Thompson, and my friend Bubba. The Wassermann Family, gave me the break I was looking for. They owned a club called *Night Move*. I decided I was ready to promote another nightclub, the thing that is so weird is it that this club's name was real close to the nightclub in Phoenix, called *Nightline*. I thought it to be, an omen so some sort.

Anyway, I needed to open this club and pull the Radio Stations and local newspapers together to promote the ultimate night spot. This night spot was a good idea but the location was plagued with bad management. I was not told until I was already accepted into the club by the owner Danny Wassermann. He was very nice but very shrewd. In this business you almost have to be. Danny on the other hand has owned this place for many years, and let's just say he ran out of steam. When I took the club over he could never really let it go completely. No one in the business wanted to work with him. That's why he chose to have me take over the club and bring it to it's maximum potential.

We named the new team; *The Underworld* along with Loving Enterprises. My friend Bubba, oversaw the Female and Male Dancer shows. Radio Stations agreed to work with us. As well as the local Entertainment newspapers. They all were great! I just had too many unresolved issues in my head. My daughters, my court case against the government seemed to take forever. This opportunity was my way of knowing that I still had the talent to be in the night club business, and to show my accusers, that I really was not involved with the crimes they indicted me for.

On the next page is an advertizement in *FLASH Magazine* for the nightclub *Night Moves*.

<u>February 1996</u>
THE NEWS WE HAVE BEEN WAITING FOR

I received a phone call from my attorney on February 13, 1996, he told me "the court ordered the United States Government to give us the information we were seeking; grand jury tapes."

I was so excited. I decided I had, enough of Virginia Beach, and I wanted to go home. It has been a few years since I left. I felt I was mentally ready for the court battle that was about to happen. I never thought I would see this day. I really did not think the court would give such an order.

It took me a few weeks but I left at the end of February. I only had $800 cash on me and all the belongings I owned still fit into my Corvette. I remember at the time I just wasn't the same person any more. The nightclub I took over was not fun any more, I did not have the control as was promised to me by Danny the owner, (who, by the way was an excellent father to his only son.) I wanted to go back home to find my twin daughters, I need them! I did not know how I would find them, but I was ready. I have now something, some reasons to come back to Phoenix with a possible new beginning for a nightclub there. I figured this was proof enough to myself, I can come back to home and try again the entertainment in Phoenix, Arizona.

My lonely journey across over 2000 miles of the United States had taken me almost a month. It was cold and rainy the first part of my journey. That was the toughest. It all started as I was driving down Highway 40 from Memphis, Tennessee. I was to interchange with Highway 30 which would have taken me through Little Rock south to where the Texarcana meets the Georgia State border. (Nearest city New Boston.) And for some unknown reason I missed the Interstate Highway change. When I noticed that I made this mistake I took the nearest exit. As I departed the highway and approached the light I noticed that I was accelerating the car, but it would not move. I misjudged the light. When I came to the stop light I said aloud

"Oh Shit , Please God Help me!" My car broke down in Conway, Arkansas, about an hour north of Little Rock. The car's transmission went completely out, as I was turning around. Some strangers helped me on the way and lead me to *Delta Transmission* and the owner a very religious man, said he would put my transmission together for under 800. Dollars, him being made aware of my financial situation and believed me. The only thing is it will take a couple of day's. I pulled in late that Friday afternoon, and they were not going to be open so that meant my car would not be finished until Wednesday or Thursday of the next week. Let me tell you I started to get those feelings, of despair and complete suffocation of thoughts. I had no other choice, I paid for the car repair up front. That way I knew it would be finished.

He had one of his employees take me to a motel. I was a complete wreck.

Everything I've done was to keep the demon's from calling upon my soul. Thoughts of giving-up all hope that nothing really changes no matter what one tries to do because, that is where these thought patterns come from. (Not demon's sent from Satan.) But just bad programing in one's thoughts, ones they wish to keep or discard like garbage. So it was then I decided not to feel sorry for myself about another damn thing. What would have happened if I made that turn, would I have been, so lucky for the way things turned out? Only God knows?

I asked God for the power, and strength to work out my homeless, unemployed, and car-less situation not to mention the 50.00, I had left in my pocket. As I sat on the edge of the road talking to God I asked him in Jesus' name to guide me through the right situations so I will arrive back home in Phoenix in my car and not a box.

The next thing I knew I rented a room and wanted to take a shower. As I was getting ready for bed and I looked into the mirror and was hiding back the fear of the uncertainties that lay ahead for me. I had to find a job, so I can stay alive for the four days my car was getting repaired. As I looked at the reflection back I saw for the first time thing weren't bad as they seem and I went to sleep.

The next morning however, the employee that dropped me off came early and asked if I needed help for transportation. He told me "I overheard my boss talking about how nice of a guy he thought you were and he hopped you find your way." He drove me to a paint store I looked on the bulletin to see if any companies are looking for experienced journeymen painter. The board had one company and I called them. The owner would not hire me because no transportation and I was not going to be sticking around. I then asked the manager of the paint store, if he knew any company, he told me there are very few painting contractors in Conway, and that I would have to drive about an hour to Little Rock, and I could possibly find work. He told me "It's going to be tough with no vehicle."

I had no luck and I know this individual, being so nice to give me a ride I could not ask him to take me. I was getting nervous. I closed my eye's and asked God for guidance. The most bizarre thing happened. As I was leaving the manager told me about a company call *Bailey Painting Company*. It became a wonderful life, I worked for them about a month and I sprayed, stained and finish coated all the woodwork in the new law library at the *University of the Ozarks* about an hours drive on Highway 40 in Clarksville, Arkansas. I met some very good people and they helped me survive for the month I was stranded. My boss who owned Baileys. Danny the foreman of the company who let me stay with his family during my stay. If these people were not born to help me who knows where I would of ended up...

June 12, 1996
FINDING MY PLACE BACK IN LIFE

Today, I turned 37 years-old as I reflect back on my life it has been definitely one full of many unbelievable situations. I thank "God" for having the powers to show me the way through life. Though my trials and tribulations are unclear for my existence on earth, and maybe one day I will see the purpose of why I was born.

This month a lot is supposed to happen. I'm waiting for the Ninth Circuit Court of Appeals to make a ruling on my appeal from the District Court of Arizona, which I filed on April 29, 1996.

A private investigator found the whereabouts of the mother of my children. I was so happy. He gave me the address of her home. I did not know what I would say I just wanted to see my daughters. It's been almost four years.

I drove to the house and sat outside, my head was spinning and I was very nervous. I did not know how Connie would react to my unannounced arrival. But I did not have a phone number for her this was the only way. Besides Connie had a lot of unanswered explanations about why she took my children from me.

I went to the door and knocked it seemed like a very long time went by before someone came to the door. Then the door opened, it was a guy.

"Can I help you?" he said.

"I need to talk to Connie, I am..."

"I know who you are, just a minute." nervously he said.

He went and got Connie, she came to the door.

"Oh my God!" "I knew some day you would find me, do you want to see your children. They are asleep but you can look in on them."

"Yes Connie, I would like to see my children" she took me to them and there they were sleeping I felt as though I was dreaming. This feeling came over me I had never felt. Actually seeing for the first time in my life "Blood Relations" I felt a bond with myself. As I approached them closer to take a better look. My heart started to hurt and my eye's started to fill with tears, these were not sadness tears. But happy tears, I couldn't believe I made such beautiful children. I had to leave before I woke them up. As I left their room I looked forward on the hallway wall facing me. I saw pictures of them in pretty dresses at Christmas time, and pictures of relatives I did not know. Connie had a boyfriend she was living with, and he was in those pictures and it was his family that was in those photos. My tears began to fall and my heart began to break. I had to leave before I broke down. Connie gave me the phone number to call and to let her know if I would call her tomorrow and I said, "Okay."

For the next few days I got to visit with my children it was a feeling I never felt before they hugged me and kissed me. To me I really think they knew who I was, even though Connie's boyfriend Robert, started to become insecure with me coming over. I noticed it a few times when Connie and me would go outside to talk, while she smoked her cigarettes. He would come back and fourth from inside the house asking if we needed privacy to talk that he would stay in the house. I told him he did not have to worry I just wanted to see my children and that he could sit in with our conversation, and Connie agreed with me. He repeated these actions many times and my response was still the same. He just could not hear what I was saying. But I knew inside my mind and heart that he was going to be the negative entity that would keep me from my children. He has a strong hold on Connie, though Connie had assured me she would never keep my children from me, now that I have found them and her. I was a little upset that she was not married to her boyfriend, and yet my little girls where calling him Daddy. He had been in my daughters lives for almost three years, (I feel they were hidden from me, but that's a whole new book). There was nothing I could do but be grateful they are allowing me to see my children.

One night we all went to eat at *Garcia Mexican Restaurant* for Fathers Day. It was Connie her boyfriend Robert, the twins and me. The girls wanted to hold my hand while we walked up to the doors. I could feel the insecurity boiling in Robert's blood. I started to feel bad for him, but these are my kids and I don't have to be ashamed or feel sorry for nobody. What about my feeling and my misfortunes of being neglected from my children's lives. Anyway, when we walked in the restaurant everyone was looking at us. The hostess commented how pretty the girls were and that we mad a cute family. The only problem is I was holding the children's hands. Robert was walking with Connie behind me, and my daughters. Robert is tall and has blond hair. He couldn't even pass for their father. The hostess was referring to me as the father. I could feel a demon stirring deep in his body. When I looked back, Robert's face was twisted in disbelief. I could feel the negative energy growing towards me. But that did not keep me from wanting my children in my life. He may have a power over the mother of my children. But he has no power over me. I just ignored his energy and held my daughters hands like it would be the last.

It was the last time I saw my children. Connie was mad that I came back into her life. She wanted me to give up my parental rights as a father, so Robert could adopt them. I told her how can he adopt my daughters if you are not even married.

She told me if I did not she had really deep pockets, and that she and Robert would take me to court.

A few months went by and Connie had gotten married to her live-in boyfriend and they both filed with the courts to have my Parental Rights severed from my children. Their claim was that I abandoned my children. This made me so upset I could not believe Connie was going through with her lies. One day she will feel the pain I am saddened with. I was no longer allowed visitations and was no longer allowed to call my children or even their mother.

Now I have to go to court and prove my innocence, I had to come up with 5,000 dollars to fight once again, false occasions of abandonment of my children. I was feeling sick again, these people lied and I can't believe they got married before they filed their claim against me. I can already see the deception these two individuals are preparing for, and the only thing I can do is watch. These people seem just like the Government, but to me they are worse, and have no right keeping my children.

When will I ever get out of this court system. I have an awaiting appeal with the Ninth Circuit Court in San Francisco, California. I have to go to court and fight for my children. They are the true victims of this conspiracy against me. I hope one day when they get older they truly understand the truths behind all the lies.

As far as my health I'm doing okay, but it truly sucks being me. I hope one day that injustices I have endured will finally go away, but I will not give up...!

July 7, 1997
NINTH CIRCUIT COURT RENDERS IT'S DECISION

I just received word from my attorney's secretary, that the Ninth Circuit Court of Appeals have rendered a decision on my appeal. She informed me that they will send me the letter from my attorney and a copy of the ruling. She told me that Dan Maynard was to busy to call me, and that after I have read his letter he would have time to talk with me, after my review, for any questions.

I could not believe it was over, I hope it turns out to be good news. I have waited along time for this moment to finally come fourth. It's been five years and five months from the first time I was arrested, for this nightmare to be finally over. This was my toughest fight ever in my life to prove my point. I have suffered greatly and lost many unreplaceable objects, not to mention the death of my child, and having my twin daughters concealed from me. I know one day it will all make sense, and I will be alive to actually see the sense it will make.

On the next few pages is the letter from my attorney Dan Maynard, and the Ninth Circuit Court's ruling.

JOHNSTON MAYNARD
GRANT AND PARKER
P.L.C.

ATTORNEYS AT LAW

3200 NORTH CENTRAL AVENUE, SUITE 2300
PHOENIX, ARIZONA 85012

DANIEL D. MAYNARD   July 11, 1997   TELEPHONE (602) 279-8500
                                                                      FACSIMILE (602) 263-8185
DIRECT NUMBER   INTERNET ADDRESS: JMGP@PRIMENET.COM

(602) 279-8519

Mr. Marcus Nelson
3208 East Wescott Drive
Phoenix, Arizona 85024

                    Re: Nelson v. USA; #63264.2

Dear Marcus:

          Enclosed is a copy of the Court's Order denying our
appeal. Basically, they said that the District Court correctly
found that the Grand Jury had before it all the information the
Government had concerning your relationship to the other suspects
and that the Grand Jury was not misled. I do not understand how
the Court can make this decision without it ever having seen the
transcript. Our contention was that the District Court erred in
not allowing us to get the transcript because we had asked for it
on numerous occasions. We told them we need it and the Court says
that we should have filed a Motion to Compel. We do not feel it is
necessary to file a Motion to Compel because we had asked for it on
a number of occasions, plus the Government had an obligation to
turn over all the documents that were relevant in the case.   I
think that this is the end of the line. I do not chance the United
States Supreme Court taking this on appeal is one in a million, so
it is a waste of time to file that appeal.

          I hope that your book does well and you can conclude that
this is the last chapter. If you have any questions, please give
me a call at your convenience.

                                   Very truly yours,

                                   Daniel D. Maynard

DDM:mbs

Enclosure

F:\USERS\DMAYNARD\DDMLTRS\3913.WPD

NOT FOR PUBLICATION

IN THE UNITED STATES COURT OF APPEALS
FOR THE NINTH CIRCUIT

FILED

JUL 7 1997

CATHY A. CATTERSON, CLERK
U.S COURT OF APPEALS

MARK A. NELSON,	)
Plaintiff-Appellant,	) No. 96-15937
v.	) DC No.CV-94-00640-PGR
UNITED STATES OF AMERICA,	) MEMORANDUM*
Defendant-Appellee.	)

Appeal from the United States District Court
for the Arizona
Paul G. Rosenblatt, District Judge, Presiding

Argued and submitted June 11, 1997
San Francisco, California

Before: SCHROEDER, KLEINFELD, Circuit Judges, and WALLACH, U.S.
Court of International Trade Judge.**

Mark A. Nelson appeals the district court's grant of
summary judgment in favor of the United States, in Nelson's
Federal Torts Claims Act ("FTCA") suit, 28 U.S.C. §§ 1346(b) and
2671, et seq. Nelson alleged malicious prosecution, negligence
and intentional infliction of emotional distress, arising out of
his indictment for extortion. The indictment was eventually
dismissed without prejudice.

_____

*This disposition is not appropriate for publication and may not
be cited to or by the courts of this circuit except as provided by
9th Cir. R. 36-3.

** The Honorable Evan J. Wallach, United States Court of
International Trade, sitting by designation.

Memorandum
NINTH CIRCUIT COURT OF APPEALS: SAN FRANCISCO, CALIFORNIA
PAGE 2

```
        Nelson first challenges the district court's denial of
his requests for discovery prior to responding to the government's
motion for summary judgment.  See Fed. R. Civ. P. 56(f).  Nelson
contends he was entitled to obtain the grand jury transcript in
order to show that his indictment was obtained on the basis of
misstatements, mischaracterizations, and omissions of clearly
exculpatory facts.  The district court did not err in refusing to
allow Nelson to conduct discovery prior to responding to the
government's motion for summary judgment because Nelson never
filed a motion to compel before the discovery deadline passed.
See Fed. R. Civ. P. 37(a).
        On the merits, the district court correctly found that
the grand jury had before it all the information the government
had concerning Nelson's relationship to the other suspects.
Therefore the grand jury was not misled either intentionally or
unintentionally by the testimony of the FBI agent who instigated
the investigation.
        AFFIRMED.
```

I guess this concludes that this is the last chapter of my book. There has been so much time, money, and emotions spent. I can't and don't have any feelings left to give. No more money, and as far as time, it was all a waste of time in the Federal Judicial System. At least I did not lose my appeal due to the merits of my case. But because Dan Maynard and his law firm did not file a motion to compel. In my opinion they did not do their job correctly. I know now that I was not to win my case with the government because it would have been a precedent case, and it would have opened the biggest can of worms in this system.

As far as the fight for my twin daughters, I lost that too! I was told by my attorney Ken Rudisill of the same law firm. That it would cost me another 5,000 dollars to fight and that I will probably lose, because the way the law is written in Arizona, I will probably lose anyway. Not to mention that Connie and Robert used the Government's case against me. I had no choice and agreed to sever my rights so that Robert could adopt my children. I was to be allowed to visit them and see progress and that never happened. But up to the date of December 25, 1997, the day I was to see my children. I was declined by Robert.

You can read more in my next two books "Abolish the Firm" and "The Unwed Father" But for now...

The End!

APPENDIXES

February 19

EXAMINING THE CREDIBILITY OF THE FBI'S CRIMINAL COMPLAINT AFFIDAVIT
PAGES 1-5 AND PARAGRAPHS 1-15

United States District Court

DISTRICT OF ____ARIZONA____

UNITED STATES OF AMERICA
V.
Michael Grant Miller,
Mark Andrew Nelson

CRIMINAL COMPLAINT

CASE NUMBER: 92-504/ M

(Name and Address of Defendant)

I, the undersigned complainant being duly sworn state the following is true and correct to the best of my knowledge and belief. On or about ____February 6, 1992____ in ____Maricopa____ county, in the _____ District of ____Arizona____ defendant(s) did, (Track Statutory Language of Offense)

knowingly and with the intent to extort money from Marc Kaplan, deposit in an authorized depository for mail matter to be sent and delivered by the Postal Service written communication postmarked February 6, 1992, addressed to Marc Kaplan and containing a threat to injure the son of Marc Kaplan that is his arm or leg would be removed, and aid and abet to the same.

in violation of Title ____18____ United States Code, Section(s) ____876 and 2____

I further state that I am a(n) ____Special Agent of the FBI____ and that this complaint is based on the following
(Official Title)

facts:

See attached Statement of Probable Cause - Exhibit A.

Continued on the attached sheet and made a part hereof: ☒ Yes   ☐ No

_____
Signature of Complainant

Sworn to before me and subscribed in my presence,

____February 19, 1992____   at   ____Phoenix, Arizona____
Date   City and State

MORTON SITVER   N000137
United States Magistrate Judge
_____   _____
Name & Title of Judicial Officer   Signature of Judicial Officer

---

Criminal Complaint: The question here is why are the passengers of Miller's and Nelson's vehicles not listed on this complaint? In fact, the passenger of the Corvette (Bonadonna), according to these FBI Special Agents made all initial contact with Miller and his passenger and Kaplan.

February 19

EXAMINING THE CREDIBILITY OF THE CRIMINAL COMPLAINT AFFIDAVIT
EXHIBIT A , PAGE 1, FIRST AND SECOND PARAGRAPHS

EXHIBIT A   92-5041m

AFFIDAVIT

1. Your affiant, Keith D. Tolhurst, is a Special Agent (SA) of the Federal Bureau of Investigation (FBI) currently assigned to Phoenix, Arizona, and has been so employed for the past 4 years. As such, your affiant is a federal law enforcement officer within the meaning of Rule 41(a), Federal Rules of Criminal Procedure.

2. Since February 7, 1992, your affiant has been participating with other SAs in an investigation involving a plot to extort $250,000.00 from Marc Kaplan of Paradise Valley, Arizona, under threat that physical injury would occur to his son. As a result of your affiant's personal participation in this investigation, and based on reports made to your affiant by other FBI Agents, law enforcement officers, and witnesses interviewed, your affiant is familiar with the facts and circumstances set forth in this affidavit.

First Paragraph: It clearly states Special Agent Tolhurst did not have the experience to head such a big investigation, but his superiors and the Federal Judicial System trusted his investigation. Here, in this Criminal Complaint Affidavit seeking the arrest of Michael Miller and myself, you will begin to see the conspiracy unfold. Unless you have already figured out the FBI's dilemma which makes you a better FBI Special Agent than the ones who investigated this case.

Second Paragraph: States that Miller and myself had been participating with others. Who were they, where were they? The FBI, at this point in the investigation, should have figured out that Miller and me, who did not know each other prior to the lake and who were both construction workers, were just relaxing for the day, because it was going to rain and we had the day off. It also states, based on "reports made to your affiant by other FBI Special Agents, law enforcement officers and wit-

nesses' interviews." Case Special Agent Tolhurst asserts that Miller and me are familiar with the case elements and circumstance she he has set forth, which is totally
<u>untrue</u>...!

February 19
EXAMINING THE CREDIBILITY OF THE CRIMINAL COMPLAINT AFFIDAVIT
PAGE 1, THIRD PARAGRAPH AND PAGE 2, FOURTH PARAGRAPH

> 3. On February 7, 1992, Marc Kaplan received in the mail a computer generated letter, postmarked Phoenix, Arizona, on February 6, 1992, wherein the sender demanded that Kaplan pay $250,000.00 in cash in one week or his son's arm or leg would be removed. This letter informed Kaplan that on Thursday, February 13, 1992, he would receive a phone call at exactly 2:00 p.m. at his business office giving him further instructions.

> 4. Based on this letter, FBI Agents obtained court orders on February 11 and February 12, 1992, directing U.S. West Communications and American Telephone and Telegraph to install
>
> N000145

> Trap and Trace devices on all the business phones of Marc Kaplan who owns and operates Health and Nutrition Laboratories at 4545 East Shea Boulevard, Suite 160, Phoenix, Arizona. A Trap and Trace device captures the incoming electronic or other impulses which identify the originating number of a wire or electronic communication and the date, time, and duration of such incoming pulses.

Third paragraph: This portion of the affidavit was true and correct.

Fourth paragraph: This information is true and correct, the recorded phone call was received at Kaplan's office at Health and Nutrition Laboratories at 2:17 P.M., on February 13, 1992.

February 19
EXAMINING THE CREDIBILITY OF THE CRIMINAL COMPLAINT AFFIDAVIT
PAGE 2, FIFTH AND SIXTH PARAGRAPH

---

5. At approximately 2:17 p.m. on February 13, 1992, Marc Kaplan received a phone call at his business office. The male caller instructed Kaplan to immediately proceed to a closed Security Pacific Bank at Tatum and Shea Boulevards in Phoenix where he would find a note attached to a pole giving him further instructions. The caller then hung up. Shortly after this phone call was terminated, an employee of U.S. West Communications advised FBI Agents this call originated from a pay telephone located at ABCO Supermarkets, 1988 North Alma School Road, Chandler, Arizona. This pay telephone was located by FBI Agents and the receiver and telephone booth processed for fingerprints by officers of the Mesa Police Department.

---

6. At approximatel 8:30 p.m. on February 13, 1992, a Fingerprint Examiner of the Mesa Police Department advised FBI Agents a fingerprint lifted from the telephone receiver removed from the telephone booth at ABCO Supermarkets matched the known fingerprints of Michael Grant Miller.

Fifth Paragraph: This portion in this affidavit is true and correct.

Sixth Paragraph: This information was never proven, though they say this individual's prints were on this phone. Miller does not recall ever using this pay phone. Not just the day in question, but in any time period. Miller, did live in this general area and it would not be against the law for him to use it; even though this phone was used in a crime. How is someone supposed to know if a public phone or any phone for that matter has been used for illegal purposes? No one ever saw Miller's actual fingerprint print.

February 19

EXAMINING THE CREDIBILITY OF THE CRIMINAL COMPLAINT AFFIDAVIT
PAGE 2 AND 3, SEVENTH PARAGRAPH AND NOTE FROM BANK

> **7.** At approximately 2:30 p.m. Marc Kaplan located the
> aforementioned note at the Security Pacific Bank, which
>
> 2   N000144

> instructed him to immediately proceed to Saguaro Lake Boat Ramp
> #2, where he would find further instructions. Kaplan was
> followed and placed under surveillance by FBI Agents as he
> departed the bank and began driving to Saguaro Lake. The area
> surrounding Saguaro Lake was also placed under surveillance by
> FBI Agents.

NOTE FROM BANK

> GET IN YOUR CAR AND DRIVE TO LAKE SAGUARO PARK. THE ROUTE WILL
> DRIVE WILL BE:
>   SHEA BLVD TO BEELINE HIGHWAY.
>   GO NORTH (L) ON BEELINE TILL YOU COME TO THE PARK.
>   MAKE A RIGHT AND FOLLOW ROAD DOWN. GO TOWARD BOAT DOCK 2
>   CONTINUE GOING AROUND LAKE UNTIL YOU VERY END.
>   GET OUT OF YOUR CAR AND GO OVER TO THE MIDDLE OF THE EATING
>   AREA.
>   LOOK UP THE HILL AND YOU WILL SEE A BLACK PAINT MARK.
>   FOLLOW THESE UP THE HILL TILL YOU SEE A BROWN PLASTIC BAG. AT
>   ONE OF THE BLACK MARKS THERE WILL BE A FISHING LINE NEAR
>   IT. THIS IS ATTACHED TO THE BAG.
>   GET BAG AND BRING BACK DOWN TO PICNIC TABLES.
>   UNLOCK SUITCAS AND READ NOTE INSIDE.

Seventh Paragraph: Case Special Agent Tolhurst reported on the note found at the *Security Pacific Bank* which instructed Kaplan to immediately proceed to *Saguaro Lake* Park go toward boat ramp #2; going around to dead end of road. Where he would find further instructions. Kaplan was followed and placed under surveillance by FBI Special Agents as he departed the bank and began driving to the lake.

This is a copy of the exact note left at the bank or location (L-2).

February 19

> 8. Prior to Kaplan arriving at Saguaro Lake, FBI Agents observed a Mercury sedan, bearing Arizona license plate AWS-090 and registered to Michael G. Miller, at the Saguaro Lake picnic area, which had arrived before the agents arrived and which was approximately 1/4 mile from Boat Ramp #2 Shortly thereafter, and before Kaplan arrived, a red Corvette, bearing Arizona license plate EVY-571 and registered to Mark A. Nelson, arrived at the picnic area and parked next to the Mercury sedan.

Eighth Paragraph: Here, FBI Special Agents observed a Mercury sedan at the *Saguaro Lake* Picnic Area. The problem with this information if the fact this vehicle and its passengers were a parked a few hundred feet away from this Marina Picnic Area. Actually Miller's car was parked sideways taking up almost three parking spaces. Miller's car was facing toward the entrance of the lake. The red Corvette after turning around in the turnaround area of the dead end road, parked next to the Mercury to talk to these two unknown individuals standing next to the Mercury drinking beer.

That is when the Corvette pulled into three spots next to the Mercury and Bonadonna got out of the car and began his opening line, "Hello, my name is Jeff Bonadonna, if I was married to Madonna, she would be called, Madonna Bonadonna". This is something he always tells people he first meets. After a few minutes the Corvette left the parking area.

Location And Events Map

MERCURY AND CORVETTE DEPARTED BEFORE KAPLAN AND THE FBI ARRIVED

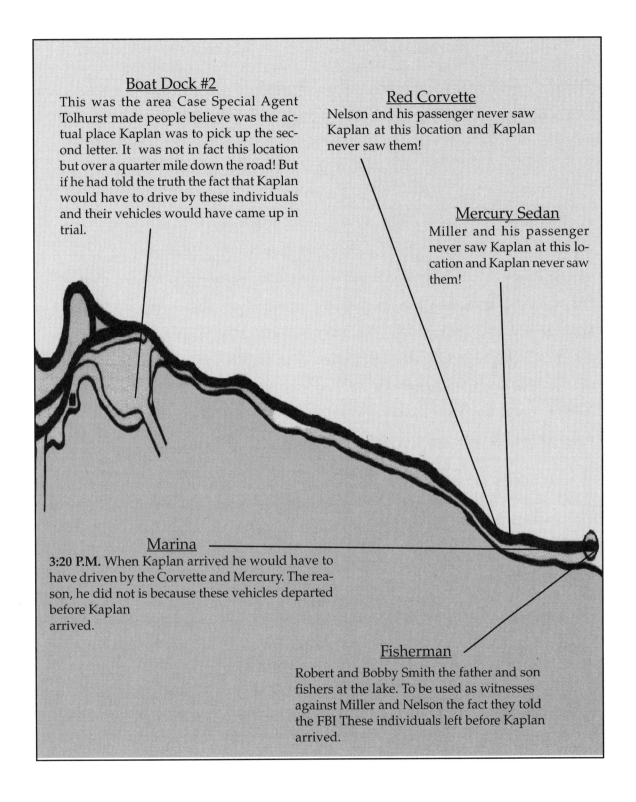

Boat Dock #2
This was the area Case Special Agent Tolhurst made people believe was the actual place Kaplan was to pick up the second letter. It was not in fact this location but over a quarter mile down the road! But if he had told the truth the fact that Kaplan would have to drive by these individuals and their vehicles would have came up in trial.

Red Corvette
Nelson and his passenger never saw Kaplan at this location and Kaplan never saw them!

Mercury Sedan
Miller and his passenger never saw Kaplan at this location and Kaplan never saw them!

Marina
3:20 P.M. When Kaplan arrived he would have to have driven by the Corvette and Mercury. The reason, he did not is because these vehicles departed before Kaplan arrived.

Fisherman
Robert and Bobby Smith the father and son fishers at the lake. To be used as witnesses against Miller and Nelson the fact they told the FBI These individuals left before Kaplan arrived.

February 19
EXAMINING THE CREDIBILITY OF THE CRIMINAL COMPLAINT AFFIDAVIT
PAGE 3, TENTH PARAGRAPH AND PAGE 4, TENTH PARAGRAPH

> 10.   The FBI Agents noted that there were very few
> people at the Lake that day, but the agents did observe four
> males at the Corvette and the Mercury conversing with each other
>
> 3

> at the Saguaro Lake picnic area, and approximately 100 feet from
> Kaplan.   One of these four males was positively identified from
> his drivers license photograph as Mark A. Nelson by FBI Agents at
> the surveillance and one fisherman at Saguaro Lake that day.
> Another of the four males was tentatively identified by one of
> the fishermen at Saguaro Lake that day as Michael G. Miller.
> Nelson was also observed by FBI Agents to be holding a hand-held
> mobile cellular telephone. Also one of the fishermen also
> identified Nelson as the driver of the Corvette.

Tenth Paragraph : Here, FBI Case Special Agent Tolhurst noted that Special Agents noted very few people at the lake; they did however observe four males at this location standing by their vehicles, the red Corvette and Mercury sedan conversing with each other. Yet, these Special Agents took pictures but none of them had these vehicles or passengers. These individuals were listed as 100 ft. from Kaplan at the *Saguaro Lake* Marina Picnic Area #3. But as you see on the map on the right, these individuals never crossed paths at this location, even though this Case Special Agent Tolhurst swore under the penalties of perjury these are true and correct facts listed in the affidavit.

At his point of the story, we can now say these are lies listed on this affidavit. This is a harsh statement, but Case Special Agent Tolhurst, knew Miller and I and especially our passengers had nothing whatsoever to this case. Special Agent Tolhurst went ahead and wrote his own observations to reflect a more positive involvement of these crimes being sought on this Criminal Complaint Affidavit against truly innocent individuals. The Case Special Agent also wrote that FBI Special Agents ob served me with my cellular telephone, making it appear like more than what it actually was, to make it look more damaging toward me. Later you will learn that even though I may have had my phone with me, there was no incriminating evidence on my phone bill either. One must note this: In this section 10 the two fisherman, the Smiths told the FBI that the red Corvette left the area before Kaplan arrived and Miller left a few minutes after the Corvette and still before Kaplan arrived. Therefore, how did the FBI see me holding a cellular phone?

February 19
EXAMINING THE CREDIBILITY OF THE CRIMINAL COMPLAINT AFFIDAVIT
PAGE 4, ELEVENTH PARAGRAPH

> 11. As Kaplan departed the Saguaro Lake Boat Dock, FBI Agents observed the Corvette and Mercury soon thereafter follow Kaplan's vehicle out of the recreation area toward the highway. Kaplan went in one direction and the Corvette and Mercury then proceeded in another direction southbound on the Bush Highway at speeds estimated to be 85 miles per hour.

Eleventh Paragraph: In this section, it clearly states, that as Kaplan departed the *Saguaro Lake* Boat Dock, FBI Special Agents observed the Corvette and Mercury soon thereafter follow Kaplan's vehicle out if the recreation area. Kaplan went in one direction and the Corvette and Mercury went in the other direction on Bush Highway. These are more lies included in this affidavit. Miller and me left before Kaplan arrived. This Conspiracy Theory if unfolding right before our eyes!

The FBI never followed the Mercury and they do not know where they went. From later information it was learned these individuals went to Miller's boss' house. Why, FBI Special Agents never followed this vehicle is strange. One reason would be the FBI was not at the lake at times they reported. The only reason the FBI Special Agents knew what these vehicles did before Kaplan and they arrived at *Saguaro Lake*, is based on the witnesses and the alibis that Miller and me told the FBI Special Agents during interrogations on February 20, 1992. Then they rewrote the *Surveillance Log* to fit their version of what they claim to have happened.

Location And Events Map
KAPLAN DEPARTS BOAT DOCK: FBI OBSERVE
CORVETTE AND MERCURY FOLLOW

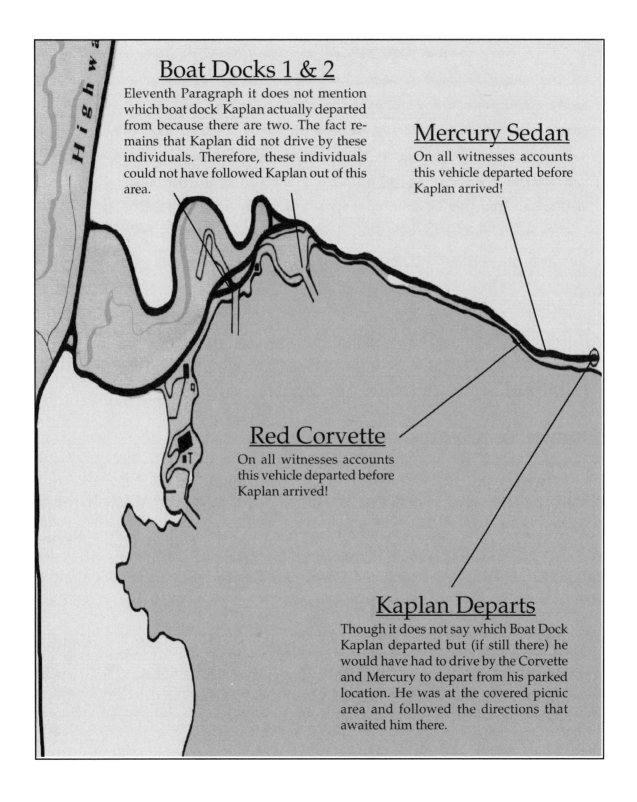

Boat Docks 1 & 2
Eleventh Paragraph it does not mention which boat dock Kaplan actually departed from because there are two. The fact remains that Kaplan did not drive by these individuals. Therefore, these individuals could not have followed Kaplan out of this area.

Mercury Sedan
On all witnesses accounts this vehicle departed before Kaplan arrived!

Red Corvette
On all witnesses accounts this vehicle departed before Kaplan arrived!

Kaplan Departs
Though it does not say which Boat Dock Kaplan departed but (if still there) he would have had to drive by the Corvette and Mercury to depart from his parked location. He was at the covered picnic area and followed the directions that awaited him there.

Highway

February 19
EXAMINING THE CREDIBILITY OF THE CRIMINAL COMPLAINT AFFIDAVIT
PAGE 4, TWELFTH PARAGRAPH AND PAGE 5, TWELFTH PARAGRAPH

> **12.** After Marc Kaplan departed Saguaro Lake en route to the Estrella Development, he stopped at a McDonald's Restaurant near the intersection of Highway 87 and Shea Boulevard. Either shortly before or after Kaplan arrived, Nelson's red Corvette also arrived at the McDonald's Restaurant and parked. An FBI Agent at this location observed a male passenger get out of the Corvette and walk within approximately ten feet of Kaplan's vehicle, and he looked briefly at Kaplan, who was sitting inside his car. At the same time, an FBI Agent began to walk towards Kaplan's vehicle. The male passenger then
>
> 4
>
> N000146

> walked back to and re-entered the Corvette, which immediately
>
> departed the McDonald's.

Twelfth Paragraph: In this section, it tells that Kaplan arrived at the *McDonalds* to make a phone call to the FBI, on route to *Estrella Mountain Park*, where he was to drop off the $ 250,000.00 in cash. Though this Case Special Agent states in his affidavit, he does not know whether it was shortly before or after Kaplan arrived, that the red Corvette arrived. Kaplan told the FBI that he saw the red Corvette just a few miles or so before he arrived at the *McDonalds* and this was the very first time he saw the red Corvette, the Corvette driver slowed down to look at him or his car (because everyone looks at his teal blue car). But he could not tell where the Corvette went after that because they left at such a high rate of speed. It is here where FBI Special Agents first saw the red Corvette and radio transmitted to fellow Special Agents: "A red Corvette left the area at a high rate of speed anyone seeing it don't let it out of your sight!" This was just a few miles before the *McDonalds*, they were in the vehicle following Kaplan on the way to *McDonalds*. Even though these Agent's identities are unknown does not limit the fact that Special Agent R. Scott Rivas and Reno F. Walker placed the Corvette at the *McDonalds* at 4:00 P.M. This is very important evidence because they also reported in their *Surveillance Log* of February 13, 1992, that they observed a passenger get out of the Corvette and begin to walk toward Kaplan's vehicle with Kaplan still in his car. This would establish that Kaplan had been there at the time the Corvette arrived according to the FBI report. This could not have happened because the red Corvette passed Kaplan on the road about a mile or so down the road. This is also a reason these Special Agents had a hard time placing Kaplan and the red Corvette together for a second time. This would ruin their made up conspiracy. The map below it to help you better understand the conspiracy against Miller and me!

Location And Events Map
KAPLAN'S ARRIVAL AT THE MCDONALDS ON SHEA BOULEVARD

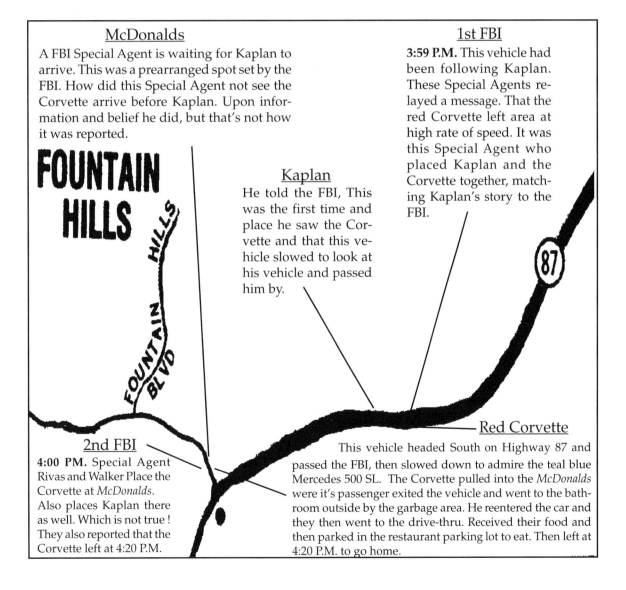

McDonalds
A FBI Special Agent is waiting for Kaplan to arrive. This was a prearranged spot set by the FBI. How did this Special Agent not see the Corvette arrive before Kaplan. Upon information and belief he did, but that's not how it was reported.

FOUNTAIN HILLS

Kaplan
He told the FBI, This was the first time and place he saw the Corvette and that this vehicle slowed to look at his vehicle and passed him by.

1st FBI
3:59 P.M. This vehicle had been following Kaplan. These Special Agents relayed a message. That the red Corvette left area at high rate of speed. It was this Special Agent who placed Kaplan and the Corvette together, matching Kaplan's story to the FBI.

2nd FBI
4:00 PM. Special Agent Rivas and Walker Place the Corvette at *McDonalds*. Also places Kaplan there as well. Which is not true ! They also reported that the Corvette left at 4:20 P.M.

Red Corvette
This vehicle headed South on Highway 87 and passed the FBI, then slowed down to admire the teal blue Mercedes 500 SL. The Corvette pulled into the *McDonalds* were it's passenger exited the vehicle and went to the bathroom outside by the garbage area. He reentered the car and they then went to the drive-thru. Received their food and then parked in the restaurant parking lot to eat. Then left at 4:20 P.M. to go home.

February 19
EXAMINING THE CREDIBILITY OF THE CRIMINAL COMPLAINT AFFIDAVIT
PAGE 5, THIRTEENTH PARAGRAPH

> 13.   After departing the McDonald's Restaurant,
> Nelson's red Corvette, still occupied by 2 males, was located by
> an FBI Agent as it proceeded into Phoenix on Shea Boulevard. The
> Agent observing this vehicle noted the driver engaged in
> maneuvers which appeared to be attempts to prevent others from
> following him. These maneuvers included changing lanes without
> signals, and delays in making a turn for no apparent reason,
> forcing others behind him to pass him. This Corvette was
> followed by the FBI Agent until it entered an apartment complex
> at 6885 East Cochise in Scottsdale, Arizona. Agents learned from
> the apartment manager that Marc A. Nelson lives in this complex.
> Furthermore, agents observed Nelson at the complex on
> February 13, 1992.

Thirteenth Paragraph: In this section, FBI Special Agents followed the red Corvette as it proceeded toward Phoenix, on Shea Boulevard. The problem is this road leads you into Scottsdale, before you can get to Phoenix. The Special Agent observed the Corvette engaging in maneuvers which appeared to the Special Agent as an attempt to prevent others from following him. Also to be noted is that the turn signal lever was broken in the Corvette and was unable to be used, and even if it wasn't broken the driver still may not have used his signals. So they should have issued the driver a ticket. The driver was doing the speed limit and as far as any delays on making a turn for no apparent reason, is a complete misrepresentation of facts.

Another fact to consider is that this Special Agent stated in this affidavit, "FBI Special Agent followed the Corvette until it entered an apartment." This did not happen! In Special Agent Rivas report of February 13, 1992, he was a 1/4 mile west of 70th Street., when the Corvette was turning South. Rivas then located the Corvette in a parking space the Corvette's licence plate registration reflected the same address. (Mark is spelled wrong, this Special Agent spelled it like the intended victim Marc Kaplan). This is just another of the many discrepancies, one of the best trained law enforcement agencies in the world should not make when it comes to gathering information to link a suspect to a crime, in this instance two innocent individuals, Miller and me.

In this Thirteen Paragraph, it states further, Special Agents observed me at the complex on February 13, 1992. This is so mind blowing, that these Special Agents can take innocent actions of law abiding citizens and shape and mold their observations and reports to fit what ever crime they are investigating. Of course, these Special Agents saw Nelson at this complex, he lived there for almost two years and on any given day or night Special Agents as well as anyone else could have seen me and my red Corvette at this location. As far as these Special Agents needing to talk to the management for verification if I lived at these apartments or not, my registration on my Corvette listed this address as my residence. Too, why would someone who knew he was being followed (as reported by the FBI) lead them to his home or drive such a noticeable vehicle with the registration and current plates? The answer is simple I had nothing to do with this crime and these FBI Special Agents conspired together to frame Miller and me to this crime.

Location And Events Map
FBI OBSERVE AND FOLLOW CORVETTE

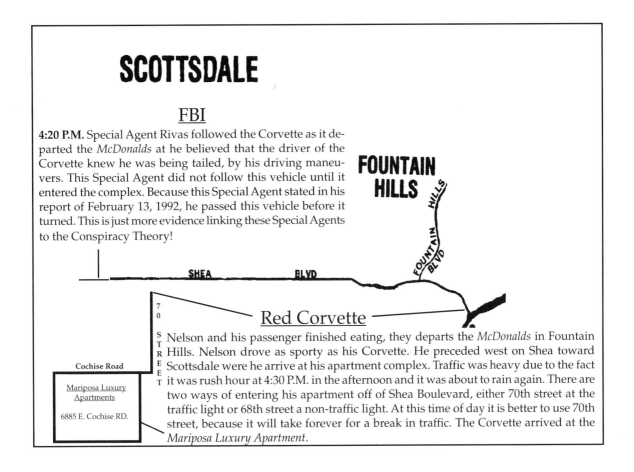

SCOTTSDALE

FBI
4:20 P.M. Special Agent Rivas followed the Corvette as it departed the *McDonalds* at he believed that the driver of the Corvette knew he was being tailed, by his driving maneuvers. This Special Agent did not follow this vehicle until it entered the complex. Because this Special Agent stated in his report of February 13, 1992, he passed this vehicle before it turned. This is just more evidence linking these Special Agents to the Conspiracy Theory!

FOUNTAIN HILLS

SHEA   BLVD

70 STREET

Cochise Road

Mariposa Luxury Apartments

6885 E. Cochise RD.

Red Corvette
Nelson and his passenger finished eating, they departs the *McDonalds* in Fountain Hills. Nelson drove as sporty as his Corvette. He preceded west on Shea toward Scottsdale were he arrive at his apartment complex. Traffic was heavy due to the fact it was rush hour at 4:30 P.M. in the afternoon and it was about to rain again. There are two ways of entering his apartment off of Shea Boulevard, either 70th street at the traffic light or 68th street a non-traffic light. At this time of day it is better to use 70th street, because it will take forever for a break in traffic. The Corvette arrived at the *Mariposa Luxury Apartment*.

February 19
EXAMINING THE CREDIBILITY OF THE CRIMINAL COMPLAINT AFFIDAVIT
PAGE 5, FOURTEENTH PARAGRAPH

---

14. The 1982 Mercury bearing Arizona license AWS-090 was observed by FBI Agents at approximately 9:30 p.m. at 1653 South Harris, Mesa, Arizona. This address was reported as Michael G. Miller's address on a Mesa police report.

Fourteenth Paragraph: FBI Special Agents observed the Mercury at 9:30 P.M. though no date was given and the fact these Special Agents already had this individual's licence plate numbers and it turns out that the registration was in Miller's name and this address was listed as his home address. What this section does not tell you is that Miller went to his boss' house, Lorenzo Gomez. He is no relation to the maid of Marc Kaplan, Carmen Gomez. Miller told his boss of meeting me and my possible need of his construction company services. Miller then gave Mr. Gomez my business card.

So the FBI did not need to wait for the 9:30 P.M. Mesa Police Report to find the location of this individual or his vehicle and if the FBI followed this individual out of the lake, why did they not follow him to his bosses house? The reason is simple. When Miller left *Saguaro Lake* the FBI did not see his vehicle or its passengers because they left before the FBI Special Agents arrived. Therefore, earlier reports of the FBI seeing this vehicle leave the lake in the opposite direction that Kaplan was heading was falsely reported. Since these Special Agents weren't at the *Saguaro Lake* as early as they claimed in the *Surveillance Log* of February 13, 1992, they did not then get to record either the Mercury or Corvette's licence plate numbers. As confusing at it may seem these Special Agents rewrote their *Surveillance Logs* and their reports to frame Miller and me to this crime. Even this Case Special Agent Tolhurst and his merry men all conspired to these event reports, the damage they caused would have never surfaced if it wasn't for the author of this book and his determination to seek the truth and to expose these Special Agents and their Case Special Agent of the Federal Judicial System for the administrative crimes they have committed against us all! Read the map on the right!

Location And Events Map

KAPLAN DEPARTS MARINA PICNIC AREA #3
FBI SEE CORVETTE AND MERCURY FOLLOW

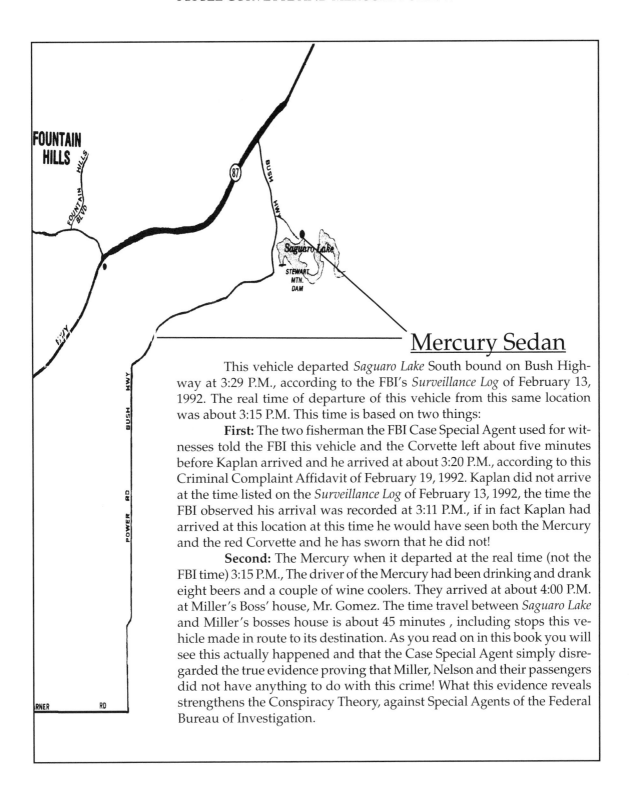

Mercury Sedan

This vehicle departed *Saguaro Lake* South bound on Bush Highway at 3:29 P.M., according to the FBI's *Surveillance Log* of February 13,
1992. The real time of departure of this vehicle from this same location
was about 3:15 P.M. This time is based on two things:

First: The two fisherman the FBI Case Special Agent used for witnesses told the FBI this vehicle and the Corvette left about five minutes
before Kaplan arrived and he arrived at about 3:20 P.M., according to this
Criminal Complaint Affidavit of February 19, 1992. Kaplan did not arrive
at the time listed on the *Surveillance Log* of February 13, 1992, the time the
FBI observed his arrival was recorded at 3:11 P.M., if in fact Kaplan had
arrived at this location at this time he would have seen both the Mercury
and the red Corvette and he has sworn that he did not!

Second: The Mercury when it departed at the real time (not the
FBI time) 3:15 P.M., The driver of the Mercury had been drinking and drank
eight beers and a couple of wine coolers. They arrived at about 4:00 P.M.
at Miller's Boss' house, Mr. Gomez. The time travel between *Saguaro Lake*
and Miller's bosses house is about 45 minutes , including stops this vehicle made in route to its destination. As you read on in this book you will
see this actually happened and that the Case Special Agent simply disregarded the true evidence proving that Miller, Nelson and their passengers
did not have anything to do with this crime! What this evidence reveals
strengthens the Conspiracy Theory, against Special Agents of the Federal
Bureau of Investigation.

February 19
EXAMINING THE CREDIBILITY OF THE CRIMINAL COMPLAINT AFFIDAVIT
PAGE 5 FIFTEENTH PARAGRAPH

15. A computerized criminal history information check on Michael Grant Miller and Mark A. Nelson reflected both had prior arrest histories for misdemeanor offenses. One of those offenses for Miller was for an arrest in 1985 for Possession of a Dangerous Weapon which was reduced to a misdemeanor.

N000147

Subscribed and Sworn to before me this 19th day of February, 1992

5

MORTON SITVER
United States Magistrate Judge

Fifteenth Paragraph: When the FBI did a computerized criminal history check on Miller and me, they found that both individuals had prior arrest histories for misdemeanor offenses. The FBI even mentioned a particular offense in 1985 for possession of a dangerous weapon which was reduced to a misdemeanor, against Miller. This offense was actually against me when I was in West Hollywood, California. I was a victim of an egotistical Sheriff of the West Hollywood Division. But that's another book.

This Criminal Complaint Affidavit is categorized evidence confirming the Conspiracy Theory. Why did this happen? Why did these Special Agents seek to destroy the lives of two innocent young men? Was it for potential promotions within the FBI? Or was it just plain malice and application of a pre-programed criminal profile that caused these FBI Special Agents to believe guilt of Miller and me and our passengers in the Mercury and Corvette? Why did these Special Agents seek arrest warrants against us? No one knows for sure, maybe someday these Special Agents will be held liable, but for now Case Special Agent Keith Tolhurst, has prepared for the arrest of Miller and me and for his statement to the Media!

February 24

6:40 A.M. RICK FAIR TURN INFORMANT SECRETLY TAPED *FRANK ALBER*
PAGES 1, 3, 5-37 AND 47

F~ ~02 (Rev. 3-10-82)

- 1 -

FEDERAL BUREAU OF INVESTIGATION

Date of transcription   2/24/92

        The following is a transcription of Tape Number 1,
which is a consensually monitored nagra recording between RICHARD
FAIR and FRANK ALBER. The conversation occurred on February 24,
1992 at approximately 6:40 a.m.:

Revised: 3/10/92

Investigation on   2/24/92   at   Phoenix, Arizona   File #   9A-PX-46497

by   SA KEITH D. TOLHURST/sm   Date dictated   2/24/92   N00019u

                                      182

```
9A-PX-46497   Tape 1              3
KDT/sm
```

	(Muffling sound)
FAIR:	Don't forget to turn on the on buttons.
UNKNOWN MALE:	Okay.
	(Muffling sound - sound of zipper)
	(UI conversation - whispering)
FAIR:	It's approximately, approximately 7:50 a.m. I'm on my way out the door to go to the 7 Eleven get some coffee and then go over to Frank's house.
	(Muffling sound - engine starting - traffic noises)
	(Beeping sound - traffic noises)
	(Long pause)
	(Door opening - muffling sound - door closing - UI noises)
	(UI voices in background)
UNKNOWN FEMALE:	Hello.
FAIR:	Mornin'. How are you?
UNKNOWN FEMALE:	Okay. How are you doing?
FAIR:	Good. Thanks.
	(Sound of cash register)
UNKNOWN FEMALE:	One twenty six.
	(Pause - sound of cash register)
UNKNOWN FEMALE:	(UI)
	(Muffling sound)

```
9A-PX-46497    Tape 1              5
KDT/sm
```

ALBER: Well no..yeah but you usually do that but you
                usually come back the next day sometime.

FAIR: Well I had that other stuff remember? That
                Mary had in the car so I had some clean
                underwear.

ALBER: Oh, I didn't know you did.

FAIR: Yeah.

                (Muffling sound)

ALBER: Anyway I told Mary you'd give her a call.

FAIR: Alright.

ALBER: She stopped in like three o'clock in the
                morning.

FAIR: Mornin'. She stopped in at three o'clock?

ALBER: Yeah (UI)

                (UI noise)

FAIR: I got a paper that says they're gonna (UI)
                thing more about that Kaplan (phonetic)
                thing.

ALBER: There isn't.

FAIR: There isn't anything in the paper...you
                looked?

                (UI noises - pause)

ALBER: (UI - voice sound far away)

FAIR: Well, Frank. Jesus Christ! I'm a you know a
                little...

ALBER: (UI)

FAIR: Well...

```
9A-PX-46497  Tape 1                6
KDT/sm
```

FAIR:	Well you make me make that call...
ALBER:	I know.
FAIR:	.....a couple weeks ago...
ALBER:	And, and...
FAIR:	I don't know why you did that to me.
ALBER:	I don't know. (UI)
	(Muffling sound)
FAIR:	I mean Frank I've been like nervous as shit.
ALBER:	(UI)
FAIR:	Frank. I slept since Friday morning when I got up and saw that thing in the paper.
ALBER:	Yeah.
FAIR:	About Katz..I've slept about...mmm...thirty minutes since that time. I mean I've been like a nervous freakin' wreck.
ALBER:	Why?
FAIR:	I have stomach pains. Why? I mean..Jesus Christ Frank I thought we were friends when you (stutters)...know.
ALBER:	Yeah. O-Okay. Listen. There..there's nothing (UI)
	(Muffling sound)
ALBER:	If, if, if they..no hold on..
FAIR:	Frank?
ALBER:	Hold, hold..will you just listen for a second.

FAIR: I'll listen.

ALBER: Alright. If they ever ask you (UI)

                    (Muffling sound)

FAIR: Tell 'em that you asked me to make the
                    call...

ALBER: Yeah.

FAIR: And if I tell 'em the truth. How am I gonna
                    know you know that if something happens here
                    Frank th-that you're gonna tell 'em the
                    truth?

ALBER: No, I'm gonna tell 'em the truth. But I'm
                    just sayin' that I won't verify that I asked
                    you to call.

FAIR: But you, you know you told me I wasn't doin'
                    anything illegal. I asked you...how many
                    times did I ask you that?

ALBER: Once.

FAIR: Oh...I thought it was more than that but...

                    (Muffling sound)

FAIR: This is pissing me off Frank that you'd do
                    that to me. I mean get me involved in it. I
                    don't even know what...

ALBER: (UI) just calm down.

FAIR: I mean we got this opportunity...

ALBER: Yeah.

FAIR: ....in San Diego. I mean I couldn't do shit
                    on that. I, I couldn't even...

ALBER: So why, why did you, yeah, come back on

```
9A-PX-46497   Tape 1              8
KDT/sm
```

                    the paper in the Mesa Tribune. Just listen a
                    minute.

ALBER: Okay.

FAIR: In the Mesa Tribune I see this freakin'
                    article. You know it's similar to the one
                    that was in there on Friday and it says they
                    gotta hundred freakin' FBI Agents workin' on
                    the thing.

ALBER: Uh-hmm.

FAIR: You don't think a freakin' hundred people are
                    gonna find something out?

ALBER: No.

FAIR: I ju..I just can't work on
                    this...thing..I..Frank! I don't know what to
                    do. I'm...

ALBER: Rick, Rick, Rick...

FAIR: ...I'm..Karen said I could stay over there.
                    I didn't tell her anything about it.

ALBER: Fine. I mean if you wanna stay over there
                    fine. I'm just sayin' there's nothing to be
                    concerned about.

FAIR: The other day I know I asked you...I said.

ALBER: Rick, Rick..Rick, Rick..just (UI) if anybody
                    asks just tell the truth.

                    (Pause)

FAIR: You told me the other day just to..

ALBER: I know. I know what day I told you and, and
                    I, and I said (UI) listen there's no sense
                    worrying about. If somebody asks ya, just
                    tell 'em the truth.

9A-PX-46497 Tape 1   9
KDT/sm

ALBER: Well I was gonna tell ya on Saturday. I was
                      gonna tell ya on Saturday but you haven't
                      been here. You haven't even called.

                      (Muffling sound)

FAIR: Quite frankly I was you know scared to even
                      come over here. I just didn't wanna be
                      around 'cause I don't...know. I don't know
                      what the hell's going on other than you know
                      you had me make this call and then I asked
                      you the other day you know you told me you
                      did one other thing.

ALBER: Oh..the o-only thing I did was this guy from
                      California asked me to make this call (UI) a
                      guy if, if (UI) don't wanna get you involved
                      any more than you are, just, just, just say
                      that that if anybody ask just say you were
                      out drinkin' and I asked you to make this
                      call. Everything can be verified. Okay?

FAIR: Le..let me say my piece.

ALBER: Okay.

FAIR: Frank we (sighs) you know you worked hard on
                      that software for about six months.

ALBER: Uh-hmm.

FAIR: You know. I know you were displeased with my
                      effort.

ALBER: Uh-hmm..

FAIR: But regardless you know there's an
                      opportunity to turn things around here.

ALBER: Right. And we, and we should be doing that.

FAIR: I mean you know we could both make some good
                      money.

```
9A-PX-46497   Tape 1                 10
KDT/sm
```

ALBER: Right.

FAIR: For both of us.

ALBER: Uh-huh.

FAIR: And then you get involved...it's, I can't
                    believe. I don't, I don't know what it is
                    you're involved in but you get involved in
                    something like this.

ALBER: (UI - voice sounds far away) involved in (UI)
                    that's why I'm saying you know I'm not, I
                    don't have a problem. I mean and, and I
                    wanted to tell you on Saturday to just say
                    the absolute truth. Just don't, don't even
                    attempt to lie.

FAIR: Why not...why not...

ALBER: Just you know you're, you're blowing this up
                    out of proportion. You're going crazy and
                    you shouldn't be.

FAIR: Yeah, I am going crazy. I'm, I'm thinkin'
                    about you know going back to Pennsylvania.
                    Go to my mothers and stuff like this.

ALBER: Why?

FAIR: Frank why don't you just tell me what the
                    hell went on so you know we could come up you
                    know with some kind of explanation for this I
                    mean so we can be successful. Now we're
                    blowing this whole damn opp...

ALBER: No, Rick, Rick you're going crazy. Will you
                    just calm down. Just calm down. But We
                    should be concentrating on the software
                    that's where our minds should be.

FAIR: Why..I don't understand I know. I thought we
                    were...

ALBER: You're there (UI) we worked hard on it and I

N000199

9A-PX-46497   Tape 1   11
KDT/sm

ALBER: ....(UI)

FAIR: ....we're supp...we're suppose to be friends
                and business partners.

ALBER: Uh-hmm.

FAIR: Yeah, we you know we've had some clashes in
                the past and basically you know promulgated
                on work and those type of things but Jesus
                Christ I mean can't you, you can't even talk
                to me. You can't even t-tell me what's going
                on. Did, did you go to that family thing
                with your, your mother, your
                mother....weren't you suppose to go to some
                family picnic or something on Saturday?

ALBER: No.

FAIR: Oh, I thought your mom called or something.

ALBER: Next weekend, which I won't be there.

FAIR: Oh, it's next, oh it's next weekend. I was
                wonderin' if you wanted (UI) freakin' did
                Bill say anything to ya about it?

ALBER: No.

FAIR: (UI) he probably didn't see anything in the
                paper.

ALBER: I, I haven't seen him.

FAIR: Did Mary Ann see anything?

ALBER: We saw it on the news and she said something
                (UI)

FAIR: Did she think you were involved or not?

                (Muffling sound)

FAIR: (Stutters) I'm just scared shitless Frank.

```
9A-PX-46497   Tape 1              12
KDT/sm
```

FAIR: Yeah. I read the paper. It says they have a
             traced some phone...

ALBER: Okay.

FAIR: ..phone in Chandler at a grocery store.

ALBER: Okay. Alright. And they had one set of
             prints and they have the guy who was there
             and also out at Saguaro Lake.

FAIR: Do you know those guys? I ask ya...

ALBER: I, I swear to God, I never heard of 'em.
             Never saw 'em. Never heard of 'em.

FAIR: Is Larry involved in this in any way? Does
             he have anything to do with this?

ALBER: No.

FAIR: 'Cause I know he worked for...

ALBER: Yeah. Just...

FAIR: ....Mark Kaplan.

ALBER: No.

FAIR: W-what were you gonna get out of the thing?
             I mean I probably shouldn't ask but you're
             probably gonna...were gonna get something
             outta it. I mean they're talking..

ALBER: I was gonna, I was gonna get five hundred
             dollars.

FAIR: Five hundred dollars?

ALBER: Yeah.

FAIR: Jesus..I mean didn't you even think?

ALBER: Rick.

9A-PX-46497   Tape 1   13
KDT/sm

ALBER: And it would be best if you don't ask
                questions that's what I'm sayin' to you. If
                you just told 'em the truth then there's
                nothing more that they can do. First of all
                they're not gonna do anything.

FAIR: Do you know what's gonna happen if Mary sees
                my name in the paper?

ALBER: Rick.

FAIR: I mean my wife is gonna go...

ALBER: What?..

FAIR: And I wanted to call her and I was afraid to
                call her...

ALBER: Why?

FAIR: ....this weekend at home. Because...I didn't
                know if she called here and I didn't know if
                anything even happened here you know I didn't
                even know if you were here. I was too scared
                you know to even leave Karen's.

ALBER: Rick.

                (Muffling sound - pause)

FAIR: Well Frank I don't think over reacting to
                possible kidnapping charges is..

ALBER: Well, but, yeah but...

                (Pause)

FAIR: What's this thing about the letter. Who
                wrote these letters and stuff?

ALBER: I don't know.

FAIR: You didn't have anything to do with that?

```
9A-PX-46497  Tape 1              14
KDT/sm
```

ALBER: That was (stutters) the message that I was
                suppose to say but I figured he would
                recognize my voice.

FAIR: Did you write that note?

ALBER: I copied it from what the person told me to
                say.

FAIR: I just can't believe that you got me fuckin'
                involved in it.

ALBER: Rick your...

FAIR: I mean I..

ALBER: ...your you know you're, you're blowing this
                up to be crazy.

FAIR: Well it is crazy.

ALBER: (Stutters) Yeah, you're making it crazy will
                you just calm down.

FAIR: How did you get involved in this thing?

ALBER: It, it sounded so simple when I first got
                involved. It, it but...

FAIR: What you do meet somebody in a bar or
                something?

ALBER: No, no, no. Nothing like that.

FAIR: You know why don't you just tell me about it?

ALBER: I got a call from a guy who, who was Mark's
                mailing partner. He did his mailings for
                Mark in California.

FAIR: What's, what's his name? Did you ever talk
                to him about me?

ALBER: No.

9A-PX-46497   Tape 1   15
KDT/sm

did Mark's mailing. And Mark fucked him
outta like forty fuckin' thousand dollars.
So what he said was he was going to, ah, it
was.   Basically he was gonna, it was like he
said sorta like blackmail. He was gonna
tell, ah, Mark's partners that Mark ripped
them off if he didn't pay the money and he
asked me to make the call.

FAIR: Well how did he get your name?

ALBER: Some how he knows somebody over in Mark's
organization and they knew that, ah, that
I..me and Mark weren't on the best terms and,
and, and so he figured hey. And that some
how he knew I was out of work. They called
and said you wanna make some extra money to
make this phone call. The only other thing
he asked me was is there any place in the
Valley that sorta like you know fairly
secluded and whatever and I had told him you
know, ah, Estrella Park. Because that's
where I ride my bicycle out there. And
that's the only other thing.

FAIR: Where is it? I don't even know where that
park is. Where is it?

ALBER: It's, ah, you take I10 'til you hit Estrella
Parkway and go left.

FAIR: Frank didn't you even think before you got
involved in something like this?

ALBER: He just..you know he said you know because
he, he explained the contact and I said God
this guy knows a lot more than I do. And I
just said shoot..it's just..one phone call
five hundred bucks I said and it, it didn't
sound like it was. First of all I felt the
guy did have the right (UI) call because he
said he was going to go through the lawyers
and everything and, and Mark, I, I know for a
fact had ripped off a lot of people.

```
9A-PX-46497  Tape 1              16
KDT/sm
```

ALBER: It wasn't that much of a grudge. The guy
                owed..was owed the money and he was just
                using you know what I though a good tactic to
                get the money.

                (Pause)

FAIR: But you knew all along what you were doing
                wasn't above board I mean...

ALBER: No it wasn't...

FAIR: You knew right from wrong?

ALBER: It wasn't quite right. But it was not
                anything like what it turned out to be.

                (Muffling sound)

FAIR: Frank this..I'll tell ya..if this blows this
                opportunity in, in San Diego..

ALBER: It..it will if you keep letting it bother you
                so much like this.

FAIR: If my name comes out in the paper for any
                reason whatsoever you know I'm finished. I
                mean San Diego's dead. I, I wouldn't have an
                opportunity to get the court administrators
                job in Maricopa. You know. I, my life would
                be just totally fucked.

ALBER: First of all just because you're name...first
                of all you're name's not gonna come out.
                Second of all...

                (Muffling sound)

ALBER: (UI) you just gotta put your mind at ease.
                Worrying about isn't gonna help and so..and
                there's nothing to worry about.

FAIR: Frank you can tell me to put my mind at ease
                until I'm blue in the face or until you're

```
9A-PX-46497   Tape 1              17
KDT/sm
```

ALBER: What, what..

FAIR: It's not gonna do anything for me and, and,
              it's easy to say forget it. But I can't. I
              mean those guys. T-those pictures I saw in
              the paper on Monday. I mean on Friday.
              Excuse me. You know looked pretty freakin'
              grungy.

ALBER: Yeah. I, I had nothing to do with that. I
              had no. Nothing! And it might be something
              totally different than what we..we had talked
              about.

FAIR: And..(sighs) I mean did you meet with this
              guy from California or what?

ALBER: No. He just called and he said he lives in
              California and asked because he didn't fly
              over and whatever. If I could do that.

FAIR: Did you get paid for it?

ALBER: No. He said when he got paid, he'd pay me.
              And I just (chuckles)

FAIR: You mean outta the two hundred and fifty
              thousand dollars?

ALBER: He was going. He was going f-for fifty
              thousand. He was owed forty two and since he
              already had legal fees and whatever to pay
              them, he, he, he said he'd be asking for
              fifty thousand.

FAIR: Okay so he was gonna fifty thousand. You're
              gonna get five hundred...

ALBER: But he was owed that money.

FAIR: Why the quarter of a million dollars?

ALBER: I don't know Rick!

```
9A-PX-46497  Tape 1              18
KDT/sm
```

FAIR: ...I want fifty thousand and I'll give you
                 five hundred and...

ALBER: Rick, Rick, Rick..

FAIR: ...we'll throw the other...

ALBER: Rick, Rick, Rick, Rick, Rick, Rick. When all
                 that came out, that was as much a surprise to
                 me as it was to you.

                 (Muffling sound)

FAIR: Well you know..that's why I told you that
                 when I saw it, I put two and two together.

ALBER: Right, right.

FAIR: I'm the guy that made that phone call...

ALBER: But...

FAIR: ....and you..

ALBER: Yeah, but you just you know you (sighs).

FAIR: You told me what I said..Frank am I doin'
                 anything illegal. You said to me..no.
                 Right?

ALBER: Right.

FAIR: But I did do something illegal.

ALBER: No, what you did. What you did was not
                 illegal. What you did was not illegal.

FAIR: Well maybe it wasn't illegal knowingly to me
                 but the fact remains it was fucking illegal.

ALBER: No it was not illegal what you did.

FAIR: If it's a part of a plot or some scheme...

ALBER: No, no, no hold on...hold on...if you..

9A-PX-46497   Tape 1   19
KDT/sm

ALBER: Right?

FAIR: No, I could still be...

ALBER: No you can't.

FAIR: How do I know that anybody's gonna vindicate
              me. Come forward and say..hey this guy had
              nothing to do with it. He was an innocent
              by-stander. How do I know anybody's gonna
              come forth and say that? How do I know
              you're even gonna come..'cause you put me in
              that position in the first God-damn place.

ALBER: (Sighs) Rick...

              (Muffling sound)

FAIR: Frank I'm....

ALBER: Rick.

FAIR: I know, I know you, you know get pissed off
              at me at some business venture.

ALBER: Yeah but that...Rick will you just..that's
              why I said if you don't know anything, then
              you are doing nothing illegal. You didn't do
              anything illegal. You had nothing to worry
              about.

FAIR: Frank I have to know something.

ALBER: You don't have to know anything.

FAIR: For my..

ALBER: Rick..that's what I'm sayin'. You just..your
              just. I don't know.

FAIR: Frank can I tell ya for my peace of mind. I
              need to know something.

ALBER: Rick, you can tell me for your peace of mind

```
9A-PX-46497   Tape 1              19
KDT/sm
```

ALBER: Right?

FAIR: No, I could still be...

ALBER: No you can't.

FAIR: How do I know that anybody's gonna vindicate
                    me. Come forward and say..hey this guy had
                    nothing to do with it. He was an innocent
                    by-stander. How do I know anybody's gonna
                    come forth and say that? How do I know
                    you're even gonna come..'cause you put me in
                    that position in the first God-damn place.

ALBER: (Sighs) Rick...

                    (Muffling sound)

FAIR: Frank I'm....

ALBER: Rick.

FAIR: I know, I know you, you know get pissed off
                    at me at some business venture.

ALBER: Yeah but that...Rick will you just..that's
                    why I said if you don't know anything, then
                    you are doing nothing illegal. You didn't do
                    anything illegal. You had nothing to worry
                    about.

FAIR: Frank I have to know something.

ALBER: You don't have to know anything.

FAIR: For my..

ALBER: Rick..that's what I'm sayin'. You just..your
                    just. I don't know.

FAIR: Frank can I tell ya for my peace of mind. I
                    need to know something.

ALBER: Rick, you can tell me for your peace of mind

9A-PX-46497   Tape 1   20
KDT/sm

FAIR: Well other than this guy, tell me honestly
             now. Other than this other guy in
             California....

ALBER: That's it...

FAIR: Do you know anybody else that's involved with
             this thing?

ALBER: No.

FAIR: Don't fuckin' lie to me!

ALBER: Okay..I, I just told you the whole story.
             The whole thing.

             (Pause)

FAIR: I'm up..somebody's gonna come here.

ALBER: No!

FAIR: Is my life in jeopardy by, by being here?

ALBER: No!

FAIR: I mean Karen could sense you know there was
             something wrong. She...

ALBER: Well, yeah because you're acting crazy.

FAIR: Well I don't think I was acting crazy. I'm
             acting scared.

ALBER: Yeah, well..and for no reason so that's sorta
             crazy.

             (Pause)

FAIR: So what was..

ALBER: And I wanted to talk to you on Saturday
             morning. To let you..you know..I said wait a
             second, it doesn't do any good to lie. So if

```
9A-PX-46497  Tape 1              21
KDT/sm
```

	you to make the phone call and you did. What's wrong with that?
FAIR:	Yeah, but that wasn't when that happened.
ALBER:	Yes it was. No it wasn't.
FAIR:	No. That was, that was...
ALBER:	We were out drinking.
FAIR:	You just picked me up for lunch that day I was at home.
ALBER:	And we went out drinkin' all afternoon.
FAIR:	And we went out. No, we went to Gallager's...
ALBER:	Uh-hmm.
FAIR:	And you kept telling me you had to make a call at two o'clock. That's what you kept sayin'. I had to make a call at two o'clock...
ALBER:	Well I said (UI) a quarter to two.
FAIR:	Right. Then we went over to the...
ALBER:	Walgreen's to get some beer.
FAIR:	Right. And then we...I don't remember if I dialed the phone or you dialed the phone or (stutters).
ALBER:	I dialed the phone.
FAIR:	You dialed the phone.
	(Pause)
FAIR:	And..did I hold the receiver?
ALBER:	Uh-huh.

9A-PX-46497   Tape 1   22
KDT/sm

FAIR: What did you wipe the phone with?

ALBER: My shirt. Just like I wiped the numbers.

FAIR: I can't even remember....

ALBER: Yeah, you made some funny comment. You
                remember? You said..

FAIR: No. I don't remember 'cause we had about...

ALBER: Okay.

FAIR: ...couple pitchers of beer.

ALBER: Okay you said what are you doing. I said I
                just don't want to take any chances. And
                then oh, no you did say you did say twice.
                You go why are you doing something illegal
                and I said no we're not.

FAIR: Okay. I can't remember..then you took me
                home. Right? Did I...

ALBER: No, we got some beers and went over my house.

FAIR: I don't even remember that 'cause I thought..

ALBER: Or did you have to pick up Ryan?

FAIR: I don't remember what it was. I, I thought
                you were driving that day 'cause Ryan had the
                car to go to school. And you picked me up.

ALBER: Didn't we come and get some beer?

FAIR: I know you stopped. All I can remember is
                that you stopped in Walgreen's. We got some
                beers and came out and you asked me to make a
                phone and I don't remember like I told ya.
                If I dialed the phone or...held the receiver
                or whatever. You know but my fingerprints
                are gonna be on something.

```
9A-PX-46497   Tape 1              23
KDT/sm
```

ALBER: Probably. Rick, will you just. Listen.
                What if what I just said. If you tell the
                truth. There's nothing they can do to you.
                There's nothing that...they won't even keep
                you. They won't even. First of
                all...they're not even gonna know who you
                are.

FAIR: If anybody...

ALBER: Nobody knows.

FAIR: Let me finish.

ALBER: Okay.

FAIR: Does anybody else involved in this scheme,
                however many people it is...

ALBER: I don't know.

FAIR: ...if you say it's one guy in California or..

ALBER: Right. That's all I know.

FAIR: ...Does that guy in California..if you say
                he's the only one that knows..does he know my
                name?

ALBER: No.

FAIR: Did he ask you...come back to you and ask you
                if the call was made?

ALBER: Uh, no.

FAIR: So no one ever talked to you after we talked
                on that phone.

ALBER: Uh-uh. Which sorta pissed me off because I
                was hoping to hear from him to get the money.

FAIR: How can...how can you get involved in
                something for five hund. I mean get involved

```
9A-PX-46497   Tape 1              24
KDT/sm
```

FAIR: And that's your total involvement in the .
                thing and..

ALBER: Yeah.

FAIR: ...and you're being honest with me? I'm
                never gonna find out anything else about
                that?

ALBER: That, that's my total involvement.

FAIR: Frank if you end up getting yourself
                arrested...

ALBER: I..alright, alright if I do.

FAIR: Whatta you gonna do? I mean San Diego's
                dead. 'Cause I can't program. You know I
                don't even know how to use the computer.

ALBER: So..

FAIR: As you said I can't even turn a computer on.

ALBER: Right. I look at it this way...all I'm gonna
                do is tell the truth.

FAIR: No..well why don't...

ALBER: What..

FAIR: Now why don't you consider go telling the
                truth now Jesus...

ALBER: Because...

FAIR: ...Christ I mean you gotta be as nervous as I
                am.

ALBER: No I'm not. No I'm not Rick.

FAIR: Well then we're two different people inside.

ALBER: (Stutters) No, I was real nervous on Friday.

```
9A-PX-46497  Tape 1              25
KDT/sm
```

ALBER: And then I said wait a second. First of all
              there's no way they know who me and you are.
              Hold on.

FAIR: Except...

ALBER: Just listen. There's no way they'd know and
              there's no way they can find out.

              (Pause)

FAIR: Frank.

ALBER: I..will, you just listen. Listen to me.
              There's no way they can know and there's no
              way they can find out. There's only one way
              they can know and one way they can find out.

FAIR: What's that?

ALBER: That's if you tell 'em.

FAIR: What if they had somebody like photographing
              or standing there and photographing us or
              something. Okay. If they knew...

ALBER: Wait a second.

FAIR: ...the damn phone. Did...

ALBER: Wait a second. They, they didn't know the
              phone.

FAIR: Oh, you just picked that one at random?

ALBER: Yeah.

              (Muffling sound)

FAIR: Well apparently...somebody had to know about
              this before I made the call. I mean there
              was...

ALBER: This, this guy asked me to make the phone

```
9A-PX-46497  Tape 1           27
KDT/sm
```

FAIR: Listen to me. I can't believe when I see
            something in the paper. It says there's one
            hundred. Over one hundred FBI Agents workin'
            on this.

ALBER: Yeah.

FAIR: That's what it said in the Mesa..

ALBER: Right.

FAIR: ..Tribune.

ALBER: That's what they said.

FAIR: A hundred people...

ALBER: Uh-hmm.

FAIR: ...are gonna find something out.

ALBER: No they won't.

            (Pause)

FAIR: (Stutters) What did this guy from California
            what did he do call you at home or something?

ALBER: Yeah.

FAIR: Just out of the blue?

ALBER: Yeah.

FAIR: Jesus.

ALBER: You know. You're just, you know that's why I
            want to talk to you on Saturday. I mean I
            couldn't...

            (Muffling sound)

FAIR: Frank when I was living here, how many
            times...

```
9A-PX-46497  Tape 1              28
KDT/sm
```

FAIR: ...did I just go away for a way or
                so...(stutters) usually I'd come back maybe
                Saturday night...

ALBER: (UI) Wait a second.

FAIR: ...or sometime Sunday.

ALBER: Wait a second. You..yeah normally you would
                play basketball.

FAIR: That's right.

ALBER: And you didn't play basketball.

FAIR: I didn't play basketball. That was..(sighs)
                the least thing on my mind was, was playing
                basketball.

ALBER: Why? Probably would've been the best thing
                for ya.

FAIR: Frank all I wanted to do was hide and not be
                seen. And that's the way I feel now. I mean
                I'm you know (sighs) If I hear anything and
                I'm here, I'm gonna freakin' be nervous as
                hell. I'm gonna be a nervous wreck for I
                don't know how long. What if they catch this
                guy in California? What's this guy's name?

ALBER: Richard Woolridge.

FAIR: And he named you...

ALBER: Okay.

FAIR: ...I mean he squeals.

ALBER: (UI)

FAIR: What did he tell ya? Did he tel..did he..

ALBER: What's he gonna..(UI) he says he called me
                and I'll just say no he didn't.

FAIR: ...did I just go away for a way or
                 so...(stutters) usually I'd come back maybe
                 Saturday night...

ALBER: (UI) Wait a second.

FAIR: ...or sometime Sunday.

ALBER: Wait a second. You..yeah normally you would
                 play basketball.

FAIR: That's right.

ALBER: And you didn't play basketball.

FAIR: I didn't play basketball. That was..(sighs)
                 the least thing on my mind was, was playing
                 basketball.

ALBER: Why? Probably would've been the best thing
                 for ya.

FAIR: Frank all I wanted to do was hide and not be
                 seen. And that's the way I feel now. I mean
                 I'm you know (sighs) If I hear anything and
                 I'm here, I'm gonna freakin' be nervous as
                 hell. I'm gonna be a nervous wreck for I
                 don't know how long. What if they catch this
                 guy in California? What's this guy's name?

ALBER: Richard Woolridge.

FAIR: And he named you...

ALBER: Okay.

FAIR: ...I mean he squeals.

ALBER: (UI)

FAIR: What did he tell ya? Did he tel..did he..

ALBER: What's he gonna..(UI) he says he called me
                 and I'll just say no he didn't.

```
9A-PX-46497   Tape 1                29
KDT/sm
```

FAIR: If Richard Wool..Woolridge says what?

ALBER: I don't know you say that he squeals and tell
                the police that I made the phone call.

FAIR: No, he gets caught.

ALBER: Okay.

FAIR: And then he comes forward.

ALBER: And says what?

FAIR: Uh...Frank Alber from Mesa, Arizona, was
                involved in this thing and made a call for
                me.

ALBER: Okay.

FAIR: You..you don't think that the police are
                gonna come out here and make an arrest?
                You're not that stupid are ya?

ALBER: What are they gonna arrest me for?

FAIR: (Sighs)

ALBER: What, w-what are they gonna arrest me for
                Rick? No..you just made the statement, I'm
                asking you a question.

FAIR: Frank I'm getting to the point.

ALBER: No, I'm asking you. You say you wanna..look
                they're gonna come out here and they're gonna
                do what?

FAIR: They're gonna bring you in for questioning...

ALBER: Okay say they bring me in for questioning..

FAIR: ..and I live here. They're gonna, they're
                gonna bring me in questioning. They're gonna
                bring anybody in that you probably know.

N000218

9A-PX-46497   Tape 1   30
KDT/sm

> me and start asking me questions. I know·
> that.

ALBER: No they're not!

          (Pause - muffling sound)

FAIR: I just hope..

ALBER: First of all. Initially you weren't living
          here. You w-weren't planning on coming back
          here.

FAIR: That's right and I wasn't you know (stutters)

ALBER: Just hold, hold on. Second of all....you
          know they're..you know I'm not quite sure how
          they're gonna..I don't know what they're
          gonna do with this guy over in California.
          I-I mean he's over in California. According
          to the paper, nobody even showed up to pick
          up anything.

FAIR: Where in California is he from, southern or?

ALBER: LA.

FAIR: LA?

ALBER: Yeah. Alright? Some how I don't know how
          these other guys got involved but I have no
          clue on who they are.

FAIR: So you're...

ALBER: All I was..all I did was make the phone call.
          You made the phone call.

FAIR: Thank you.

ALBER: Okay. Now, now.

          (Muffling sound)

```
9A-PX-46497  Tape 1              31
KDT/sm
```

FAIR: No what..whatta you gonna say Rick Fair did
                     it?

ALBER: No. I'm just gonna say no I didn't do it.

                     (Muffling sound)

FAIR: Just tell me this.

ALBER: No. All I'm gonna say is no I didn't do it.
                     And if they say do you know anybody who did
                     it. Of course I'm gonna say no I do not.

FAIR: Well let's look at this scenario Frank.

ALBER: Okay lets hear this scenario.

FAIR: Lets say..you know they do find out that
                     you're...

                     (Side A of tape cuts off)

9A-PX-46497   Tape 1   32
KDT/sm

(Side B of tape starts)

ALBER: Then they're gonna..who do you think they're gonna (UI)

FAIR: No what...whatta you gonna say Rick Fair did it?

ALBER: No. I'm gonna say no I didn't do it.

(Muffling sound)

FAIR: Just tell me this.

ALBER: No. All I'm gonna say is no I didn't do it. And if they say do you know anybody who did it. Of course I'm gonna say no I do not.

FAIR: Well let's look at this scenario Frank.

ALBER: Okay lets hear this scenario.

FAIR: Lets say..you know they do find out that you're involved.

ALBER: Okay. Just...we're going with this scenario.

FAIR: And for some reason whatever...

ALBER: Uh-hmm. Go on.

FAIR: ...my name comes up.

ALBER: Why would it come up?

FAIR: Don't worry about it   How would it come up?

ALBER: Alright. But first of all you gotta tell me how it's gonna come up.

(Pause)

```
9A-PX-46497   Tape 1                33
KDT/sm
```

ALBER: Well...I don't know how you think they're
                gonna do that. Th-there's, ah, two hundred
                million people in this country Rick.

FAIR: First of all you didn't let me fini..finish
                my scenario.

ALBER: Okay. Lets go on with your scenario

FAIR: They do come up with my name.

ALBER: Okay, they come up with your name.

FAIR: And they got your name.

ALBER: Yeah, they got my name.

FAIR: Are you gonna come forward and tell them that
                I had nothing to do with this?

ALBER: Absolute. One hundred percent.

FAIR: And that what I did and what I asked you..

ALBER: Right.

FAIR: You know..

ALBER: I will tell 'em the absolute truth when it
                pertains to you.

                (Muffling sound)

ALBER: I swear to you that there will be no
                deviation from that. And that's what I
                wanted to tell you on Saturday.

FAIR: 'Cause I you know I told...

ALBER: That's what I wanted to tell you on Saturday.
                Okay? But you weren't here. I thought about
                it and I said why..why put Rick in any
                position. I said put him at ease. Just
                say...tell him to tell the truth. No lies.

                                              N000222

```
9A-PX-46497  Tape 1           34
KDT/sm
```

ALBER: No, I, I, I know that. All you have to do is
                if they ask you anything. If they ask you.

FAIR: I'm gonna tell the truth Frank.

ALBER: Wait a second. You just..let me finish. If
                they ask you, you tell 'em the truth. Okay?

                (Muffling sound)

FAIR: Alright. Just as long as you're, you know
                you're..

ALBER: I just told...

FAIR: ..you're..

ALBER: I told you what I did. It would've been
                better for you if I didn't tell ya.

FAIR: And you didn't do anything else?

ALBER: I didn't do anything else.

                (Pause)

FAIR: But you told me you went to this..did you go
                to this Estrella Par..w-what is it Es...es..

ALBER: Well I go out there all the time.

FAIR: Did you go out there and meet anybody?

ALBER: ~~Not (Stutters) Rick:~~

FAIR: Is that where you got the note? Is that what
                you said?

ALBER: Nah, I didn't...

FAIR: Oh...

ALBER: ..get any note. The guy called me on the
                phone.

```
9A-PX-46497   Tape 1              35
KDT/sm
```

FAIR: So when he called you he told you what,
                what..

ALBER: Yeah.

FAIR: ..to say.

ALBER: Yeah.

FAIR: Oh, okay. You didn't make it up?

ALBER: No!

FAIR: Alright.

ALBER: How..how would I, how would I make that up?
                I would have to know something else.

FAIR: T-that's all I need to know. As long as you
                can assure me. One hundred percent that
                you're telling me the truth.

ALBER: I'm telling you the truth.

FAIR: Well then I can live with that and as long as
                I'm not gonna become involved in this thing.
                Which I already fucking am.

ALBER: Just..(UI) if anybody asks..any you know
                police ask..just keep it to yourself unless
                somebody asks. If somebody asks you tell 'em
                the truth.

                (Muffling sound)

FAIR: Alright I'll, I'll let it at that.

ALBER: Huh? Just...I mean. I, I wanted to go over
                with this on you Saturday. I figured you
                definitely be back on Sunday. I went over to
                check you didn't play basketball. I just
                wanted to be you know I just said wait a
                second. You're probably a little nervous. I
                told you to tell a lie. Which is stupid. I

                                                      N000224
```
```

```
9A-PX-46497   Tape 1              36
KDT/sm
```

FAIR: Well that's...what happened it's...

ALBER: What did..I said to tell the truth. Okay?

FAIR: Alright. Was my son playin' basketball?

ALBER: I didn't see him.

FAIR: Now I'm afraid to call home.

ALBER: Why?

FAIR: (Sighs) (UI) why is not...

ALBER: Stop. (UI) Mary's not workin' by the way.

FAIR: She's not?

ALBER: Not today. No.

FAIR: Took the day off?

ALBER: Or she had off or something.

             (Pause)

ALBER: Rick. You did not do anything wrong.

FAIR: Frank I know that.

ALBER: Wait a second. That's what you need to just,
             just tell yourself. You did not do anything
             wrong. Hold, I know what your going...but
             you just need to sit there and say I did not
             do anything wrong. You didn't. There's no
             reason for you to be nervous.

FAIR: It, it's not so much the fact that I didn't
             do anything wrong. Which I didn't. But if
             my name came out in the paper...

ALBER: Uh-hmm.

FAIR: ..you know I'd be devastated.

```
9A-PX-46497  Tape 1              37
KDT/sm
```

	involved in something like that and I was involved in that..
ALBER:	You weren't involved.
FAIR:	Well I know that..
ALBER:	And...
FAIR:	..but I'm gonna have to explain that to her.
ALBER:	Well I know and if you go and just say the truth to whoever asks you..then there's not a problem. There might be more of a problem for me but there's absolutely no problem for you.
FAIR:	Yeah, if I tell truth I'm gonna say..
ALBER:	Right.
FAIR:	....Frank Alber made..
ALBER:	And, and, and that's, I said for you to tell the truth. Okay?
FAIR:	You know I would've never made that call if I wouldn't had some drinks. You know (sighs) you know we had a couple pitchers of beer you know but I kept, like I said I kept reiterating with you..am I doing anything wrong here Frank you said no. I guarantee you or something to that affect. You're not doing anything wrong. Isn't that what you told me?
ALBER:	I said you're not doing anything wrong. Now..and you weren't. Now if you know just put your mind at ease. Because A...there is..first of all there's no way how they're gonna find you. Just go with that flow for a second. Alright? There's no way. Okay? Rick? Rick?

February 24

```
9A-PX-46497  Tape 1              47
KDT/sm
```

FAIR:	Thank you. I'll see you a little later.
ALBER:	Rick (UI - voice sounds far away)
FAIR:	Alright. I'll see ya.
	(UI noises - beeping sound - UI noise - traffic noises)
KEITH TOLHURST:	Well you did good.
FAIR:	Well thank you.
UNKNOWN MALE:	Real good.
TOLHURST:	(UI) gonna take this stuff and...
FAIR:	Okay.
TOLHURST:	...get it turned off here.
	(UI noise - UI conversation)
FAIR:	Okay
	(Sound of zipper - UI conversation)
FAIR:	(Laughing) Dropping my drawers in front (UI)
R. SCOTT RIVAS:	Okay, ah, this is SA Rivas it's, um, what is it..February 24, 1992. Approximately 8:00 in the morning. We're here with the CW and we're gonna be turning this recorder off. Any second here...
	(UI noises - Tape cuts off)
	(END OF TRANSCRIPT)

N000236

February 26
GRAND JURY TESTIMONY

BEFORE THE FEDERAL GRAND JURY

DISTRICT OF ARIZONA

GRAND JURY TESTIMONY OF   )
)
KEITH D. TOLHURST   )
)
In re the matter of a Grand Jury)
Investigation.   )
_____)

                    Phoenix, Arizona
                    February 26, 1992
                    9:40 o'clock a.m.

            REPORTER'S TRANSCRIPT OF PROCEEDINGS

                              WHITE & ASSOCIATES
                            CERTIFIED COURT REPORTERS
                              932 South Stapley
                             Mesa, Arizona 85204

PREPARED FOR: CHARLES F. HYDER   464-1035

                         BY: Peggy Tryon

                                        N000419

February 26
GRAND JURY TESTIMONY
PAGE 11

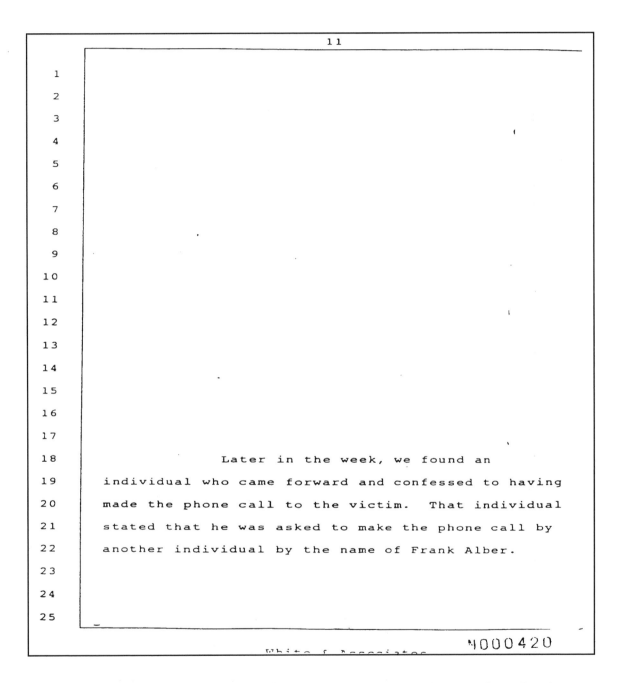

```
                                              11

 1
 2
 3
 4
 5
 6
 7
 8
 9
10
11
12
13
14
15
16
17
18              Later in the week, we found an
19    individual who came forward and confessed to having
20    made the phone call to the victim.   That individual
21    stated that he was asked to make the phone call by
22    another individual by the name of Frank Alber.
23
24
25

                                                      4000420
```

This individual who came forward was *Rick Fair*. Who confessed to having made the phone call to Marc Kaplan on Feb. 13, 1991.

February 26
GRAND JURY TESTIMONY
PAGE 12

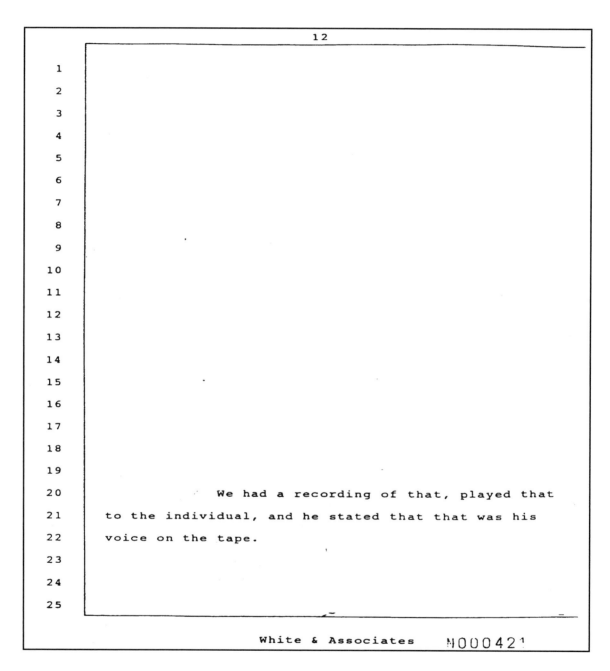

```
                                    12

 1

 2

 3

 4

 5

 6

 7

 8

 9

10

11

12

13

14

15

16

17

18

19

20              We had a recording of that, played that

21       to the individual, and he stated that that was his

22       voice on the tape.

23

24

25


                   White & Associates     N000421
```

The voice on tape was *Rick Fair*, this was the recording of the advisory phone call made to Kaplan at his office, from the *ABCO Supermarket* in Chandler, Arizona on Feb. 13, 1991.

February 26
GRAND JURY TESTIMONY
PAGE 14

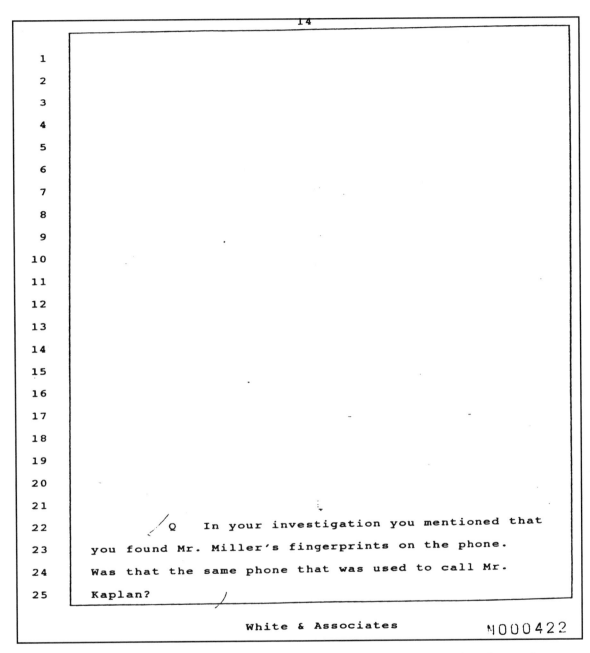

```
                              14
 1
 2
 3
 4
 5
 6
 7
 8
 9
10
11
12
13
14
15
16
17
18
19
20
21
22      /  Q    In your investigation you mentioned that
23   you found Mr. Miller's fingerprints on the phone.
24   Was that the same phone that was used to call Mr.
25   Kaplan?              /

              White & Associates            N000422
```

Though the FBI claims they found Miller's fingerprint on the phone that was used to call Kaplan, yet these prints were never verified as actually being Millers in court.

February 26
GRAND JURY TESTIMONY
PAGE 15

```
                              15

1          A    Yes.  The fingerprints that Mr. Miller

2     had left on the telephone was the same phone that was

3     used to make the extortion call.  However, we've

4     determined that Mr. Miller did not make the call, but

5     it was his print on the same phone, and it was also

6     him out at Saguaro Lake at the same time as the

7     victim.

8          Q    Other than the evidence that you have

9     related at this time, seeing Mr. Nelson and Mr.

10    Miller at the lake where Mr. Kaplan was instructed to

11    go, has your investigation revealed at this time any

12    prior relationship between these individuals?

13         A    No, it hasn't.

14         Q    Has your investigation revealed any

15    prior relationship of Mr. Nelson to Mr. Alber?

16         A    At this point it isn't conclusive, but

17    we have -- we do know that Mr. Alber was attempting

18    to promote a concert with some large-name musical

19    acts in the Mesa area, and we also know that Mark

20    Nelson claims to be a music promoter of some type,

21    but we have not confirmed any connection to those two

22    yet.

23         Q    Has your investigation revealed any

24    prior connection with Michael Miller and Frank Alber?

25         A    The only connection that we really have
```

White & Associates   N000423

The answer to the question on line 14, *Frank Alber* was never attempting to promote a concert in Mesa or any other city. Nowhere does it say so in any report and *Alber* himself never gave such information to the FBI. How could he, he was too busy fooling everyone investigating this extortion plot!

February 26
GRAND JURY TESTIMONY
PAGE 16

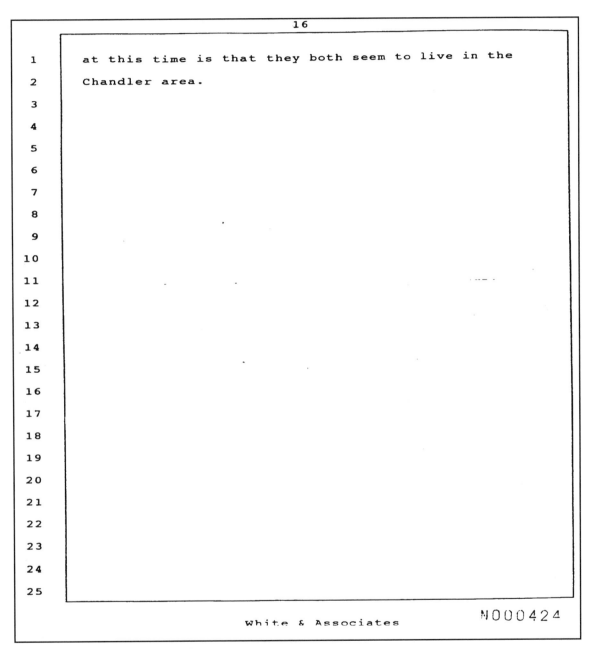

```
                              16

 1      at this time is that they both seem to live in the

 2      Chandler area.

 3

 4

 5

 6

 7

 8

 9

10

11

12

13

14

15

16

17

18

19

20

21

22

23

24

25

                White & Associates            N000424
```

The question from page 15 line 23, the only connection with Michael Miller and *Frank Alber* at this time, is that they both seemed to live in the Chandler area. According to the FBI, if you even live in the same area as a suspected criminal, you may have this information used against you in a court of law!

February 26
GRAND JURY TESTIMONY
PAGE 19

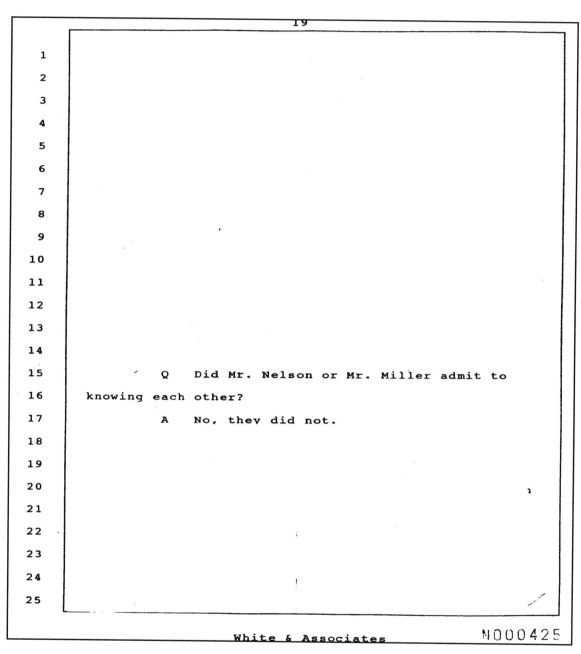

One juror asked the question about Miller and me admitting knowing each other, FBI Case Special Agent replied, No, they did not.

February 26
GRAND JURY TESTIMONY
PAGE 20

```
                                    20

1              Q    So at this particular point, Agent

2    Tolhurst, have you presented to the Grand Jury all

3    the evidence that you have with regard to Mr. Miller

4    and Mr. Nelson and Mr. Alber and their connection

5    with this matter and with each other?

6              A    I believe so.

7

8

9

10

11

12

13

14

15

16

17

18

19

20

21

22

23

24

25

                       White & Associates

                                            N000426
```

Case Special Agent Tolhurst answered the question on line 1, he has presented all the evidence that he had with regard to Michael Miller and Mark A. Nelson and *Frank Alber* and their connection with this matter and with each other!

February 26

GRAND JURY TESTIMONY
PAGE 23

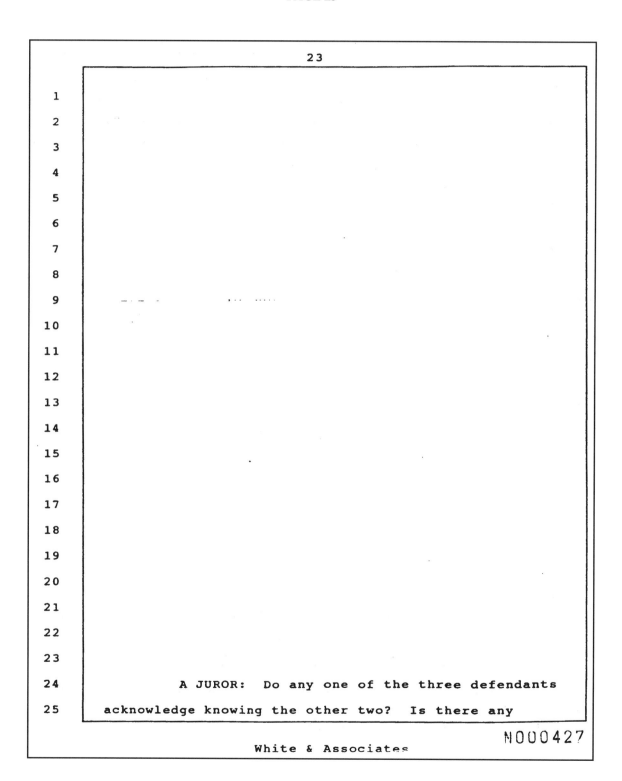

23

24   A JUROR: Do any one of the three defendants

25   acknowledge knowing the other two? Is there any

White & Associates

N000427

February 26
GRAND JURY TESTIMONY
PAGE 24

```
                                    24
  1   acknowledgment of any of them toward each other?
  2            THE WITNESS:  No, sir.  The only
  3   acknowledgment at all is that Mr. Alber acknowledges
  4   knowing the victim and vice versa.
  5
  6
  7
  8
  9
 10
 11
 12
 13
 14
 15
 16
 17
 18
 19
 20
 21
 22
 23
 24
 25
```

White & Associates   N000430

A juror asked on page 23, line 24, did any of the three defendants acknowledge knowing the other two and is there any acknowledgment of any of them toward each other? Case Special Agent Tolhurst answered on this page 24, line 2. No, sir. *Alber* knows Kaplan and vice versa.

February 26
GRAND JURY TESTIMONY
PAGE 29

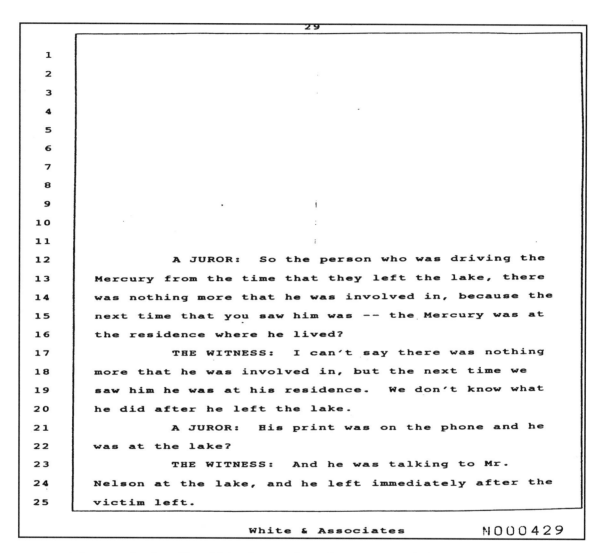

```
                              29

 1
 2
 3
 4
 5
 6
 7
 8
 9
10
11
12          A JUROR:  So the person who was driving the
13   Mercury from the time that they left the lake, there
14   was nothing more that he was involved in, because the
15   next time that you saw him was -- the Mercury was at
16   the residence where he lived?
17          THE WITNESS:  I can't say there was nothing
18   more that he was involved in, but the next time we
19   saw him he was at his residence.  We don't know what
20   he did after he left the lake.
21          A JUROR:  His print was on the phone and he
22   was at the lake?
23          THE WITNESS:  And he was talking to Mr.
24   Nelson at the lake, and he left immediately after the
25   victim left.

                  White & Associates              N000429
```

A juror asked on line 12 in short when the Mercury left the lake, you know of nothing more he was involved with, next time you saw him was at his home? Tolhurst answered: "He couldn't say there was nothing more that he was involved in, we don't know what he did after he left the lake." The reason the FBI did not know what Miller did after the lake, because he left before the FBI and Kaplan arrived at *Saguaro Lake*. Additionally, Tolhurst stated on line 23, that Miller was talking to me at the lake and he left immediately after Kaplan left. We know this could not have happened like this Special Agent said, because Miller and me were not at the lake at the time the FBI and Kaplan arrived. Further, lines 1-11 were omitted. *Why*?

April 12

TRANSCRIPT OF SENTENCING FOR *FRANK ALBER*
PAGE 1

COPY

```
___ FILED          LODGED
___ RECEIVED  X  COPY

    FEB  8 1994

CLERK U S DISTRICT COURT
   DISTRICT OF ARIZONA
_____ DEPUTY
```

1

2
                    UNITED STATES DISTRICT COURT
                       DISTRICT OF ARIZONA
3

4   THE UNITED STATES,   )   No. CR-92-80/3-PHX-RCB
)
               Plaintiff,   )   Phoenix, Arizona
5   )   April 12, 1993
         vs.   )   9:31 a.m.
6   )
    FRANK R. ALBER,   )
7   )
               Defendant.   )
8   _____)

9

10

11   TRANSCRIPT OF SENTENCING
          BEFORE THE HONORABLE ROBERT C. BROOMFIELD
12   UNITED STATES DISTRICT JUDGE

13 APPEARANCES:

14 For the Plaintiff: By: Charles Hyder
                              U.S. ATTORNEY OFFICE
15   230 North First Avenue, 4th Floor
                              Phoenix, AZ 85025
16
    For the Defendant: By: Michael Black
17   3101 N. Central Ave., Suite 530
                              Phoenix, AZ 85012
18
    Court Recorder: Rose Huckaby-Cotton
19
    Transcription Service: A/V Tronics, Inc.
20   34 W. Monroe, Suite 600
                              Phoenix, AZ 85003
21

22

23

24
    Proceedings recorded by electronic sound recording,
25 transcript produced by transcription service.

A\V▾TRONICS
Professional Court Reporting
& Transcription
Phoenix, Arizona

April 12
TRANSCRIPT OF SENTENCING FOR *FRANK ALBER*
PAGE 15

15

1 MR. HYDER: If the Court is not -- if the Court is

2 of the opinion that Mr. Alber is to receive credit or

3 acceptance of responsibility, which the Government has argued

4 against, the Government then harkens back to the nature of

5 this crime and the effect that it's had. And this particular

6 crime, as I stated before, there are more than one victim.

7 There are multiple victims in this case. The Government

8 submits that it is engaging in an esoteric exercise of

9 intellectual stimulation to say that you can threaten harm to

10 a person's family, specifically to a member of that family

11 and because a letter wasn't received by the intended victim,

12 but only by one member of the family, that there can be no

13 resultant harm to the true victim of this matter, the true

14 subject of this matter, which would be the boy. Certainly

15 Mr. Kaplan suffered, his wife suffered, the whole family

16 suffered, because all of a sudden they're faced with this

17 demand from people they have no idea of their identities at

18 the time. There's no way that they can give the FBI any

19 assistance in particular -- in particularity with identifying

20 who is involved. So it resulted in a whole disruption, if

21 you will, and I think that's a mild adjective, of their

22 family life. It's supplanted by great fear and insecurity,

23 which exists today. The FBI, as I stated, had to do some

24 in-house protection with regard to the family, not knowing

25 who was involved. The Kaplans themselves had to hire

April 12
TRANSCRIPT OF SENTENCING FOR *FRANK ALBER*
PAGE 16

16

1 | bodyguards to be at the home and at the school with their

2 | children. They suffered great psychological injury to the

3 | whole family, because all of a sudden, as most of us tend to

4 | ignore, their vulnerability and the vulnerability of all of

5 | us was shown and exposed because they didn't know what they

6 | were facing or who they were facing. But it appeared at the

7 | time as a highly organized and sophisticated group of

8 | individuals bent upon violence. To ignore that type of harm

9 | to a family unit and to ignore who are the true victims of

10 | this particular type and nature of a crime, I submit to you

11 | is to ignore reality, and it is to exalt form over substance

12 | within the confines of the guidelines. There is no way to

13 | describe the fear that a family would face in this particular

14 | situation. And today -- I mean, even if Mr. Alber goes to

15 | prison, whether Mr. Nelson and Mr. Miller are further

16 | indicted, or whether they're not, there is no way that the

17 | irreparable harm that has been occasioned by this incident

18 | will dissipate. Because there will always be that lingering

19 | doubt as to whether or not all the responsible parties have

20 | been dealt with by the law, and then there's that resulting

21 | fear of having to face this again if perhaps Mr. Alber -- or

22 | upon his release. This is a type of psychological damage

23 | that is utilized by terrorists. And it's just basic

24 | psychology, that if you send this message and expose the

25 | vulnerability of the people, whether we're dealing with this

April 12

TRANSCRIPT OF SENTENCING FOR *FRANK ALBER*
PAGE 18

1   might be involved, to be faced with that at the time they

2   were, and to try to address that issue and protect that

3   family and to try to make a determination of who might

4   possibly be responsible, and to provide the type of

5   protection they did and be able to carry out the

6   investigation, was almost an inhumane and impossible thing to

7   do. By mere fortunate circumstances was Mr. Alber even

8   caught in this particular matter. Had not Mr. Fare come

9   forward, it's doubtful whether Mr. Alber would have been

10 caught. I don't know whether the Court has had the

11 opportunity, and perhaps the Court should review it before

12 passing sentence, but the conversation which was recorded

13 between Mr. Fare and Mr. Alber is enlightening as well. I

14 submit to you it shows a person who has no remorse, who saw a

15 need, he believed, to enrich himself, and picked innocent

16 people as victims. People who had done him no harm, people

17 who had in fact been friends of his, people with whom he

18 really had no malice or any bone to pick. I'm not as

19 articulate as I'd like to be, but I just tell you that the

20 threat of this type of crime is not adequately dealt with in

21 the guidelines per se. I think it's adequately dealt with by

22 the statute in it's maximum term. To carry out this plot,

23 had it succeeded, would've necessitated at least the

24 kidnapping and physical violence, and to say that -- well, we

25 should say that there's no harm, no foul because there was no

April 12

TRANSCRIPT OF SENTENCING FOR *FRANK ALBER*
PAGE 19

1   kidnapping or no physical violence in this case, again is to

2   ignore reality, because the basis of extortion is the threat.

3   It's the living with the terrifying threat that if you don't

4   carry this out, something's going to happen, and if it

5   doesn't happen today it may happen in the future. I submit

6   to you, in this case there's no redeeming value to

7   Mr. Alber's actions, and there's no reason that the

8   psychological harm to Mr. Kaplan's family as a whole should

9   not be consideration when passing sentence and does not --

10 and does deserve an upward departure, substantial upward

11 departure, because it's a particular crime which everybody's

12 vulnerable to, and which -- it's a continuing threat. It's

13 not one, in which we have in crimes of violence, from our

14 experience shows once that crime is committed, once

15 conviction is obtained, that that's usually the end of it.

16 In the minds of the victims, there is no end to this

17 particular thing. And I respectfully submit that the Court

18 should upwardly depart substantially in this particular case

19 and take into consideration the effect that this action has

20 had upon the victim's family. Thank you.

21   THE COURT: Mr. Black.

22   MR. BLACK: Thank you, Your Honor. I think it's

23 altogether inappropriate for the Government to come in here

24 and tell this Court, and liken Mr. Alber's conduct to the

25 bombing of the World Trade Center in New York. I think

April 12

TRANSCRIPT OF SENTENCING FOR *FRANK ALBER*
PAGE 20

1   that's absolutely inappropriate in an attempt to get you to

2   depart upward in this fashion. Mr. Hyder said at least three

3   times in his remarks to you, that by exalting form over

4   substance -- that is, by following the guidelines that

5   adequately take into consideration Mr. Alber's behavior --

6   that you're not -- I'm sorry, did the Court say -- I'm sorry.

7   That by repeating that at least three times, indicating that

8   we're exalting form over substance by following the

9   guidelines, and not taking into consideration this harm to

10   the family, that Mr. Hyder presents to you isn't taken into

11   consideration, it is. The pre-sentence report more than

12   adequately explains what harm there was to this family,

13   whether they used bodyguards or not to protect the child till

14   Mr. Alber was apprehended, or the others were apprehended, I

15   maintain is of no consideration to this Court to the extent

16   that there is an upward departure. Mr. Hyder tells the Court

17   that it is doubtful that Mr. Alber would be apprehended, had

18   it not been for Mr. Fare. I submit there is nothing to

19   indicate that that is grounds for an upward departure which

20   he was arguing for. He was simply giving a closing argument

21   to the Court. Now if Mr. Hyder had thought or the Government

22   had thought that this was so serious, it could've been

23   indicted as a kidnapping offense as opposed to what it was

24   indicted as. Moreover, as far -- if I may at this point too,

25   I'd like to dovetail in and ask the Court -- and tell the

April 12

TRANSCRIPT OF SENTENCING FOR *FRANK ALBER*
PAGE 21

1	Court why I think there should be a downward departure. The
2	Government simply cannot accept the fact that they made a
3	mistake and that there are no other people involved. For
4	Mr. Alber to enter into this plea with no bargain from the
5	Government on the other side, no benefit -- simply to plead
6	straight up to at least one count of the indictment that's
7	sustainable without any type of a bargain from the
8	Government -- shows his good faith. Had he been the bona
9	fide criminal who come before the Court, these courts all the
10	time, he would've asked for a 5(k)(1) departure by simply
11	saying, "Okay, I did it, I'll provide substantial assistance
12	against whomever," -- he simply could not do that because
13	there are no other folks involved other than he. And the
14	Government simply cannot accept along with the FBI that they
15	made a mistake with regard to Mr. Miller and Mr. Nelson, and
16	now they think that because they made that mistake, a fact
17	they cannot accept, that Mr. Alber is perpetuating a lie,
18	that there were others involved. I submit that it would've
19	been the prudent thing for him to do, if he could've done it,
20	to seek a departure, agree to testify, but he couldn't do
21	that because it didn't happen, and he indeed would've been
22	committing perjury. I would submit, Your Honor, that he
23	should be rewarded for coming to the Court and acknowledging
24	that he did what he did, so that two genuinely innocent folks
25	wouldn't stand the possibility of getting convicted -- being

A\V▾TRONICS
Professional Court Reporting
& Transcription
Phoenix, Arizona

April 12
TRANSCRIPT OF SENTENCING FOR *FRANK ALBER*
PAGE 22

1   convicted for something they genuinely did not do. Not just

2   folks against the Government who could say they're not

3   guilty, but two genuinely innocent young men who stood the

4   possibility, because of Mr. Alber's clear guilt and his

5   acknowledged guilt, who stood the chance of getting convicted

6   and going to prison for an equally long period of time. And

7   in Mr. Alber's letter to you, Your Honor, he indicates that

8   the reason he didn't come -- one of the reasons he didn't

9   come forward is that he could not conceive of the Government

10   continuing a prosecution against those two individuals. It

11   was almost ineffable to him. So I would submit that these

12   generalized notions that the Government makes about the

13   psychological harm to the Kaplan family has been adequately

14   dealt with by Mr. Nebgen who has talked to them. I have not.

15   Had there been what Mr. Hyder maintains is that type of harm,

16   it surely would've found it's place into the pre-sentence

17   report, and the Court would have heard it there and seen it

18   there, rather than from Mr. Hyder's words. I think that part

19   of his request for the upward departure, part of it -- a

20   majority of it stems from his inability to believe that

21   Mr. Alber acted alone. And that disbelief is fostered by the

22   fact that it's the Government's position that Mr. Alber's

23   taking of the polygraph exams wasn't as successful as they

24   would've liked it to be. Now you can call it inconclusive or

25   a failure. My dissatisfaction with polygraphs started -- and

A\V▾TRONICS
Professional Court Reporting
& Transcription
Phoenix, Arizona

April 12

TRANSCRIPT OF SENTENCING FOR *FRANK ALBER*
PAGE 23

1 I'd like to share this with you to show why they shouldn't be

2 admitted, and perhaps it will assuage some of the

3 Government's fears. As a young prosecutor right out of law

4 school, I prosecuted a manslaughter case where a young man

5 was seen by four individuals during the day to be a driver of

6 a vehicle, the driver that saw him, got out of the driver's

7 side car that hit a car and killed a pedestrian. That young

8 man, despite the eye witness testimony of these four folks,

9 took a polygraph and passed it, and ever since that day,

10 since my prosecutorial days, I have been a firm non-believer

11 in polygraphs, although as a condition of entering into this

12 we agreed to do it. Whatever reason, he didn't do as well on

13 those polygraphs, but he would maintain to the "enth" degree,

14 and he will tell the Court here in a moment if you chose to

15 sentence him, that there was no one else involved. And

16 lastly, I think it is fearmongering of the first order for

17 Mr. Hyder to suggest to the Court that there should be an

18 upward departure because the Kaplans, even after Mr. Alber is

19 released from jail, to be worried that he's going to do it

20 again. I see nothing in the case law and nothing in the

21 guidelines that would reflect that that is a ground for an

22 upward departure. I think he should be rewarded by a

23 downward departure of four levels for coming forward and

24 exonerating two clearly innocent individuals.

25   THE COURT: Anything else on the departure

April 12

```
                                                                 26

 1    regard to analogies used.  With the exception of this, that

 2    Government just wants to make it clear -- as inarticulate as

 3    Government counsel is -- that the threat to these people,

 4    Mr. Kaplan and his family, is just as great as the threat

 5    that anybody else would experience under similar

 6    circumstances, regardless of who made the threat.  And the

 7    Government is only asking that the Court keep that in mind

 8    when it passes sentence on Mr. Alber, and it believes that

 9    Mr. Alber deserves to receive an upward departure because of

10    the resultant harm to these people.  Thank you.

11         THE COURT:  Thank you.  Anything else before I

12    resolve the contested issues?

13         MR. BLACK:  I have one, just enquiry of the Court.

14    Is there a victim -- is there a victim statement that was

15    given to the Court that I haven't seen?  You mentioned it in

16    one of the other cases preceding us, and I wondered if I -- I

17    had seen where Mr. Nebgen wrote about his contacts with the

18    victim, but is there a separate sheet dealing with that?

19         THE COURT:  There's no victim witness report in the

20    usual sense, that I'm aware of.

21         MR. BLACK:  Okay.

22         MR. HYDER:  No, that's correct, Your Honor.

23    Mr. Kaplan and his family has not returned that questionnaire

24    to us.

25         THE COURT:  Thank you.  I'll make certain findings
```

A|V▾TRONICS
Professional Court Reporting
& Transcription
Phoenix, Arizona

April 12

1   at this point. In my view there are two clearly relatively

2   close questions that I must decide, and the decision there,

3   in great measure, determines what some of the other contested

4   guideline facts are and the other objections that are

5   imposed. And those deal with the conspiracy, whether there

6   in fact was a conspiracy or whether this was the conduct of

7   Mr. Alber alone; and the second one deals with the request

8   for a departure. First, I find by a preponderance of the

9   evidence, that there is sufficient evidence of a conspiracy

10   without designating the partners or the co-conspirators, but

11   to include at least Mr. Alber and one or more other

12   individuals. The letter itself is evidence of conspiratorial

13   conduct, to be sure. One acting by himself or herself in a

14   letter could appear to involve others, when in fact they are

15   not, but it is evidence of a conspiracy. Polygraph

16   examinations were taken. There were several questions where

17   the examiner suggested they were either inconclusive or there

18   was evidence of deception. By itself, polygraph evidence

19   would not be something that I would rely upon; however, here

20   there was a stipulation that if Mr. Alber were to be called

21   to testify, his responses could be used. But more important

22   to me is it would be difficult, but certainly not impossible,

23   for a single individual to hatch, plan, carry out the

24   conspiracy that occurred in this instance. Also, it just is

25   too coincidental for this Court to accept that Mr. Miller and

April 12

TRANSCRIPT OF SENTENCING FOR *FRANK ALBER*
PAGE 28

28

```
 1    Mr. Nelson just happened to be at Saguaro Lake and left
 2    Saguaro Lake at the time they did, immediately after
 3    Mr. Kaplan did.  And that at least one of them, perhaps
 4    both -f it's unclear -- stopped at the same place where
 5    Mr. Kaplan stopped to make a telephone call.  The fact that
 6    Mr. -- I don't recall whether it's Mr. Miller's fingerprint
 7    or Mr. Nelson's fingerprint was on the telephone where the
 8    threatening call was made, probably is coincidence, although
 9    in fact it could be further evidence to show that there was a
10    conspiracy.  I do find the conspiracy, by a preponderance.
11          I find with respect to paragraph 21 that the
12    applicable offense guideline is 2(b)3.2, and I find that the
13    enhancements indicated in paragraphs 22 and 23 have been
14    appropriately given.
15          With respect to the Government's argument that
16    there should be a further enhancement under 2(b)3.2, 3(b), I
17    will overrule that objection.  What is not borne out by the
18    evidence, although it in fact could be true -- it just simply
19    isn't borne out by the evidence that's been offered to me,
20    that there was in fact preparation to carry out the serious
21    bodily injury that was in fact threatened.  So I'll overrule
22    that objection.
23          With respect to the Government's request or
24    objection to the failure to include an unusually vulnerable
25    victim, I think the guidelines do not permit me to consider
```

A|V▾TRONICS
Professional Court Reporting
& Transcription
Phoenix, Arizona

This was the end of the transcripts given to the defence team. The defendant *Frank Alber* was sentence to 12 years to a Federal Prison and will not be released until the year 20005.

Whitewash

Why is a prosecutor who seems to have gone way over the line still plying his trade as an assistant U.S. attorney?

by Roger Parloff

The Honorable Janet Napolitano
United States Attorney for the District of Arizona
Phoenix, Arizona

Dear Ms. Napolitano:

I am writing to ask you to explain an unusual situation that exists in your office.

You have an employee, assistant U.S. attorney Charles Hyder, who may be the only active federal prosecutor today who has himself attempted to commit a capital crime.

I may be wrong about that, and, if so, I would like some dispassionate Arizona lawyer to explain to me in writing why I'm wrong.

At this point, you are the only reasonable candidate.

A judge who might have explained it to me, superior court judge Frederick Martone—who has since been elevated to the Arizona supreme court—chose not to do so for good reasons after holding a misconduct hearing in July 1991. Martone, in fact, may have even agreed with me about what Hyder did. Martone was then presiding over the retrial of John Knapp, whose 1974 capital murder conviction had been overturned in 1987, due to newly discovered evidence. After hearing five weeks of testimony in 1991 about peculiar goings-on when Hyder prosecuted Knapp at his first two trials—resulting in a hung jury in September 1974 and then a conviction in December 1974—Martone wrote that "there was substantial evidence in this case in connection with withheld evidence, the destruction of evidence, and inaccurate representations." Remember, winning the execution of an innocent man by means of intentionally inaccurate representations—that is, by committing or suborning perjury—was itself a capital crime in Arizona in 1974. Nevertheless, Martone withheld decision on whether Hyder was actually guilty of misconduct because, as he read the law, he was not legally empowered to do anything even if Hyder was guilty of such misconduct. All he could do was give Knapp a new trial, which Knapp was already getting. "The remedy for professional misconduct lies with another body," he wrote, alluding to the State Bar of Arizona.

Earlier this year the State Bar of Arizona dismissed a

Roger Parloff, a senior reporter at The American Lawyer, *is writing a book about the John Knapp case, to be published jointly by American Lawyer Media, L.P., and Little, Brown & Company.*

Assistant U.S. attorney Charles Hyder

disciplinary charge that was filed against Charles Hyder stemming from the accusations I am referring to. So, evidently, someone at the bar *does* disagree with me. But because of the Arizona Supreme Court's confidentiality rules, the bar cannot even confirm to me that a disciplinary charge was ever brought against Hyder, let alone how it was disposed of, or why. Indeed, the only reason I know that the charge was dismissed was that Hyder's lawyer, Donald Daughton of Phoenix's seven-lawyer Daughton, Hawkins, Brockelman, Guinan & Patterson, violated those confidentiality rules by telling me so on the record.

Writing, as every law student discovers, disciplines the thinking process. Only when lawyers write their opinions down can they judge whether their beliefs are defensible or merely the product of bias. It makes me deeply uncomfortable that no disinterested lawyer in Arizona is ever going to explain publicly and in writing why Hyder should or should

not be sanctioned for wrongdoing in the Knapp case.

So I am writing, by default, to you, Ms. Napolitano.

The situation is not your doing, of course. You didn't hire Hyder. He was there when you came into office in July 1993, long after the alleged wrongdoing. I have even heard rumors that Hyder's transfer to the inglorious intake unit of your office shortly after your arrival may reflect your judgment that Hyder should no longer serve as a trial prosecutor. But your chief assistant, Virginia Mathis, categorically denies that there is any truth to such rumors. Hyder did not return four phone calls. (Mathis also denies that Hyder's transfer has anything to do with his controversial 11-month prosecution of a former Scottsdale man for extortion before finally dropping the charges on the eve of trial in January 1993. The defendant, Mark Nelson, filed a civil rights suit this year accusing Hyder of concealing exonerating evidence from his federal grand jury in February 1992; Hyder has previously denied wrongdoing.)

I know I am dredging up the past and refusing to forgive and forget, but capital crimes have a way of getting under people's skin, and this one has gotten under mine. While other journalists have moved on to stories about appearances of impropriety in Washington vis-à-vis appearances of impropriety in Arkansas, I still want to know why federal prosecutor Hyder is going unprosecuted, unpunished, unsanctioned, unchided, and un-wrist-slapped for conduct that looks to me like the most heinous crime any lawyer can commit.

On a cold morning in November 1973, there was a fire in a bedroom at the home of John and Linda Knapp in Mesa, Arizona. The fire killed their two little girls, ages 3 ½ and 2 ½ ["They Still Want to Kill Him," July/August 1991, and "Innocent Man on Death Row," December 1983].

After interpreting of the burn damage, fire inspectors soon suspected that either John or Linda had emptied an entire gallon of Coleman fuel around the bedroom. Since their utilities had been cut off for nonpayment, the Knapps were using Coleman appliances for cooking, heating, and lighting.

Both John and Linda, on the other hand, told matching stories that suggested that the children might have started the fire accidentally, while playing with matches. The Knapps speculated that the children might have been trying to keep warm; it was 44 degrees outside that morning, and the Knapps had no heat.

John and Linda stuck to these stories through several interrogations, but 11 days after the fire, under extremely odd circumstances, Knapp confessed to committing the crime in exactly the manner fire inspectors had been telling him it had to have been done—by pouring, and then lighting, a gallon of fuel from a Coleman can from the living room closet. Knapp later said that he confessed to protect his wife, whom he feared may have had something to do with the fire, and while not thinking clearly due to an extremely severe headache—a recurrent medical condition for which Knapp had been hospitalized three months before the fire, and for which his doctors had prescribed Darvon and Percodan. At the suppression hearing detectives testified that Knapp had complained of a severe headache during the interrogation, and that he had been screaming, tearing hair out of his head, and complaining of seeing spots at the time he confessed. Knapp recanted the confession within an hour of making it.

As motive—Knapp had no insurance on his daughters—the state theorized that Knapp killed them to save his marriage, by eliminating the expenses of raising them.

At trial Knapp's lawyers argued that either the children set the fire or, alternatively, that his wife, Linda—who had a history of mental instability and severe and dangerous child neglect—might have set the fire, either accidentally or intentionally. Linda, though still a suspect, was not charged.

Knapp's first capital murder trial, prosecuted by then-deputy county attorney Hyder, ended in a mistrial in early September 1974.

At the second trial, however, Hyder succeeded in convincing then-superior court judge (now senior federal district judge) Charles Hardy not to permit the second jury to see the key defense evidence, which he had permitted the first jury to see—filmed fire tests that showed that if a single match fell in the right spot, it would ignite the synthetic carpet and pad in the Knapp children's room. Those furnishings would then burn ferociously and mimic many of the characteristics of a flammable liquid fire.

Without that evidence, Knapp was convicted. In early 1975 he was sentenced to die in the gas chamber, and in late 1976 Hyder was elected Maricopa County attorney—the county's chief prosecutor.

In his 12 years on death row Knapp weathered five warrants of execution. He came within 36 hours of death in 1977 and within five days of death in 1983. He won a new trial in 1987, after new scientific evidence strongly suggested that the fire could, indeed, have been accidentally set by the children playing with matches just as John and Linda had claimed. That trial—Knapp's third—ended in a hung jury in 1991. With the state gearing up for a fourth trial, Knapp pleaded no contest in late 1992 in exchange for time served—i.e., freedom.

But when the state first decided to reprosecute Knapp in 1990, the new prosecutors turned over from the state's files a great deal of information that had, for one reason or another, never come before the jury when your employee Charles Hyder prosecuted the case. These documents and tapes weren't in the defense files that Knapp's *pro bono* lawyers at Phoenix's Meyer, Hendricks, Victor, Osborn & Maledon inherited when they took over the case in 1981. All of Knapp's defense lawyers over the years swore they had never seen these tapes or documents before.

Meyer, Hendricks's Larry Hammond brought a motion to dismiss the new case against Knapp, because of Hyder's alleged prosecutorial misconduct at the 1974 trials. That motion led to the five-week misconduct hearing in June and July 1991 before Judge Martone, to which I have already alluded.

There, Hyder and his courtroom champion, deputy Pima county attorney David White—Knapp's then-prosecutor—argued that Hyder had properly turned over everything as required, but that Knapp's original two lawyers failed to employ any of the exculpatory or useful portions of those materials out of oversight or incompetence or some now unfathomable strategic choice. When those lawyers claimed never to have seen those documents before, they were either lying or mistaken, White argued. They or their successors, White theorized, must

John Knapp: Once sentenced to die

Prosecutor Hyder repeatedly—and falsely—communicated to the jury that convicted Knapp and to the judge that sentenced him to death that fingerprints found on the alleged murder weapon were unidentifiable.

have also lost all the material in question before the defense files reached Meyer, Hendricks in 1981.

Indeed, there was evidence that at least *some* materials *had* been lost from the defense file as it had been passed from attorney to attorney. And, fortunately for Hyder, an additional unusual circumstance lent superficial plausibility to Hyder's contention that the original defense lawyers may have inexplicably failed to use materials they had possessed. One of Knapp's original defense lawyers was Charles Diettrich. Though Diettrich was an experienced, highly regarded trial lawyer at the time of the Knapp case—and his performance at trial was complimented by Judge Hardy at the time of sentencing—Diettrich's life fell apart after Knapp's conviction and, in part, because of it. Diettrich, who had strongly believed in Knapp's innocence, descended into alcoholism, manic depression, and drug addiction. He was convicted of cocaine possession and disbarred in 1981.

So in 1991 Hyder and prosecutor White claimed that it was Knapp's own incompetent lawyers who had effectively concealed the exculpatory evidence from the jury, not prosecutor Hyder. Diettrich's mental and physical demise rendered Hyder's implausible accusation just barely conceivable with respect to Diettrich. Nevertheless, it remained a mystery why Diettrich's younger co-counsel, David Basham of the public defender's office, would also have failed to use any of the tapes or documents in dispute, if he had actually ever seen them.

The prosecutorial misconduct allegations against Hyder are too massive and multifaceted for me to ask you to respond to all of them in detail. I will therefore ask you to respond to my written opinion about only one narrow aspect of those allegations.

Accordingly, I will assume, for the sake of argument, that Hyder dutifully turned over to the defense in 1974 the two dozen witness statements and sundry tape recordings that the defense inexplicably never used at either 1974 trial. I will make that assumption even though one of those documents contains startling exculpatory information—a prosecution witness told state investigators that she had seen one of the Knapp children light matches four or five times—and even though transcripts show that both defense lawyers stated during the 1974 trials *without contradiction from Hyder at the time* that they had never received any prior statements from that witness.

I will further assume that there were innocent explanations for the loss or destruction of at least three hours of the state's taped interrogation of Linda Knapp, and for the fact that the only surviving tapes of that interrogation appeared to an electronics expert to have been edited copies from which material had been deleted. I will also assume that there was an innocent explanation—though Hyder himself never offered one during the 1991 misconduct hearings—for the fact that Hyder never turned over to the defense a videotape he had had made of a state fire test performed in April 1974, that that tape was then inexplicably erased or obliterated while in Hyder's custody during trial in August 1974, and that Hyder stood mute while his fire expert falsely told the jury that none of the state's fire tests had ever been videotaped.

I will focus only upon one false, material statement that your employee, Hyder, repeatedly communicated to the jury that convicted John Knapp, and to the judge that sentenced him to death.

Hyder's story at trial was that the fingerprints on the Coleman fuel can were smudged, adult prints. It was therefore possible to eliminate the children as suspects—they could not, for instance, have spilled fuel around their room while playing with the can—but it was not possible to identify which adult had touched the can.

That story was false. In June 1990 the new prosecutors discovered that the original fingerprint analysis report for the can from the closet—the alleged murder weapon—clearly stated that there were, in fact, 11 lifts taken from this can, and all of them were identifiable.

Since John Knapp, according to his confession, had poured a gallon of fuel from this can all over the room, had returned the can to the closet, and had then started the fire, he would have been the last to touch that can. One might have expected that if his confession were true, his prints would be among those found on the can.

When comparisons were performed in June 1990—sixteen years and five warrants of execution after they might have done Knapp some good—several of the prints were found to belong to neither John nor Linda; they may have been those of the fire investigators who first found the can.

All the other prints were Linda's. None were John's.

Later, in September 1991, state fingerprint analysts finally found one of John's prints on the can, but it was underneath one of Linda's, meaning that Knapp still could not have left that print when committing the alleged crime.

All the results tended to disprove the confession.

Since it was known in 1974 that the prints were identifiable, why had no comparisons been done at the time? Or had comparisons been done, and the results concealed? How had the false story started in the first place? How had it been preserved?

In the days following the fire, investigators had seized three Coleman fuel cans from the Knapp house to test them for identifiable fingerprints, and to see if there were any children's prints on them. On *one* can—which was still full and, therefore, could not have been the murder weapon—there really were smudged, adult prints. A police report referring to the fingerprint analysis for *this* can *was* turned over to the defense in 1973 or 1974, and it was found in the defense files when Meyer, Hendricks inherited them in 1981.

But the fingerprint reports for the other two cans, including the alleged murder weapon, stated that numerous identifiable lifts were taken from each can. These reports were *not* found in defense files. (In 1990 all the prints on the half-full can from the bookshelf were also found to be Linda's; none were John's.)

John Knapp was arrested early in the morning on November 28, 1973, and was fingerprinted during the routine booking process. In addition, investigators took his *palm* prints—which was not routine. Since there were latent palm prints on the alleged murder weapon, it might seem as if someone wanted to run comparisons.

Comparing prints on the alleged murder weapon to the suspect's prints is about as basic a homicide procedure as can be imagined. Nevertheless, the comparisons were either never performed when your employee, Charles Hyder, handled Knapp's case in 1974—or they *were* performed, but the results, because they tended to show that John Knapp's confession was false, were kept secret.

How was it that the defense lawyers never realized that the fingerprints were identifiable in the first place? Hyder's answer at the misconduct hearings before Judge Martone in 1991 was predictable: The defense lawyers were incompetent.

Hyder asserted that the original prosecutor at the local justice court, where the case was filed before being transferred to superior court, had presumably turned over those fingerprint reports to the defense in December 1973, before Hyder even got involved in the case.

Knapp's lawyer Hammond, who had brought the misconduct motion before Martone, interviewed the former prosecutor at the justice court, Hugo Zettler, in March 1991. At that time Zettler told Hammond that fingerprint reports were not always sent directly to the prosecutor and that he could not say whether he had ever actually possessed them while he was handling the case.

Nevertheless, by the time of the prosecutorial misconduct hearings before Judge Martone three months after that interview, Zettler had refreshed his recollection during two evening preparation sessions at Hyder's home, and he had concluded that he would have both possessed those reports and turned them over to the defense at the December 1973 hearing. He was certain of this, even though the only notation on the case log for that date reads, "Defendant had copies of our DRs [police reports]—not all, only the ones I had on this date."

Under Hyder's theory, defense lawyers Basham and Diettrich then either failed to look at those reports or forgot about what the reports said. Then they lost them, so that they were never passed along to future defense lawyers.

While, personally, I have trouble with Hyder's scenario, I could certainly understand your giving Hyder the benefit of the doubt, Ms. Napolitano, if that were where the story ended.

But it's not. Hyder's scenario, even if true, doesn't exonerate him. Whether Hyder actively concealed the fingerprint reports from the defense lawyers or merely took advantage of the lawyers' oversights or incompetence, he still wasn't allowed to defraud a judge and jury in a capital case, which is exactly what it looks like he did at the second 1974 trial, as we shall see. So let's keep following the story.

In early August 1974, when Diettrich was trying to suppress Knapp's confession at a pre-trial hearing, Diettrich mentioned his—mistaken—understanding that all the prints were unidentifiable. Hyder did not correct Diettrich. Hyder ultimately *conceded* at the 1991 misconduct hearings that he had known that Diettrich was telling the judge incorrect information about the fingerprints, but Hyder testified that he had effectively set Judge Hardy straight several moments later when he said, "Mr. Diettrich's . . . appreciation of the evidence is much different than mine."

At the first trial in 1974, Hyder called as a witness the fingerprint analyst who had examined the alleged murder weapon. In Hyder's private trial folder—which was turned over to Hammond in March 1991—there was a piece of paper on which Hyder, in his famously methodical way, had typed out the questions he planned to ask and the answers he expected the expert, William Watling, to give. The planned examination would have elicited that there were numerous identifiable prints on the can.

Yet at trial Hyder did *not* follow that script. Instead, Hyder tiptoed through the examination in a way that did

not reveal that the prints were identifiable.

During Diettrich's cross-examination of Watling, Diettrich's ignorance of the true situation became apparent. And seemingly to keep Diettrich ignorant, Watling's responses became patently misleading.

"And you found no fingerprints on the can you could identify?" Diettrich asked.

"I found some latent prints on the can," Watling responded, "but none that could be considered to have been made by a child of the ages listed."

"Were you able to identify the prints you found on the can?" Diettrich persisted.

"No, sir, I was not."

Watling wasn't telling the whole truth. He was *able* to identify those prints, he had just never been *asked* to identify them, as both Watling and Hyder knew. Hyder conceded at the 1991 misconduct hearings that he knew the

If Hyder concealed evidence at Knapp's trials, then he illegally buried Knapp alive for 12 years and came within a hair's breadth of killing him.

fingerprints were identifiable at the time Watling gave this misleading answer. But he claimed—*in 1991*, Ms. Napolitano, not in 1974—that he still saw nothing misleading about Watling's testimony. Watling asserted at the misconduct hearings in 1991 that his answer would have been correctly understood by a fingerprint specialist, although he conceded that it may have been misleading to lawyers, judges, and jurors.

At the second 1974 trial, Hyder did not traverse the same perilous ground.

Instead of calling Watling again, Hyder and Diettrich entered into a *stipulation* to have Judge Hardy simply tell the jurors what Watling supposedly would have said if called. Hyder falsely told the jury that Watling would say that he had found only adult, smudged prints on the can. Defense lawyer Diettrich, still in the dark, consented to the stipulation. Then Judge Hardy relayed Hyder's false message to the jurors who would convict Knapp: "You can take it as a fact," he told them, "there were no children's fingerprints on any of these cans, and the fingerprints that were there were so smudged they could not be identified."

Shortly before entering the false stipulation, Hyder had also stood by silently as defense lawyer Diettrich was misled yet again about the truth regarding the fingerprints, this time by Hyder's chief investigator on the case, Sergeant Robert Malone. Malone falsely testified on cross-examination that fingerprint analysis showed only "smudged fingerprints of adults and no fingerprints of children" on the fuel cans. Finally, in his summation, Hyder falsely argued to the jury that "a lot of smeared, unidentifiable adult prints were found on the cans. No children's prints."

Didn't Hyder do everything within his power to commit a capital crime during that trial, Ms. Napolitano—to win the execution of a possibly innocent man by suborning or committing perjury?

Now, of course, you might argue that, technically, to commit or suborn perjury Hyder would have to have offered false sworn testimony, while the false stipulation was merely his avowal as a lawyer, which he was offering as a *substitute* for sworn testimony. Similarly, his jury argument wasn't sworn, and perhaps standing mute in the

face of Malone's false testimony did not amount to "suborning"? Are those the reasons, Ms. Napolitano, you don't feel it's fair to accuse Hyder of doing everything within his power to commit a capital crime?

Or is it that you don't consider Knapp "innocent"—a prerequisite for rendering Hyder's apparent crime capital, as opposed to a mere felony punishable by up to 14 years' imprisonment? Perhaps you reason that, having accepted complete freedom in exchange for a no contest plea, Knapp has now officially licensed the state to score his prosecution as a "conviction," and, therefore, you don't feel we should look past the formalism?

Or is it that you think Hyder's false stipulation, false jury argument, and silent tolerance of false testimony from Malone were all "honest mistakes," as Hyder maintained at the 1991 hearings? Let's examine that possibility.

Hyder's responses to the gradually snowballing mass of evidence against him evolved over time. Originally, when Hammond interviewed him in March 1991, Hyder said that he had never realized that the prints were identifiable. Hyder said that the fingerprint expert must have misled him by falsely telling him that the prints were unidentifiable.

But Hyder later changed his mind in light of the documents Hammond obtained from Hyder's trial file showing that in 1974 Hyder himself had written out the answers he expected Watling to give—including the fact that the prints were identifiable.

Hyder then acknowledged that, in fact, he must have known during both the suppression hearing and the first trial that the prints were identifiable. He testified, however, that *he must have forgotten that fact during the month-and-a-half hiatus between the first trial and the second trial.*

That's the honest mistake theory. Do you believe that, Ms. Napolitano?

But there is still another wrinkle in the story I'd like to hear your insights on. Since Hyder now concedes that he knew the prints were identifiable before and during the first trial, the question arises: Why had he never asked that they be compared to Knapp's?

At the misconduct hearings before Judge Martone in 1991, prosecutor White argued that the fact that there were identifiable prints on the murder weapon was, in context, meaningless. He maintained that since everyone knew the cans belonged to John and Linda, one would expect their fingerprints to be on the cans. All the investigators cared about was whether there were children's prints on the cans. As long as the children's prints weren't there, the children could be eliminated as suspects.

Do you accept that argument, Ms. Napolitano? To me, that argument seems mistaken in the same sense that the proposition $2 + 2 = 5$ is mistaken. The presence or absence of John Knapp's prints on the can from the hall closet provided evidence that, while not conclusive, would either tend to corroborate or tend to disprove Knapp's confession.

White forcefully and shamelessly argued that, because it is physically possible for someone to touch a can and not leave fingerprints, the absence of Knapp's fingerprints was literally meaningless. White's argument hinged upon the false assumption that evidence is meaningless unless it completely resolves an issue beyond any shadow of a doubt—which no single piece of evidence ever does. Evidence can have weight without being dispositive. Though it was conceivable Knapp had handled the can and left no prints, the jury was entitled to make its own judgment about just how likely or unlikely that was. At least four of the jurors who voted to acquit Knapp in 1991 thought it was highly unlikely, they told me.

Indeed, if the absence of John's prints were literally meaningless, then the absence of the children's prints would also have been meaningless, and Hyder would have been conning the jurors in arguing that they could eliminate the children as suspects because of the absence of their prints on the cans. To the extent there is any force at all to White's argument, it doesn't exonerate Hyder; it only changes the focus of the fraud Hyder was perpetrating upon the jury.

If the absence of the children's prints on the cans *eliminated* the children as suspects, why didn't the absence of John Knapp's prints on the cans eliminate *him* as a suspect?

There seems to be no intelligible rejoinder. Judge Martone sought one from the state's witnesses at the misconduct hearings in 1991, but in vain. He tried most persistently with the witness Joseph Howe, who was an administrative deputy in the county attorney's office during Hyder's first prosecution of Knapp in 1974. Howe, a former evidence professor, had become a superior court judge in Phoenix by the time of the misconduct hearings. Judge Martone asked Judge Howe to explain why the absence of the children's prints had meaning, but the absence of Knapp's prints didn't.

"Well," Howe responded, "I think probably because the presence or absence of adult prints belonging to the parents would not tend, from an impact standpoint to the jury, to mean much. But I think that the absence of any children's prints at all, to the jury, would tend to be important."

Judge Howe was speaking gibberish. Can you do any better, Ms. Napolitano? And what if, for the sake of argument, Hyder really did follow some variant of Judge Howe's contorted reasoning? What do you think of a prosecutor who resorts to this sort of rationalization rather than just find out whose prints are on the alleged murder weapon?

The notion that there could have been a plausible, innocent reason that homicide investigators seemed to perform no comparisons between the latent and known prints in 1973 or 1974 suffered a severe setback on June 27, 1991, midway through the misconduct hearings. That's when it came out that, in fact, comparisons *had* been done in 1973 or 1974.

That truth was finally volunteered by John Jolly and his supervisor. Jolly was the fingerprint examiner who, in June 1990, had compared the latent prints from the Cole-

man fuel cans to known prints from John and Linda Knapp. When Jolly had gone into the old latent print files in June 1990 and fished out the cards from the Knapp case, he had discovered that a number of the cards were *folded.* Folding was something that was done during the process of *comparing* two sets of prints. The cards were folded so that the analyst could put two prints next to each other under a magnifying glass.

Ironically, Jolly's supervisor, Carey Chapman, had been aggravated about Jolly's discovery from a purely bureaucratic perspective. He was annoyed that Jolly was wasting his time on redundant comparisons.

But then he and Jolly discovered that there was no earlier comparison report. And that was very strange. It was contrary to procedure to perform a comparison and not draw up a report.

Despite this new information, neither Hyder nor prosecutor White conceded that comparisons had, in fact, been done between the latents and John Knapp's prints in 1973 or 1974. Apparently, at some level of consciousness Hyder and White realized that the absence of Knapp's prints on the murder weapon was not quite as meaningless as they were claiming; they were not about to admit that Hyder or state investigators actually *knew* in 1974 that that was the true state of affairs.

Instead, prosecutor White's deadpan response to Jolly's revelation was to postulate that perhaps the analysts in 1974 had compared the latent prints *not* to John Knapp's prints, but to other *latent* prints. Though such a possibility had never occurred to either Jolly or his supervisor, White managed to secure from the original fingerprint analyst Watling the concession that, indeed, analysts sometimes *did* compare latents to latents. They might do so, Watling explained, if they found latents on several different objects and wanted to find matches in order to make their job easier *when the time came to compare those latents to known prints.*

But doing such a latent-to-latent comparison would still only make sense, then, if the analysts anticipated

eventually comparing latents to known prints—which Hyder claimed had never been done or planned.

A latent-to-latent comparison in the context of the Knapp case didn't seem to make any sense. Still, it was a scenario White could cling to, rather than concede the horrendous, obvious alternative.

As I understand it, then, to believe that Hyder was not guilty of extraordinary, verdict-altering, life-destroying wrongdoing in the Knapp case, the unknown hearing officer at the State Bar of Arizona must have believed the following:

Justice court prosecutor Zettler turned over the fingerprint reports to Knapp's defense lawyers, who didn't look at them, or forgot what they showed, and then lost them. Hyder knew that there were identifiable prints on the murder weapon, but chose not to compare them to John Knapp's prints, seeing no point to it. Comparisons were performed, however, between those latent prints and other unknown latents for unknown reasons, and the results of that comparison were never recorded anywhere. Then, sometime during the month-and-a-half break between the first and second 1974 trials, both Hyder and his chief investigator forgot that the prints were identifiable and told the judge and jury that they were smudged.

Is that an accurate summary of your beliefs, Ms. Napolitano?

I understand that Hyder is popular among his colleagues. Is that the real reason that nobody at the state bar or in your office will take any action to censure Hyder publicly?

If Hyder intentionally concealed exculpatory evidence at Knapp's 1974 trials, then he illegally buried Knapp alive for 12 years, and came within a hair's breadth of killing him.

Isn't the public entitled to an explanation of why Hyder is still a prosecutor in your office?   ∎

FILED _____ LODGED
_____ RECEIVED _____ COPY

MAR 2 9 1996

CLERK U S DISTRICT COURT
DISTRICT OF ARIZONA
BY _____ DEPUTY

IN THE UNITED STATES DISTRICT COURT

FOR THE DISTRICT OF ARIZONA

MARK A. NELSON,   )
)
            Plaintiff,   )   CIV 94-640 PHX-PGR
)
      v.   )   ORDER
)
UNITED STATES OF AMERICA,)
)
            Defendant.   )
_____)

Pending before the Court is Defendant's Motion for Summary Judgment. Plaintiff filed his response to the motion on March 28, 1996. The Court finds that no reply is necessary, and thus issues its decision on the motion.[1]

BACKGROUND

On or about February 7, 1992, the Federal Bureau of Investigation ("FBI") began an investigation into alleged extortion activities directed at Marc Kaplan ("Kaplan"). Keith Tolhurst ("Tolhurst") was the FBI agent in charge of the investigation. On February 19, 1992, Tolhurst appeared as a complainant in <u>United States v. Michael Grant Miller; Mark Andrew Nelson</u>, CR 92-5041M (D.Ariz.) before Magistrate Judge Morton Sitver. Tolhurst provided an affidavit of probable cause, alleged that Miller and Nelson (hereinafter "Plaintiff") violated 18 U.S.C. §§876 and 2 with respect to an extortion of money from Kaplan. Based upon Tolhurst's affidavit

_____

[1] Plaintiff also filed a Request for Oral Arguments with his response. However, the Court finds that oral arguments would not assist the Court in its decision and Plaintiff's request is denied.

1   of probable cause, Magistrate Judge Sitver issued an arrest warrant for Plaintiff,

2   who was arrested on February 20, 1992. Plaintiff was released to his father's

3   custody on February 27, 1992; however, Plaintiff was required to wear an electronic

4   monitoring bracelet on his ankle from May 26, 1992, until the time the indictment

5   was dismissed.

6   On February 26, 1992, Tolhurst testified before a federal grand jury as to

7   Plaintiff's alleged involvement in the Kaplan extortion. Plaintiff was indicted by the

8   grand jury in a two-count indictment charging violations of 18 U.S.C. §§876 and 371,

9   extortion and conspiracy in the case of United States v. Alber, et al., CR-92-080-

10 PHX-RCB. On January 14, 1993, Charles Hyder ("Hyder"), the Assistant United

11 States Attorney who was prosecuting the matter, filed a motion to dismiss the

12 criminal case as to Plaintiff without prejudice. The motion was granted.

13   On March 25, 1994, Plaintiff filed a complaint against the United States of

14 America, the FBI, the United States Attorney's Office for the District of Arizona,

15 Hyder, and Tolhurst.[2] Plaintiff alleged malicious prosecution, negligence, and

16 intentional infliction of emotional distress pursuant to the Federal Tort Claims Act

17 ("FTCA"). Plaintiff contends that Tolhurst and Hyder knew Plaintiff was not involved

18 in the Kaplan extortion, but that Tolhurst intentionally misled the grand jury to issue

19 the indictment, and Hyder condoned Tolhurst's actions.

20   Upon unopposed motion of the FBI and the United States Attorneys' Office,

21 this Court dismissed these two parties on June 10, 1994. See Doc. #13. On that

22 same day, again upon unopposed motion, the Court also substituted the United

23 States of America as the Defendant in place of Hyder and Tolhurst. See Doc. #14.

24 . . . .

25

26 _____

    [2] Jane Doe Hyder and Jane Doe Tolhurst were also named as the spouses of Hyder
27 and Tolhurst.

28   2

On October 17, 1994, Defendant filed a Motion for Summary Judgment. Plaintiff filed a Rule 56(f) affidavit requesting discovery prior to filing a response to the motion for summary judgment. This Court denied all pending motions. On August 24, 1995, Defendant again filed a Motion for Summary Judgment, asserting that Plaintiff's claims are barred by the discretionary function exception to the FTCA. Additionally, Defendant asserts that findings of probable cause preclude the malicious prosecution claim, and that because the intentional infliction of emotional distress claim does not exist independent of the malicious prosecution claim, this claim is also precluded.

Plaintiff again filed a Rule 56(f) affidavit, as well as a Motion to Compel in relation to discovery he had requested from Defendant one year prior to the filing of the motion. Defendant did not respond to the motion to compel, but rather claimed, in response to the 56(f) affidavit, that no discovery was necessary in order to respond to the motion for summary judgment. This Court granted the motion to compel and gave Plaintiff an extension of time to respond to the motion for summary judgment.

Defendant then filed a motion for an extension of time to file a motion for reconsideration, as well as a motion for extension of time to produce documents. Defendant asserted that the documents requested by Plaintiff were protected by various privileges, and therefore this Court had to reconsider its order compelling Defendant to produce such documents. The Court granted the motions for extension, and subsequently granted the motion for reconsideration. The Court ordered that Defendant need not produce any documents, and that Plaintiff must respond to the motion for summary judgment.

Plaintiff filed his response on March 28, 1996. Plaintiff claims that the discretionary function exception does not apply because the Department of Justice

1 | has a policy in place which prevents its employees from lying to a grand jury, which

2 | is the gist of Plaintiff's complaint. Plaintiff also states that investigative functions by

3 | their nature are not subject to the discretionary function exception. Finally, Plaintiff

4 | contends that any finding of probable cause is rebutted by the showing of fraud

5 | and/or falsification of evidence, as Plaintiff contends Tolhurst and Hyder did.

6 | Plaintiff has also filed a renewed Declaration Pursuant to Rule 56(f) and

7 | Motion for Reconsideration. Plaintiff claims that he must be allowed discovery to

8 | adequately respond to the motion for summary judgment, and that this Court should

9 | reconsider its Order granting Defendant's Motion for Reconsideration.

10 | DISCUSSION

11 | A. Motion for Reconsideration

12 | A party seeking a motion for reconsideration must (1) demonstrate some

13 | valid reason why the court should reconsider its prior ruling and (2) set forth

14 | substantial facts or law to persuade the court to reverse its prior decision. Bahrs. V.

15 | Hughes Aircraft Co., 795 F.Supp. 965, 967 (D.Ariz. 1992). Plaintiff has failed to

16 | make either showing. As will be discussed *infra*, the issues contained in

17 | Defendant's Motion for Summary Judgment, i.e. the discretionary function exception

18 | and the availability of the state tort remedies to Plaintiff, can be determined based

19 | upon the motion and the response filed by Plaintiff. Therefore, the Court will deny

20 | Plaintiff's Motion for Reconsideration.

21 | B. Motion for Summary Judgment

22 | 1. Standard

23 | Summary judgment may be granted if the movant shows that "there is no

24 | genuine issue as to any material fact and that the moving party is entitled to

25 | judgment as a matter of law." Rule 56(c), Federal Rules of Civil Procedure.

26 | . . . .

27 |

28 | 4

1   Summary judgment is proper if the nonmoving party fails to make a showing

2   sufficient to establish the existence of an essential element of his case on which he

3   will bear the burden of proof at trial. <u>Celotex Corp. v. Catrett</u>, 477 U.S. 317, 322

4   106 S.Ct. 2548, 2552, 91 L.Ed.2d 265 (1986). The disputed fact(s) must be

5   material. <u>Id.</u>

6   Substantive law determines which facts are material. "Only disputes over

7   facts that might affect the outcome of the suit under the governing law will properly

8   preclude the entry of summary judgment." <u>Anderson v. Liberty Lobby</u>, 477 U.S. 242,

9   249, 106 S.Ct. 2505, 2510, 91 L.Ed.2d 202 (1986).

10   Moreover, the dispute must be genuine. A dispute about a material fact is

11 genuine if "the evidence is such that a reasonable jury could return a verdict for the

12 nonmoving party." <u>Liberty Lobby</u>, 477 U.S. at 249, 106 S.Ct. at 2510. There is no

13 issue for trial unless there is sufficient evidence favoring the nonmoving party. If the

14 evidence is merely colorable or is not significantly probative, summary judgment

15 may be granted. <u>Liberty Lobby</u>, 477 U.S. at 249-50, 106 S.Ct. at 2510-11. In a civil

16 case, the issue is:

17   whether a fair-minded jury could return a verdict for
            the Plaintiff on the evidence presented. The mere
18   existence of a scintilla of evidence in support of the
            Plaintiff's position will be insufficient; there must be
19   evidence on which the jury could reasonably find for
            the Plaintiff.
20
    <u>Liberty Lobby</u>, 477 U.S. at 252, 106 S.Ct. at 2512.
21
        The opposing evidence must be "such that a reasonable jury could return a
22
    verdict for the nonmoving party." <u>Liberty Lobby</u>, 477 U.S at 242, 106 S.Ct. at 2510;
23
    <u>Aydin Corp. v. Loral Corp.</u>, 718 F.2d 897, 902 (9th Cir. 1983).
24
        2. Application
25
        In the absence of consent the United States is absolutely immune from suit.
26
    <u>United States v. Testan</u>, 424 U.S. 392, 299, 96 S.Ct. 948 (1976). The Federal Tort
27

28   5

1 | Claims Act ("FTCA"), 28 U.S.C. 2671 et seq., provides a waiver of sovereign

2 | immunity for suits arising out of common law torts committed by federal employees

3 | acting within the scope of their employment. 28 U.S.C. §§ 2671, 2674, 2679. It is

4 | subject, however, to certain specific exceptions designed to protect "critical"

5 | governmental functions. See 28 U.S.C. § 2680; Wright v. United States, 719 F.2d

6 | 1032, 1034 (9th Cir. 1983); Kosak v. United States, 465 U.S. 848, 852, 104 S.Ct.

7 | 1519 (1984). If a plaintiff's claim falls within an exception, the court lacks subject

8 | matter jurisdiction. Wright at 1034.

9 | a. Discretionary function exception

10 | Defendant's first contention is that the actions of Hyder and Tolhurst fall

11 | within the discretionary function exception to the FTCA. Section 2680 of the FTCA

12 | states in part:

13 | The provisions of this chapter and section 1346(b) of
this title shall not apply to--

14 | (a) Any claim based upon an act or omission
of an employee of the Government, exercising due

15 | care, in the execution of a statute or regulation,
whether or not such statute or regulation be valid, or

16 | based upon the exercise or performance or the failure
to exercise or perform a discretionary function or duty

17 | on the part of a federal agency or an employee of the
Government, whether or not the discretion involved

18 | be abused.

19 | 28 U.S.C. § 2680(a).

20 | In order for an act of a government employee to fall within the discretionary

21 | function exception, certain elements must be established. The United States

22 | Supreme Court has addressed the breadth of the discretionary function exception:

23 | The exception covers only acts that are
discretionary in nature, acts that "involv[e] an element

24 | of judgment or choice," *Berkovitz [v. United States,*
486 U.S. 531, 108 S.Ct. 1954 (1988)], *supra*, at 536,

25 | 108 S.Ct., at 1958; see also *Dalehite v. United
States*, 346 U.S. 15, 34, 73 S.Ct. 956, 967, 97 L.Ed.

26 | 1427 (1953); and "it is the nature of the conduct,
rather than the status of the actor" that governs

27 |

28 | 6

whether the exception applies. *Varig Airlines [United States v. Varig Airlines*, 467 U.S. 797, 104 S.Ct. 2755 (1984)], *supra*, at 813, 104 S.Ct., at 2764. The requirement of judgment or choice is not satisfied if a "federal statute, regulation, or policy specifically prescribes a course of action for an employee to follow," because "the employee has no rightful option but to adhere to the directive." *Berkovitz*, 486 U.S., at 536, 108 S.Ct., at 1958-1959.

Furthermore, even "assuming the challenged conduct involves an element of judgment," it remains to be decided "whether that judgment is of the kind that the discretionary function exception was designed to shield." *Ibid.* See *Varig Airlines*, 467 U.S., at 813, 104 S.Ct., at 2764. Because the purpose of the exception is to "prevent judicial 'second-guessing' of legislative and administrative decisions grounded in social, economic, and political policy through the medium of an action in tort," *id.*, at 814, 104 S.Ct., at 2765, when properly construed, the exception "protects only governmental actions and decisions based on considerations of public policy." *Berkovitz*, *supra*, at 537, 108 S.Ct., at 1959.

U.S. v. Gaubert, 499 U.S. 315, 322-23, 111 S.Ct. 1267, 1273-74 (1991).

Plaintiff contends that the acts of Hyder and Tolhurst cannot fall within the discretionary function exception because the Department of Justice has a policy and mandate that its employees, when aware of substantial evidence that is inconsistent with the guilt of the suspect, must present or otherwise disclose such evidence to a Grand Jury prior to seeking an indictment against the suspect. Plaintiff claims that because Tolhurst and Hyder withheld information from the Grand Jury, i.e. the taped phone conversation between Frank Alber[3] and Richard Fair in which Alber admits he does not know Plaintiff, their actions were not within the discretionary function exception.

However, Plaintiff's reliance on the excerpts of the taped conversation between Alber and Fair as demonstrating that Hyder and Tolhurst withheld information from the Grand Jury or lied to the Grand Jury is misplaced. Plaintiff also

---

[3] Frank Alber subsequently pled guilty to the extortion crime against Kaplan.

1   provides excerpts from the Grand Jury transcript which were provided to him by

2   Hyder as exculpatory evidence which states the following:

3   Q. Other than the evidence that you have related at
             this time, seeing Mr. Nelson and Mr. Miller at the lake
4   where Mr. Kaplan was instructed to go, has your
             investigation revealed at this time any prior
5   relationship between these individuals?

6   A. No, it hasn't.

7   Q. Has your investigation revealed any prior
             relationship of Mr. Nelson to Mr. Alber?
8
             A. At this point it isn't conclusive, but we have -- we
9   do know that Mr. Alber was attempting to promote a
             concert with some large-name musical acts in the
10   Mesa area, and we also know that Mark Nelson
             claims to be a music promoter of some type, but we
11   have not confirmed any connection to those two yet.

12   ***

13   Q. Did Mr. Nelson or Mr. Miller admit to knowing each
             other?
14
             A. No, they did not.
15
             ***
16
             A JUROR: Do any one of the three defendants
17   acknowledge knowing the other two? Is there any
             acknowledgement of any of them toward each other?
18
             THE WITNESS: No, sir. The only acknowledgment
19   at all is that Mr. Alber acknowledges knowing the
             victim and vice versa.
20
See Plaintiff's Separate Statement of Facts in Opposition to Defendant's Second

21   Motion for Summary Judgment, Exhibit B (emphasis added).

22   Based upon these excerpts, Tolhurst testified that the only connection

23   between Plaintiff and Alber was the fact that they were observed at Saguaro Lake at

24   the same time Kaplan was asked to go there in connection with the extortion

25   demands. This is the same information which can be ascertained from the

26   conversation between Alber and Fair, which Plaintiff relies upon as establishing that

27

28   8

1	Tolhurst and Hyder lied to the Grand Jury. However, Plaintiff does not dispute the
2	facts contained in Tolhurst's affidavit which led to the issuance of the arrest warrant,
3	i.e. that he was at Saguaro Lake on the day in question. The Grand Jury found that
4	even though the only evidence was that Plaintiff was observed at Saguaro Lake that
5	day, there was still enough probable cause to indict Plaintiff. This information does
6	not show that Hyder or Tolhurst intentionally lied to or misled the Grand Jury, and
7	therefore Plaintiff's theory that their actions in "withholding" this information from the
8	Grand Jury violates a Department of Justice policy which would negate the
9	application of the discretionary function exception must be rejected.
10	Clearly the actions of Hyder would fall within the purview of the discretionary
11	function exception. "The decision whether or not to prosecute a given individual is a
12	discretionary function for which the United States is immune from liability." Wright v.
13	United States, 719 F.2d 1032, 1035 (9th Cir. 1983). Therefore, any liability based
14	upon the actions of Hyder fall within the discretionary function exception and
15	Defendant has not waived immunity as to those claims. Thus, this Court is without
16	jurisdiction over Plaintiff's claims with respect to Hyder.
17	However, the discretionary function exception, as applied to the actions of
18	Tolhurst, is not so clear cut. In Garcia v. U.S., 826 F.2d 806 (9th Cir. 1987), the
19	Ninth Circuit Court of Appeals stated, in relation to the actions of a border patrol
20	agent during an arrest:
21	While law enforcement involves exercise of a certain amount of discretion on the part of the individual
22	officers, such decisions do not involve the sort of generalized social, economic and political policy
23	choices that Congress intended to exempt from tort liability. *See Caban v. United States*, 671 F.2d 1230
24	(2d Cir. 1982) (INS decision whether to detain alien based on alien's appearance and ability to answer
25	questions about his homeland not a discretionary function under FTCA).
26	
27	Garcia, 826 F.2d at 809.
28	9

1   Additionally, the Ninth Circuit has found that the discretionary function

2   exception did not apply to the actions of an IRS agent who was implementing the

3   decision of the prosecution to seek indictments against an individual who allegedly

4   failed to file income tax returns and who allegedly made false statements with

5   respect to his tax returns. The court stated:

> The decision whether or not to prosecute a given
> individual is a discretionary function for which the
> United States is immune from liability. *See Smith v.*
> *United States*, 375 F.2d 243 (5th Cir. 1967), *cert.*
> *denied*, 389 U.S. 841, 88 S.Ct. 76, 19 L.Ed.2d 106
> (1967). The conduct of agent Fletcher in
> implementing that decision, however, including the
> nature of his testimony before the grand jury, is not
> immune as a discretionary function. *See Liuzzo v.*
> *United States*, 508 F.Supp. 923, 930-33 (E.D.Mich.
> 1981) (claims concerning FBI agents implementation
> of governments' informant policy not barred by
> discretionary function exception). Unlike the decision
> to prosecute, an agent's conduct, both before and
> after that decision is made, is susceptible to judicial
> evaluation. *See Driscoll v. United States*, 525 F.2d at
> 138.

15   <u>Wright v. United States</u>, 719 F.2d 1032, 1035 (9th Cir. 1983).

16   Based upon this case law, the discretionary function exception would not

17   apply to the actions of Tolhurst. Therefore, this Court has jurisdiction over those

18   claims, and Defendants' Motion for Summary Judgment based upon the

19   discretionary function exception with respect to the actions of Tolhurst must be

20   denied.

21   <u>b. No basis for claims</u>

22   Although the discretionary function exception to the FTCA does not apply

23   with respect to actions of Tolhurst, Plaintiff's claims are without merit and therefore

24   summary judgment is still appropriate as to Defendant's liability based upon the

25   actions of Tolhurst. Further, even if the discretionary function exception did not

26   apply to the actions of Hyder, which it does, Plaintiff's claims would still have to be

27

28   10

dismissed as to Hyder's actions. Under the FTCA, Defendant USA is only liable to the extent a private person would be liable under the law of the place where the act or omission occurred. See 28 U.S.C. § 1346(b). Therefore, any finding of liability under the FTCA must be based upon state law. Brock v. United States, 601 F.2d 976, 979 (9th Cir. 1979).

In order to state a claim for malicious prosecution under Arizona law, Plaintiff must establish the following:

> that a prior prosecution terminated in favor of the plaintiff, that the defendant was the prosecutor, that it was actuated by malice, that there was no probable cause and that damages were sustained.

Frey v. Stoneman, 150 Ariz. 106, 109, 722 P.2d 274, 277 (Ariz. 1986). The failure to establish any one element requires dismissal of the entire claim.

The actions of Tolhurst could not result in a claim for malicious prosecution as Tolhurst was not the prosecutor in Plaintiff's case. Therefore, one essential element of the claim for malicious prosecution is not met with respect to Tolhurst.

Although Hyder was the prosecutor for Plaintiff's case, there clearly was probable cause for Plaintiff's arrest. Not one, but two, probable cause determinations were made in relation to Plaintiff's case: Magistrate Judge Sitver found probable cause at the time of the issuance of the warrant for arrest, and the grand jury found probable cause at the time of the issuance of the indictment. Therefore, the element of lack of probable cause necessary to bring a malicious prosecution claim is lacking, and Plaintiff's claim against Hyder is insufficient.

Plaintiff contends that because Hyder and Tolhurst did not make a full disclosure to the Grand Jury with respect to the taped conversation between Alber and Fair, a finding that probable cause existed is rebutted because the withholding of this information shows that the indictment and/or arrest warrant was based on fraud or on failure to disclose exculpatory evidence. However, as discussed *supra*,

11

the alleged failure to disclose[4] the taped conversation does not show fraud or

failure to disclose information. Therefore, the finding of probable cause is not

rebutted in this case.

Additionally, a malicious prosecution claim against Hyder is barred by the

FTCA. Section 2680 of the FTCA states:

> The provisions of this chapter and section 1346(b) of
> this title shall not apply to--
> ***
>   (h) Any claim arising out of assault, battery,
> false imprisonment, false arrest, malicious
> prosecution, abuse of process, libel, slander,
> misrepresentation, deceit, or interference with
> contract rights: *Provided*, That, with regard to acts or
> omissions of investigative or law enforcement officers
> of the United States Government, the provisions of
> this chapter and section 1346(b) of this title shall
> apply to any claim arising, on or after the date of the
> enactment of this proviso, out of assault, battery,
> false imprisonment, false arrest, abuse of process, or
> malicious prosection. For the purpose of this
> subsection, "investigative or law enforcement officer"
> means any officer of the United States who is
> empowered by law to execute searches, to seize
> evidence, or to make arrests for violations of Federal
> law.

---

[4] Also contained in the Grand Jury excerpts provided to the Court by Plaintiff is the following:

> Later in the week, we found an individual who came forward
> and confessed to having made the phone call to the victim.
> That individual stated that he was asked to make the phone
> call by another individual by the name of Frank Alber.
>
> ***
>
> We had a recording of that, played that to the individual, and
> he stated that that was his voice on the tape.

See Plaintiff's Separate Statement of Facts in Opposition to Defendant's Second Motion for Summary Judgment, Exhibit B (emphasis added).
     Therefore, Tolhurst may have disclosed the existence of the tape recorded conversation to the Grand Jury, but simply did not expand on that disclosure.

12

28 U.S.C. § 2680(h).

Clearly the malicious prosecution claim is barred against Hyder. There is no evidence in the record before the Court that Hyder is an "investigative or law enforcement officer" as defined in 28 U.S.C. § 2680(h). Therefore, a malicious prosecution claim against Hyder is prohibited by the exceptions to the FTCA.[5]

Therefore, based upon the foregoing discussion, there is no claim for malicious prosecution against either Hyder or Tolhurst, and therefore no cause of action for malicious prosecution can be had against Defendant based upon Hyder and/or Tolhurst's actions.

Plaintiff's claim for "negligence" is also without merit. Under Arizona law, there is no recognized tort of "negligence"; the negligent acts Plaintiff alleges are subsumed within the other named torts, i.e. malicious prosecution and intentional infliction of emotional distress.[6]

> Plaintiff may not recover under broad general principles of negligence, however, but must proceed by way of the traditional remedies of false arrest and imprisonment and malicious prosecution. Her right to be free of restraint or unjustified and unreasonable litigation is limited by the obvious policy of the law to encourage proceedings against those who are apparently guilty of criminal conduct and to let finished litigation remain undisturbed and unchallenged. . . . To that end, plaintiff's recovery must be determined by established rules defining the torts of false arrest and imprisonment and malicious prosecution, rules which permit damages only under

---

[5] Although 28 U.S.C. § 2680(h) does not shield the actions of Tolhurst under the FTCA, Tolhurst's actions cannot provide a basis for malicious prosecution because he was not the prosecutor, as discussed *supra*.

[6] Although Plaintiff refers to a "wrongful arrest" and "wrongful incarceration" under the discussion of Count II, Negligence, Plaintiff has not specifically pled a cause of action for false arrest or false imprisonment. However, even if Plaintiff had pled these torts, both would be barred by the finding of this Court that probable cause existed for Plaintiff's arrest and subsequent indictment. See Hockett v. City of Tucson, 139 Ariz. 317, 678 P.2d 502, 505 (Ariz.App. 1983); Whitlock v. Boyer, 77 Ariz. 334, 271 P.2d 484, 487 (1954).

13

1 circumstances in which the law regards the
   imprisonment or prosecution as improper and
2 unjustified. . . .

3 Boose v. City of Rochester, 71 A.D.2d 59, 62, 421 N.Y.S.2d 740, 744 (App.Div.

4 1979) (citations omitted).

5   Additionally, the Ninth Circuit Court of Appeals has addressed the issue of

6 labeling a tort by one name in order to create a cause of action when, in reality, the

7 label is merely disguising a tort which is prohibited by the FTCA. In Thomas-Lazear

8 v. F.B.I., 851 F.2d 1202 (9th Cir. 1988), the Ninth Circuit stated:

9   [T]he Supreme Court has implied that section
               2680(h) bars claims arising out of either negligent or
10   intentional commission of the enumerated torts. See
               United States v. Neustadt, 366 U.S. 696, 706-707, 81
11   S.Ct. 1294, 1300, 6 L.Ed.2d 614 (1961) (claim for
               negligence barred as actually stating a claim for
12   negligent misrepresentation). This circuit looks
               beyond the labels used to determine whether a
13   proposed claim is barred. See, e.g., Alexander v.
               United States, 787 F.2d 1349, 1350-51 (9th Cir.
14   1986); Leaf v. United States, 661 F.2d 740, 742 (9th
               Cir. 1981) (negligence claims actually
15   misrepresentation), cert. denied, 456 U.S. 960, 102
               S.Ct. 2036, 72 L.Ed.2d 484 (1982). In this case, the
16   claim for negligent infliction of emotional distress is
               nothing more than a restatement of the slander claim,
17   which is barred by section 2680(h). Put another way,
               the Government's actions that constitute a claim for
18   slander are essential to Thomas-Lazear's claim for
               negligent infliction of emotional distress. See Metz v.
19   United States, 788 F.2d 1528, 1535 (11th Cir. 1986)
               (concluding there is no difference in acts underlying
20   claims for false arrest and intentional infliction of
               emotional distress), cert. denied, __ U.S. __, 107 S.Ct.
21   400, 93 L.Ed.2d 353 (1986). Here, as in Metz,
               "[t]here is no other government conduct upon which
22   such claims can rest." Id.

23 Thomas-Lazear, 851 F.2d at 1206-07.

24   As stated supra, Plaintiff cannot recover against Defendant based upon a

25 theory of malicious prosecution; as will be discussed infra, Plaintiff can also not

26 recover against Defendant based upon a theory of intentional infliction of emotional

27

28   14

distress. Therefore, absent any cause of action under these recognized Arizona

torts, Plaintiff cannot recover under the guise of a tort of "negligence" independent

of these causes of action. The actions which Plaintiff claims establish the

"negligence" cause of action are no more than the actions Plaintiff complains

resulted in the malicious prosecution and the intentional infliction of emotional

distress. Thus, Plaintiff's cause of action for negligence must also be denied.

The final tort claim upon which Plaintiff seeks relief is the intentional infliction

of emotional distress ("IIED"). In Arizona, the three required elements for an IIED

cause of action are:

> First, the conduct by the defendant must be "extreme"
> and "outrageous"; second, the defendant must either
> intend to cause emotional distress or recklessly
> disregard the near certainty that such distress will
> result from his conduct; and third, severe emotional
> distress must indeed occur as a result of defendant's
> conduct.

Ford v. Revlon, 153 Ariz. 38, 43 (1987).

Plaintiff cannot establish the necessary elements to obtain relief under an

IIED cause of action. As stated supra, there was probable cause to issue the arrest

warrant and the grand jury indictment. Tolhurst, seeking an arrest warrant based

upon the facts attested to in his affidavit, and Hyder, seeking to prosecute a case

against Plaintiff based upon the information attested to in his and his supervisor's

affidavit, i.e. the affidavit of Roslyn Silver[7], did not act "extremely" or "outrageously".

Nor is there any evidence that either Hyder or Tolhurst intended to cause any

emotional distress or that they recklessly disregarded that such distress would result

from their conduct. Their jobs necessary require them to cause distress to every

---

[7] It should be noted that Plaintiff has failed to provide any evidence contrary to the affidavits provided by Defendant in support of its Motion for Summary Judgment, i.e. an affidavit from Plaintiff himself.

15

criminal defendant investigated and charged; to claim that by doing their job they

are inflicting emotional distress upon these individuals would result in a breakdown

of the criminal justice system.

Therefore, because there was probable cause for the arrest and the

indictment, and because Hyder and Tolhurst did not act extremely, outrageously, or

with intentional or reckless disregard of Plaintiff's alleged emotional distress, Plaintiff

has failed to establish the necessary elements for a claim of IIED and this claim

must be denied.

IT IS THEREFORE ORDERED denying Plaintiff's Request for Oral

Arguments, filed March 28, 1996.

FURTHER ORDERED denying Plaintiff's Motion for Reconsideration, filed

March 28, 1996.

FURTHER ORDERED granting Defendant's Motion for Summary Judgment

[Doc. #39]. Plaintiff's complaint and cause of action shall be dismissed as to

Defendant. The Clerk of the Court shall enter judgment accordingly.

DATED this _31_ day of March. 1996.

_____

HON. PAUL G. ROSENBLATT
United States District Judge

16

SURVEILLANCE LOG -- PHOENIX DIVISION

DATE: 2/13/92   DAY: THUR.

WEATHER: CLEAR   CASE #: 9A-A-46497

STARTING (Street) 4545 E. SHEA BLVD.   CASE AGENT: K. TOLHURST
LOCATION:

(City) SCOTTSDALE, AZ.

PERSONNEL BATEMAN (4), COWAN (3), MACDONALD (7), BEITER (8), PETERSON (2),
INVOLVED: RIPLEY (PC), HENDERSON (10), WHITE (1)   PAGE 1 OF 2

INIT	TIME	OBSV	ACTIVITY OBSERVED	PHOTOS ATTEMPTED ROLL #	EXP
TAB	1:45p	4,10	SURVEILLANCE INSTITUTED AT 4545 E. SHEA BLVD, SCOTTSDALE (L-1)		
TAB	2:25p	4,10	MARC KAPLAN (M-1) DEPARTS L-1 DRIVING A TEAL BLUE MERCEDES BENZ, AZ/GWS676 (V-1).		
	2:28p	1, PC	V-1 OBSERVED AT A CLOSED SECURITY PACIFIC BANK N.W. CORNER OF TATUM AND SHEA (L-2).		
	2:3?p	PC	V-1 OBSERVED IN THE MIDDLE DRIVE-THRU OF L-2 WITH M-1 TAKING A PIECE OF PAPER OFF THE NORTHERN POLE.		
	2:29p	PC	M-1, AS HE DEPARTS FROM L-1, IS OBSERVED TO TALK TO THE DRIVER OF A WHITE CADILLAC, AZ/ KFTY (V-2).		
TAB	3:01p	4	OBSERVED PARKED PAST RAMP 2 (SAGUARO LAKE MARINA), FAR EASTERN END IS A DARK COLORED MERCURY (V-3)		
TAB	3:03p	4	A RED CORVETTE (V-4) IS NOW OBSERVED PARKED NEXT TO (V-3). 4 WHITE MALES ARE OBSERVED AROUND THESE VEHICLES. ONE OF THE W/M'S IS CARRYING A CELLULAR TELEPHONE, ANOTHER IS DESCRIBED WITH LONG PERM HAIR WITH A PONY TAIL, AND ONE W/M IS WEARING A BASEBALL CAP BACKWARDS.		
BM	3:11p	4,7,12	V-1 ARRIVES L-3.		
TAB	3:14p	4	M-1 IS OUT OF V-1 AND IS OBSERVED NORTH ON THE HILL FROM SAGUARO LAKE (EAST END). M-1 IS OBSERVED OPENING A GREY PLASTIC TRASH BAG AND THEN		

258

SURVEILLANCE LOG -- PHOENIX DIVISION

DATE: 2/13/92   **DAY:** THUR.   **CASE #:** 9A-PX-46497

CASE AGENT: K. TOLHURST

PAGE 2 **OF** 2

INIT	TIME	OBSV	ACTIVITY OBSERVED	PHOTOS ATTEMPTED ROLL #	EXP #
			REMOVING A DARK BAG FROM IT.		
TSA	3¹⁵p	4	M-1 WALKS BACK DOWN THE HILL TO THE AREA WITH		
			COVERED PICNIC TABLES WITH THIS BAG.		
TMB	3¹⁶p	4	OVER THE NEXT FEW MINUTES M-1 IS OBSERVED		
			TO GO BACK AND FORTH BETWEEN V-1 AND THE		
			COVERED PICNIC TABLE AREA.		
TMB CM	3²⁶p	4,10	M-1 LEAVES A DARK COLORED BAG ON THE TABLE		
			AND DEPARTS AREA IN V-1.		
TB CM	3²⁷p	4,10	V-4 DEPARTS L-3 WITH 2 OF THE WHITE MALES.		
			V-4, FURTHER DESCRIBED AS HAVING LICENSE PLATE		
			AZ/EYV571, TURNS LEFT (WEST) UPON EXITING		
			L-3 AREA.		
CM	3²⁹p	3,10	V-3, FURTHER DESCRIBED AS A MERCURY ZEPHYR, AZ/		
			AWS 096, DEPARTS L-3 WITH 2 WHITE MALES,		
			HEADING IN THE SAME DIRECTION AS V-4.		
	3⁴⁰p		SURVEILLANCE DISCONTINUED, LOG MAINTAINED BY		
			CARL HENDERSON.		
			Carl R. Henderson, S.A. F.B.I. A. AZ		
			Thomas A. Bateman, SA, FBI, PX, AZ		
			Duane McdonaId SA, FBI, PX, AZ		
			Lial J. Peterson, SA, FBI PX AZ		
			Harold F. Bents SA FBI PX AZ		
			Dunn J white SA, FBI, PX AZ		
			Reg, Myler, PSR PX AZ		
			Terry B. Camm, SA, FBI, PX, AZ -44		